China-EU Law Series

Volume 1

For further volumes:
http://www.springer.com/series/11933

Xiang Li • Jigang Jin

Concise Chinese Tort Laws

Springer

Xiang Li
China University of Political Science and Law
Beijing, China

Jigang Jin
Skadden, Arps, Slate, Meagher and Flom LLP
San Francisco, CA, USA

ISSN 2198-2708 ISSN 2198-2716 (electronic)
ISBN 978-3-642-41023-9 ISBN 978-3-642-41024-6 (eBook)
DOI 10.1007/978-3-642-41024-6
Springer Heidelberg New York Dordrecht London

Library of Congress Control Number: 2014933046

Printed on acid-free paper

Springer is part of Springer Science+Business Media (www.springer.com)

To my uncle, Shaoxia Zhang – your insights on life and enduring support mean so very much.

– Xiang Li

Preface

Ten years ago, I went to the Minnesota Law School after graduation from the Fudan Law School. On a social event as the school just started, I had a casual chat with a law professor, who was interested in the Chinese students from the mainland, then an almost invisible minority in the student body. When I told him that I studied law for 4 years in China, the professor shrugged his shoulders and asked me, "O ye, is there any law in China?" I knew he did not mean it but he did hurt me. I might maybe not blame his ignorance of the law in China, but I really dislike his blind pride as if only the US laws should be worthy of worship while China was nothing but a desert where no good law could exist.

Fairly speaking, the professor might not be blamed. In spite of the fact that China's economy has been growing rapidly in the past 30 years and China has been viewed as an emerging power in the world, the most people of the western world did not know the dramatic changes that had occurred in China's law and society, and they still viewed China as a strange place full of mysteries, even many law professionals believed that there were many hidden rules and practices in Chinese legal system. With respect to this situation, it is the Chinese scholars who should be blamed because they did not work hard enough to introduce the Chinese legal culture to the world along with Chinese goods exported to the overseas market.

Ten years after, now, with this book I can finally give a well-founded response to that professor (and those having negative views of Chinese law) that I can say that at least in the Tort Law area, Chinese legislation is quite descent, and the judicial system is also functioned very smoothly. In this book, I present to the readers the complete and true pictures of Chinese Tort Law, so the readers can see what happened in China in this aspect. Although I hope that some readers of this book will no longer hold bias towards China after reading this book, the key motive I write this book is to keep the door of communication and exchange of ideas between Chinese law scholars and their foreign peers open, because I believe that only open-minded discussions and change of ideas will benefit healthy development of the Chinese legal system, while hollow patriotic propaganda will never bear constructive result to anyone.

I write on torts for two reasons: firstly, Tort Law can be a caliber to gauge the overall development of Chinese legal system. As a part of the Civil Code of China, the Tort Law of the People's Republic of China was passed on December 26, 2009, by the Standing Committee of National People's Congress and implemented from July 1, 2010. This new law is an outstanding milestone that marked the latest legislation technicalities and the prevailing legal philosophy in China. Secondly, torts are rooted deeply in the social life, and the law of torts concerns basic rights and interests of the general public. Therefore, the Tort Law embodies variety of mutually conflicting value concepts and the compromise thereof. By reading this law we can perceive in depth various conflicts that whole Chinese society is witnessing during a dramatic transit process.

The book adopted creative layouts to provide mutlidimensional prospective to readers and to present the complete picture of Tort Laws in China. This book is divided into three parts: Part I, Torts in Theory, conveys mainstream viewpoints of Chinese Tort Law research scholars; Part II, Torts in Statue, defines hard-core clauses of the Chinese Tort law and provides case examples; and Part III, Torts in Practice—attempts to showcase the practical performance of Tort Laws in China by giving the most typical cases. In short, the author wanted to convey no prejudicial doctrines or creed, but to give readers the utmost initiative to read and to judge, in hopes of enabling readers to see Tort Laws in the daily life of Chinese people.

During the writing of the book, many have helped me along the way. The list begins with my family. I would like to thank my wife Vivian Cheng for her practical comments and suggestions and for reading the manuscript. The China-EU School of Law is generous in its financial support. In addition, the following students provided valuable research assistance: Jo Audrey Lee, Wang Zhang, Han Gao, Yue Ma, Jixin Ji, Anqi Zhou, Yaowen Qin, Chaoying Wen, Yang Gao, Da Shi, and Wei Cheng.

Beijing, China
23 August 2012

Xiang Li

Contents

Part I Torts in Theory

Part I
Torts in Theory

Chapter 1
The Development of Tort Law in China

The Concept of Tort Liability in Ancient China

The relationship between a country's law and its culture is like the relationship between plants and soil. In order to understand China's Tort Law, we must first examine what kind of social culture China's Tort Law is planted in. That is, according to Chinese people's traditional thoughts, what is tortious act and what liability would it incur?

Although having 5,000 years of history, China did not enact its first Tort Law until 2009. However, that is not to say that the Chinese people had no idea on the concept of tort liability before 2009. On the contrary, if we pay a little attention to China's traditional philosophies and thoughts, we would find numerous traces of Chinese people's unique interpretation of tort liability with Chinese wisdom. Even today, many of these thoughts are not outdated in the eyes of western legal scholars.

Confucianism had always been treated as the orthodox in ancient China, and it formed the core value and mainstream thoughts of Chinese culture. Even within this 2,000-year-old philosophy, there are some ideas similar to today's Tort Law concepts. From a macro perspective, the core idea of Confucianism is harmony. That is, no one lives in this world alone and people are interconnected via consanguinity, property, profession, or other things. It is through these connections that a person assumes his role in the society. And if everyone can strictly fulfill the obligations of his role, e.g., taking care of his parents, loyal to his friends, and kind to others, harmony would be easily achieved in our society. Not surprisingly, is not this what we are striving for today by specifying the legal relationships among people to better protect people's rights? Looking at these similarities, we cannot help praising the wisdoms of those ancient Chinese saints.

From a micro perspective, we can find similar or equivalent provisions in modern Tort Law for many principles or norms promoted by Confucianism. For example, the Analects of Confucius say: "if one does not like to be treated by others in certain ways, he should not treat others in those ways." Is not this the most straightforward explanation of the so-called reasonable person standard in modern

X. Li and J. Jin, *Concise Chinese Tort Laws*, China-EU Law Series 1,
DOI 10.1007/978-3-642-41024-6_1, © Springer-Verlag Berlin Heidelberg 2014

Tort Law? Also said in the Analects of Confucius is everyone should control his inappropriate desire, impulse, and words and voluntarily abide by the law and norm to avoid hurting others. This is exactly what the duty of care is in Tort Law. Indeed, there are plenty of examples like these in ancient Chinese philosophies and thoughts. And we can easily find the counterparts in modern Tort Law for these codes of conduct that had been followed for thousands of years in China. Indeed, we cannot help being filled with respect for our ancient ancestors.

As can be seen, although tort is a concept borrowed from the west, the idea of tort liability is not strictly western only. Respecting other's basic rights and maintaining social order had existed in ancient Chinese philosophies and thoughts. These ideas were even summarized as specific codes of conduct, which had influenced people's behavior for thousands of years and become part of Chinese civilization. In this sense, Tort Law is not invented but discovered in China because its gene has been branded in the heart of every inheritor of the Chinese civilization.

The Legislation of Tort Law in Ancient China

Ancient Chinese laws absorbed the core values and thoughts of Confucianism and formed a content-rich and structure-complete legal system. They naturally included some tort rules and specifications, and some of which even reached the highest legislative level during that period of history.

The earliest confirmed tort case in ancient China occurred in the Zhou dynasty. A story engraved on a bronze tripod recorded such a tort case: during a famine, a person sent his slave to rob another person's barn, and as a result that person was sued in the court; the court not only ordered him to return the grains robbed from the victim but also ordered him to pay equivalent amount of grains to the victim as a punishment. Unquestionably, this is the most typical damage compensation caused by infringing on other people's properties.

In the following Qin dynasty, Tort Law received further development and included provisions requiring not only damage but also subjective fault as an element for establishing tort liability. For example, the "Qin Code" expressly provided the following: a borrower of a piece of farming equipment does not need to compensate the owner for any damage on the equipment if such damage is caused because the farming equipment is too old. This provision adequately reflected the spirit of the fault liability principle. Also, various defenses appeared in the law. For example, if public property is damaged as a result of irresistible natural force, such as fire, the user (or renter) of the public property is not held liable for such loss, which is treated as a write-off instead. Another example, to kill a livestock that is about to hurt someone is considered a self-defense if the livestock was instigated to attack; otherwise, it is treated as necessity. Either way, the person, who killed the livestock, is not liable.

In the Tang dynasty, China's law system reached its peak. The Tang dynasty laws, as represented by the "Yong Hui Code," formed the model for ancient

Chinese law system, which was the most advanced and scientific legal system in the world during that time. Tort Laws included in the "Tang Code" also reached such level. Compared with the "Corpus Iuris Civilis," the "Tang Code" was more advanced in several areas: first, it was the first law system that systematically provided the rules on tortious act and emphasized causation relationship as an element for tortious act; second, it was the first law system that consciously distinguished intentional tort and negligence, and eventually led to the removal of negligence out of the scope of criminal penalty; and third, it was the first law system that specified in detail the various defenses and methods for assuming liability; it even provided the gain and loss offset principles, which only appeared in western law systems recently. With its advanced legal ideas and legislative skills, the "Tang Code" is indisputably a milestone in China's ancient legal history. It became a legislative example or basis for all countries under the Confucianism influence. Its specification regarding tortious liability led its time, and its leading status was not terminated until the "Napoleonic Code" was born 1,200 years later.

During the long time after the Tang dynasty, the rulers of each dynasty continued improving the Tort Law, which reached its peak in the Qing dynasty. After several thousand years of cultural precipitation and accumulation, the Tort Law of the Qing dynasty included the essence of all ancient Chinese Tort Laws. The "Qing Code" had very detailed and systematic specifications on Tort Law, including 4 categories and 15 specific rules, which covered property damage compensation, compensation for inflicting bodily injury on others, various methods for assuming tort liability, and defenses against tort liability. It was a very detailed and rigorous legal system and reached its peak during China's feudalism period.

If we put all ancient Chinese Tort Laws in front of us, we would find that the development of these laws had always followed a fixed structure and maintained a very stable legal system—the Chinese Tort Law system. Although new rules were frequently introduced and developed into the Tort Law during the several thousand years of feudalism period since the Qin dynasty, these developments were limited to improvements on details and specific contents of the law, and the major structure of the law had never changed in any significant way. Thus, we can easily summarize the characteristics of ancient Chinese legislations on Tort Law:

1. A significant characteristic of ancient Chinese legislation is that all laws, including its civil law and criminal law, were mixed together. Provisions of Tort Law appeared sporadically and separately in the law. As a result, there may be a portion of a provision relating to criminal law and another portion of the same provision relating to Tort Law. In this sense, there was not a separate Tort Law in ancient China. The Tort Law provisions were dispersed among the criminal law provisions and existed as auxiliary of the criminal law. Because of this legislation style, it was not difficult for the Tort Law to carry many characteristics of the criminal law, particularly in the respect that the element requirement for establishing tort liability was very strict.
2. Although ancient Chinese Tort Law was not very organized, it had a relatively independent and complete system and had remained highly stable and followed

its own logical core in its development throughout ancient Chinese history. Various rules of the Tort Law had changed frequently, but they were closely interconnected, and formed a very strict civil right protection system. Either from the perspective of its liability system or from the perspective of protecting civil rights, the ancient Chinese Tort Law was very systematic and comprehensive.

3. Looking at the development of ancient Chinese Tort Law, we can easily find a path with clear logic—the transition from emphasizing more on punishment to emphasizing more on compensation. By the late feudalism period, the function of tort compensation had almost completely focused on compensation. Whether it was personal injury or property damage, a perpetrator was almost always ordered to assume liability by making monetary compensation. This practice reflected the perfect handling on tort cases by ancient Chinese. Besides those, ancient Chinese Tort Law showed its incredible advanced nature on certain specifications, including indirect damage compensation, causation relationship, offset on gains and losses, etc., which are major western Tort Law principles but appeared in ancient Chinese Tort Law thousands of years ago.

The Legislation of Early Modern Chinese Tort Law

After the first Opium War, China faced a huge change that had not occurred for 3,000 years. The imperial powers broke open China's door with warships and guns and quickly turned China into a half-colonial half-feudalism country. Western culture flooded into China and drove China's legal system to near collapsing point. Under such situations, the Qing government was forced to reform itself to adopt western technologies. From then on, China had abandoned its thousand-year's legal tradition and started integrating into the European continental law system.

By learning from the civil codes of Germany, France, and Japan, China finished the "Qing Civil Code Rough Draft" in August 1911. It was the first time for China to abandon the tradition of mixing criminal and civil laws and to adopt western legislative technique. The "Qing Civil Code Rough Draft" had very comprehensive specification on damage compensation, which included four parts: part one specified the fault liability imputation principle—the first ever in Chinese history; part two provided various types of special tortious acts; part three specified the determination on the amount of compensation and methods for assuming liability; and part four provided the statute of limitations on tort cases. However, before the "Qing Civil Code Rough Draft" was enacted, the Qing dynasty collapsed.

After the Republic of China was founded, the laws of the previous dynasty were adopted. The 1926 "Civil Code Rough Draft of the Republic of China" was largely based on the "Qing Civil Code Rough Draft." The Tort Law did not change that much, except that several provisions were deleted. However, the "Civil Code Rough Draft of the Republic of China" adjusted its structure to move the subject matter of "damage compensation," which existed as a separate chapter previously, into Paragraph 2, Section 1 ("the generation of debt") of Chapter 1 ("the general provision"). This approach has affected the later structures of Tort Law since then. Because of political reasons, the parliament was dissolved and this law was never enacted.

Then, based on the above two rough drafts, the government of the Republic of China enacted the "Civil Code of the Republic of China," which was considered the first civil law in Chinese history. The "Civil Code of the Republic of China" generally followed the structure of the "Civil Code Rough Draft of the Republic of China," still treating "damage compensation" as part of the "generation of debt." Content wise, the two laws were largely the same, including general tortious act, special tortious act, principles and methods for assuming liability, and statute of limitations. However, the "Civil Code of the Republic of China" streamlined and combined a lot of the provisions to make the langue more concise and accurate.

Although the legislation of early modern Chinese Tort Law lasted only about 40 years, it went through three different civil laws and had a very important transition role in Chinese legal history because it was the transformation of China's Tort Law from ancient feudalism nature to early modern or modern law nature. Even though these three laws had heavy traces of copying from others, they were great achievements of Chinese people given the tremendous legislative difficulties during that time. Given the tradition of ancient Chinese legislation was so deeply rooted in Chinese society, it was commendable that the Chinese people broke through the manacle of that closed system and adopted those advanced western legal theories and principles.

The Legislation of Modern Chinese Tort Law

The founding of the People's Republic of China in 1949 changed China again and drove the development of Chinese Tort Law into a completely different historical direction. After the communist took power, China completely abolished all laws used in the Republic of China, including the civil code, which was no longer applicable in mainland China, leaving a legal vacuum in China for a long time. Because of the lack of legislative technique and being heavily influenced by legal nihilism, the People's Republic of China did not undertake any Tort Law legislation during the first several decades of its history but borrowed some legal theories from the Soviet Union and compiled a couple textbooks on civil law issues to be used as guidance in trial practice. Since the beginning of the Cultural Revolution, all laws had ceased to exist in mainland China and disappeared completely.

Between 1949 (when the People's Republic of China was founded) and the end of 1978, China had almost no Tort Law legislation. It was not until the end of 1978 that the Chinese government started its economic and legal reform, including restoring the legislation on Tort Law. In April of 1986, the "General Principles of Civil Law" was passed by the People's Congress and became effective on January 1, 1987. It used more than one chapter to specify the general principles and relevant issues of Tort Law. This law was the first systematic legislation on Tort Law after the founding of the People's Republic of China and created the most basic expression and specification of Chinese Tort Law for the next 20 years.

The "General Principles of Civil Law" has four parts relating to Tort Law: firstly, it provided the imputation principles on tort, including fault liability, no-fault liability, and equitable liability; secondly, it specified the form of and compensation for tortious act, covering the infringement of personal rights, property rights, and intellectual property rights; thirdly, it specified special torts and liability, involving product liability, environmental pollution liability, high-risk liability, etc.; and lastly, it provided the defenses relating to the determination of tort liability, including self-defense, necessity, and contributory negligence, etc.

Because the content of the "General Principles of Civil Law" is relatively simple and cannot satisfy the need for judicial practice in real life, the Supreme People's Court successively published various judicial interpretations, which improved the Tort Law system. Among those judicial interpretations, the important ones include "Interpretation of the Supreme People's Court on Several Issues about the Trial of Cases Concerning the Right of Reputation," "Interpretation of the Supreme People's Court on Problems regarding the Ascertainment of Compensation Liability for Emotional Damages in Civil Torts," "Interpretation of the Supreme People's Court of Some Issues concerning the Application of Law for the Trial of Cases on Compensation for Personal Injury," etc. Besides those, regarding certain special torts, China had adopted special laws for regulating such legal issues, such as "Product Quality Law," "Road and Traffic Safety Law," "Consumer Right Protection Law," etc.

These laws temporarily satisfied the Chinese society's need for Tort Law legislation but started revealing their shortcomings in face of the fast social development in China, including the following: (1) most provisions are very abstract and focused on elaborating certain theoretical ideas rather than on providing practical guidance in actual judicial practice; (2) various tort compensation rules appear in all sorts and levels of legal documents, conflict with one another, and create difficulties for the courts during judicial practice and for legal scholars in their analysis, interpretation, and summarization of tort issues; and (3) because China has enjoyed fast social and economic development since it started its reform, various tort issues appeared and the development of Tort Law has not always been keeping a good pace with the reform; thus, certain provisions appear obsolete, and there were even no rules to apply to certain tort issues in some situations; the law is clearly lagging behind the social development.

To deal with the above problems and provide a matching law for the future civil code, China started the enactment of the "Tort Law" in 2002. After 7 years of drafting and four times deliberating, the "Tort Law" was eventually adopted during the 12th meeting of the 11th National People's Congress standing committee and has been in force since July 1, 2010. This was another major law passed by the People's Congress in China after the "Property Law" was enacted. It is closely related to each Chinese citizen's rights, including the right to life, right to health, privacy right, patent right, inheritance right, etc., and provides protection to a series of personal and property rights. It indicated another big step of China on building a legal society.

The "Tort Law" has two chapters and 92 articles. It combined the continental law system's structure and Anglo-American law system's practical use into one. On the one hand, considering the relatively independent feature of Anglo-American Tort Law, China's legislative body drafted China's "Tort Law" as a separate law, not part of the debt law as the continental law system did. The purpose of this is to increase the status of the "Tort Law." On the other hand, China's legislative body followed continental law system's structure, adopting the generalization legislation method in drafting the "Tort Law," i.e., specifying the general provisions first to summarize the major and general tortious acts and then specifying special provisions for special torts, a general-specific structure.

With respect to specific provisions, the "Tort Law" includes a broad range of specifications, covering medical malpractice, traffic accident, product liability, an object thrown or falling from a building, network-based libel, environmental pollution, etc., which are closely related to people's everyday life and public social interests. Although very complicated, the "Tort Law" is not just a collection of old rules. It includes many new rules and specifications and provides resolutions of new social issues. For example, it is the first to create the right to request compensation on mental distress, acknowledge the equal-life-equal-value compensation principle in major accidents, and clarify the legal liability for disclosing other's privacy on the internet, etc.

In sum, the enactment of the "Tort Law" has great significance not only on China's current social and economic development but also on China's future development. We know that the core of law has always been specifying public rights and protecting private rights, and the "Tort Law" is exactly such a law that provides complete protection over people's civil rights; a law that is filled with humanities, care, and love; and a law that provides relief to people when their rights are infringed. The creation of this law not only represents a symbolic step towards the creation of a full-blown civil law but also emphasizes the care of people's life and health. It provides the very basis for resolving our current social conflicts and building a more fair, stable, and harmonic society.

privacy right, patent right, inheritance right, etc., and provides protection to a series of personal and property rights. It indicated another step of China to building a legal society.

[illegible]

Chapter 2
Tortious Act and Tort Liability

The Concept of Tortious Act

On a mountain near the Greek town of Delphi, there stands the Temple of Apollo. The ancient Greek people deemed the temple a place to communicate with the Gods. Within the temple, there is an old slate with unknown age, bearing on it seven commandments allegedly from Gods. Among them, the most famous one is "people, know yourself!" Indeed, how on earth can we know ourselves?

Even now, this is an unanswered question. In the eyes of people from different professions, identities, or social statuses, the view can be very different. But, in the eyes of legal scholars (particularly Tort Law scholars), a human being is more often treated as an abstract host having a set of legal rights, such as the right to life, personal rights, right to image, privacy right, etc. These rights, when added together, form a legal person.

Thus, everyone in this world is a collection of legal rights. Although these rights are complicated and may change from time to time, the common valuable effect of these rights is the endowment of autonomous power to people. It is this autonomous power that protects us as independent and free people, allows each one of us to be the owner of our own soul, and prevents outside forces to interfere with our acts or control our will. We can not only control our bodies to participate any type of activities but also manipulate our mind to travel freely in the spiritual world. We can even use our free will to not do anything. Everyone is naturally born with this autonomous power. The protection of this power is again and again confirmed by law. No one is allowed to deprive it from other people or harm it.

Any act that disturbs this autonomous power or harms people's legitimate rights, whether intentionally or negligently, is considered a tortious act, which will trigger the rules of correction based on damage and compensation to punish the perpetrator's illegal act, restore the normal social and societal order, and compensate the victim's damage. It is not difficult to see that tortious acts are the kind of acts that breach one's legal obligation, infringe on other people's legitimate rights, and should be punished according to the law. The purpose of studying tortious acts and creating

X. Li and J. Jin, *Concise Chinese Tort Laws*, China-EU Law Series 1,
DOI 10.1007/978-3-642-41024-6_2, © Springer-Verlag Berlin Heidelberg 2014

specialized law is to establish a fair and reasonable mechanism that provides remedies and compensations to damages caused by tortious acts.

As a legal term, "tort" is a foreign concept in Chinese language. It came from the Latin term "tortus," which means distorted or bended. French also has the term "tort," which means hurt or fault. Thus, tortious act in nature is an improper or wrongful act and causes damage to other people. But to use it as the definition for tort is probably too broad. In fact, both criminal acts and breach of contract have similar characteristics. Then, what acts are tortious acts?

Firstly, tortious act is a kind of illegal act. Illegality is the most essential feature of tortious act, i.e., tortious acts must be against the law. Because legal acts do not violate any legal rights and obligations that may exist among people, they cannot be tortious acts. Tortious act may be due to either a breach of a specific obligation specified by law (i.e., breach of legal obligation) or a breach of a general obligation specified by a legal principle (i.e., violation of public norm or custom). Either way, as long as an act violates the law on protecting civil rights, the act has broken the authority of law and therefore is illegal.

Secondly, tortious act is a fault-based behavior. Generally, a perpetrator has certain subjective fault when committing a tortious act and therefore is morally reprehensible. It may be due to negligence, overconfidence, or even intention. Thus, most tortious acts are based on fault, and only under certain situations specified by law can tortious act be no-fault based. These situations include product liability, environmental pollution, animal attacks, etc. We should not simply think that these special situations do not require fault. A more accurate description should be "no inquiry of fault." The purpose for not inquiring whether the defendant is at fault is to help the victim to more easily obtain remedy for his/her damage.

Thirdly, tortious act is an objective act. Tortious act is an objective act committed by a person following his/her own will. Pure mental activity without any physical doing cannot constitute tortious act. On the other hand, no matter how destructive it is, a natural disaster cannot be a tortious act as long as there is no human participation. Even when there is a human factor in it, damage caused purely by nature should be disregarded and only the remaining damage should be covered by the perpetrator. As an objective act, tortious act may be expressed in different ways. It can be a feasance act or nonfeasance act. The difference lies on the nature of legal obligation the perpetrator owed to others.

Lastly, tortious act is a harmful act. Tortious act may cause many different types of damages, but in nature they are all damages or injuries to a victim's civil legal rights. Thus, the perpetrator must bear liability to compensate the victim whatever damage he/she has caused. When the tortious act has posed a danger to a person, that person may request the other side to eliminate the danger; when the tortious act has hindered or obstructed a person to exercise his/her rights, the person may request the other side to eliminate the hindrance; when the tortious act has caused damage or injury to a person, the person may request the other side to compensate his/her damage or injury.

According to the above, we can summarize "tortious act" as an act committed by a person with fault or without fault under certain situations specified by law, which breaches the person's legal obligation and infringes on other person's personal or property rights, and as a result the person is held legally liable. Articles 6 and 7 of the "Tort Law of the People's Republic of China" (hereinafter, the "Tort Law") clearly accept this view, stating: "[o]ne who is at fault for infringement upon civil rights or interests of others shall be subject to the tort liability; if any law provides one shall assume the tort liability for infringing others' civil rights or interests, whether at fault or not, he/she shall be subject to such statutory provisions."

As discussed earlier, "tortious act" and "breach of contract" are very similar to each other, and they have also been frequently confused in judicial practice. Thus, further comparison on these two will help us understand the legal content of tortious act better: (1) from the perspective of the breached legal obligation, "breach of contract" breaches an agreed obligation between the contractual parties, whereas "tortious act" breaches a legal obligation imposed by law to each and every person; (2) from the perspective of whether a contractual relationship exists, we should determine whether such a relationship exists beforehand; if so, the case is a contract case; otherwise, it is a tort case; (3) from the perspective of what has been infringed, "breach of contract" violates a relative right, whereas "tortious act" violates an absolute right, which is outside the scope of contract or debt rights; and (4) from the perspective of damage, if an illegal act causes property damage and the victim seeks remedy, damage is limited to reasonably foreseeable damage in the case of breach of contract, but in the case of tort, actual damage is recovered.

The differences between "tortious act" and "criminal act" are relatively more obvious and they are the following: (1) from the perspective of legal basis, "criminal act" is the violation of criminal law, whereas "tortious act" is the violation of Tort Law; (2) from the perspective of objects being violated or infringed, the scope of objects that can be violated by "criminal act" is very broad, whereas "tortious act" may only violate or infringe on two types of rights—personal rights and property rights and no other social relation may be the object of "tortious act"; (3) from the perspective of social harm, "criminal act" must carry some degree of social harms, but it is not necessarily true for "tortious act," which only requires that certain damage or harm has been caused; and (4) from the perspective of subjective wrongfulness, "criminal act" has higher degree of subjective wrongfulness and is mostly intentional, but "tortious act" only requires that the perpetrator has subjective fault, which in most cases is only negligence.

In sum, the most accurate understanding of "tortious act" is a person's civil wrongful act causes remediable personal or property damage to other people and such act is a breach of this person's obligation imposed by law. On this point, there is no major difference between the continental law system and the Anglo-American law system. But notably, China's legal scholars generally accept the continental law system's view and consider "tortious act" a factor for causing debt. Stated differently, when a tortious act occurs, there exists a special right-obligation relationship between the perpetrator and the victim—the perpetrator has an obligation to compensate the victim's damage and the victim has the right to request for remedy based on the damage caused by the perpetrator. This right-obligation relationship forms the so-called debt due to a tortious act.

Types of Tortious Acts

Tortious acts are very complicated illegal civil acts, having many different forms and types. Thus, categorizing tortious acts according to different standards helps us to more clearly understand their characteristics and differences and further helps us to summarize their formation and study the relevant legal consequences. The most common categorizing methods include the following:

1. Depending on the elements, tortious acts may be categorized into general tortious acts and special tortious acts. General tortious acts are specified in the general provisions of the Tort Law. They are committed out of a perpetrator's own fault, and fault liability and general tort elements are usually applicable. In such cases, damages are usually caused by the perpetrator's own fault. Thus, the perpetrator is held liable for these damages. To commit a general tortious act, the perpetrator must have civil capacity and can clearly appreciate the intent and consequence of his/her act. Also, the perpetrator must be at fault, which can be either intentional or negligent, and the fault can be the basis for imposing liability on the perpetrator. Lastly, the law determines whether there is any infringement based on the general tort elements: illegal act, damage, causation, and subjective fault.

   As to special tortious acts, although these acts are not wrongful in nature, damages are clearly caused by these acts, events, or other special reasons. In these cases, the perpetrators are held liable due to specific provisions in the Tort Law. The major differences between special tortious acts and general tortious acts are reflected on the elements and the principles of tort liability. Special tortious acts have lesser elements than general tortious acts, and presumed fault liability or no-fault liability imputation principle applies. Also, because the law may reduce or reverse the burden of proving certain elements, special tort cases are generally much easier to prove than general tort cases in actual practice.
2. Depending on the number of perpetrators, tortious acts may be categorized into singular tortious acts and plural tortious acts. As its name reflects, a singular tortious act is committed by a single person, and this person can be either a natural person or a legal person. A plural tortious act is committed by two or more persons based on joint fault or conscious cooperation. A plural tortious act harms other people's legitimate rights and causes the same damage. It should be noted that the difference between a singular tortious act and a plural tortious act is not just the increase of number of perpetrators. The much deeper difference is reflected on the complexity of the legal relationships. The court not only needs to decide whether these perpetrators shall be held liable for the victim's damage but also needs to determine how to distribute liability among these perpetrators—whether they shall bear joint and several liability, liability proportional to each perpetrator's fault, etc. It is easy to appreciate the difficulty to make a fair and reasonable judicial decision.

3. Depending on the rights being infringed, tortious acts may be categorized into property right-based tortious acts and personal right-based tortious acts. Property right-based tortious acts lead to property damages; therefore, only property-based remedies may be requested. Here, property right includes real right, debt right, intellectual property right, etc. Property right-based tortious acts include trespassing, nuisance, misappropriation, destruction, plagiarism, counterfeiting, tampering, etc. Personal right-based tortious acts may not only lead to property damages but also cause mental distress; therefore, a victim in this situation may not only get property damage relief but also request remedy on the mental distress. Personal right-based tortious acts may further be categorized into personality rights-based tortious acts and identity rights-based tortious acts. Personality right includes the right to life, right to health, bodily right and other material personality rights, as well as the right to name, the right to image, the right to privacy and other spiritual personality rights. Identity right includes the authorship right, the honorary right, and the right to marriage, etc.
4. Depending on the nature of the acts, tortious acts may be categorized into feasance type of tortious acts and nonfeasance type of tortious acts. By committing a feasance type of tortious act, a person breaches his/her obligation not to do something and actively commits an illegal act. Stated differently, the law forbids certain harmful or wrongful acts to protect people's legitimate civil rights and interests, but the perpetrator actively committed such an act. By committing a nonfeasance type of tortious act, a person breaches his/her duty to act and causes damage or injury to a victim. In some situations, the law has imposed certain duties or obligations on some special groups of people. Not carrying out these duties or obligations would constitute a tort. The obligations or duties must be expressly specified in the law, and they are usually created under three situations: (1) obligations based on certain special personal relationships, (2) obligations based on certain special professions or positions, and (3) obligations based on previous activities.

The Concept of Tort Liability

Tort liability is a concept built upon tortious acts. It refers to a person's legal obligation to take responsibility for the legal consequences of infringing on other people's property or personal rights. Thus, the existence of a tortious act is the precondition for the formation of tort liability, and tort liability is the possible consequence that may be caused by a tortious act. The two have a causation relationship. Thus, the main characteristics of tort liability are as follows:

Firstly, tort liability is the legal consequence a person should bear for breaching his/her legal duties. Civil duties can be categorized into legal duties and contractual duties. Legal duties are created by the specifications or prohibitions of law and regulation. These duties generally apply to all natural or legal persons. Breaching such duties leads to tort liabilities.

Secondly, tort liability is preconditioned on tortious acts. Without tortious act, there is no tort liability. The purpose for creating tort liability is to punish tortious acts, protect people's civil rights, and restore the damaged property or personal relationships. Thus, tort liability is the legal consequence that a perpetrator shall be held liable for committing the tortious act.

Thirdly, relative to contract liability, tort liability is a separate and individual civil liability, with strong legality and enforceability. Different from the contractual nature of contract liability, tort liability is established based on the Tort Law or other special laws. Forming and assuming tort liability must meet all conditions and means specified by law.

Lastly, remedies for tort liability are mainly in the form of damage compensation but are not limited to so. To ensure that the victims can receive adequate remedies, tort liability may also be enforced in other forms such as cessation of the infringement, elimination of nuisance, returning of properties, removing danger, apologize, etc.

It should be noted that although tortious acts may cause liabilities to the perpetrators and the victims may receive various remedies including damage compensation, the liabilities cannot be established automatically and the victims must actively pursue the claims. This relates to the issue of a victim's right to request relief for any damage caused by a tortious act. Pursuant to this right, the victim is entitled to request the perpetrator to compensate whatever damage caused. To this end, Article 3 of the "Tort Law" specifically states: "[t]he victim of a tort is entitled to require the tortfeasor to assume the tort liability." This provision straightforwardly endows a victim the right to request damage relief from the perpetrator of the tortious act and clearly specifies the route to achieve such relief.

The right to request relief in a tort case is based on the fact that a person's civil right is infringed. The civil right can be either property right or personal right. Once there is damage, the victim has the right to request compensational relief from the perpetrator, and the perpetrator has the obligation to compensate the victim's damage. The creation of the right to request relief is critical to a victim because it gives the victim the right to sue in court and also is the starting point for calculating the statute of limitations.

As can be seen, the key to determine whether the right to request relief on torts exists is whether the perpetrator has violated someone's civil rights protected by law. Thus, what kind of civil rights are protected by law is the most important issue. Article 2 of the "Tort Law" lists 18 types of protected rights, including personal and property rights and interests such as the right to life, right to health, rights associated with names, reputational rights, honorary rights, right to one's image, right to privacy, right to marital autonomy, right to guardianship, ownership rights, usufruct, collateral rights, copyrights, patent rights, exclusive rights to use trademarks, discovery rights, equity rights, and inheritance rights. In other words, the "Tort Law" provides the strictest protection to these 18 types of rights. As long as an act has violated any of these rights and met the requirements for tortious act, the perpetrator shall be held liable provided there is no defense or privilege. It should be noted that these 18 rights are not exhaustive. There are other unlisted rights protected by law. But it is quite difficult to foresee and define them. We can only rely on the judges for finding and determining them in judicial practice.

In reality, people often encounter a question in exercising the right to request relief—the concurrence of legal liabilities. This concept refers to a question that which provision or provisions should apply when an illegal act violates multiple provisions of the law. If only one provision applies and others are excluded, it is called conflicting concurrence of legal liabilities and usually occurs within a same legal department, e.g., the concurrence of tort liability and contract liability. If multiple provisions apply, it is called non-conflicting concurrence of legal liabilities, which usually happens across different legal departments, e.g., the concurrence of civil liability and criminal liability. Paragraph 1, Article 4 of the "Tort Law" specifies the non-conflicting concurrence of legal liabilities: "[e]ven if a tortfeasor is required to assume administrative liability or criminal liability for the same conduct, it shall not prejudice the tort liability that the tortfeasor shall legally assume." Thus, when a perpetrator shall bear both administrative and tort liabilities (or criminal and tort liabilities) for the same act, a tort suit collateral to administrative suit (or criminal suit) should be brought against the perpetrator.

Even though tort liability, administrative liability, and criminal liability may stay independent and separate when concurrence of liabilities occurs, conflict may still exist when a perpetrator's property is not adequate enough for satisfying fine, confiscation, and other penalties. Then, there is a question of priority among these liabilities. On this point, Paragraph 2, Article 4 of the "Tort Law" states: "[w]here a tortfeasor's assets are not adequate for payments for the tort liability and administrative liability or criminal liability for the same conduct, the tortfeasor shall first assume the tort liability." Under that provision, when tort liability conflicts with administrative or criminal liability, tort liability takes priority in terms of remedy or compensation. This reflects the legislative principle of putting people's civil and private rights first.

Responsive to the categorization of tortious acts into general tortious acts and special tortious acts, the "Tort Law" also establishes two basic liability forms: general tort liability and special tort liability. General tort liability governs general tortious acts; special tort liability governs special tortious acts. They have different elements, imputation principles, defenses, and privileges:

1. General tort liability usually uses fault liability as its imputation principle. The existence of fault is the precondition for such liability. Defenses against general tort liability include contributory negligence, victim's intention, third party's fault, force majeure, self-defense, and necessity.
2. Special tort liability is specially created for public policy reasons by legislative bodies. It is usually not based on fault. The burden of proof may sometimes be shifted to a defendant to reduce plaintiff's burden. Reduction or elimination of liability must be based on specific statutes of the law.

The Concept and Function of Tort Law

The concept of Tort Law has a general version as well as a special version. The special version only refers to the "Tort Law" passed by the standing committee of the National People's Congress on December 26, 2009. The general version refers to all laws and rules regarding tortious acts and liabilities thereof, including standardizing the definition and types of tortious acts, determining what constitute tortious acts, and specifying remedies and liabilities for the consequences of tortious acts. Characteristics of Tort Law include the following:

First, it protects civil rights, which not only include those rights specifically listed in Article 2 of the "Tort Law" but also should include other unlisted but legitimate personal and property rights. That is, Tort Law's protection system is open and can cover those tortious acts that may occur in the future.

Second, it is essentially a liability law, which addresses not just the tortious acts but more importantly the consequences of those acts. Thus, Tort Law specifies not only various different types of tortious acts but also rules of liability, including imputation principles of liability, elements, methods for assuming liability, remedies, and defenses.

Third, the main purpose of Tort Law is to provide relief for victims through imputation of liability. Tort law's major form of remedy is damage compensation. It also provides cessation of the infringement, elimination of nuisance, returning properties, removing danger, apologies, etc.—providing relief to victims both spiritual wise and property wise.

In different times and at different locations, the function of Tort Law has been different throughout history. For example, the function may be expiation, punishment, intimidation, and education, compensating or preventing damages and reflecting the social economic situation at that time as well as the people's ethical and moral attitudes. Generally speaking, Tort Law has four major functions:

Firstly, it has the function of compensating damages. Emphasizing this function is an important trend of modern Tort Law. The original purpose of Tort Law was to provide remedy or relief to any person whose right was infringed. Thus, the primary function of Tort Law is to ensure that a plaintiff's damage will be compensated. And this is accomplished by establishing civil liability and by providing various means of compensation to restore the infringed right or damaged interest back to its previous condition. Depending on the nature of the infringed right or damaged interest, the means may be different: as to property right, the means include returning the property at issue, restoring the property back to normal or previous condition, or compensating the damage; as to personal right, the means include eliminating the effect, restoring reputation, apologizing, or compensating the damage to reduce or remove the victim's mental grief.

Tort law's basis for imposing liability on a perpetrator is that the perpetrator's victim is entitled to remedy or relief for the damage caused by the perpetrator. The direct purpose of the liability imputation principle is to identify the person who should be liable. Once that person is identified, the amount of remedy should not change whether the person acted intentionally or negligently. In other words, Tort Law's liability imputation principle is not created to punish perpetrators but to provide quick, complete, and substantial remedies to victims so that their infringed rights or damaged interests may be restored as close to pre-infringement conditions as possible. Shifting of proof of burden, no-fault tort liability, liability insurance, and rationalization of compensation amount—these modern Tort Law rules were all established for the purpose of making it easier to provide remedies to victims.

Secondly, Tort Law has the function of distributing damages and balancing interests. By applying rules such as perpetrator's general liability, joint and several liability, third party's liability, mixed liability based on plaintiff's and defendant's fault, shared liability when no party is at fault, and beneficiary's liability to bear damage, Tort Law is able to transfer victims' damages in whole or in part to perpetrators or other relevant parties to achieve its damage distribution function. While focusing on protecting people's personal and property rights and providing remedies or relief, Tort Law also provides the function of balancing social interests. This function is achieved by issuing judicial judgment and determining the amount of compensation. Whether compensation is needed and how much is needed directly affect the economic interests between or among the parties. To certain degrees, it is a redistribution of social wealth.

Thirdly, Tort Law has the function of curbing or controlling illegal acts or activities. One of the core purposes of Tort Law is to hold perpetrators liable for their infringing acts. This civil liability does not carry punishment in principle. It just requests the perpetrator to compensate the victim any damage in full amount. Even so, the perpetrator still needs to face two unfavorable results: first, because the perpetrator's act is deemed an illegal act by the law, the perpetrator will often receive certain negative response from the society, and second, the perpetrator is requested to perform certain obligations, either in the form of making a compensation (paying certain amount of money, or return or restore the victim's property) or in the form of nonmonetary performance (e.g., eliminating the effect of his/her tortious act, restoring the victim's reputation, apologizing). All of these are not favorable to the perpetrator (or defendant). Thus, Tort Law can admonish perpetrators and urge them not to commit tortious or infringing acts again. For example, no-fault liability causes corporations or manufacturers to improve the quality of their products; shifting the burden of proof encourages underground construction workers to exercise reasonable care. While admonishing perpetrators, Tort Law also admonishes all members of our society.

Lastly, Tort Law has the function of protecting and creating civil rights. Early Tort Law only specified personality rights narrowly. With the development of social civilization, people started realizing the importance of personality rights (e.g., privacy right, honorary right, etc.) Because the Tort Law system is open ended, every country has been constantly creating new types of civil rights through legislation or case law precedents and absorbing them under its protection. For example, in recent years, the objects of Tort Law's protection were no longer limited to those civil rights specified or recognized by traditional civil law. Certain legitimate rights, such as a deceased's rights, were also under its protection.

Application of Tort Law

General Tort Law is a system having very rich contents, including not only those fundamental and principle-guiding laws such as "General Principles of Civil Law" and "Tort Law" but also many specific Tort Laws, administrative laws, as well as judicial interpretations. Although these laws jointly contribute to the completeness of our Tort Law system, they also cause many issues in actual applications. Thus, because there exist potential conflicts among these laws in different levels, we need to clarify and sort out the relationships among them:

1. The relationship between the "Tort Law" and the "General Principles of Civil Law": as part of the debt law in the "Specific Provisions of the Civil Law," the "Tort Law" absorbed and replaced those provisions relating to tort liability in the "General Principles of Civil Law." Thus, after the "Tort Law" was in effect, the tort-related provisions in the "General Principles of Civil Law" were no longer applicable. But, provisions in debt law that are applicable to tort liabilities and sections in the "General Principles of Civil Law" that are corresponding to the general provisions of civil law should still be applicable. For example, Paragraph 3, Article 18, of the "General Principles of Civil Law"—if a guardian does not fulfill his duties as guardian or infringes upon the lawful rights and interests of his ward, he shall be held responsible; if a guardian causes any property loss for his ward, he shall compensate for such loss—should still be applicable.
2. The relationship between the "Tort Law" and special Tort Laws: according to the scope of law's efficacy, laws may be categorized into general laws and special laws. In principle, with respect to laws created by a same institute, special laws override general laws when there are conflicts. On this point, Article 5 of the "Tort Law" specifies: "[w] here other laws provide otherwise for any tort liability in particular, such special provisions shall prevail." As said above, the "Tort Law" is a general law relating to tort liabilities. Other laws such as "Road Traffic Safety Law" or "Product Quality Law," which has special rules relating to tort liability, are special laws. Thus, following the above specified principle, special Tort Laws override the "Tort Law" when there are conflicts between them.
3. Relationship between the "Tort Law" and subordinate laws: being enacted by the standing committee of the National People's Congress, the "Tort Law" is only subordinate to the constitution with respect to legal efficacy. Administrative rules, local rules, administrative regulations, autonomous ordinances, and specific regulations are all subordinate laws relative to the "Tort Law" in terms of legislative rank. According to Article 8 of the "Legislation Law," as the basic civil system, Tort Law should be enacted or amended only by the National People's Congress and its standing committee. Such enactment and amendment cannot be achieved through subordinate laws. However, because administrative rules and judicial interpretations have played important roles in China's judicial application, they should still be reasonably followed.

Relationship between the "Tort Law" and administrative laws: many administrative laws, such as the "Measures on Handling of Road Traffic Accident" and "Measures on Handling Medical Malpractice Cases" promulgated by the State Council of the People's Republic of China, specify rules governing specific tort cases because of the lack of rules or for experimental purposes. The law sometimes authorizes the State Council to make certain rules or regulations. And the State Council regularly makes regulations and details for the implementation of existing law to make it more specific. Thus, in the application of the "Tort Law," administrative laws shall not be overlooked or neglected. Rather, it should be determined whether these administrative laws apply according to the content and specifications of these laws. With respect to a rule or provision that is specified in an administrative law but not in the "Tort Law," we should determine whether it conflicts with the legislative intent and principles of the "Tort Law." If so, such rule or provision can be applied to resolve the relevant tort issue. Otherwise, it should not be applied. With respect to a rule or provision that is specified in both an administrative law and the "Tort Law," the "Tort Law" should be applied according to the principle that a superior law has higher priority than a subordinate law.

Relationship between the "Tort Law" and judicial interpretations: to ensure accurate and unified applications of laws in judicial practice, the People's Supreme Court of China frequently provides interpretations of laws. Judicial interpretations completely and accurately interpret the laws' basic spirit and even fill in the holes in the laws. Certain rules in "Tort Law," such as the duty of care rule, were established first by judicial interpretations. In the application of the "Tort Law," judicial interpretation has a critical role. Thus, those judicial interpretations, which were created before the enactment of Tort Law and conform to the basic legislative spirit of the "Tort Law," shall still be followed. The interpretations that do not conform to the spirit are not applicable, and in those cases, the "Tort Law" should be applied. Interpretations after the enactment of the "Tort Law" shall be applicable.

Chapter 3
Imputation Principles of Tort Liability

Concept

The nature of Tort Law is to impose civil liability on people who have committed wrongful or illegal acts so that injured parties may receive damage compensation as a way of recovery. As such, it is not difficult to see that this policy is based on the principle of attributing liability to the perpetrator (i.e., wrongdoer) for his wrongful act. Otherwise, even if a person's act has caused damage to another person's legitimate interest, we simply do not have authority to punish that person. Thus, what standard(s) should be applied in determining whether a person's act is wrong and therefore the person should assume liability for other's injury or damage is the most important issue in every country's Tort Law system—this is the so-called imputation principles of tort liability.

As the name suggests, imputation principles of tort liability are the rules of determining and attributing liabilities. With respect to tort, these principles deal with the general rules and standards of a perpetrator's responsibility to compensate the damage or injury he has caused to other people. They are the guiding principles for determining whether a person should be held responsible for the damage he has caused and therefore should assume civil liability. Stated differently, the imputation principles of tort liability solve the difficult issue of what kind of act gives rise to civil liability.

The task of determining tort liability seems awfully complicated but can be reduced into two questions: should a person be liable and how much liability should the person have? The first question—should a person be liable—is answered by the imputation principles of tort liability. That is, after injury or damage has been caused, what standard(s) should be followed to determine whether it is the perpetrator, the victim, or other people in our society who should be responsible for the injury and/or damage? It is only after the first question has been answered that the second question is submitted for resolution in accordance with the rules of compensation.

X. Li and J. Jin, *Concise Chinese Tort Laws*, China-EU Law Series 1,
DOI 10.1007/978-3-642-41024-6_3,

To appreciate the importance of the imputation principles of tort liability, we shall look no further than the image of Lady Justice carrying the balance scale of truth and fairness. If Lady Justice were adjudicating a tort case, then what is carried on each end of the balance scale would be "act" and "liability," respectively. And the beam of the scale would be the imputation principles of tort liability because only by relying on it could we determine which side of the balance scale is heavier. As can be seen, the imputation principles of tort liability are critical within Tort Law. They specify the adjudicating criteria and set the prerequisites for imposing liability on a perpetrator. In practice, these principles serve a decisive role in resolving tort cases.

Specifically, the imputation principles of tort liability serve at least three major functions in Tort Law:

Firstly, they set an order—the relevant positions of each type of act and its consequences in the universe of Tort Law—and reflect the values of a country's social justice as well as the spirit of its Tort Law.

Secondly, they provide a standard. In judicial practice, these principles will become a measuring scale for properly assessing various conducts and then determining the corresponding consequences. Thus, the significance of applying the principles lies with the appropriate characterization of the various acts, which is clearly the prerequisite of whether we can apply Tort Law in our actual social life.

Finally, they are the core of the Tort Law system, exist in each operative step of the process, and serve as its base, on which each and every element of the system is built. Although the principles do not always lead to the finding of liability, whether a person is liable or not will always be the result of these principles' effect.

As can be seen, the imputation principles of tort liability is the absolute "commander in chief" in the theories of Tort Law and determines the basic profile of a country's Tort Law system. In other words, what type of Tort Law we have is governed by what type of imputation principles of tort liability we use.

Significance of the Principles

The imputation principles of tort liability have provided not only theoretical guidance on determining tortious acts and assumption of liability but also significant implications in practice. It is no exaggeration to say that all rules of Tort Law are based on these principles. Specifically:

1. These principles determine the categorization and application of tortious acts. Depending on the imputation principle of tort liability, tortious acts can be categorized into general tortious act and special tortious act. Fault liability generally applies to the former one. Presumed fault liability, no-fault liability, and strict liability generally apply to the latter one.
2. They define the elements of tort liability. Different imputation principles of tort liability have different elements for establishing tort liability. For example,

elements for fault liability include fault, tortious act, causation, and damage. But for no-fault liability, the elements include tortious act, causation, and damage—"fault" is no longer required.

3. They determine who bears the burden of proof. Under the theory of fault liability, a plaintiff has the burden of proof. But under the theory of presumed fault liability, the burden of proof shifts to a defendant, who must prove that he has no fault. This is designed to protect certain disadvantaged plaintiffs in special tort cases.
4. They govern the reduction or elimination of liability and the scope of damage. Depending on the imputation principle of tort liability, different defenses may be applied for reduction or elimination of liability. The scope of defenses available for fault liability can be relatively broader than that for no-fault liability, which may even provide no such defense in certain occasions.

In sum, the establishment of Tort Law system affords different legal meanings to different subjects. The goal of a country's legislation on the imputation principles of tort liability is generally to manifest its different treatments to different tortious acts: applying fault liability to general tortious act indicates Tort Law's traditional functionality, whereas applying no-fault liability to tortious acts involving ultrahazardous activities, vicious animals, or environment polluting activities indicates modern Tort Law's policy to safeguard the interests of vulnerable groups and maintain social justice.

From the perspective of judicial practice, it is helpful for judicial officials to correctly grasp the imputation principles of tort liability so that right in the beginning of a case they can determine the issues such as whether the plaintiff has the burden to prove the defendant's fault, what the defendant can rely on to reduce liability, the scope of damage, and the cap of damage. As such, these officials can correctly handle the litigation and issue a judgment in compliance with the law. It is also helpful for the parties in the case to be clear on what imputation principle of tort liability applies here so that they can collect the right evidence, properly exercise their rights and obligations, and raise appropriate requests.

The System of Tort Liability

What kind of imputation principles of tort liability a country should choose eventually depends on the social functionality its Tort Law system is expected to achieve, and that is mostly determined by the country's social and economic development status. Because most people expect multiple social functions from the Tort Law, many countries had felt that a single imputation principle of tort liability would not be able to serve the need of their fast-moving society. As such, countries have turned to systemized imputation principles of tort liability. While acknowledging fault liability as the basic imputation principle, they have created other types of tort principles for special cases. China is one of these countries.

Articles 6–7 of the "Tort Law" specify the imputation principles of tort liability, which include fault liability, presumed fault liability, and no-fault liability. Therefore, China's system of tort liability is composed of fault liability, presumed fault liability, and no-fault liability.

However, it should be noted that although the above three principles are all part of China's Tort Law system, they are not parallel to each other, they do not carry the same weight, and they are applicable to different situations. Overall, we can characterize their relationships as the following: fault liability is the fundamental imputation principle of tort liability and presumed fault liability and no-fault liability are supplementary principles.

To say so is because fault liability is the most important one among the imputation principles of tort liability. As shown, fault liability is a principle that is generally applicable to all tort cases unless the law expressly says that presumed fault liability or no-fault liability applies. It is therefore a catchall principle. The "Tort Law" is very clear on this point. Fault liability is created as a general provision and holds a dominant position therein. It is the core of general torts. Presumed liability and no-fault liability are all special rules for certain special situations. Therefore, they belong to specific provisions and are only supplementary rules for special tort cases.

Presumed fault liability was originally derived from fault liability. Its judging criteria and elements are no different from those of fault liability, but there are important differences between the two: (1) The burden of proof is different. The burden of proof for fault liability lies solely on a plaintiff's shoulder, whereas the burden of proof for presumed fault liability is shifted to a defendant, who must present evidence to prove his innocence. (2) The scope of applicability is different. Fault liability is applicable to the majority of general torts, whereas presumed fault liability only applies to certain special torts. Because of these differences, the "Tort Law" specifically included presumed fault liability as an independent imputation principle of tort liability.

No-fault liability should also be treated as an independent imputation principle of tort liability because it was developed as a result of fault liability's inability to meet certain social needs. It reduces the difficulty for victims to proffer evidence in certain special situations and therefore makes it easier for them to recover their damages. Because of that, the law strictly defines the scope and condition for its application—this principle can be used when and only when the "Tort Law" or other special law specifically allows. Otherwise, this principle must not be applied.

These three principles serve their functions independently and are applied flexibly, forming a special characteristic of China's Tort Law legislation. In the specific provisions of the "Tort Law," each type of tort is specified according to special imputation principles of tort liability. As such, they work in complementary with each other and may form multilayer tort liabilities in certain situations. In medical malpractice cases, for example, fault liability, presumed fault liability, and no-fault liability may apply in different situations depending on the reason that caused the injury. Such kind of legislation is clearly more considerate than the one with just a single imputation principle of tort liability, as it considers different interests under different situations and achieves a balance of interests between patients and medical institutes.

Besides the above three imputation principles of tort liability, there is an equitable liability that needs our attention. In certain cases, there was no fault on the perpetrator's side and the damage or injury was not caused by any special legal fact. But to provide appropriate compensation to the victim, courts can consider factors such as the perpetrator's and the victim's financial status to issue a judgment requesting the perpetrator to pay the damage in whole or in part to achieve equity and justice. Equitable liability only applies to those rare situations, where it is difficult to apply fault liability and there is no basis (or legal fact) to apply presumed fault liability or no-fault liability. In these situations, it is necessary to grant equitable power to the judge so that he can reasonably distribute the damage among the parties.

Regarding the issue of whether equitable liability is part of the tort liabilities, there have been many different opinions among China's law scholars in the past. With the introduction of the "Tort Law," this issue became moot because the "Tort Law" has adopted a separate approach—it specified fault liability, presumed fault liability, and no-fault liability in the provisions for the formation of liability, but specified equitable liability in the provisions for assumption of liability. As can be seen, the current Tort Law legislation has not treated equitable liability as part of the tort liabilities but a liability that serves as a supplementary rule for loss/damage allocation.

Fault Liability

Fault liability is a principle of determining a perpetrator's civil liability based on whether the perpetrator is at fault. Basically, if there is no fault, then there should be no liability. In other words, fault is the basis for a perpetrator to assume liability and a necessary element for finding tort liability. In general torts, the reason to impose civil liability on a perpetrator is that there is fact establishing the perpetrator's subjective fault. On the other hand, if a perpetrator is not at subjective fault, he should not be liable even though his act has caused damage and there is causation relationship between his act and the damage.

Fault liability first appeared in the "French Civil Code" of 1804 and was considered a great development in Tort Law. This is because:

1. Individually: It reflects a strong individualism and respect for self-determination and free will. It emphasizes that each person is a complete and independent individual and therefore should be responsible for his behavior. If a person has committed a wrong while interacting with others in a society, that person should of course be liable for any damage or injury so caused. On the opposite, if that person has fulfilled all necessary obligations, he should not worry and the law should not hold him responsible.

2. Socially: It is a subjective responsibility and makes everyone aware of the consequence of his act. As such, it serves a guiding and warning function for people with respect to their acts and presents a safe and encouraged social lifestyle. With the guidance of fault liability, people can avoid tort liabilities by exercising reasonable care before doing something, therefore protecting our whole society as a much safer place.
3. Economically: It grew up together with capitalism and served as well as protected the industrial economy's development. The rule to determine liability purely based on damage or injury had severely impeded the progress of reform and innovation in the past for fear of being responsible for huge reparation if something went wrong. But now, if one has exercised reasonable care, he can try all kinds of new technologies or inventions to improve productivity, without worrying about liability even if there is damage caused. Thus, fault liability actually serves the function of limiting liability. It protects free competition and innovation and promotes economic development.
4. Morally: It maintains a balanced relationship between law and moral, making the two close enough so that the law conforms with moral values in general (i.e., any wrongdoing should be punished) but not so mixed up that the two be treated the same. The "wrong" we are talking about here is not the same as "sin." As long as a person has committed no legal wrong, then moral fault does not necessarily lead to legal penalty.

In sum, what fault liability establishes is a standard that people should be able to follow in the real world generally, a standard that can provide guidance and restriction to people's behavior, a standard that fits well with our traditional moral norm, and a standard that promotes economic development and encourages innovation. No wonder many American and European countries choose fault liability as their primary imputation principle for tort liability, and same does China.

Article 6, Paragraph 1 of "Tort Law" says: "[o]ne who is at fault for infringement upon civil rights or interests of others shall be subject to the tort liability." This is the basic specification of fault liability in China's Tort Law—it embodies the following meanings:

1. With respect to its place, fault liability is the basic imputation principle of tort liability in Tort Law. It applies to general tort cases, and only when there is a specific provision can other principle of tort liability apply. That is to say, fault liability is the primary imputation principle in Tort Law, and any other imputation principle of tort liability is supplementary. When the law is silent on which principle applies, the default principle is fault liability.
2. With respect to its content, fault liability is founded on two important tenets: the first one is that there is liability only when there is fault—the law attributes liability for any injury or damage caused by a wrongful act to a person who is at fault and holds the person responsible for the injury or damage; therefore, establishing a person's fault is the precondition for requesting that person to be liable for the injury or damage; and the second one is that no fault no

liability—if a perpetrator has no subjective fault on causing the damage or injury, he cannot be held liable. Even if the perpetrator's act directly caused the victim's damage or injury, the victim does not necessarily get compensated as it also depends on whether the perpetrator is subjectively at fault.

3. With respect to its function, fault liability uses fault as its ultimate element and an important factor for determining the scope of the perpetrator's liability. This includes two layers of meaning: Firstly, fault is considered an element of proving liability. Proving whether a perpetrator is at fault is at the core of determining liability. If the person is not at subjective fault, there is no liability because of the lack of the fault element. Secondly, fault is a factor to be considered in determining how much liability the perpetrator must be accountable—ensuring that the perpetrator's liability is roughly consistent with the degree of the person's fault and achieving a reasonable and equitable liability sharing among the parties.

Fault liability is a subjective principle in nature. It starts with the fact that a person has consciously committed a wrongful act. Therefore, the "wrongful act" (or simply "fault") discussed here is a subjective condition. It is the perpetrator's state of mind when he committed the wrongful act (i.e., the perpetrator's subjective attitude towards the harmful consequence of his act). Generally speaking, subjective fault can be divided into two mental statuses: *intentional*—a person can foresee the harmful result of his act and intends the occurrence of the result or let the result occur without any intervention and *negligence*—a person should have foreseen the harmful result of his act, can foresee the harmful result but did not foresee it because of carelessness, or already foresaw them but overconfidently and wrongfully believed that the harmful result could be avoided and therefore caused damage or injury.

No matter which subjective fault is at issue, a plaintiff (or victim) bears the burden of proof and a defendant (or an accused party) does not. If the victim cannot prove by sufficient evidence that the defendant was at subjective fault when he committed the act, then the defendant's act is considered appropriate. Even if there is damage or injury, the defendant is not liable.

Presumed Fault Liability

In certain special situations specified by law, a perpetrator is presumed to be at fault based on his tortious act and therefore is held liable for the damage or injury caused—i.e., the "presumed fault liability." That is, the perpetrator's subjective fault is inferred from the fact that a victim's legitimate interest has been harmed by the perpetrator's act. According to this principle, if the victim can prove damage or injury, illegal act, as well as causation, and the perpetrator cannot prove that there was no intention or negligence relating to the act and damage, then the judge can make the presumption that the perpetrator is at fault and order him to pay for the damage.

Presumed fault liability was created by a French judge named Domat in the seventeenth century. It was initially adopted by the "French Civil Code" and has been adopted by most countries' Tort Laws by now. Presumed fault liability originated from fault liability majorly for handling situations where fault liability was insufficient. With its application scope getting broader and broader later on, presumed fault liability became an independent tort principle. As an extension of fault liability, presumed fault liability did not completely fall off the track of fault liability. It still considers the perpetrator's subjective fault and is just an extended application of fault liability. China adopted the same philosophy in Tort Law legislation—Paragraph 2, Article 6 of the "Tort Law" states: "[o]ne who is at fault as construed according to statutory provisions and cannot prove otherwise shall be subject to the tort liability." This is China's legal account of presumed fault liability.

The significance of presumed fault liability is that it puts victims on a more advantaged litigating position, by shifting certain litigation burdens to perpetrators to protect the victims' legitimate interests and punish tortious activities. Although fault liability is the main liability imputation principle, it is not a principle that can be applied to all types of tort cases, especially for cases where the parties' litigating powers are off-balanced or it is so difficult for a plaintiff to bear the burden of proof that it cannot possibly establish the elements for fault liability. If we continue following the old rules without any reform in such cases, it is equivalent to refuse these victims the remedies of Tort Law. Thus, if these victims are still deemed as eligible for recovery under Tort Law, we should try to change the structural unfairness and reform the rules so that the victims have a chance to compete with the well-positioned perpetrators on the same ground in courts. This is what the Tort Law should deliver in our social justice system. By applying the presumed fault liability to presume fault on a perpetrator's side, a victim is relieved of the burden of proof and is placed on a more advantaged position, whereas the perpetrator's overall obligation is increased because the burden of proof is shifted to him. This mechanism helps on protecting victims' legitimate interests.

Since presumed fault liability derives from fault liability, its elements of proof are exactly the same to those of fault liability. They are damage or injury, causation, illegal act, and subjective fault. These four elements must be met before finding liability, but in cases where presumed fault liability applies, courts will presume subjective fault on a defendant's side after a plaintiff has established the first three elements. At this point, the defendant must offer evidence to prove the opposite regarding the subjective fault element. Otherwise, the plaintiff wins and the defendant is liable for the plaintiff's damage or injury.

As can be seen, the biggest difference between presumed fault liability and fault liability lies on the issue of how the subjective fault element is established. With respect to presumed fault liability, courts do not require a victim to bear the burden to prove the fault element. Rather, courts directly presume subjective fault on a perpetrator's side from the very existence of any damage or injury and its causation relationship with any illegal act. If the defendant maintains his allegation that he is innocent, he should offer evidence to prove so. Two opposite results can occur: on the one hand, the defendant alleges that he is innocent and is able to offer evidence to prove so, then the presumption is overruled and the defendant is not liable for whatever damage or injury occurred; on the other hand, if the defendant cannot offer sufficient evidence to prove its innocence, then he must pay for the damage or injury.

Although presumed fault liability embodies a policy that is more beneficial to the victims and offers more protection to them, it does not mean that this principle has imposed liability on the defendants for no reasons whatsoever, because it does provide a defendant an opportunity to exonerate himself. The law recognizes the effect of a defendant's evidence refuting his fault before presuming the fault on his side. Only when damage and causation exist, and the defendant cannot refute the fault element, would fault be presumed on his side. In other words, if the defendant can offer evidence to prove that he was not at fault, then the defendant is not liable. Also, the application of presumed fault liability is limited to situations expressly specified by law, where it is usually the perpetrator who is more familiar or knowledgeable with the facts relating to the causation of damage or injury. And therefore, the perpetrator has the convenience to raise argument and offer evidence to prove his innocence. Thus, it cannot be said that presumed fault liability is clearly unfair to defendants.

According to the "Tort Law," presumed fault liability applies to the following situations: (1) a person lacking civil capacity suffers a bodily injury while studying or living in a school or other educational institution, (2) medical ethics liability in medical malpractice, (3) a person is harmed by an animal in a zoo, (4) a driver of a non-motor vehicle or a pedestrian is harmed by a motor vehicle in a traffic accident, and (5) any bodily injury caused by a building, a hanged object on a building, a stacked material, a damaged tree, or any underground facility.

No-fault Liability

Under certain situations specified by law and based on any damage or injury already occurred, a person who has caused such damage or injury is held liable whether or not he is at fault. This is the so-called no-fault liability. Under different occasions, we may call no-fault liability "determined fault liability," "danger liability," or "strict liability." They have the same or similar meanings but are from different perspectives regarding tort liability. Determined fault liability is based more on the perspective of preventing tort; danger liability is based more on the perspective of the basis for attributing liability; and strict liability is based more on the nature of the liability.

It is notable that no-fault liability and absolute liability are not the same concept. Absolute liability refers to the kind of liability in Tort Law or misdemeanor law, which is enforced by statute. Further, the degree of care or precaution that has been taken is not considered, and no evidence of fault is required in establishing absolute liability. The major differences between no-fault liability and absolute liability are the following: the former is applicable to many types of special torts, while the latter is applicable to only a few exceptional cases; the former is stricter compared to fault liability, but less strict than the latter; and certain defenses and exclusion of liability exist for no-fault liability, but almost none exists for absolute liability.

The basic principle of no-fault liability is to determine liability based on the damage or injury caused—fault on the perpetrator's side is not a required element for finding liability. The purpose to have the no fault element is to increase the perpetrator's liability in certain situations specified by law and make it easier for the victim to obtain remedy. Under this principle, fault is not the basis for liability but the fact of damage or injury is. Stated differently, if there is damage or injury, then there is liability; otherwise, there is no liability. In these cases, the victim does not need to prove the perpetrator's fault. Even if the perpetrator can prove that he has no fault, the end result will not change, unless the perpetrator can prove that the damage or injury was intentionally inflicted by the victim itself. As can be seen, no-fault liability puts a victim on a more advantaged position in tort litigation. The reason for doing so is closely related to the principle's origination.

No-fault liability was originated in the nineteenth century. Rapid economic development of western capitalism provided tremendous social and material achievement but at the same time led to numerous industrial disasters, increased the frequency of traffic accidents, created serious public hazard endangering people's health, and produced large quantities of defective products that caused injuries on consumers. With respect to the accidents caused by these advanced technologies, the industrial or economic activities themselves were not wrongful in nature. Therefore, it was difficult to determine liability via the fault-based legal concept. As such, victims were not readily compensated for their damages or injuries by applying traditional fault liability or even by objectivizing fault concept and shifting the burden of proof. Furthermore, because corporations had control over production and could reduce the dangers and risks associated therewith, and they had hugely benefited from these production activities, they should contribute certain percentage of profit into insurance policies so that victims can be compensated for whatever damage or injury caused. Because of these reasons, people started thinking outside the box of fault liability and using a new approach to remedy a victim. This new approach is called no-fault liability in the continental law system and strict liability in Anglo-American law system.

Of course, besides the social and economic reasons illustrated above, there were fundamental theoretical reasons for the creation of no-fault liability. Fault liability achieves civil justice through certain requirements on people's subjective behavior and therefore fits in the notion of justice from the traditional and natural law's perspective. On the contrast, no-fault liability achieves civil justice by balancing the interests between the vulnerable groups and strong groups and by reducing social instability via eliminating problems. Therefore, it reflects a new kind of civil justice in a highly modernized and productive society and carries the mark of social jurisprudence. Thus, if fault liability embodies the philosophy of classical liberalism and is the application of natural law in torts, then no-fault liability embodies the philosophy of realism in law.

Article 7 of the "Tort Law" states: "[i]f any law provides one shall assume the tort liability for infringing others' civil rights or interests, whether at fault or not, he/she shall be subject to such statutory provisions." It is noted that the most important condition for no-fault liability's application is the express specification of the law. In other words, only when the law specifically states so can no-fault liability be applied.

The significance of no-fault liability is that it increases a perpetrator's liability so that a victim's complaint is quickly addressed and any damage or injury is readily compensated. With respect to this point, a comparison between no-fault liability and presumed fault liability is telling that the "fault" in presumed fault liability is presumed to be true. That is, the fault element is still a necessary element to prove fault liability, but that only the burden of proof is shifted from a plaintiff to a defendant. If the defendant can prove otherwise, he is relieved from the liability. But for no-fault liability, there is no opportunity for a defendant to refute its fault. In fact, the "fault" element is not even required here. As long as the defendant's act has caused damage or injury to the plaintiff and there was no defense recognized in law, it is inevitable for the defendant to assume liability.

According to the imputation principle of no-fault liability, a perpetrator's subjective fault is not relevant. As long as there is causation relationship between the perpetrator's act and his victim's damage or injury, the perpetrator's liability is established and must be responsible for the damage or injury. Thus, in most cases where no-fault liability applies, the most important element to prove is the causation element. And because the fact of damage or injury and the fact of the perpetrator's act are easy to establish, the major fight between the plaintiff and the defendant would be to establish the causation between the two facts.

In sum, the elements to prove liability under the imputation principle of no-fault liability are reduced to three: damage or injury, illegal act, and causation. A victim must offer evidence to prove the above three elements but does not need to prove a perpetrator's subjective fault. As soon as the victim has fulfilled its obligations, the burden is shifted to the perpetrator to prove the opposite or to establish whatever exemption (or defense) allowed by law. Because of the strictness of no-fault liability, the law provides different exemptions (or defenses) for different special tortious acts. Except for these exemptions allowed by law, a perpetrator has no other defenses.

According to the "Tort Law," no-fault liability applies to the following situations: (1) manufacturer's liability to its defective products; (2) liability to environmental pollutions; (3) liability to highly dangerous activities; (4) animal keeper or manager's liability to other's injury caused by a domestic animal; (5) a guardian to a person who lacks civil capacity or has limited civil capacity is liable to another person's injury caused by the person lacking such capacity; and (6) liabilities of an employer, a party that uses dispatched labor, and a dispatching party.

Chapter 4
Elements of Tort Liability

Overview

Elements of tort liability are the basic components for establishing tort liability and the necessary prerequisites for a perpetrator to assume liability. Whether to hold a perpetrator liable after he has committed illegal act or caused damage should not be determined solely based on the illegal act or the damage. Rather, imputation of tort liability should be determined by examining all elements of tort liability. It is only after all elements have been proved that a perpetrator can be held liable and ordered to compensate the damage. Thus, it is not the case that a perpetrator must bear liability if he has committed illegal act or caused damage. Only when certain conditions are met the perpetrator can be held liable, and these conditions are the very elements of tort liability.

As can be seen, the most important function of these elements in Tort Law is to serve as the basis for determining whether a perpetrator should be held liable for any damage caused. This depends on what elements are required for the specific tort liability the perpetrator is facing. Then, our court can objectively judge the perpetrator's act based on the required elements in the actual case. No matter how the elements change, the principle of applying them is the same—only when all elements are met can a perpetrator be held liable; otherwise, there is no liability.

From the three-element theory to the seven-element theory, there is no consensus on how many and what types of elements are required for tort liability among China's Tort Law scholars. Even the "Tort Law" has not resolved the dispute on this issue as Article 6, Paragraph 1, of the "Tort Law" does not clearly specify the elements for general torts. However, based on the legislative spirit and judicial interpretation of the statute by China's courts, we can safely conclude that there are four elements for tort liability, including a perpetrator's subjective fault, damage, illegal act, and causation. Thus, in determining whether there is tort liability, all four elements must be proved. Otherwise, there is no liability.

It should be noted that the elements may change depending on the type of tort liability applied. Thus, the elements for general torts are different from those for

X. Li and J. Jin, *Concise Chinese Tort Laws*, China-EU Law Series 1,
DOI 10.1007/978-3-642-41024-6_4, © Springer-Verlag Berlin Heidelberg 2014

special torts. For no-fault liability, the "fault" element is not required. If presumed fault liability is applied, then all four elements are required except that the "fault" element is presumed and the victim does not need to offer evidence to prove it.

To study the elements of tort liability is not only important in theory but also significant in practice. During litigation, parties' claims and defenses should all be focused on and relevant to these elements. A plaintiff generally needs to offer evidence to prove all elements before the court can be persuaded to adjudicate the case in his favor. In contrast, a defendant should raise defenses to refute one or more of these elements, therefore convincing the court that he should not be held liable. In sum, these four elements for general torts are like lighthouses in the sea of Tort Law, firmly holding the boundary between liability and no liability and providing the direction and steps for proving or disapproving it.

Illegal Act

Illegal act is an act by a natural person with civil capacity that infringes other person's legitimate civil right or interest. It is one of the elements for finding tort liability and therefore a prerequisite for the same. If there is no illegal act, then there is no basis for the causation element, not to mention liability. Thus, if a person's act is not illegal, the person cannot be held liable even though the act has caused damage or injury to another person. For example, demolishing a neighbor's house to prevent a fire from spreading and pushing away a pedestrian to prevent a car accident are the kind of acts recognized by law and are not considered illegal.

As suggested by its name, illegal act must include two coexisting elements—"illegal" and "act"—at the same time. That is, an illegal act must be an act first. Natural events or ideas simply cannot be illegal act. Secondly, the act must objectively violate the law. Let us discuss "act" and "illegal" a little bit further below.

An act is a feasance or nonfeasance expression in the objective world by a human being or a human group under its will and through itself or someone else under its control or manage. As an element of illegal act, an act also includes an implied condition—it must be performed by someone who is above a certain legal age specified by law, has civil capacity, and can recognize and control his behavior, or performed by a social group as a legal person. "Civil capacity" is a person's capacity to be responsible for the legal consequences of his act. In Tort Law, minors or insane persons are not responsible for their act because they lack the knowledge and capability to understand the legal consequences of their act.

Usually, a person is responsible for his own act under the principles of Tort Law. That is, a perpetrator is liable for any damage or injury caused by his own act. Of course, this covers not only a perpetrator's active act that causes damage but also any damage caused by anything under the perpetrator's control. For example, if the falling or collapsing of an object hanged or placed on a building causes any damage to a person, the owner or manager of the object is liable. This is to impose liability based on the perpetrator's nonfeasance and lack of precaution. Under certain situations, however, a person should also be responsible for any act of a person under his control or manage. For example, an employer is liable for any damage caused by its employee in the course of the employee's work. This is the so-called "vicarious liability" principle. In sum, tort liability is generally based on a perpetrator's own act, but there are exceptions under the law that someone's act can be the basis for another person's tort liability.

According to its expression, illegal act can be either feasance or nonfeasance. Feasance is a person's active act. If the act is against the law and the person has actively committed it, then the act is an illegal act. Nonfeasance is the inaction of a person who has the obligation to do something (i.e., act) but failed to fulfill it and the inaction allows or results in damage or injury. The inaction is a nonfeasance type of illegal act. In Tort Law, feasance is the major illegal act. The precondition for a person's inaction to be considered as an illegal act is that the person must have a legal duty to act in the relevant situation. Moral obligations do not give rise to such duty.

In most cases, the law does not force a person to actively protect another person's right or interest. Even if the latter is in danger, the former's inaction is not illegal. But in a few situations, inaction may be considered illegal. Such legal obligation originates from (1) special relationships such as the relationship between a common carrier and passengers; (2) the danger originally created by the perpetrator, for example, a motor vehicle driver's obligation to rescue a victim in an accident caused by the driver; (3) statutory obligations, for example, parents' obligations; (4) voluntarily assumed obligations, for example, if a volunteer already jumped into the water to save a drowning person, the volunteer cannot stop in the middle for no reason; (5) promise, for example, if a person has promised to provide help to another when in danger, then he has the obligation to deliver the promise; (6) commercial relationships such as the relationship between a shopping market and its customers; and (7) professional requirements, for example, an employer has obligations to control its employees' behavior.

The second element of illegal act is "illegal." That is, the act must be objectively against the law and have caused damage to another person's legitimate right or interest. The illegal trait can be expressed in the following major ways: (1) actively or passively violating what the law prohibits, (2) actively or passively omitting legal obligations, and (3) actively or passively violating the good customs. Please note that acts that have caused damages or harms on other persons' bodies or properties are illegal because they generally violate what the law requires. But the law also specifies that in certain situations, a person's act is not illegal because such act is specifically allowed under the law as a defense or privilege even though the act has caused damage or injury. Therefore, the act does not have the illegal trait that is required for tort liability. Such defenses or privileges are narrowly specified in the "Tort Law," and only two types of such defense/privilege are allowed: self-defense and necessity. But in theory, there are several others including self-help, performing duties by law, victim's consent, and voluntary service.

Damage

Damage is the element for each and every type of tort liability—if there is no damage, there is no liability. Normally, we can interpret damage broadly as any negative change of a victim's legally protected interest, including bodily, personal, and property rights. The nature of damage is the diminishing or even complete loss of a person's property interest or non-property interest. Damage is different from danger. Danger is a possibility of causing damage, but damage is the actual result of violating or infringing a victim's right or interest. Therefore, the result is detrimental or unfavorable to the victim. Such result includes death, bodily harm, damaged reputation, emotional stress, pain, and other types of property loss. It does not matter whether the loss can be evaluated in money, as long as a victim's bodily, personal, or property right has been affected negatively, there is damage caused.

The importance of the damage element cannot be overstated because the very purpose of Tort Law is to provide remedies for people who suffered damage as a result of torts. Thus, if there is no damage, there is no remedy. In other words, the precondition for tort remedy is damage. But tort liability cannot be solely based on damage because there is a requirement of degree and the establishment of other necessary elements.

Thus, the purpose to study the damage element is to determine whether a plaintiff has suffered injury or loss within the remedial scope specified by law so that the plaintiff has the right for compensation. Specifically, damage, as an element for tort liability, has the following properties:

1. Damage is the negative result of infringing or violating a victim's legitimate bodily or property right. The Tort Law cannot protect the kind of right or interest prohibited by law. Thus, if the victim's source of profit or interest is not recognized by law, the damage cannot be remedied. Therefore, infringing or violating illegitimate interest cannot be the basis for finding tort liability.
2. According to the result of the damage, there is necessity and possibility to remedy it legally. On the one hand, the damage must exceed certain degree for eligibility of legal remedy. On the other hand, there must be objective possibility for the legal remedy. For example, the law has included such damage within the scope of legal remedy, and there is actual means for the remedy.
3. There is certainty and objective authenticity on the damage. As an element for tort liability, damage must be real and actual damage, not possible damage. There are three layers of meaning here: Firstly, damage must be a fact already occurred. The occurrence of the fact is the precondition for determining the existence of damage—regarding any damage that will occur in the near future, one can only request for prevention means, not compensation. Secondly, damage must be objectively authentic and cannot be subjective speculation. Thirdly, damage must have a negative effect on the victim. Stated differently, the victim's bodily or property right has changed negatively compared to its status prior to the damage's occurrence.

According to different criterion, damages can be categorized into different groups. The most well-known one is to divide damages into bodily injury, property damage, and mental distress.

Bodily injury is the fact of harm to a person's bodily right, the right to health, or the right to life. It can be an injury on a natural person's physical body or health, or even the loss of life—the material personality right of a person has been violated, and the violation has caused damage on the integrity of the person's organs or the normal life-supporting physiological functions, or even death. Bodily injury can also cover any damage related to medical malpractice injury, funeral cost, loss of working time due to disability or injury, or loss of future income due to death. Further, bodily injury can also cause mental pain, e.g., mental distress suffered by close relatives of the deceased, mental distress suffered by an injured victim, etc.

Property damage is the fact of economic loss resulted from the infringement on a person's property right. Appropriation of property and destruction of property are the main reasons of property damage. Appropriation of property is the illegal act of taking possession of something owned or lawfully possessed by a person with the intent to deprive the person's ownership or right of possession. Destruction of property is destroying or lessening the value of someone else's property without transferring the possession of it. Further, infringement on property rights other than ownership and possession is also becoming more and more common.

Property damage is mainly in the form of property loss, which includes direct loss and indirect loss. Direct loss is the kind of property loss caused by an infringing act's direct effect on a victim's property right (e.g., the total loss of personal property), or the necessary expense the victim needs to extend to remedy the situation. Indirect loss is the loss of profit or revenue of a victim as a result of the tortious act. In other words, interest (e.g., operative profit) that can be obtained by the victim in the future is no longer obtainable because of the perpetrator's tortious act. In Tort Law, direct loss is generally fully compensated. With respect to indirect loss, it depends on how likely the victim would receive such future interest.

Mental distress is the kind of harm to a civil subject's spiritual activities, including injuries to one's personality rights (i.e., the right to name, image, likeness, privacy, etc.) as well as identity right. Mental distress can be in the form of a victim's mental pain or the loss or attenuation of the victim's spiritual interests. There are two sources for mental pain/distress: the first source is a victim's physical pain caused by a tortious act (a natural person's physical or physiological pain or discomfort, including dizziness, weakness, insomnia, etc.), and the second source is emotional pain (negative emotional or spiritual feelings of a natural person, including anger, fear, worry, sadness, etc.). Loss or attenuation of spiritual interests is the destruction of a victim's effort to maintain his/her personality rights or identity right, which leads to damage on such rights, such as infringement on one's likeness, leak of private information, or damaged reputation, etc. Mental distress may or may not lead to property damage. But in both situations, the damage is a legal fact of mental distress.

Causation

Among the elements for tort liabilities, causation is an extremely important one. It serves the function of finding a bridge between a perpetrator's act and a victim's damage and provides the legitimate reason for shifting the damage from the victim to the perpetrator. Therefore, no matter which imputation principle of tort liability is applied, causation is always an indispensable element. On the one hand, causation determines whether there is tort liability and provides the legitimate basis for the imputation of liability. Since a civil subject can only be held responsible for his own act, if there is no causation between a perpetrator's act and damage suffered by a victim, the perpetrator cannot be held liable for the damage. On the other hand, causation can also determine the scope of the liability, becoming a tool for the fair distribution of damage. Particularly, when there are several factors that jointly caused the damage, the amount of liability a perpetrator should assume is determined based on the weight each factor has contributed to cause the damage. In sum, causation serves the important binding function in determining tort liability. A tort liability without causation cannot stand.

Causation is initially a concept in philosophy. Philosophers believe that the world is an integrated entity comprising moving natures or social events with general connections and mutual restraints. If these natures or events are extracted from the general connections and studied in isolated state, the constantly changing movements will appear: one is the cause and the other is the result. Thus, in the field of philosophy, the concept of causation reflects the general connections and mutual restraints among events. Whether it is in nature or human society, the occurrence of any event is caused by another event. Generally, the event causing another event is called "cause," and the resulted event is called "result." This relationship is called causation.

Since any event in the world is caused by another event, tort liability is not an exception. There has never been an infringement that does not have a cause. The occurrence of damage must have a connection with some sort of activity. As such, legal scholars adopted the concept of causation and introduced it into the Tort Law. It has been an indispensable element for tort liability and has been used for illustrating the relationship and objective connection between an illegal act as cause and damage as result. Thus, causation relationship is actually the objective connection between an illegal act and damage, that is, whether certain damage is caused by a perpetrator's act. Only when that is the case, the perpetrator can be held liable.

However, causation in legal field is different from causation in philosophy field. Objectively, in a causation relationship, the cause event always happens before the result event. But subjectively, people often find the result first and then try to find the cause. This explains our purpose of studying causation when establishing tort liability—to find the illegal act and then the perpetrator from the damage. Thus, cause in tort is limited to human activities and does not include natural events that have no connection with any human activity, and damage in tort is limited to material or spiritual damage that has certain connection with human.

There had been many theories about causation relationship during the long development history of the Tort Law of the continental law system. Because each theory had certain difficult-to-overcome issues, majority of them had disappeared. Now, the leading theory in China is the "adequate causation" theory, which was proposed by a German legal scholar von Kries in the late nineteenth century and was adopted by majority of the continental law countries.

According to the "adequate causation" theory, causation cannot be established just based on an isolated case, in which a first event caused a second event under a certain circumstance. Instead, it must be proved that there is strong reason to believe that the first event, if occurred again under the same circumstance, would cause the second event according to common sense. In other words, causation exists between an act and damage if such act would usually cause such damage. As can be seen, what the "adequate causation" theory emphasizes is how likely a same illegal act can cause the same damage under the same circumstance. If the likelihood is high and the illegal act has indeed caused the damage in reality, there is causation between the illegal act and the damage.

When applying causation theories in actual cases, judges are usually concerned with two issues: (1) whether a plaintiff's damage was indeed caused by a defendant's act and (2) whether the injurious result would occur under the same condition (s) (i.e., whether the outcome is consistent with people's common knowledge or experience). In China, these two issues are expressed as "condition relationship" and "certainty." According to common sense, a condition is considered as causing a result only if the same result would occur when the same condition exists. Thus, certainty is actually a limit to condition relationship. The purpose for that is to form a bifurcated testing standard, wherein condition relationship relates to the issue of whether the illegal act is a necessary condition for the outcome of damage and certainty relates to the issue of whether the act is enough to produce such damage—if so, there is causation between the two; otherwise, there is no causation. As for when the act is considered enough to produce such damage, judges will rule based on the combination of common sense and social experience.

Generally, the victim bears the burden to prove the causation element. Only if the proffered evidence meets the corresponding causation test can liability be proven. But in certain special cases, causation can be presumed. That is, as long as the victim has offered enough evidence, it will be presumed that the causation between the perpetrator's act and the victim's damage exists. Thereafter, the burden shifts to the perpetrator to prove that his act did not cause the victim's damage. Such a mechanism usually applies in situations, where victims are clearly disadvantaged and therefore cannot prove all elements of causation. Such law-specified situations include environmental pollution cases, joint dangerous activities, and medical malpractice disputes.

Besides determining liabilities, the causation element also serves the function of distributing such liabilities, particularly when there are multiple factors that caused the same result. Although these factors have all contributed to the occurrence of the result, they carry different weights, which depend on the nature of each factor, distance, and strength. For example, direct one is heavier than indirect one, near one is heavier than far one, and major one is heavier than minor one. Obviously, the heavier the factor is, the more liability the perpetrator should have and vice versa.

Subjective Fault

Fault is the subjective element in the formation of tort liability. It reflects a perpetrator's state of mind while committing a tortious act, and such state of mind deserves to be condemned. With respect to fault liability, fault is the necessary condition and legal basis for a perpetrator to assume liability. As long as a perpetrator has subjective fault while committing a tortious act, the perpetrator must be held liable for damage caused by his act. On the contrary, if a perpetrator would not be able to recognize or prevent the danger of his act even enough reasonable precaution has been taken, he is not liable for the damage caused by his act, and the case has to be treated as an accident. With respect to presumed fault liability, fault is still an element for establishing liability, although the burden of proof is shifted to a defendant. And as for no-fault liability, a perpetrator must bear liability whether or not the perpetrator is at fault. But if a victim is found at fault, a perpetrator's liability can be reduced.

As can be seen, fault has always played a very important role in Tort Law. Because it is an analysis of a perpetrator's subjective state of mind, it should be treated as a subjective concept, which distinguishes itself from illegal act. The former is a negative assessment of the perpetrator, whereas the latter is a negative assessment of the act. In Tort Law, the same act can carry a different legal consequence if an actor has a different state of mind. It must be noted that although illegal act can be an objective testing criterion in determining whether a perpetrator has subjective fault, we should never treat illegal act and fault the same—fault reflects an actor's state of mind; it is a subjective concept.

As a reflection of a perpetrator's state of mind during his tortious act, subjective fault can be in one of two basic forms—intentional and negligent. "Intentional" is a state of mind of a person, who knowingly did something to deliberately cause some consequence even though he was fully aware that such consequence would follow. Specifically, if a perpetrator knew with a reasonable certainty that his act would cause certain consequence but still acted, the consequence should be treated as what the perpetrator intended. However, if the perpetrator was not very sure whether his act would cause the consequence, the act should be treated as "negligent."

Thus, this "intentional" concept in Tort Law contains two layers of meaning: (1) "intentional" is a state of mind concerning a specific type of result (the perpetrator intended the result to happen through his/her own act), and (2) it is based on the perpetrator's subjective self-confidence (the perpetrator not only hoped for the intended result but also firmly believed that it would happen). Because this kind of state of mind utterly lacks consideration and respect for other people's legitimate rights and interests, the law condemns it and provides a legal basis for imputing liability. If not, we would all be living in a world filled with animosity.

"Negligent" is a type of tort liability, according to which a person has caused damage to another person because he has not exercised the kind of care a reasonable person would have exercised under the same circumstance. This type of tort liability was created for the reason that a person has the obligation not to create unreasonable danger to others while he acts in the everyday social and interpersonal life. If the person breaches such obligation and causes damage to others, he should be held liable for the negligence unless there is any exception for this.

Just from the definitions, we have already seen the clear difference between "intentional" and "negligent." "Intentional" is the state of mind of a person who hopes to cause certain damage and believes such damage will happen, i.e., knowingly committing the wrongdoing. In contrast, "negligent" does not carry such mentality. On the contrary, the perpetrator might want to try hard to prevent such damage from happening. But because of his negligent act, the damage nevertheless resulted; therefore, he should bear the responsibility. Thus, if a person's act has only caused the risk of a foreseeable damage, and the risk may or may not become reality, it must be negligent.

The subjective fault of negligence can be further divided into two states of mind: careless and slack. "Careless" refers to the situation where a person can or should have foreseen the danger but did not, while "slack" refers to the situation where the person can foresee the danger but wrongfully and readily believed that the danger could be avoided. Whether the damage was caused because of the perpetrator's carelessness or slackness, the perpetrator's act is treated as negligence—the breach of one's obligation of reasonable care to others in our society. Of course, because the degree of breach is different, negligence can have three different levels: (1) gross negligence (breach of the general level of duty of care that a common person in our society would have exercised in like circumstances), (2) specific negligence (breach of the higher level of duty of care that a person would have exercised in handling his/her own affairs), and (3) abstract negligence (breach of the highest level of duty of care that a prudent administrator would have exercised in like circumstances).

Besides being an element for establishing tort liability, subjective fault is also used for determining and distributing liability. The former function is to determine whether a perpetrator should be held liable, whereas the latter function is to determine how the perpetrator should be liable. In joint tort cases, for example, although the joint tortfeasors bear joint and several liability, the distribution of the liability should be determined internally among them. Not only should the weight of each tortfeasor's contribution be considered, the degree of each one's subjective fault should also be determined and serve as the primary basis for the distribution. Also, in contributory negligence cases, since a plaintiff may also bear part of the blame, a defendant's share of the liability may be reduced accordingly.

Chapter 5
Joint Tort Liability

Overview

In the previous chapters of this book, most scenarios we have used in explaining theories or discussing cases involve only one perpetrator, who has committed tortious act against a victim and caused damage to the victim's bodily or property right and shall be liable for the damage. But in reality, the scenario may be more complicated than that. In a lot of cases, a victim's damage was caused by multiple tortfeasors by coordination or coincidence. They have caused the victim's damage jointly and should be jointly liable for the damage. This creates the issue of joint liability.

Joint tort liability is the kind of civil liability imposed on multiple tortfeasors for their joint tortious act. Joint tortious act is the kind of tortious act committed by two or more than two perpetrators and is an undividable reason for causing damage. It is also called "joint fault" or "joint illegal act" in different occasions. Under normal situations in Tort Law, a single tortfeasor is held liable for a certain caused damage alone. As an exception, multiple independent perpetrators are jointly liable for the same damage. Article 8 of the "Tort Law" states: "[w]here two or more persons jointly commit a tort, resulting in damage to other persons, they shall be liable jointly and severally."

The history of joint liability can be traced back to the Roman law system, according to which a victim could sue not only the direct perpetrator but also the person who had encouraged or incited the perpetrator to commit the tortious act. Although the "French Civil Code" did not directly mention the term "joint tort liability," it specified the joint and several liability in detail to solve the issue of how to distribute liabilities among people whose faults in combination caused damage. It was the "German Civil Code" that first created the modern rule of joint tort liability, clearly defined the concept of joint tortious act, and clearly specified that joint tortfeasors shall have joint and several liability for the relevant damage. The German approach was followed by other countries in the continental law system in creating their own joint Tort Laws.

X. Li and J. Jin, *Concise Chinese Tort Laws*, China-EU Law Series 1,

DOI 10.1007/978-3-642-41024-6_5,

China's rules relating to joint tort liability were also influenced by the German model. This can be traced back to Article 130 of the "General Principles of Civil Law," which states: "[i]f two or more persons jointly infringe upon another person's rights and cause him damage, they shall bear joint liability." Thereafter, Article 148 of the "Opinions of the Supreme People's Court on Several Issues concerning the Implementation of the General Principles of the Civil Law of the People's Republic of China" and Article 4 of the "Some Provisions of the Supreme People's Court on Evidence in Civil Procedure" specified incitement, assistance, and common danger activities. Article 3 of the "Judicial Interpretation of Damages for Personal Injuries" extended the content of Article 3 of the "General Principles of Civil Law," specifying:

> If two or more persons intentionally or negligently, jointly infringe upon another person's rights and cause him damage, or if their infringing acts worked together directly in causing the same damage, they have committed joint tort and shall bear joint and several liability according to article 130 of the General Principles of the Civil Law. If two or more persons did not commit joint intentional or negligent tort, but their independent acts indirectly combined and caused the same damage, each person shall bear the amount of liability according to how much contribution the person's act had.

Until the creation of the "Tort Law," China established the joint tort rules with Chinese characteristic by summarizing past experiences and learning from other countries' legislative experience. Article 8 of the "Tort Law" specifies joint tortious act, Article 9 specifies incitement and assistance, and Article 10 specifies common danger. Together with other specifications, they formed a quite complete system.

The difference between joint tort and single-perpetrator tort is not just the number of tortfeasors involved. The more important effect by the increased number of tortfeasors is the increased complexity of distributing the liability. When a victim's damage was caused by multiple perpetrators' acts, whether these acts constitute tort liability, whether all of part of these perpetrators should be held liable for the damage, and how to distribute liability among them are all practical issues need to be solved by the rules of joint tort liability. As can be seen, there is great significance to study the rules of joint tort liability.

First, the rules strengthen the remedy to a victim and place him on a more advantaged position. Compared with single-perpetrator tort, joint tort may cause a much higher social risk and generally cause much more serious damage to a victim. Therefore, the law demands that all perpetrators of a joint tort, disregarding their roles, must bear joint liability to the victim's damage. This avoids the possibility that the victim will not be adequately compensated for his damage because a single tortfeasor is not capable of doing so. As long as there is another tortfeasor liable for the same damage, that tortfeasor must also bear the responsibility to compensate the victim. As a result, the victim has more chances to be fully compensated for his damage.

Second, by increasing the liability for joint tort, the rule reduces the occurrence of such tortious activities. Compared with single-perpetrator tort, tortfeasors in joint tort usually possess more subjective malice and cause more destruction to social stability or harmony. By increasing the punishment and therefore influencing the perpetrators' choice of act, we can prevent joint tort to the highest degree and help to establish a safer and stable society. The essence of joint tort liability is to hold a perpetrator fully responsible for the damage, not just the share he/she has contributed, as long as the perpetrator has participated in the underlying tort activity. The victim can seek remedy not only from all perpetrators as a group but also from any individual one, who must bear the full liability to the damage.

Last, we must pay attention not to abuse the rules of joint tort liability so that the parties' interest can be maintained in a balanced way. Elements for joint tort liability are quite strict. This is to prevent the abuse of the rules and overbroad implication of people. Also, within the group of the joint tortfeasors, liability is still distributed depending on the weight of each tortfeasor's contribution to the damage. And from the capability's perspective, the tortfeasors are more capable of compensating the victim's damage as a group. Thus, the mechanism of joint tort liability fully considers balancing the interests between the victim and the tortfeasors and reduces the law's operating cost by distributing the risk.

The precondition for applying joint tort liability is the existence of joint tortious act. Thus, how to determine joint tortious act is the most important issue in joint tort. Based on the traditional rules of Tort Law, the elements for establishing joint tortious act are as follows:

1. Multiple perpetrators. There must be two or more than two perpetrators for joint tort. When there is only one perpetrator, there is no joint tort. It is worth noting that a perpetrator can be a natural person or a legal person.
2. The perpetrators have joint subjective fault—intentional or negligent. This requirement demands that the perpetrators have direct conscious cooperation or conspiracy, which distinguishes it from tort cases involving multiple perpetrators without any conscious cooperation or conspiracy. Whether the victim is at fault has no effect on the establishment of joint tort liability. If the victim has fault, joint tort liability may still be established, but the liability can be reduced accordingly based on the degree of the victim's fault.
3. Commonality of the perpetrators' tortious acts. The perpetrators' acts are interconnected, comprising a combined reason for causing the victim's damage, and each perpetrator's act individually contributed the occurrence of the damage. If any perpetrator's act has no causation relationship with the damage, that perpetrator is not a joint tortfeasor and is not liable for joint tort with other perpetrators. However, it is noted that some perpetrator's act may be a major factor for the tort and other's may be minor, and the act can be feasance or nonfeasance.
4. Same damage. The damage result of the joint tortfeasors' acts is undivided. Even there may be multiple damage results, these results were jointly caused by the perpetrators and no particular damage result can be attributed to a particular perpetrator.
5. The liability has joint attribute. According to the law, joint tortfeasors bear joint liability to damage. Thus, the formality of joint liability is different from that of general tort liability. Because each tortfeasor must bear liability not only for his

own act but also for other tortfeasors' acts, he is essentially liable for the full damage. Therefore, joint liability is an increased liability.

However, with the Tort Law's development increasingly in line with the social progress and development, the law of joint tort has changed substantially. The most notable change is related to the issue of what type(s) of conscious cooperation is required among the joint tortfeasors.

Initially, the leading theory on this issue is the "conscious cooperation" theory. This theory believes that conscious cooperation is the necessary condition for joint tort liability; to combine the perpetrators' acts as a joint act requires the existence of a related motivation or wish, i.e., joint conscious cooperation or joint intention. Only if there is joint intention can there be unification of wills and acts among the multiple perpetrators and can there be joint tort liability. In other words, if there is no joint intention, there is no joint liability. This is a very strict standard and the narrowest interpretation of joint tort liability.

Thereafter, the "joint fault" theory replaced the "conscious cooperation" theory as the leading theory among scholars. According to this theory, as long as there is conscious cooperation or joint fault among the tortfeasors, the case shall be processed as a joint tort case. Joint fault occurs when multiple perpetrators have common knowledge of their acts or corresponding consequence(s) or they should have taken reasonable care to prevent a potential risk but did not. It includes joint intention and joint negligence. Joint negligence includes two different scenarios: (1) Each perpetrator should have known or foreseen the risk that his act may cause damage but still acted and caused the damage because of carelessness or lack of attention. (2) When multiple perpetrators acted jointly to cause damage but their joint intention cannot be established, it may be determined that they have joint fault according to the actual fact of the case. The "General Principles of Civil Law" has adopted the "joint fault" theory—both joint intention and joint fault can lead to joint tort liability.

Later on, a new theory—the "relevance collaboration" theory—came out and stirred a big debate among scholars. According to this theory, joint tort liability shall not rely on conscious cooperation as a necessary condition. Rather, as long as the perpetrators objectively committed joint tortious act and caused the same and undividable damage, they shall bear joint civil liability. Stated differently, although the perpetrators did not have conscious cooperation, because their acts have a relevant collaborator (i.e., they caused the same damage and it is impossible to determine which act caused which part of the damage), the perpetrators should bear joint liability. This theory changed the principle upheld since the creation of the "German Civil Code" that joint tort liability must be based on the subjective collaboration (i.e., there must be conscious cooperation among the multiple perpetrators.) According to this theory, which emphasizes the integration of the perpetrators' acts, as long as each act is part of the relevant reason for causing the same damage, there is joint tort liability even if these acts lack the necessary coordination in time and place. The typical legislation embodying this theory is Article 3 of the "Judicial Interpretation of Damages for Personal Injuries," which greatly extended the traditional rules of joint liability in the "General Principles of Civil Law"—if two or more persons did not have joint intention or joint negligence but their acts combined directly caused the same damage, they shall bear joint tort liability. This article changed the joint Tort Law from a subjective standard to an objective standard. Although many scholars support this theory given it enlarges the scope of joint tort liability and provides more protection for victims, there are also many scholars opposing it, believing that this theory cannot justify itself and it is hard to apply it in practice.

In recent years, a "middle ground" theory slowly evolved from the "relevance collaboration" theory. According to this theory, the nature of joint tortious act is defined as relevance collaboration, but the concept of relevance collaboration is divided into subjective one and objective one. With respect to subjective relevance collaboration, there was conscious cooperation among the multiple perpetrators (i.e., joint intention, but joint fault is not included and is treated as objective relevance collaboration). Therefore, there was common guiding thought while they were committing the tortious acts. With respect to objective relevance collaboration, although there was no conscious cooperation among the multiple perpetrators, their acts were correlated and created a joint force for causing an undividable damage. In other words, the perpetrators did not have a joint intention to commit a tortious act, but their acts in direct combination caused the damage. In such a situation, although each act was individually committed, the perpetrators may be held for joint liability because each perpetrator's act is the joint reason for causing the damage and the damage is undividable.

It is a pity that Article 8 of the "Tort Law" did not choose a clear ground. Because of its vague language, we do not know which theory was selected by the legislators. Thus, the debate on which theory is better continues among China's scholars. But undoubtedly, the trend of joint Tort Law is to extend the scope of the concept of joint tortious act so that joint liability can be more broadly applied and victims' interests can be more readily protected.

It should be noted that joint tort cannot be based solely on the fact that there are multiple perpetrators in the case. If other conditions are not met, the case shall be treated as a multi-perpetrator tort case—the situation where two or more than two perpetrators acted separately and caused the same damage but no joint tort can be established. The "Tort Law" specifies two types of multi-perpetrator tort. One is the scenario specified in Article 11: "[w]here two or more persons commit torts respectively, resulting in the same damage, but each one's act is sufficient to cause the entire damage, the tortfeasors shall be held liable jointly and severally." In this scenario, because the connections among the perpetrators' acts are indirect, there is no joint tort. The other one is what Article 12 specifies: "[w]here two or more persons commit torts respectively, resulting in the same damage, if the seriousness of liability of each tortfeasor can be determined, the tortfeasors shall assume corresponding liabilities respectively; or if the seriousness of liability of each tortfeasor is difficult to be determined, the tortfeasors shall assume the compensatory liability evenly." Article 12's difference with Article 11 is that although the perpetrators' acts all individually caused the same damage, not each act was serious enough to cause the whole damage but only part of it. In this type of multi-perpetrator tort case, each perpetrator bears his own share of liability.

Joint tortious act is a general concept. It can be further divided into simple joint tortious act, complex joint tortious act, and joint dangerous act. In simple joint tortious act, all perpetrators are acting parties; in complex joint tortious act, perpetrators are grouped into acting parties, inciting parties, and assisting parties; joint dangerous act is that two or more than two persons jointly committed a dangerous act that caused damage, but the real person(s) who caused the damage cannot be determined. We will separately discuss these concepts below.

Simple Joint Tortious Act

Joint tortious act is two or more people's illegal infringing act against someone's legitimate right. It can be further divided into simple joint tortious act and complex tortious act. In the case of simple joint tortious act, two or more persons engage in direct tortious acts that cause the same and undividable damage, and each person's act is part of the undividable cause for the damage. Simple joint tortious act and complex joint tortious act have clear differences: the perpetrators in the former case are all acting parties—each perpetrator has committed tortious act that caused the victim's damage—and under joint intention. Although each perpetrator may have its own role and task, their acts are all direct infringing acts and they are all acting parties. In the case of complex joint tortious act, perpetrators are grouped as acting parties, inciting parties, and assisting parties.

Simple joint tortious act is called "simple" not only because it is the most common form of joint tortious act, but also because it fits into the most classical form of joint tortious act. This is reflected by the fact that each perpetrator must have directly performed the tortious act. That said, the perpetrators' roles, functions, and importance can be different. As long as there is joint intention directing their thoughts, each perpetrator's act must be deemed the group's act. It should be noted that even though the joint tortious act is composed of each perpetrator's tortious act, each act must be a part of the undividable reason that caused the damage—without it, the very damage will not occur or some other kind of damage may be resulted. Thus, regarding simple joint tortious act, all perpetrators' acts must be part of the undividable reason for causing the damage.

Simple joint tortious act is a multi-perpetrator tort that carries joint and several liability. Thus, to impose civil liability on each perpetrator, we must first determine whether the perpetrator's act has met the requirement for the particular tort liability. After that, we can talk about the special requirement for joint tortious act. Thus, besides the requirements that the perpetrators must directly perform the acts and the damage must be the same, a multi-perpetrator tort must meet the following conditions to become a simple joint tortious act:

1. Multiple perpetrators. There must be two or more than two perpetrators in the case. They can either be natural person or legal person. An entity that is not a legal person and has no civil capacity cannot be liable for the joint tort's damage. The person who is responsible for the entity's act shall bear the liability.

2. There is subjective joint fault or objective relevance collaboration among the perpetrators. Since Article 8 of the "Tort Law" is not clear on this issue, two standards for determining joint tortious act shall be followed according to Article 3 of the "Judicial Interpretation of Damages for Personal Injuries": one is joint fault, including joint intention and joint negligence; the other is the direct combination of multiple acts. Where damage was caused by indirect collaboration of multiple perpetrators' acts, the case is treated as a multi-perpetrator tort with no conscious cooperation among the perpetrators. The difference between direct combination and indirect collaboration is whether the act individually affects the outcome. If the perpetrators' acts cannot be divided with respect to the occurrence of the damage and are the necessary condition for the outcome, then it is direct combination and each act is the joint reason for the damage. If the perpetrators' acts have individual effects on the occurrence of the damage, their contribution to the outcome can be determined and evaluated relatively, and if they are not the necessary condition, then it is indirect collaboration.
3. The perpetrators' acts must all meet the requirement for the corresponding tort liability. If fault liability is applied, all acts must meet the elements for fault liability, including subjective fault, illegal act, causation, and damage. Therefore, if one of the perpetrators has no legal capacity, his liability cannot be so determined and he shall not be held responsible. Or if one of them has an affirmative defense, liability shall be shared by the rest of the perpetrators.

The form of liability resulted from joint tortious act is joint and several liability. It is an enhanced liability to tortfeasors to increase a victim's chance of being compensated. That is, the victim of a joint tortious act can request compensation for his damage from all joint tortfeasors or anyone of them. After the victim is fully compensated for the damage, his right for remedy ceases to exist and all perpetrators are released from the liability. Of course, those perpetrators who had made the compensation have the right to ask for repayment from those who had not.

Articles 13 and 14 of the "Tort Law" specify the complete set of rules of joint and several liability. Article 13 specifies the external relationship—each perpetrator shall bear the full liability without consideration of share and ranking, and any perpetrator's compensation for the full damage will release all perpetrators from liability. If a victim waives his claim against any perpetrator, then the rest of the perpetrators do not bear joint and several liability to the former perpetrator's share. Article 14 specifies the internal relationship—joint tortfeasors shall share liability internally. Although joint liability is a whole liability externally, it is shared internally among the perpetrators. The amount of compensation to be paid by each perpetrator shall be determined according to the extent of his respective liability. If it is difficult to determine the extent of each perpetrator's liability, each shall be liable to pay an equal amount of compensation. And if a perpetrator has paid more than the amount for which he is liable, that perpetrator has the right to recover from other jointly and severally liable perpetrators.

Inciting and Assisting Acts

Inciting and assisting acts are complex joint tortious acts, or the so-called constructive joint tortious acts. The reason to call them so is that the law considers these types of multi-perpetrator tortious acts as joint tortious acts for certain special purposes, although they are not the typical joint tortious acts according to the basic principles of joint tort liability. In cases where two or more persons acted with conspiracy or joint intention, each person may have assumed different role during the action—some performed the actual acts and others incited or assisted them in carrying out the acts. In these cases, there was collusion among the perpetrators, their acts correlated with each other in becoming an undividable unit, and these acts all pointed to the same damage. As a result, the law treats these cases as joint tort cases so that all joint perpetrators must bear joint and several liability. Article 9 of the "Tort Law" states: "[i]nciting or assisting another person in committing a tort, one shall be liable jointly and severally with the tortfeasor."

Because inciting and assisting acts are specified by law as constructive joint tortious acts, there are some differences between the elements for them and the elements for simple joint tortious act. There are two main differences: (1) The inciting or assisting party did not directly perform the infringing act, but he has formed a common intention with the performing party or parties via the incitation or assistance. As such, their acts became a combined and undividable unit, and the inciting or assisting act has undoubtedly contributed to the occurrence of the damage. Accordingly, he should bear joint and several liability with the acting party or parties. (2) The inciting or assisting party must have acted with subjective intention; he must have recognized that his act would affect the person(s) being incited or assisted and the possible damage that would be caused by the person(s) but still actively pursued his inciting or assisting activity. Negligence cannot be the basis for inciting or assisting acts. Otherwise, the scope of complex joint tortious act would be enlarged without limitation, a danger that would lead to the abuse of joint tort liability.

Incitation and assistance have different legal meanings. Inciting is to enlighten, persuade, stimulate, induce, or instigate someone to perform an infringing act. Incitation must be carried out in an active mode. Passive nonfeasance cannot be an inciting act. Inciting act can be through mouth, by writing or other expression means, openly or secretly, and in person or via others. Thus, the inciting party is the source for intention in joint tort and serves the planning, strategizing, and instigating functions. It was under the inciting party's guidance that the performing party carried out the infringing act and achieved the goal.

Assisting is to provide help to others such as providing tools or instructions so that the assisted person can carry out the infringing act easily. Assisting act is usually carried out in an active mode. But if a person who has a duty to act does not act intentionally, the person's nonfeasance can also be considered as an assisting act. The assistance can be material or spiritual. It can be provided before the infringing act or during the act. Thus, the assisting person is someone who provides material or spiritual support to the acting person or creates helpful conditions for the acting person to achieve the infringing goal. If a person already possessed the will to commit a tortious act but only that his will was not strong enough, the one who emboldened the person and made him determined to commit the tort is an assisting party, not an inciting party.

The legal consequences for inciting or assisting acts are the same as those for simple joint tortious acts—joint and several liability. In determining the internal share of liability for an inciting or assisting party, the degree of his fault and the weight of his contribution to the damage, not his role, are the factors to be considered. However, an inciting or assisting party's share of liability can be different depending on the person(s) being incited or assisted by him. According to Article 9 of the "Tort Law," there are two scenarios:

1. Assisting or inciting a person having full civil capacity. The assisting or inciting person and the performing person bear joint and several liability, just like in simple joint tort cases.
2. Assisting or inciting a person having no or partial civil capacity. The assisting or inciting person bears full liability. Of course, if the guardian of the assisted or incited person has failed his obligation for being the guardian, the guardian shall also bear certain portion of the liability. The assisting or inciting person shall bear the major portion of the liability; the guardian shall bear the minor portion; and the overlapped part is joint liability. The assisting or inciting person usually pays the full damage and then recovers the corresponding portion from the guardian later.

Joint Dangerous Act

Joint dangerous act, which is also called semi-joint tortious act, is the case where two or more persons committed infringing acts against a victim's legitimate right, but only one or some of the persons' acts caused the damage and it cannot be determined whose act(s) was responsible. In such a case, all perpetrators shall bear joint and several liability according to the law.

In a multi-perpetrator tort case, if it can be determined that only one perpetrator's act is the actual cause of the damage and all other perpetrators' acts have no causation relationship with the damage, the case is an individual tort case; if the evidence shows that all perpetrators' acts combined are the cause, the case is a joint tort case; if the evidence shows that one or some of the perpetrators caused the damage but cannot determine who, the case is a joint dangerous act tort case.

Article 10 of the "Tort Law" specified the basic rules and legal consequences of joint dangerous act. The elements for it include the following:

1. Multiple perpetrators. There must be two or more people involved. They can be natural persons or legal persons. A single perpetrator cannot lead to a finding of joint dangerous act. Perpetrators of joint dangerous act are an undividable unit

created by their common negligence for failing to take reasonable care to protect other people's rights.

2. The act is dangerous in nature. The danger of joint dangerous act is the possibility of infringing other people's legitimate rights. It should be noted that there is no joint intent among the perpetrators of joint dangerous act. Rather, they acted individually without any common knowledge and will regarding the damage. Since there is no conscious cooperation, one perpetrator's act cannot speak for all other perpetrators. Therefore, each perpetrator's act must be able to cause the whole damage and meet all elements of the corresponding tort liability.
3. One or some of the perpetrators caused the damage. The victim does not need to prove that there is causation between each perpetrator's act and the damage. However, he must prove that certain or some of the perpetrators' acts caused the damage—there is causation between the perpetrators' acts as a whole and the damage; otherwise, the dangerous acts are not the cause of the damage, and the perpetrators bear no liability to the damage.
4. It cannot be determined which perpetrator's act caused the damage. In a case of joint dangerous act, damage must be determined and that the damage is caused by the joint dangerous act must also be determined. But which perpetrator's act caused the damage cannot be determined. It is because of this difficulty that the law only requires the victim to prove that each perpetrator's act may cause his damage, and as such requires that the perpetrators bear joint and several liability if the victim has proved so.

The law is very clear that the legal consequence of joint dangerous act is joint and several liability. But if a defendant can prove by evidence that his act does not meet the elements of tort liability, he can be released from the liability.

Chapter 6
Affirmative Defenses Against Tort Liability

Overview

Creating law is like making difficult movements on a balance beam. In a sense, it is an art with an emphasis on the balance of justice. A good set of laws must be impartial and objectively just, treating both a plaintiff and a defendant by the same standard so that they can litigate in the court on an equal ground. The making of Tort Law must follow the same principle, avoiding excessively protecting one side or suppressing the other side. Both the plaintiff and the defendant should be given equal and reasonable rights so that the plaintiff can get full compensation for his damage and the defendant is not held liable for what he did not do.

Thus, after specifying the elements of liability in Chapter II, the "Tort Law" lists six different circumstances where no liability or mitigated liability arises in Chapter III. These circumstances are "contributory negligence" in Article 26, "injured party's deliberate intent" in Article 27, "third party" in Article 28, "force majeure" in Article 29, "self-defense" in Article 30, and "necessity" in Article 31. Usually, we also call these circumstances "affirmative defenses," which may be used by a defendant during litigation against a plaintiff's claim. However, these six circumstances do not cover the whole scope of affirmative defenses. There are many other affirmative defenses that have already been acknowledged or applied in practice. Also, the "Tort Law" does not include the statute of limitations, which should still be governed by the "General Principles of Civil Law."

An affirmative defense allows a defendant to refute a plaintiff's claim so that he may bear no or mitigated liability in the case. In determining tort liability, we often found that although a defendant's act truly infringed someone else's legitimate right, because there was a legitimate and justifiable reason for the act, the defendant could raise it as a defense to request a ruling of no or mitigated liability. These types of legitimate reasons, which were later summarized by law, are called affirmative defenses.

X. Li and J. Jin, *Concise Chinese Tort Laws*, China-EU Law Series 1,
DOI 10.1007/978-3-642-41024-6_6, © Springer-Verlag Berlin Heidelberg 2014

In a broader sense, an affirmative defense is raised by a defendant against a plaintiff's claim for damage. It includes three layers of defense: (1) whether the damage is caused by the defendant's act; (2) whether the act is a tortious act; and (3) when it has been established that the act is a tortious act, tort liability shall not be established because of the occurrence of a special event. As can be seen, even though there are many different types of affirmative defenses, the nature of their efficacy is all focused on the issue of whether the act is a tortious act or whether the liability should be established. As such, there may be a conflict between the two sides of litigation—a conflict regarding act and a conflict regarding liability. The first two layers are conflicts regarding act, a passive defense; the latter one is a conflict regarding liability, an aggressive defense.

Affirmative defenses were created in accordance with the different imputation principles of tort liability and their corresponding elements. No matter how many types or variations of affirmative defenses there are, they must all meet two conditions: (1) adversarial—an affirmative defense must counter the element(s) of a tort liability, destroy the formation of the whole civil liability, and cause a plaintiff's claim to topple so that a defendant is released from the whole or part of the liability, and (2) objective—it must be an objective fact, not speculated by a defendant or not yet occurred. Besides those two, an affirmative defense must be specified by law. However, because there are many affirmative defenses not yet specified by the "Tort Law," this condition is temporarily questionable.

There are many types of affirmative defenses. The most well known are general affirmative defenses and special affirmative defenses. General affirmative defenses refer to those situations where a defendant actually caused the damage but his act is legal and appropriate. General affirmative defenses include authorized act, self-defense, necessity, consent, and self-help. Special affirmative defenses refer to the situations where the damage is caused by an external factor, not the defendant's act. Special affirmative defenses include victim's fault, third party's fault, force majeure, and accident.

Contributory (Comparative) Negligence

Contributory negligence is also called comparative negligence in Anglo-American Tort Law. When a victim's own negligence contributed to causing the damage, a defendant may raise it as a partial defense to reduce his liability. Article 26 of the "Tort Law" states "[i]f the victim's fault also contributes to the occurrence of damage, the liability of the tortfeasor may be mitigated." This affirmative defense makes common sense as it is unfair to hold a defendant liable for the whole damage when a victim contributed to the damage through his own fault. As such, the defendant's liability should be reduced accordingly.

The legal basis for contributory negligence is that a victim's fault also contributed to the occurrence or expansion of the damage. Stated differently, when it is determined that a perpetrator is liable because his tortious act has caused damage to a victim, the victim is considered contributorily/comparatively negligent if his own fault contributed to the occurrence or expansion of the damage. The legal consequence of contributory negligence is fault offsetting. The nature of contributory negligence is that each person shall be liable for the part of the damage caused by his own fault. Thus, the part of the damage caused by the victim's own fault shall be reduced from the whole damage. The perpetrator is only liable for the damage caused by his fault.

As can be seen, contributory negligence has the following legal traits: (1) both plaintiff and defendant's faults are considered and they are compared according to their weights in causing the damage, (2) the precondition to raise this affirmative defense is that the victim's fault also contributed to causing or expanding the loss, and (3) the result of contributory negligence is the reduction of the defendant's liability.

Two factors need to be considered in the application of contributory negligence. One is whether a defendant's act has caused tort liability. This is the precondition for contributory negligence, and only after the defendant's liability is established, we may proceed to study the victim's fault. The other is whether the victim is actually at fault and what liability he should bear. There are several elements for establishing a victim's liability: (1) the victim must be at fault—the victim could foresee or should have foreseen the danger of his own act but still proceeded without proper care—(2) the victim's fault is part of the reason to cause or expand the damage. Here, even when the damage has already occurred, if the victim's own fault has caused the expansion of the damage, contributory negligence also applies.

When both factors are met, the specific steps of applying the doctrine of contributory negligence may be carried out. Now, not only the degrees of the parties' faults but also their weights in causing the damage need to be compared so that shares of liability may be more accurately determined. If it is determined that the victim has 30 % of the fault, then the defendant is only required to bear 70 % of the liability in the end. But by no means, the defendant can be totally absolved. His liability is only reduced proportionally to the amount of the victim's fault. Also, it should be noted that the continental law system endows its judges the power to apply the doctrine of contributory negligence on their own even though the defendants did not raise the defense.

Victim's Deliberate Intent

The victim's deliberate intent is an affirmative defense against a victim's claim in a case, where the victim knew that his act would cause damage to himself but still proceeded with the intent to cause so or without any intervention to prevent the damage from occurring. Under this situation, it would be unfair for a defendant to bear liability for the damage intentionally caused by the victim's own act because there is no causation between the defendant's act and the damage. Thus, all countries treat it an affirmative defense in their Tort Laws. Article 27 of the "Tort Law" also specifies "[i]f the damage is caused intentionally by the victim, the actor is not liable."

Particularly, a victim's deliberate intent may be direct or indirect. In the case of direct deliberate intent, a victim subjectively seeks to cause damage to himself. Whereas in the case of indirect deliberate intent, a victim already knew that his act would cause damage to himself but still proceeded with the act and let the damage happen anyway. No matter which type of deliberate intent it is, the victim's act is the sole causation of the damage. Therefore, the defendant shall not be held liable.

As an affirmative defense, the application of the victim's deliberate intent defense has the following characteristics: (1) the victim has subjective intent and he actively seeks to cause damage to himself or let the damage to occur without any intervention, (2) the damage is completely and solely caused by the victim's own intentional act, and (3) the defendant bears no liability as a result.

The victim's deliberate intent defense applies to both fault liability and no-fault liability. When it is applied to no-fault liability tort, as long as the damage is intentionally caused by the victim, the defendant bears no liability. For example, when any damage is caused by a civil aircraft, the operator of the said civil aircraft does not bear liability if the victim deliberately incurred the damage. Another example, if a victim's damage related to any water pollution is intentionally incurred by himself, the polluter bears no liability to such damage. In the case of fault liability, if the defendant has general fault, he can be completely released from any liability by raising this affirmative defense; if the defendant also has deliberate intention, the doctrine of contributory negligence should be applied; if the defendant has committed gross negligence, some scholars believe that he can still be completely released from liability, but others think that the doctrine of contributory negligence should be applied here.

Third Party's Fault

Third party's fault refers to a situation where a third party (i.e., a party other than the perpetrator and the victim) is at fault in causing or expanding the victim's damage. In a tort case, a defendant can raise the defense that the victim's damage was partially or wholly caused by a third party to reduce or avoid liability. Article 28 of the "Tort Law" provides the legal basis for this affirmative defense: "[i]f the damage is caused by a third party, the third party shall assume the tort liability."

As a broadly used affirmative defense, third party's fault has the following characteristics: (1) The third party is someone other than the perpetrator and the victim (i.e., neither the defendant nor the plaintiff). It should be specifically noted that the third party shall not be affiliated with the defendant. For example, if an employee of an employer caused damage to a victim during the course of his employment, the employer cannot allege that the employee is a third party and raise the third party's fault defense. (2) The damage was caused by the third party's fault. The fault mentioned here includes both intentional fault and negligence. And there should not be any fault connection between the third party and the defendant. If they caused the damage based on their conscious cooperation, they shall be treated as joint tortfeasors to bear joint and several liability to the damage. (3) The third party's fault is the basis for reducing or discharging the defendant's liability.

The third party's fault defense can be applied in not only fault liability torts but also no-fault liability torts. In fault liability torts, if a defendant can prove that a victim's damage was completely caused by a third party's tortious act and the third party's tortious act was the whole reason for causing the damage (i.e., there is direct causation relationship between the third party's tortious act and the victim's damage), the defendant shall be completely discharged from any liability and the third party shall be held liable for the damage. In no-fault liability torts, the tortious activity's degree of danger controls the result. As to extra dangerous activities, even though the victim's damage was completely caused by a third party's wrongdoing, the law demands that the perpetrator of the extra dangerous activity or the possessor of extra hazardous material must first bear the liability. With respect to a perpetrator of general dangerous activity, if he can prove that the damage was completely caused by a third party's wrongdoing, he shall be completely discharged from any liability and the third party shall bear all liability to the damage.

Article 28 of the "Tort Law" established the general rule of third party's fault defense: if the third party's wrongdoing is the sole reason for causing the victim's damage and the defendant has no fault, the defendant shall not bear liability; if the third party's wrongdoing is only part of the reason, the defendant's liability can only be reduced but not completely discharged.

However, the "Tort Law" also specified the special rules for third party's fault defense in its subsequent provisions. There are three major scenarios: (1) Application of quasi joint and several liability—for example, in environmental pollution torts, if the pollution was caused by a third party's wrongdoing, the victim can seek damage from the third party or the polluter. In the latter case, the polluter has the right to seek reimbursement from the third party. (2) Application of supplemental liability, for example, managers of public places such as hotels, shopping markets, banks, bus stations, and entertainment venues and the organizers of mass activities shall bear tortious liability for injury or damage caused to other people as a result of their failure to fulfill their duty of care. Where the injury or damage is caused by a third party, the third party shall bear tortious liability, and where the manager or organizer fails to fulfill its duty of care, it shall assume supplementary liability. (3) Application of prepayment responsibility—for example, if a product's defect is caused by a transporter, a warehouse, or another third party, the producer or the seller may, after paying compensation, claim the same from the third party.

Force Majeure

Force majeure refers to those forces that cannot be stopped or resisted by human, including natural or social events. It is a very traditional type of affirmative defense in Tort Law and has become a universal example in every country's legislation—since damage was caused by force beyond a party's control, the party should not be held liable. Article 29 of the "Tort Law" specifies "[i]f any damage to other persons is caused as result of force majeure, no liability shall be assumed. Where the law provides otherwise, such provisions shall prevail."

The legitimacy of force majeure being an affirmative defense is self-evident. From a perspective of the elements of tort liability, if force majeure is the complete reason for the damage, there is no causation relationship between a defendant's act and a victim's damage. Thus, the defendant has no fault and no tort liability can be established. To hold the defendant liable for the damage is therefore unfair.

The main purpose to provide force majeure as an affirmative defense is to keep a balance between personal freedom and public interest threatened by force majeure. To force a party taking liability for something it cannot foresee and prevent is morally unfair and against justice, although it is beneficial for protecting victims. Also, from an economic perspective, this approach will put restrictions on freedom and stifle innovation—against the principle of freewill deeply embedded in the judicial system. Since there is no dispute regarding force majeure being an affirmative defense in torts, the main purpose of the law is to define the scope, in which no liability shall arise for damage sustained by any party as a result of natural or social events. In other words, what obligations or degree of care does a party have to resist natural disaster and protect other people's personal and property right from being violated by such disaster? To establish this degree, not only the relationship between personal freedom and social security should be considered, but also the comparison between the prevention cost and relevant gains shall be taken into account.

Generally speaking, force majeure is independent from a person's act. It is not governed by a party's will and is a force irresistible by human being. According to the interpretation of Article 153 of the "General Principles of Civil Law," force majeure is an objective condition that cannot be foreseen, prevented, and overcome. Only if an objective condition meets all three prongs of this definition, it can be treated as force majeure so that a defendant may be discharged from liability. Specifically, force majeure must meet the following conditions:

1. Unforeseeability is the subjective condition for force majeure—the occurrence of a future event is not governed by people's will; this is the critical factor for determining whether a party is subjectively at fault. If the occurrence of the event and the consequential damage can be foreseen by the party but the party still proceeded with his act or ignored the obligation to prevent them, the party's deliberate intent becomes the subjective element for tort liability according to the principle of fault liability. Not only cannot the force majeure defense be raised here, the party will not be discharged from liability also. Thus, the subjective element for force majeure must be that the occurrence of a future event is greatly unexpected by the party, or in other words, the party cannot predict it with normal logic and social experience. It should be noted that the unforeseeability should be determined based on the current level of technologies. Also, because different people have different capabilities in foreseeing certain future events, an average person's capability should be treated as the standard.

2. That the event cannot be prevented and overcome is the objective element for force majeure. What is emphasized here is that a party cannot control whether or not the future event will occur. Even after the party has made the best effort and taken every possible measure, the occurrence was still inevitable; then, the party has no choice but to leave it to God. In fact, this objective element also includes the assessment of the party's capability, i.e., the party does not have enough capability to prevent and overcome the future event caused by certain natural or social forces, and therefore demonstrates the inevitability of the future event's occurrence and consequential damage.
3. The event must be an objective condition. Force majeure should be independent from people's will, and it is an objective condition existing externally to an acting party (i.e., the externality property). It is easy to determine externality for natural events, but determining externality for social events is frequently difficult. The purpose of force majeure's externality property is to clarify the boundary between the acting party's own act and other party's or society's act. To emphasize force majeure's objectiveness and externality property is to affirm the intervention of an objective event, which breaks the causation relationship between the acting party's act and damage.

In modern societies, because the range of human activities is becoming much wider, civil activities have been increasingly influenced by nature. Also, with the growing of human economic activities, social conflicts are becoming more and more complicated. Wars, strikes, and governmental policy changes all affect civil activities. Among these natural and social events, which should be included within the scope of force majeure as a legally specified affirmative defense? Neither the "Tort Law" nor the "Principles of Civil Law" lists the types of force majeure. But according to common understanding, force majeure has the following different types:

1. Major natural disasters: earthquake, tsunami, typhoon, flood, plague of locusts, rainstorm, hail, sandstorm, volcanic eruption, landslide, avalanche, mudslide, etc. It should be noted that not all natural disasters can be force majeure. Those minor natural disasters, which have not caused difficulty for the parties to exercise their obligations, are not qualified to be force majeure.
2. Abnormal social events: war, armed conflict, riot, etc. With respect to whether strikes can be force majeure in China, there are still disputes because they are foreseeable in most cases.
3. In certain situations, some countries' or governments' acts may be qualified. This refers to those damages caused as a result of a country or government carrying out its executive or judicial function. As to what is covered under this category, it is determined by a judge on a case-by-case basis.

The general principles of applying force majeure as an affirmative defense include the following:

1. In tort cases based on fault liability: if force majeure is the whole reason for causing damage, a defendant is completely discharged from any liability;

however, if force majeure is only part of the reason, the defendant's liability may only be reduced and he must bear the remaining liability.

2. In tort cases based on no-fault liability, there are two different situations: (i) Force majeure cannot be raised as defense—for example, postal service must compensate damage related to remittance or insured mails even the loss or damage is caused by force majeure. (ii) The scope of force majeure is limited—for example, with respect to damage caused by civil nuclear facilities, the operator may be discharged of liability only if the damage is caused by war, armed conflict, enemy's act, or riot; natural disasters do not count.

Self-Defense

Self-defense has existed as a legally recognized affirmative defense for a long period of time. To prevent a state's or public's interest or a person's own or other people's bodily or property right from being harmed by any illegal activity, the person may take reasonable act to defend against such illegal activity. In regular situations, the act pursued in self-defense is illegal if it causes injury to others. But because the self-defense act is aimed at stopping or preventing an illegal act, it breaks the logical relation between the self-defense act and any tort liability, blocks the creation of any civil liability, and therefore becomes a reason for no liability.

Article 30 of the "Tort Law" states "[a]nyone who causes harm to another for exercising self-defense shall not be subject to tort liability. If the self-defense exceeds the necessary limit, causing any undue harm, the person exercising self-defense shall assume appropriate liability." As a defense for reducing or discharging liability, self-defense is built on the reasonableness and legitimacy of the self-defense act, indicating that the self-defense actor is not at fault subjectively. Self-defense is a citizen's legal right of self-protection and is encouraged by law. Its purpose is to protect the acting person himself or someone else from being harmed by any illegal activity.

To be qualified as self-defense, the following conditions must be met:

1. It must be to protect the self-defense actor's or other people's bodily or property right from being harmed by illegal activities. Although relevant legislation in China does not expressly specify whose interest may be the target of protection by the self-defense act, various countries' legislative experiences and China's actual judicial practice have indicated that self-defense may be carried out for protecting the self-defense actor's or other people's bodily or property right.
2. There must be an illegal tortious act occurring. The term "illegal tortious act" means the kind of act that causes harm to certain legitimate right or interest, including crime and other types of illegal harmful act.
3. It is necessary and urgent to take the self-defense act against the ongoing illegal tortious act. The purpose of self-defense is to stop or prevent illegal tortious act and possible damage that may be caused. Thus, the illegal tortious act must be ongoing; it cannot be finished or not yet started. Otherwise, self-defense is

inappropriate in terms of timing and the self-defense actor must bear civil liability.

4. The self-defense act must be targeted towards the person who is committing the illegal tortious act; it cannot be taken towards a third person, who is not committing any illegal tortious act.
5. The purpose of taking the self-defense act must be protecting legitimate interest—preventing legitimate bodily or property right from being harmed by illegal tortious act when there is no opportunity to ask for help from the state.
6. The self-defense act must be reasonable in degree. Self-defense act is legitimate and is beneficial to society. However, it must not exceed the degree that is necessary to stop or prevent the illegal tortious act.

The general principles of applying self-defense are as follows: if the act constitutes self-defense, the self-defense actor bears no liability and if the act exceeds reasonable degree (i.e., excessive defense), the actor must bear reasonable amount of liability. The term "reasonable amount of liability" means that the self-defense actor will not be liable for the whole damage, but will be held liable for the portion of damage exceeding the limit according to the degree of his fault and other case-related facts including the situation he was in, his mental status, and reasonableness of his act.

As can be seen, the limit to self-defense is the most important issue. Generally speaking, self-defense act should be limited to and not more than what is necessary for a person to stop or prevent the harm. There are several principles in practice that can provide us some guidance: (1) a person can only take self-defense act against an ongoing harm or attack (i.e., the harm or attack has started but not yet finished); the defendant cannot take act against a harm that has not yet started or already finished; (2) if the attacking person has stopped or given up his illegal tortious act, a person cannot use self-defense as an excuse to abuse force; (3) a person cannot use force as self-defense against oral attack; (4) only when a person reasonably believes that his life is under threat can the person use deadly force; and (5) during the act of self-defense, a person cannot intentionally harm a third person.

Necessity

In order to prevent the public's, one's own, or other people's legitimate interest from being damaged by an ongoing danger, a person has to take an emergency measure that causes small damage to someone else's interest; the person, however, is not held liable for the damage or is only liable to a reduced amount of damage. This legal principle is called necessity. Stated differently, under a sudden and urgent situation and with no alternative option, a person may take reasonable measures or action to sacrifice someone else's interest for the purpose of protecting his own or other people's life or property, and the law does not hold the person liable for the damage after facts. Danger may sometimes come from people's activities or from nature, but no matter where it comes from, it is reasonable and legitimate for a person to take measures to avoid or exclude the danger; and almost all countries provide necessity as an affirmative defense in torts.

Article 31 of the "Tort Law" states "[w]here any damage is caused by the conduct of necessity, the person giving rise to the danger shall be liable. If the danger is caused by natural phenomena, the person causing the damage for necessity shall not be liable or shall make appropriate compensation. If improper measures of necessity are taken or a necessary limit is exceeded, causing any undue damage, the person causing the harm for necessity shall assume appropriate liability." As can be seen, necessity is in essence a principle of choosing the lesser of two evils. When two legitimate interests are both under threat of danger and only one can be saved, the law allows saving the more important interest by sacrificing the other one.

It is easy to see that there are similarities between self-defense and necessity—both are designed to save one interest by harming the other. What is different is that a plaintiff in necessity is completely innocent—it was not him but other external factor(s) that put a defendant in danger. Thus, the law should be more beneficial to a plaintiff and put more restrictions on the use of necessity by a defendant. For example, a very important restriction is that the defendant cannot be related to the occurrence of the emergency situation. If the emergency situation was created as a result of the defendant's fault, the necessity defense does not apply.

Elements for necessity include the following:

1. The intent or purpose must be to protect a legitimate interest—to protect public's, one's own, or other people's bodily or property right from being harmed by danger. Relevant legislation in China does not expressly specify whose interest may be the target of protection by necessity, but various countries' legislative experiences and China's actual judicial practice have indicated that necessity may cover public's, one's own, or other people's bodily or property right.
2. Necessity action can only be taken in face of ongoing danger. If the danger has not occurred or has already gone or it has occurred but will not cause any harm to any legitimate interest, necessity action cannot be taken.
3. There is no other better alternative. When facing an ongoing danger, a person has to take action to save a bigger interest protected by law, and there is no other better alternative solution.
4. The action taken cannot be excessive—not more than what is necessary. The essence of necessity is preventing a greater harm by sacrificing something less important. Thus, the harm caused by the necessity action must be smaller than what the danger may have caused. Generally speaking, bodily interest is greater than property interest.

As to the consequences of necessity, the law is quite clear and they can be categorized into the following different cases according to the source of the danger: first, if the danger is caused by nature, the necessity action taking party shall bear liability to the portion of damage exceeding the necessary level, and the benefited party shall reimburse the victim the portion of damage within the necessary level; second, if the danger is caused by a third party, the necessity taking party shall bear liability to the portion of damage exceeding the necessary level, and the danger causing party shall reimburse the victim the portion of damage within the necessary level; and third, if the danger is wholly caused by the necessity action taking party, then the action taking party shall bear liability for the whole damage.

Other Affirmative Defenses

Besides the six types of affirmative defenses specified in the "Tort Law," there are other affirmative defenses recognized and applied broadly in judicial practice. The most typical ones are as follows:

Actions pursuant to official duty: an official bears no liability for actions that are necessary and taken pursuant to authorization or specification by law even these actions cause damage to other people's bodily or property interest. The elements for this defense are the following: (1) there must be authorization by law, (2) the procedure and means of carrying out the official duty must be legal, (3) it must be necessary, and (4) damage is usually inevitable.

Self-help: under emergency situation and no opportunity to request help from relevant government offices, a person may take reasonable measures to detain or constrain other people's property or freedom with the purpose of protecting his own right. Elements for self-help include the following: (1) the purpose must be to protect someone's own right, (2) the situation must be urgent and there is no chance to request help from the governmental offices, and (3) the self-help action must be targeted towards debtor's property or body, (4) allowed by law and morality, and (5) not be excessive.

Accident: an event occurred as a result of something other than a defendant's deliberate intent. Elements for accident include the following: (1) the event is unforeseeable, (2) the event is caused by something external to the defendant, and (3) the event is accidental.

Victim's promise: A victim has voluntarily promised that he/she will bear certain liabilities beforehand. Victim's promise, as long as it does not violate the mandatory rules and good morals, should be recognized and upheld by law.

Elements: (1) The victim must have the authority and capacity to exercise the relevant right, (2) the victim must expressly indicate his intent and truthful will, (3) the damage has not exceeded the scope and degree agreed by the victim, and (4) the victim's promise does not violate law and morality.

Statute of Limitations

Because the "Tort Law" has no specification regarding statutory limitation, the relevant rules are still governed by the "General Principles of Civil Law." Three types of statutory limitations are specified therein: (1) the general statutory limitation is 2 years, (2) special statutory limitation of 1 year applies to bodily injury type of torts, and (3) the longest statutory limitation shall be 20 years.

Also, certain special laws have specified statutory limitations for certain special infringement activities. In those situations, the specially enacted rules shall control. For example, "Environment Protection Law" specifies that statutory limitation for environment pollution litigations shall be 3 years; "Product Quality Law" specifies that statutory limitation for product liability-related cases may be as long as 10 years, etc.

Chapter 7
General Tort Liability

Overview

General tort liability is specified by the general provisions in Tort Law. General tort liability follows when a person intentionally or negligently commits an illegal act and causes damage as a result. Looking at the organizational structure of the "Tort Law," it is not difficult to see that there are basic types of tort liabilities specified therein: the general tort liability specified by the general provisions and the specific tort liability specified by the specific provisions. General tort liability governs general tortious acts, and specific tort liability governs special tortious acts. The two are different in the application of imputation principles of tort liability, elements, affirmative defenses, etc.

Specifically, general tort liability is usually based on fault; a perpetrator's subjective fault is the precondition for such liability; relevant affirmative defenses include contributory negligence, victim's deliberate intent, third party's fault, force majeure, self defense and necessity, etc. In contrast, special tort liabilities are created by specific legislations with certain public policy considerations. They are usually not based on fault; and in certain situations, the burden of proof is shifted from victim to defendant. Basis for liability reduction or discharge must come from specific provisions in law.

As can be seen, general tort liability is a concept relative to the concept of special tort liability. There are two reasons for naming it "general": (1) It is the most common or typical type of tort liability, each and every element must be established before liability can be found, and all affirmative defenses apply here. (2) It is defined by general provisions of law; tortious acts that are not covered by any special situations specified by law are governed by general tort liability.

But it should be noted that the "Tort Law" adopted an approach different from the ones adopted by other continental law countries. It includes two general provisions—Article 2 and Paragraph 1 of Article 6. Article 2 is the major general provision, covering all types of tort liabilities. Its main function is to emphasize the illegal characteristics of tortious acts and that they should be punished according to

X. Li and J. Jin, *Concise Chinese Tort Laws*, China-EU Law Series 1,
DOI 10.1007/978-3-642-41024-6_7, © Springer-Verlag Berlin Heidelberg 2014

the law. Paragraph 1 of Article 6 is the minor general provision, prescribing the elements for general tort liability. Its main function is to distinguish general tort liability from special tort liability and provide the remedy basis for the former.

Because general tort liability is the most simple, most common, and most typical type of liability, majority of the tort cases are general tort liability cases. Therefore, it has a very close relationship with people's everyday life, and every person might have a close contact with it once in a while in his/her life. Next, let us go over several very common types of general tort liability.

Liability for Infringing Personal Rights

Personal rights are the rights owned by a civil subject according to law. These rights are inseparable from the civil subject and are based on interests relevant to the personality and identity relationships. Because every personal right is a specific embodiment of a citizen's basic rights in the area of civil law, the purpose of protecting personal rights is not just to defend an individual's identity, interest, and dignity; it is also to maintain a normal social order. After all, "personal rights" is not a virtual concept, but a combination of a series of concrete and specific rights, including personality rights and identity rights.

Let us take a look at "personality rights" first. They are based on a person's personality interests and are indispensable for protecting a civil subject's independent personality. Further, personality rights can be divided into material personality rights and spiritual personality rights. The former refers to a natural person's nontransferable ownership of material personality elements-related interests, including the right to life, bodily right, the right to health; the latter refers to a natural person's nontransferable ownership of spiritual personality elements-related interests, including rights associated with names, the right to one's image, the right to privacy, honorary rights, the right to marital autonomy, etc. Below, we will first discuss liabilities for infringement on the three major material personality rights; then, we will discuss similar issues regarding the right to names, the right to one's image, honorary rights, and the right to privacy.

Infringement on the right to life refers to a tortious act that illegally harms a person's body and causes the person's death. The right to life includes the protection of life safety and limited control over life-related interests. It is a citizen's most important political and civil right, as well as the precondition for the citizen's activities and being a civil subject with political and civil capacity. Infringing on a person's right to life—illegally harming the person's body and causing death—is not only a crime but also a serious tortious act. The perpetrator must bear both criminal and civil liabilities.

Infringement on a person's right to life usually leads to a general tortious liability. Its legal characteristics include the following: (1) A tortious act that harmed a victim's right to life. The tortious act can be either an active feasance or a passive nonfeasance. When a perpetrator has the obligation to protect a person's life, but neglected or ignored such duty, and as a result caused the person's death, the perpetrator has committed a nonfeasance type of tortious act infringing on the victim's right to life. The tortious act must be targeted towards a living person—a natural person who is considered biologically alive. (2) Fault exists. In most cases, infringement on a person's right to life requires that a perpetrator has subjective fault, including intentional and negligent. The type of the fault has no effect on formation of the liability, but has major effect on damage and compensation. For intentional or grossly negligent acts, there can be punitive damage or relatively high solatium. (3) Death has occurred. In Tort Law, the only difference between infringement on the right to life and infringement on the right to health is the result of death. A case, where no death occurred, is considered an infringement on the right to health. If death occurred, the case is considered an infringement on the right to life.

Infringement on the right to health is a tortious act that harms a person's health. This kind of act must be illegal and can be distinguished from other similar but legal acts. Some legal acts may cause harm, but they are not considered infringements on someone's right to health, e.g., a doctor operates on a patient to remove an organ. Such a tortious act can be either feasance or nonfeasance. In practice, most tortious acts infringing on the right to health are feasance type of acts. If a party has the obligation to act to protect someone from being harmed but did not act, and as a result harm was caused, the party has committed a nonfeasance type of tortious act.

Infringement on the right to health may cause many different aspects of injurious results, including (1) temporary injury (some minor infringements may just cause temporary injuries to victims, such as organ dysfunctions, mental disorders, bleedings, tissue ruptures, infections, etc.), (2) permanent injury (some more serious infringements may cause injuries that cannot be fully cured even after appropriate medical treatments), (3) disability or loss of working capability (serious harm may cause the partial or complete loss of certain bodily functions, which leads to a victim's partial or complete loss of working capability), (4) pain and mental anguish (infringement on the right to health does not necessarily always cause physical harm; sometimes, it may only cause pain or mental anguish—but the perpetrator still needs to be held liable and compensate for such damage), and (5) property damage (property damage associated with infringement on the right to health may usually include the following: medical expenses, lost income for loss of working time, lost income of nursing persons, and loss of future income for partially or completely losing working capabilities).

Infringement on bodily right is also a very common general tort liability. Bodily right is a citizen's right to maintain the integrity of his body and freely utilize each part of the body. It is not difficult to understand that the most important part of bodily right is to maintain a body's integrity and completeness. Thus, the meaning of bodily right includes two aspects: The first aspect is that a citizen has the right to protect and maintain his body's completeness and integrity. A body comprises limbs, organs, and other tissues, and the completeness of a body is protected by law. In certain situations, although a perpetrator's act has not harmed a victim's health, it has broken the completeness of the victim's body, e.g., intentionally cutting someone's hair without permission. The second aspect is that a person has the control right over his body. A person's willingness to donate his organs after death is such an expression of the control right over his body. But the execution of control right must not harm health; otherwise, it would not be allowed under the law.

Usually, the legal characteristics of infringement on bodily right include the following: (1) It is a fault-based liability. To establish liability for a perpetrator's infringement on a person's bodily right, the perpetrator must be at fault. Because this type of tort requires intentional violation on someone else's body, only intentional acts can lead to this liability. (2) Acts violating other's bodies are usually feasance type of acts. That is, a perpetrator takes a definite action, by using his body part or by any tool, to substantially touch or hit someone else's body. Violating means maliciously infringing on or colliding without the other person's permission. Violating other people's body is illegal—the perpetrator has violated his legal obligation not to infringe on other people's bodily rights. (3) No need for any objective result of damage. As long as the perpetrator's body part or tool has offensively touched or hit the victim's body, the tortious act has been committed.

The above three tort liabilities are all liabilities for infringement on material personality rights. In judicial practice, they can be very easily confused with each other. Then, what are the differences between them? First, the distinctions between infringement on the right to life and on bodily right are bodily right protects the completeness of a body's parts—limbs, organs, tissues, etc.—whereas the right to life protects the normal activities of life; simply put, a body is infringed because of inflicted injuries and a life is infringed because death is caused; infringement on bodily rights can be reversed, but the infringement on the right to life cannot. Second, the distinctions between infringement on the right to health and on the right to life are the right to health protects the well-being of a body's biological and physical functions; the right to life protects a life from being terminated. After infringement occurred, if life continues, the infringement is to the right to health. If the infringement causes death, it is infringement on the right to life. Last, the distinctions between infringement on the right to health and on bodily right are infringement on bodily right refers to illegally offending someone else's body or violating the integrity or completeness of that person's body; infringement on the right to health refers to harming a victim's physical or mental health by active or negative means, causing the victim's health to deteriorate. Thus, intentionally ripping off a person's artificial limb violates the person's bodily right, whereas intentionally harming someone's mental health is infringement on right to health.

Infringement on spiritual personality rights will certainly lead to general tort liability. Among others, the right to names is a natural person's legal right to decide, use, and change his name. Infringement on the right to names refers to a case where a perpetrator intentionally or negligently interferes with a person's right to decide or change his name, abuses or impersonates other person's name, etc. Generally speaking, the right to names includes four major rights: the right to have a name, the right to decide the name, the right to use the name, and the right to change the name. Take the right to use the name as an example, it refers to the exclusive right of a person to use his name and no other people can use it unlawfully. Stealing another person's name or unlawfully impersonating this person is a violation of this person's exclusive right to use his name. A perpetrator unlawfully uses another person's name to gain profit is a typical type of infringement on that person's right to names.

Similar to the right to names, the right to images is also protected by law. It is the right of a natural person to own, produce, and use his own images. Infringement on a person's right to images refers to the activities of using or disfiguring that person's images. The right to images has double legal characteristics. It includes not only spiritual interest but also material interest. The kind of interest protected by law is primarily the spiritual interest, and the material interest is a derived interest therein. The right to images generally includes the exclusive right to produce someone's images, the exclusive right to use them, and the right to protect the interests derived from the images.

It should be noted that there are personal image and group image. An individual has the right to claim his personal image. But no person in a group is allowed to individually claim the group's image. This is mainly based on the theory that an individual's personality is absorbed by the group's commonality. Thus, unless it can be determined that the purpose of using the group's image is to pinpoint to a single person among the group (e.g., by close-up or tagging), no one in the group can individually claim the right to the image.

Activities that infringe on a person's honorary right are equally intolerable. Honorary right is a civil subject's right to protect and maintain the interests related to the social assessment or self-evaluation over his personal traits or values. Infringement on a person's honorary right refers to a perpetrator's intentional act aimed at ruining that person's reputation to cause the decline of that person's social assessment. Because honorary right is an absolute right, the law does not require a person to make positive effort for the purpose of improving other's reputation. Thus, infringement on honorary right is always a feasance type of act. Nonfeasance cannot cause infringement on someone else's honorary right. Honorary right includes the right to maintain reputation (keep one's reputation at the best level, keep it from declining, prevent it from being damaged, or improve it), the right to protect reputation (preclude infringement and use legal procedures to enforce), and the right to utilize reputation (utilize one's reputation to gain benefit or interest).

Honorary right concerns a civil subject's human dignity. The law's protection over honorary right is to ensure that every person is respectfully treated in our society. When the opposite occurs—someone's honorary right has been infringed and the person is not getting the respect he deserves—the law provides necessary remedy to the person so that he will get fair assessment from the society. Compared with other personality rights, honorary right has many notable characteristics: First, its subject includes all civil subjects; both a natural person and a legal person can have honorary right. Second, honorary right's object is a civil subject's honorary interest. To a natural person, it refers to the person's morality, capability, etc. To a legal person, it refers to its business condition, performance capacity, commercial creditability, etc. Third, although honorary right is not directly a property, it often has a strong connection with property interests. In cases relating to honorary right, there are often subject matters regarding property interests. Property damage resulted from infringement on someone's honorary right shall be compensated.

Defamation is the most common way of infringing on a person's honorary right. It refers to a perpetrator's act of disseminating untruthful information about a person to a third party to damage the person's reputation. As can be seen, the evil of defamation is that it can damage a person's good reputation. The most major characteristic of defamation is that it creates something nonexisting, and that is the major difference between defamation and insult. The former needs to create something untruthful, but the latter does not—as long as the information damages reputation in the eyes of a normal member of the society, disseminating it constitutes insult.

Elements for defamation include the following: (1) A perpetrator has disseminated untruthful information. It requires that the perpetrator has committed an act of disseminating the information to the public; and the information must be a statement of fact; the stated fact is untruthful; and the statement is targeted towards a certain person, including a category of people who can be characterized. (2) The act has caused damage to the victim's reputation. Such damage includes not only the objective aspect of reputation (i.e., the decline of social evaluation) but also the subjective aspect (i.e., loss of sense of honor). (3) There is causation relationship between the act and the damage. (4) The perpetrator intentionally committed the act. It should be noted that if a plaintiff is a public figure, the court will usually increase the standard of establishing defamation, such as requiring establishing malice from the defendant. At the same time, there are two affirmative defenses against defamation: one is called "absolute privilege"—such as working-related speeches during legislative procedures or judicial proceedings, discussions between a married couple, victim's consent, etc.; the other is called "conditional privilege"—such as to protect one's own, other's, or the public's interests, etc.

Insult can also infringe on a person's honorary right. It is an intentional act that belittles a person's personality or harms his reputation by using violence, language, or words. Elements for insult include the following: one, the perpetrator has committed an act that harms someone's reputation and the act is targeted towards people within a certain scope; two, the insulting act must be known to a third person unless the act is so serious that the harm done to the victim is very evident. Relevant defenses include the stated fact is true, victim's consent, local language custom, etc.

The concept of the right to privacy was not proposed until 1890 by two American scholars and was not recognized until 1905 in a legal case. Thereafter, it developed very quickly and has been recognized by almost all countries in the world. Infringement on the right to privacy leads to legal liability. Previously, China had protected the right to privacy as part of the honorary right. The enactment of the "Tort Law" expressly put this right within the scope of legally protected civil rights and therefore recognized it by means of basic law.

Privacy is a private area that a person does not want others to know or interfere with. The right to privacy is a type of personality right established by law and owned by a natural person. According to this right, a natural person has control over interests related to his personal secrets and life as well as power to exclude others' interferences. Thus, privacy is in essence irrelevant to public interest; it is information that a person does not want others to know or an area he does not want others to interfere with. There are three major types of privacies: personal information, private activities, and personal territory.

As a specific personality right, the right to privacy has the following basic meanings: (1) The right to conceal privacy. This type of concealment right specifically refers to a person's right to not disclose his privacy to others. Because privacy right is irrelevant to public interest, the owner of the right has the right to conceal his privacy, and this is also for the need to maintain his personality interest. (2) The right to use privacy. Under this right, the owner of the right may use his personal information or allow others to use such information to satisfy personal, spiritual, or material needs, for example, to disclose someone's own diary or use life experience to create literary works or to allow others to use his own body to paint or photograph. The right to use privacy must be a legitimate use; otherwise, it is not protected by law. (3) The right to maintain privacy. It is the right of an owner to keep his privacy from being violated and the right to seek legal remedy when such violation occurs. (4) The right to control privacy. A citizen has the right to control his privacy by his own will, including the right to decide when to disclose his privacy, whom to disclose it to, and how to disclose it.

Infringements on the right to privacy can be divided into three categories: the first category includes illegal collection, distribution, and utilization of personal information; the second category includes interfering, tracking, photographing, videotaping, and other illegal disturbing activities; and the third category includes peeping; disseminating other person's diary, physical defect, or communication; illegally searching other's house, luggage, baggage, or body; breaking into other's house or bedroom without permission; installing tapping or monitoring devices; and other activities that infringe on someone's private territory. However, no right is unlimited or without restriction, and privacy right is no exception. When the right to privacy has a conflict with another right, the balance of interest does not automatically tilt to the side of privacy. In today's society, every country is paying more attention to protecting national security and public interest as well as safeguarding citizen's right to information. Sometimes there is indeed a contradiction between privacy and public interest. While paying attention to protect privacy right, each country is also increasing the degree of protection over public interest, national security, and citizen's right to information.

Lastly, let us take a look at the identity right. Identity right is the right of a person to maintain his identity interest. It is based on the person's identity relationship and is exclusively owned by the person. The object of this right is the person's identity interest. Stated differently, an identity relationship refers to a civil subject's status within a particular family and relative group. But not all identify relationships are protected by law. For example, friendship is not a right because it is not recognized by law and therefore not protected by law. But to those identity relationships that are recognized and protected by law, if they are infringed by illegal acts, such acts usually cause general tort liabilities.

A civil subject's identity right usually includes parental right, spousal right, kinship, etc. Parental right refers to a parent's obligation and right to protect and teach his minor children, including the right to take care of them and take custody of their property. Spousal right refers to the civil right mutually enjoyed by a married couple during their legal marriage. It includes the following: each side has the right and obligation to live with the other side; each side has the right to request the other side to be loyal; and each side has the right to request the other side's help, care, and cooperation as well as the obligation to help, care, and cooperate with the other side. As to kinship, it refers to a civil subject's right based on his special identity created out of consanguinity or adoption—the right and obligation based on identity created out of relationships other than spousal relationship or parent-minor child relationship—as well as interests associated with the identity.

Infringement on Property Rights

Infringement on property rights refers to an act that infringes on other's property interest and causes damage. China's constitution and law protect not only public property but also private citizen's legitimate income, savings, house, and other properties from being infringed. Article 2 of the "Tort Law" specifically lists the following property rights: ownership rights, usufruct, collateral rights, copyrights, patent rights, exclusive rights to use trademarks, discovery rights, equity rights, and inheritance rights. If these property rights were infringed by others, the infringements usually cause general tort liabilities and the victims are entitled to relief that is enough to cover the entire damage.

Compared with infringement on bodily rights, infringement on property rights has the following major legal characteristics:

1. The subject matter being infringed is property right. The civil rights defined by civil law include property rights and personal rights. According to the current law, property rights include real rights, debt rights, inheritance rights, intellectual property rights, and possession rights.
2. The consequence is property damage. Property damage may include direct damage and indirect damage. Direct damage in property right refers to the decrease of currently owned property interests (e.g., the decrease of value of a victim's property); indirect damage in property right refers to the decrease or loss of property interests that may be acquired by the victim (e.g., property interests that could be acquired by the victim in normal situation but are lost because of the infringement).
3. Civil methods for assuming liability with a property nature should apply. Relevant sections of the "Tort Law" specified in detail the methods for assuming liability applicable to property infringement liabilities, such as returning property, restoration to the original state and compensation for losses, etc. These methods for assuming liability reflect the principle of using property-based liabilities for remedies.
4. The liability scope of property infringement is determined based on the resulted damage. According to the principle of equal value exchange and the law of market value, all property damages need to be compensated.

According to different standards, we can divide property infringements into different categories. For example, based on the nature of the infringed property right, there are infringements on state-own property right, group-own property right, and private-own property right. The first two categories concern public properties and the latter one concerns private property. Although the natures of these properties are different, the law must treat and protect them equally. As another example, based on the content of the infringed property right, there are infringements on real rights, debt rights, and intellectual property rights. The significance of this kind of categorization is that, with the property right's content being different, the elements for liability, method for assuming liability, and remedy will be different, too. Yet another example, based on the form of the property right, there are infringements on real property right and personal property right. Infringement on personal property right is the most common property infringement, whereas infringement on real property right includes, besides its overlapping part with infringement on personal property right, infringements on natural resource right and adjacent right.

It should be noted that intellectual property right infringement refers to a perpetrator's infringement on a natural person's, a legal person's, or other organization's copyrights, trademark rights, patent rights, discovery rights, invention rights, and other technological achievements by plagiarizing, tampering, counterfeiting, etc. Intellectual property right has certain special characteristics. It is both a personal right and a property right. Thus, infringement on intellectual property right may not only cause direct property damage but also spiritual damage to a victim. Accordingly, some scholars put intellectual property right infringement neither in the property infringement category nor in the personal right infringement category, but treat such infringement as a unique category by itself. Even having so many special characteristics, intellectual property right infringement does not always create special tort liability as people think. Because the specific provisions of the "Tort Law" does not include any specification or suggestion regarding intellectual property right infringement, such infringement still creates general tort liability and the fault liability principle applies.

The most common property infringements in our everyday life are trespass, obstruction, misappropriation, and destruction. The first two are related to real property and the latter two are related to personal property. Trespass is an infringement against real property; what's infringed is a person's right of ownership, possession, and use over his land or building. Trespass is a type of feasance act and sometimes may lead to the infringement of the victim's privacy right also. Obstruction refers to a perpetrator's illegal disturbing activities towards a victim's right to peaceful enjoyment of his land, such as setting obstacles on a road to block people's passage. Misappropriation refers to taking possession of other person's personal property illegally or without permission to deprive the person's right of possession. What the perpetrator is trying to do here is to take away the personal property that belongs to the victim. Destruction means that a perpetrator destroys or damages someone else's personal property so that the property no long exists or loses its original value or function. Of course, property right infringement is not limited to the above four types. As long as there is an illegal act committed under fault and it has infringed on legitimate property right and caused damage, the act shall be deemed as a general tortious act and the perpetrator shall bear the corresponding civil liability.

Chapter 8
Special Provisions on Liable Parties

Overview

Chapter 4 of the "Tort Law" is called "Special Provisions on Liable Parties," which, from Article 32 to Article 40, specifies six specific tort liabilities: (1) guardian's responsibility; (2) temporary loss of consciousness or control by a person with full civil capacity; (3) employer's liability; (4) infringement via Internet; (5) breach of duty of care; and (6) school injuries. The reason to specifically organize these six tort liabilities in one chapter is because they are very different from other tort liabilities in form—they are all vicarious liabilities, accompanied with a little bit supplemental liabilities and joint and several liability. Thus, it is not difficult to understand why the title of this chapter includes "Special Liable Parties"—most liabilities specified in this chapter are in the form of vicarious liabilities.

Vicarious liability means that a person is held liable for damage caused by another person's act or an object under the person's control. Simply put it, the real meaning of vicarious liability is a person has committed tortious act and caused damage, but instead of that person, someone responsible for him is held liable for the damage, and therefore an identity inconsistency between the actual tortfeasor and the ultimate liable party is created, for example, an employer is held liable for its employee's tortious act, parents are held liable for their children's tortious acts, etc. Generally speaking, vicarious liability has the following legal characteristics:

First, the liable party and the perpetrator (or the damage-causing object) are separate entities. In general torts, the liable party is the perpetrator. A single perpetrator bears the liability by himself, and joint perpetrators bear the liability jointly. When damage is caused by an object, the object usually has a relationship with the perpetrator. For example, when a person causes a dog to attack someone, the dog is not the perpetrator but the tool of the person to commit a tortious act. The dog's act is then the natural extension of the person's act, and the perpetrator and liable party are still the same entity. But vicarious liability is different. Its precondition is that the perpetrator and the liable party are two different entities, and the perpetrator has no direct relationship with the damage-causing object. Here, the liable party does not

X. Li and J. Jin, *Concise Chinese Tort Laws*, China-EU Law Series 1,
DOI 10.1007/978-3-642-41024-6_8, © Springer-Verlag Berlin Heidelberg 2014

have the intent to cause harm or damage. The direct cause of damage is the perpetrator who is different from the liable party or the damage-causing object. This situation—the perpetrator (or the damage-causing object) and the liable party are separate—is the objective basis for transferring liability to the liable party.

Second, the condition for a liable party to bear liability for a perpetrator or a damage-causing object is the existence of certain special relationship between them. Between a liable party and a perpetrator, this special relationship may be employment relationship, guardianship, agency relationship, affiliation relationship, etc. Between a liable party and a damage-causing object, this special relationship may be property relationship such as possession, ownership, or custody. In terms of causing damage, these relationships are not direct causation relationships, but have certain indirect connections. Without these indirect connections, or beyond these indirect connections, there is no basis for the liable party to bear the vicarious liability. For example, a person incites another person to cause injury to a victim. Because there is no certain indirect relationship between the two persons, they have committed joint tort. Another example, a person did not provide help when he saw a victim was being attacked by an animal. Because the person has no special relationship with that animal, he bears no liability but only moral condemnation.

Third, the liable party bears the obligation to compensate for the damage. In general torts, a perpetrator bears the obligation to make the necessary compensation. But in a case of vicarious liability, whether damage is caused by a person or animal, a victim's right is directed at a party who did not directly cause the damage but has a certain relationship with the person or animal that caused the damage. When an animal, building, or machine causes damage, the owner, manager, or possessor should be liable. When a person causes damage, a party that has a special relationship with the person is held legally responsible. Joint and several liability does not apply here, and the victim can only seek remedy from the liable party.

A liability can be considered a vicarious liability only if it has all of the above characteristics. Once that is established, the liable party must be responsible for all damages caused by the perpetrator. However, after the liable party has made necessary compensation, if the perpetrator is found at fault, the liable party may seek remedy from the perpetrator. Generally speaking, there are two types of vicarious liabilities: human-related vicarious liability and animal-related vicarious liability. Liabilities specified in Article 4 of the "Tort Law"—guardian's responsibility, temporary loss of consciousness or control by a person with full civil capacity, employer's liability, etc.—are all human-related vicarious liabilities. We will discuss them in detail below.

Guardian's Liability

Under Chinese law, having civil capacity is the condition for a civil subject to participate in civil activities. A natural person who is above a certain age and is capable of taking care of his affairs is considered a person having civil capacity.

According to a natural person's age and mental health, civil capacity may be in three different forms: full civil capacity, limited civil capacity, and no civil capacity. A minor who is 10 years old or older is treated as a person having limited civil capacity and can participate civil activities corresponding to his age and mental capacity. The minor's other civil activities are managed or controlled by his legal representative. A minor under the age of 10 lacks civil capacity and is represented by his legal representative for all affairs. To make up the lack of civil capacity, the civil law established the guardianship rule which specifies that the legal representative of a person with limited or no civil capacity is his guardian.

A guardian is held liable for any damage caused by his ward. Article 32 of the "Tort Law" states:

> If a person without civil capacity or with limited civil capacity causes any damage to other persons, the guardian shall assume the tort liability. If the guardian has fulfilled his duties, his tort liability may be mitigated.
>
> If a person without civil conduct capacity or with limited civil conduct capacity, who has property, causes any damage to other persons, the compensations shall be paid out of his own property. The guardian shall make up any shortfall of the compensations.

Compared with Article 133 of the old "General Principles of Civil Law," the above provision has no substantive difference. It serves as the basic rule for guardian's liability.

Guardian's liability is based on the existence of a guardianship relation. A minor's guardian is his parents, direct relatives, close friends or relatives, or other organizations. A mentally ill's guardian is his close relatives or other organizations. If it is unclear who the guardian is, the party in the front of the row and having the capacity should bear the responsibility. Even when the guardianship responsibility is entrusted to another party, the guardian is still held liable for the ward's acts. Other than those, the elements for guardian's liability are pretty simple—they are the following: the ward has committed illegal act and the guardian is at fault; the victim has suffered damage or injury; and there is causation between the ward's illegal act and the victim's damage.

It is not difficult to determine from the law that guardian's liability has the following characteristics: (1) the presumed fault liability principle applies here—the guardian's fault is presumed from the fact that the guardian's ward has caused damage or injury to other people; if the guardian contends otherwise, he should bear the burden to prove so; (2) it distributes damage on a fair basis—even the guardian has no fault at all, his liability can only be reduced but not totally negated; (3) it is preconditioned on the fact that the ward has committed an illegal act, but whether the ward is at fault is not important; and (4) it is in the form of vicarious liability—because the guardian is held responsible for his ward's act not his own, this type of liability is a typical vicarious one.

Specifically, the assumption of guardian's liability is guided by four rules: the first one is that when a ward caused damage to other people, the guardian shall be liable for the damage; the second one is that if the guardian has exercised due care, his liability may be reduced; the third one is that if the ward has property, then compensation should come from the ward's property; and the fourth one is that when the ward's property is not enough for the compensation, the rest comes from the guardian's property.

Thus, cases regarding guardian's liability can be divided into two scenarios in actual practice: (1) when the ward has no property, the guardian will be liable for the full damage if all tort elements are established and (2) when the ward has property, but not enough to cover the whole damage, the guardian will be responsible for compensating the uncovered portion of damage. For example, a minor inherited some property from his deceased parents. The local community committee is the guardian for this minor. If the minor committed an illegal act, damage shall be covered by the property he inherited. However, the minor shall be left with enough financial resource to support his necessities so that his normal living and studying condition will not be affected. If the minor's property is not enough to cover the full damage, the guardian is responsible for the uncovered portion. Of course, general rules apply in these situations, such as contributory negligence and the principle of deduction of collateral benefits, etc.

Temporary Loss of Consciousness or Control by a Person with Full Civil Capacity

Temporary loss of consciousness or control by a person with full civil capacity occurs when the person temporarily loses consciousness because of fault, abuse of alcohol, or the misuse of narcotic or psychotropic drugs and causes damage or injury to other people. Therefore, the person shall bear liability for the damage or injury he has caused. Article 33 of the "Tort Law" specifies this special tort. Its content includes the following: first, if a person having full civil capacity causes damage or injury to other people because his own fault induced his temporary loss of consciousness or control, the person shall bear liability; second, if the person is not at fault, he shall bear corresponding liability to the extent his financial capability allows; and third, the person shall bear full liability for any alcohol- or narcotic drug-induced loss of consciousness or control.

There are four conditions for this liability: (1) the perpetrator must have full civil capacity; if the person only has limited civil capacity or no civil capacity, his legal representative shall bear the liability; (2) the victim has suffered damage or injury, including property damage, bodily harm, or mental distress; (3) the damage was caused because the perpetrator temporarily lost consciousness or control; and (4) the perpetrator cannot prove that he was not at fault regarding his temporary loss of consciousness or control.

Given the situations that may cause a person to temporarily lose his consciousness are very complex, Article 33 of the "Tort Law" specifies the corresponding liability for each of these situations:

1. It was the perpetrator's fault that led to his temporary loss of consciousness or control. Under this situation, the perpetrator shall bear liability. For example, a

person has suffered a stroke and needs to take medicine everyday according to doctor's instructions. But he did not take medicine consecutively for several days. As a result, he suffered another stroke and passed out while driving. And consequently he hit a pedestrian. In this case, because this person has fault in leading to his temporary loss of consciousness, he should bear liability according to the degree of his fault. The fault at issue here refers to the fault that led to the loss of consciousness, not the fault occurred after that. If a person having full civil capacity loses his consciousness because of his own fault, he shall bear liability for whatever damage he has caused after his loss of consciousness.
2. It was not the perpetrator's fault that led to his temporary loss of consciousness or control. Under this situation, the perpetrator is not liable for the damage. For example, a person did not know he was allergic to certain pollen. But one day he inhaled this type of pollen and got into an allergic reaction, which harmed someone else. Although he was not at fault here, he should still bear a share of the damage for fairness reasons. The size of the share is determined based on each party's financial capability—if he is in a better financial situation, he should compensate more; vice versa. But it should be noted that what is required is reasonable amount of compensation, not full amount.
3. The perpetrator's temporary loss of consciousness or control was caused by abuse of alcohol or the misuse of narcotic or psychotropic drugs. Under these situations, the perpetrator shall bear full liability, because he knew or should have known that alcohol and narcotic or psychotropic drugs can affect a person's central nerve system and cause the temporary loss of consciousness or control. By ignoring the possible consequence of causing harm to others, the person shall not be allowed to use his loss of consciousness or control as an excuse but shall be held liable for his fault of indulgence.

Employer's Liability

Articles 34 and 35 of the "Tort Law" specify the special tort of employer's liability—an employer is held liable for its employee's tortious act committed during the course of the employee's work. Specifically, employer's liability includes employer liability, liability of a party using dispatched labor, and liability of a party receiving individual labor. Their common characteristics are, although a tortious act was committed by a laborer, the consequence is borne by a party employing the laborer. Thus, this tortious liability is a typical vicarious liability.

Employer's liability is not a new type of tortious liability. It already existed in the "General Principles of Civil Law" and the "Judicial Interpretation of Personal Injuries." But the "Tort Law" made some major adjustments on these provisions:

First, it provided a uniform specification on these different types of employer's liabilities. Before the enactment of the "Tort Law," employer's liability is triggered by three different tortious acts: a government official's tortious act committed while discharging his duty, a tortious act committed by an employee of a nongovernmental entity during the course of the employee's work, and a tortious act committed by an employee of a nonlegal-person entity during the course of the employee's work. But the "Tort Law" specifies that Article 34 applies to all employers, including governmental entities, legal-person entities, nonlegal-person entities, proprietorships, and partnerships. Besides the above, Article 35 further specifies the tortious liability of a party receiving an individual's labor service when the labor-serving individual caused damage to others.

Second, the employee who is at fault does not bear joint and several liability externally. Before the enactment of the "Tort Law," an employer's tortious liability was handled in two different ways when its wrongdoing employee has gross negligence or intent. If the employer is a legal person, then the employee does not bear joint and several liability. Otherwise, the employee shall bear joint and several liability. After the employer has made compensation for the damage, it has the right to recover part of the compensation from the employee. But the "Tort Law" has changed this rule—the employer shall bear full liability for its employee's tortious act during the employee's course of work. Even if the employee is at fault, he/she does not bear joint and several liability.

The significance of the changes can be summarized into two points: (1) Simplicity. The "Tort Law" simplified the legal relationships, which were quite complicated under the old rules. (2) Fairness. Whether it is a government entity, a nongovernmental legal-person entity, or a nonlegal-person entity, the law applies to them equally.

According to Article 34 of the "Tort Law," the employer must bear liability whether it has fault or not. Therefore, it is a no-fault tortious liability. But the employee at issue must have committed a tortious act and caused damage. Otherwise, the employer has no liability. The employee's tortious act can be either fault based or no-fault based. Besides these, we should also pay attention to four points when determining the employer's liability:

First, the employer discussed here may be an enterprise, institute, government office, social organization, partnership, proprietorship, contractor, etc. Stated differently, except for individual labor contract relationships, all employer-employee relationships are covered by Article 34 of the "Tort Law." And, an employee can be a full-time employee, a part-time employee, or a temporary employee.

Second, the employee's tortious act is related to the work within the scope of his employment. The employee must act in accordance with the employer's instruction, and the consequence is borne by the employer. On the contrary, if the employee's act has nothing to do with his work, even if the act occurred during the timeframe of the employee's work, the employer is not responsible. For example, if a person beats up a victim while at work for private reason, the victim should seek remedy from the person directly. In practice, two factors are considered in determining whether a person's act is related to his work: whether the act is authorized by the employer or within the scope of the person's work and whether it is for the purpose of achieving a work-related task or it is internally related to the work, even though it is not authorized by the employer or is outside the scope of his work.

Third, with respect to tortious acts committed by government officials during the course of their work, one type of these tortious acts is related to their official capacity; the other type of these tortious acts are related to the corresponding government unit's civil capacity. As to the former case, the government entities need to make reasonable compensation to the victims according to the relevant provisions of the "State Compensation Law." As to the latter case, the government entities need to bear reasonable civil liabilities.

Last, the employee does not bear joint and several liability, even if he has intent or gross negligence. However, after the employer bears the liability, it can recover damage from the employee. Although this rule is not expressly specified in law, it may be undoubtedly derived from the legislative intent.

According to Paragraph 2, Article 34 of the "Tort Law," parties that use dispatched labor shall bear tortious liability for any injury or damage caused to other people by the dispatched personnel during the course of their work and the labor dispatch period; the labor-dispatching party shall bear corresponding supplementary liability where it is at fault. Here, the labor-dispatching party enters into a contract with a worker and sends the worker to the party that uses the worker. The major characteristic of labor dispatching is the separation of hiring and using of the worker. The labor-dispatching party is a contracting party, but the party that uses the worker is not.

Although the labor-dispatching party contracts with the worker, it does not directly manage or use the worker. During the dispatching period, the dispatched worker works for the party that uses and manages him and provides him certain working conditions and protections. It is therefore not difficult to understand that the party using the worker shall bear liability for the worker's tortious act during the course of his work. Also, if the labor-dispatching party is at fault on dispatching the worker, it should bear corresponding supplemental liability.

It should be noted that the supplemental liability includes two different meanings: (1) The party using the worker is the primary one on bearing liability and the dispatching party is secondary. Only when the party using the worker is not financially capable of covering the full damage, the dispatching party is held liable for the rest. (2) The labor-dispatching party only bears corresponding supplementary liability, i.e., the amount of liability corresponds to its fault and contribution to the damage.

Article 35 of the "Tort Law" specifies:

> Where, in a labor relationship formed between individuals, the party providing labor services causes any damage to other persons due to the labor services, the party receiving labor services shall assume the tort liability. If the party providing labor services suffers any damage to himself/herself due to his/her own labor services, both parties shall assume corresponding liabilities according to their respective faults.

This provision only applies to labor relationships formed between individuals, such as nannies, tutors, etc., similar to the independent contractors in US tort law. It is not difficult to see, Article 35 specifies two different scenarios:

First, the party to whom labor is provided shall bear tortious liability when the labor-providing party causes an injury or damage to another person. The precondition for the liability is that the labor-providing party's tortious act is related to the work. If the tortious act is the labor-providing party's personal act and has nothing to do with the work, the labor-receiving party does not bear the liability. For example, a nanny went out for fun during a weekend and hit someone accidentally on the road. Because the nanny's tortious act has nothing to do with the nanny work, the nanny should bear the liability.

Second, where the party providing labor causes injury or damage to himself as a result of his labor services, liability shall be borne by both parties in light of their respective degree of fault. Here, the fault-based liability principle is applied. Thus, if the labor-providing party and the labor-receiving party are both at fault, they should each bear corresponding liability according to the degree of fault. The more faults the person has, the more liability he should bear. No fault, no liability.

Network-Based Tortious Liability

Network-based infringements are various activities occurred on the Internet that infringe upon people's civil rights. The most common network-based infringements are libel, disclosing other people's personal information, uploading pirated music and video works, etc. With the Internet becoming more and more popular in people's everyday life, various types of network-based infringements have sharply increased in recent years. And the law fighting against network-based infringements is becoming one of the fastest developing areas of the Tort Law. In this regard, the "Tort Law" responded progressively and specified the corresponding liabilities of network users and network service providers in Article 36. However, because the provisions of the "Tort Law" are too abstract, we have to rely mainly on the Supreme People's Court's "Several Issues Concerning the Laws Applicable to the Trial of Copyright Disputes Involving Computer Networks Interpretations" and the State Council's "Regulation on the Protection of the Right to Network Dissemination of Information" in practice.

Paragraph 1, Article 36 of the "Tort Law" provides Internet users and Internet service providers shall bear tortious liability in the event they infringe other people's civil rights and interests through the Internet. This provision governs the Internet users' and Internet service providers own tortious acts, which are general torts, and the fault-based liability imputation principle applies here. With respect to the Internet service providers, two types of tortious acts are most common: one type of tortious act is using technology to infringe on other people's right and interest, such as destroying other's technology protection measures, using technology to attack other's networks, stealing other's information, etc.; the other type is using content to infringe on other's right, such as creating false information to defame other people, infringing on other's copyright, etc.

Network users' most common infringing activities are the following: (1) infringement on personality right, such as stealing or impersonating other people's names, using other people's portraits without permission, publishing insulting or defaming articles against other people, hacking other people's computers, illegally intercepting other people's message or transmissions, and disclosing other people's private information without permission; (2) infringement on property right, such as stealing money from other people's online banking accounts, or infringing on other people's network-based virtual properties (e.g., virtual money or equipment in computer games); and (3) infringement on intellectual properties, such as transmitting other's work digitally without permission, circumventing technical measures, infringement on copyright or database, infringement on other's trademark rights to mislead consumers, and maliciously register trademarks or domain names that are similar to other's legitimate trademarks or domain names.

Paragraphs 2–3, Article 36 of the "Tort Law" specify two situations, under which the Internet service providers shall bear joint and several liability on Internet users' tortious acts committed on the providers' networks—the notification rule and the knowledge rule. Obviously, these two rules are replicates of the safe harbor and red flag rules of the US "Digital Millennium Copyright Act." Therefore, the principles of their applications are the same.

According to the notification rule, Internet service providers are usually not aware of users using their networks to commit infringement acts. Thus, the victims have the obligation to inform the service providers that the contents of the providers' websites have infringed on their rights and request the providers to remove the infringing contents. After receiving such notifications, the service providers must act accordingly to remove, disconnect, or shield such infringing contents. If the service providers did not take necessary measures to stop the infringements, therefore allow the infringement activities to continue, they shall bear tortious liabilities to those expanded damages and joint and several liability with the infringing users. If the service providers did not receive such notifications or if they took necessary measures after receiving such notifications, they shall not bear liabilities.

According to the knowledge rule, if the Internet service providers knew that certain users were committing infringing activities via the providers' networks, but did not take any necessary measures to stop them, therefore caused damage to other people, then the service providers shall bear joint and several liability with the users. To determine whether the service providers have the knowledge, the following principles shall be followed: (1) Depending on the different types of service providers according to the technology platforms, the standards should be different, but the overall standard should be a high standard—unless the infringing activities raise a red flag, knowledge is not attributed to the service providers. (2) Depending on the different types of protected rights, the standards are different. For example, regarding copyright, unless the infringement is clear, if the service providers did not edit the uploaded infringing content, they would not be considered as having the knowledge (3) The service providers do not have a general auditing obligation, i.e., no duty to actively search and find the infringing activities on their networks.

It should be noted that the joint and several liability borne by the service providers may have differences under different situations. Under the notification rule, the service providers bear joint and several liability only to the expanded damages. But under knowledge rule, they bear joint and several liability with the infringing users to the whole damages.

Liabilities for Breaching the Duty to Safeguard

Managers of hotels, shopping centers, banks, bus or train stations, entertainment venues, and other public places have the duty to provide reasonable safety measures to protect people's lives and properties. Therefore, breach of such duty will lead to tortious liabilities if any injury or damage is caused to people as a result of the breach. Based on Article 6 of the "Judicial Interpretation of Personal Injury and Compensation," Article 37 of the "Tort Law" specifies this liability via two provisions.

First, managers of public places such as hotels, shopping markets, banks, bus stations, and entertainment venues and the organizers of mass activities shall bear tortious liability for injury or damage done to other people as a result of their failure to fulfill their duty of care. This is a nonfeasance type of tortious liability and the fault liability imputation principle applies here. Thus, the elements for breaching the duty to provide safety measures include the following: breach of the duty of care, the victim suffered damage or injury, there is causation relationship between the breach and the damage or injury, and the party that breached the duty of care is at fault.

To establish these elements, the most difficult task is to prove the existence and content of the duty of care. Generally speaking, the content of the duty of care may be explicitly specified by law, based on contract, or created due to the good faith principle. Because the parties owing such duty of care involve many different industries, their duty of care can be different to different groups of people. Accordingly, the law lacks specific rules. In practice, factors such as general acceptable standard in the relevant industry, the local condition, the scale of the organized activity, the nature and degree of the tortious act, and capabilities of the party owing the duty of care as well as measures taken before and after the tortious act should all be considered.

Also, Paragraph 2 specifies that "[w]here the injury or damage is caused by a third party, the third party shall bear tortious liability, where the manager or organizer fails to fulfill its duty of care, it shall assume supplementary liability." This provision is also reasonable and fair because the third party should bear liability for his own tortious act anyway. And the party owing the duty of care did not exercise reasonable care, either. Therefore, it should bear supplementary liability. As stated above, the manager or organizer is only liable to the extent corresponding to its fault and contribution to the damage, not the whole damage.

School Injuries

A kindergarten, school, or other educational institution must fulfill its educational and management duties to students who have no civil capacity or limited civil capacity during their living or studying there. If it fails to fulfill such duties and as a result any student is injured, the kindergarten, school, or educational institution is held liable for the injury. Article 38–40 of the "Tort Law" specify three different school injuries, respectively.

First, Article 38 specifies the scenario when a student having no civil capacity is injured. Here, the kindergarten, school, or educational institution shall bear liability, except if it can prove that it has exercised due care. This indicates that the law applies presumed fault liability imputation principle when the injured student has no civil capacity. In other words, if a student is less than 10 years old, the student's school is presumed at fault if the student is injured while living or studying there, and the school is held liable. If the school can provide evidence to prove that it has exercised due care, then it is released from the liability.

Second, Article 39 specifies the scenario when a student with limited civil capacity is injured. Here, if the school failed to exercise reasonable care, it shall bear liability. Thus, the fault-based liability imputation principle applies here, and the result is obvious.

Last, Article 40 specifies the scenario when a student having no or limited civil capacity is injured by a third party while the student is studying or living in the kindergarten, school, or educational institution. Here, the third party shall bear the liability. But if the kindergarten, school, or educational institution has failed to exercise due care, it should bear corresponding supplementary liability. In certain situations, a person who is not related to a school may sneak in and harm the students there. Students organized by their school for a fun trip outside may be harmed or injured by someone not related to the school. Under these situations, the person who has caused injuries to the student(s) should undoubtedly bear the tortious liability. However, because the students were still in school or under the school's care while the tortious act occurred, the school should bear supplementary liability if it failed to exercise its duty of care.

Chapter 9
Special Tort Liability

Overview

Special tort liability is defined in relative to general tort liability. It lacks certain elements for general tort liability and applies presumed fault liability or no-fault liability imputation principle. In most cases, special tort liabilities are indirect liabilities, requesting a defendant to bear liability caused by the person(s) he is responsible for, properties he manages, and dangerous conditions controlled by him. Special tort liabilities are special because of the following:

1. Applicable liability imputation principles are special. For general tort liabilities, fault liability applies. But for special tort liabilities, presumed fault liability (injuries caused by property) or no-fault liability (e.g., product liability, environmental pollution, etc.) applies so that victims' legitimate rights may be better protected.
2. Elements for establishing these liabilities are special. Elements for establishing special tort liabilities are not determined according to the elements for general tort liabilities, but according to the laws and based on the specific conditions. These special conditions are not generic, and each type of special tort liability has different special conditions—without these special conditions, that type of special tort liability cannot be established.
3. Special rules on burden of proof. Because special tort liabilities use either presumed fault liability or no-fault liability imputation rule, the burden of proof is usually shifted from plaintiffs to defendants. That is, the defendants have the burden to prove that they are innocent; and under no-fault liability rule, the defendants even need to prove that the damages or injuries were caused by some third parties.
4. The forms of the liabilities are special. General tort liabilities are direct liabilities; special tort liabilities are indirect liabilities, requesting a defendant to bear liability caused by the person(s) he is responsible for, properties he manages, and dangerous conditions controlled by him.

X. Li and J. Jin, *Concise Chinese Tort Laws*, China-EU Law Series 1,
DOI 10.1007/978-3-642-41024-6_9, © Springer-Verlag Berlin Heidelberg 2014

According to the rules for general tort liabilities, each person is only liable for damage or injury caused by his own fault, and a victim bears the burden to prove that. With the development of our modern society, more and more things are becoming the source for tortious damages or injuries, and the contributing factors are growing in multiple directions. As a result, many victims find themselves incapable of meeting their burden of proof, and some cannot even find who the perpetrators are. Under these conditions, justice and fairness cannot be maintained if the rules for general liabilities are enforced here. Thus, special tort liabilities were developed. By adjusting the elements for establishing liabilities, burden of proof, and form of the liabilities, our system can better protect victims' legitimate rights, therefore serving the development of our modern society.

Besides those special tort liabilities specified in Chapter 4, the "Tort Law" specifies seven different special tort liabilities in the following seven chapters: product liability, motor vehicle traffic accident liability, medical malpractice liability, environmental pollution liability, high-risk operation liability, liability for damage caused by domestic animals, and liability for damage caused by objects. In the interest of brevity, we will only briefly introduce these liabilities below.

Product Liability

Manufacturers or sellers are held liable for damage or injuries caused by defective products they manufactured or sold. Such liability is called product liability. In the early times, in order to protect consumers against infringements caused by defective products, the law used contract theories for such remedy, including express warranty and implied warranty theories. However, with the social economic connections becoming more and more complicated, a victim is not always the direct purchaser of the defective product. That is, the victim does not have a contract relationship with the producer or seller of the defective product. Therefore, neither the express warranty nor the implied warranty applies here. Because of the limits of the warranty theories, many countries have started establishing product liability rule within their tort law systems, making product liability a tort liability in whole or in part and introducing strict liability as the imputation principle. China follows the same approach and has specified product liability in Articles 41–47 of the "Tort Law."

Although the "Tort Law" treats product liability as a special tort liability, there are more than one imputation principles for product liability. And for different liable parties, a different liability imputation principle is applied. For example, a manufacturer bears no-fault liability; a seller bears fault liability. This multilayer processing platform serves the judicial system's need better.

1. No-fault liability is applied. According to Article 41 of the "Tort Law," manufacturers shall bear tortious liability for damage caused to others by their defective products. This provision explicitly establishes the no-fault liability

for manufacturers with respect to their defective products. When a victim who has suffered injury or damage caused by a manufacturer's defective product requests relief, the manufacturer cannot defend itself by claiming it has no fault, and the victim is not required to prove the manufacturer's fault.

2. Fault liability is applied. According to Article 42 of the "Tort Law," a seller shall bear tortious liability for damage caused to others by defective products where the seller is at fault. Obviously, this shows that a seller's liability on defective products is based on fault. Only when a seller is the one causing the products defective can it be held liable. Also, Article 42 specifies that "where the seller is unable to identify either the producer or the supplier of defective products, the seller shall bear tortious liability." In this scenario, the seller is obviously at fault because it has not strictly controlled its procurement process.

As a special tort liability, product liability is special with respect to its establishing elements, including the product is defective, damage is caused by the defect(s), and causation relationship exists between the damage and the product's defect(s).

First, product defect is the necessary precondition for establishing product liability. Although the "Tort Law" does not include a concrete definition for defective product, in light of the "Product Quality Law" and other relevant regulations, product defect refers to the unreasonable danger of a product that may cause injury or damage to a consumer. If there is government standard or industrial standard relating to the protection of personal health and property safety, a defective product is considered as not meeting the standard. Thus, product defect actually has three different meanings: (1) defect means unreasonable danger, so reasonable danger is not a defect; (2) this danger endangers people and property safety; other than that, a danger is not a defect; and (3) the standard for determining whether a product is defective can be either a general standard or a legal standard. The general standard uses people's reasonable expectation as the standard, i.e., a reasonable person's expectation on a product's safety aspect under normal circumstances; the legal standard is a government or industry's mandatory requirement on product safety, and if a product does not meet the standard, the product is deemed as having unreasonable danger. In practice, if there is legal standard, the legal standard is applied; otherwise, the general standard is applied.

If categorized by the type of a defect, product defect can be design defect, manufacturing defect, or marketing defect. Design defect means that a product has unsafe and unreasonable factors in its design, e.g., the structure is unreasonable, design material is improper, no additional safety measure, etc. Manufacturing defect occurs when the product material or components are defective or the assembling process has certain error in it and therefore caused the final product to contain unreasonable danger. Marketing defect means that a manufacturer has not provided enough warnings and description and therefore caused its products to pose unreasonable danger during their shipment, storage, and use.

Secondly, damage is indispensable in establishing product liability. In other words, the use of a defective product must have caused the victim's death, bodily harm, property damage, or other serious damage. If general injuries were caused, the perpetrator must pay for the victim's medical expenses and loss of income; if permanent injury was resulted, the perpetrator must also make compensation for disability living allowance (besides the medical expenses and loss of income); if death was caused, the perpetrator is further responsible for funeral cost, pensions; if the victim was dead or disabled, the perpetrator must also be responsible for the necessities of the person(s) depending on the victim. For property damage, the remedy must cover both direct and indirect damages; the perpetrator bears the burden of proof regarding the existence and scope of the damage. When there is mental distress caused, the perpetrator is held liable for that as well. That is what is called other serious damage.

Finally, there must be causation relationship between damage and the product defect at issue. The causation relationship is a required element that a victim needs to prove. According to this element, the product defect is the factor that caused the victim's injury or damage; there is direct causation relationship between the victim's damage and the product defect at issue. To make his case, a victim must prove that he has used the defective product and must prove the damage caused by the defective product. Then, he needs to prove that the use of the defective product is the reason for causing the injury or damage.

For the convenience of the victim, he can use two different ways to obtain relief according to the "Tort Law": one way is to request compensation from the manufacturer; the other way is to request compensation from the seller. In other words, if the damage is caused by a defective product, the victim can get remedy from either the manufacturer or the seller; if they refuse to make compensations, the victim can sue either one of them. Of course, if the product defect is caused by the manufacturer, after making necessary compensations to the victim, the seller may retrieve damage from the manufacturer. Also, even if the defect was caused by the shipper, storage manager, or other third parties, the victim may ask for remedy from the manufacturer or seller. The manufacturer or seller may later recover the damage from the shipper or storage manager to the extent they were at fault in causing the defect.

A defective product may have two effects: One is actual damage or injury, which already existed and can be remedied by compensation; the other one is the threat to someone's bodily and property safety, which is a potential damage that has not occurred yet. Under the latter situation, the person under threat can ask the manufacturer or seller to remove the danger or threat.

Another common scenario is that, when products were put on the market, the manufacturer and sellers did not find the defect(s) due to some technical reasons or lack of certain technologies, but found the defect(s) afterwards. Under such scenario, the manufacturer and sellers must provide timely and effective warnings to people or recall these defective products to prevent any potential harm or damage to customers. However, if the manufacturer or sellers knowingly ignore the risk and continue manufacturing or selling the defective products and as a result cause deaths or serious injuries to consumers, the victims can request punitive damages. Obviously, the condition for applying punitive damage under Chinese law is very restrictive. Not only must a perpetrator have subjective malice, but also a victim needs to suffer death or serious bodily harm.

Although not explicitly specified in the "Tort Law," in light of the "Product Quality Law" and other relevant regulations, defenses against product liability recognized by Chinese law generally include the following: products have not been put on the market, defect(s) did not exist at the time the products were put on the market, existing technologies cannot detect the defect(s) when the products were put on the market, and another is victim's fault—including misuse, abuse, overuse, ignoring the warning against modifying or disassembling the products, etc.

Motor Vehicle Traffic Accident Liability

Motor vehicle traffic accident liability refers to the special tort liability that should be borne by a person who negligently or intentionally created a traffic accident and caused injury or damage to others. Chapter 6, Provisions 53–58 of the "Tort Law," specifies the motor vehicle traffic accident liability generally. But because of the limited specification, these provisions are quite abstract and lack particularity. Therefore, other laws or regulations including the "Road and Traffic Safety Law" are still the main basis for processing motor vehicle traffic accident liabilities.

Chapter 6 of the "Tort Law" can be divided into three parts. First, although the content of Article 48 is very simple—for damage caused by motor vehicles in traffic accidents, liability to pay compensation shall be determined in accordance with the relevant provisions of the Road Traffic Safety Law—it actually establishes the basic rule, elements, and imputation principle.

According to Articles 17 and 76 of the "Road Traffic Safety Law," the government mandates the motor vehicle third party insurance rule—insurance companies are required to make appropriate compensations within the amounts specified in the insurance agreements first. In other words, with respect to accidents between motor vehicles and motor vehicles, motor vehicles and non-motor vehicles, as well as motor vehicles and pedestrians, insurance companies are to make the compensations within the insured amounts, and the perpetrators are only held liable for the rest of the amount that cannot be covered by insurance. This has significance on timely compensating victims and distributing the risk among motor vehicle drivers. This is the so-called "insurance first" rule for motor vehicle traffic accident liabilities.

According to the "Road Traffic Safety Law," elements for motor vehicle traffic accident liability include the following: (1) the traffic accident-causing vehicle must be a motor vehicle, i.e., a wheeled vehicle that uses motor power to drive or haul and is used on a road for carrying people, shipping goods, or accomplishing professional operations; (2) it must occur on a road—only traffic accident occurred on a road, a city street, or a place, although controlled by an organization but public traffic is allowed, can be the basis for motor vehicle traffic accident liability; (3) there must be a victim who has suffered death, injury, or property damage from the traffic accident; (4) the perpetrator must have subjective fault and actually violated the traffic rules; if neither party violated the traffic rules, the traffic accident is an accidental event and neither party shall bear liability; and (5) there must be causation relationship—in practice, the "but for" rule is generally applied, i.e., "but for this act, the damage usually does not happen" and "because of this act, the damage usually will happen."

The fault liability and presumed fault liability imputation principles are generally applied for motor vehicle traffic accident liabilities. And the no-fault liability imputation principle applies for only a small number of cases involving motor vehicle traffic accidents. As to the question of which principle applies, it depends on the parties involved in the traffic accident and whether they were at fault.

1. For accident between motor vehicles, the party at fault shall bear the liability; when both parties were at fault, they should share the liability according to the amount of fault each party has. As can be seen, for accident between motor vehicles, fault liability imputation principle applies. That is, when two motor vehicles were involved in a traffic accident where damage or injury was caused, it is important to determine which party's fault led to the accident. Then the party who was at fault should bear the liability. And if a party was not at fault, it does not need to bear liability.
2. The presumed fault liability imputation principle generally applies for accidents between motor vehicles and non-motor vehicles and between motor vehicles and pedestrians. At the same time, the motor vehicle parties bear a certain part of no-fault liabilities. In practice, when an accident occurred between a motor vehicle and a non-motor vehicle or pedestrian, the presumed fault liability imputation principle applies first. That is, the non-motor vehicle driver or pedestrian only needs to prove the fact that his injury or damage was caused by the collision, but the subjective factor—which party was at fault—is left for the motor vehicle party to prove. If the motor vehicle party cannot prove that it is not at fault, it should bear the liability. If it can prove the other side was at fault, then its liability is reduced accordingly. Even if the motor vehicle party can prove that it was not at fault, it still should bear not more than 10 % of the liability. As to this part of the liability, it is no-fault liability. Only if the motor vehicle party can prove that the accident was intentionally caused by the non-motor vehicle driver or pedestrian, it can be discharged from all liabilities.

Second, the second part of the content is Article 49 through Article 52, which discuss the scenarios where the owner and driver of the motor vehicle are two different entities and who should bear the liabilities when a traffic accident occurs.

Article 49 specifies the scenario where the owner and driver are different entities because of leasing or borrowing. In such case, the insurance company shall make necessary compensation within the amount specified in the insurance agreement first. The driver then shall be responsible for the part that cannot be covered by the insurance policy. But if the owner was at fault with respect to the occurrence of the accident, the owner shall bear corresponding liability. This is actually requiring the owner of the motor vehicle to make reasonable investigation before leasing the motor vehicle to the driver, e.g., does the driver have a driver's license, etc. Also, the owner should make sure that the motor vehicle is safe to drive, e.g., making sure the braking system works, etc. If the owner did not meet the above duty, he was at fault.

Article 50 specifies the scenario where the motor vehicle has been sold by the owner to another party, but the transfer of ownership has not been registered yet. If an accident occurs and the motor vehicle party is held liable, the insurance party should make necessary compensation within the amount specified in the insurance policy first; the driver of the motor vehicle should bear the rest that cannot be covered by the insurance policy. The ownership transfer was already effective when the transaction occurred. Registration is only a procedural requirement. The original owner is not the possessor of the motor vehicle anymore, does not have any control over the motor vehicle, and cannot prevent the occurrence of any traffic accident. Thus, when accident occurs, the actual possessor or driver of the motor vehicle should bear the liability.

Article 51 specifies the scenario where an assembled motor vehicle or a motor vehicle that is due to be scrapped is sold or transferred by other means, the transferor and the transferee shall be jointly and severally liable for damage caused by said vehicle in a traffic accident. Because assembled motor vehicles or motor vehicles due to be scrapped do not meet the safety standard for road driving, they can easily cause traffic accidents, causing injury or damage to pedestrians, non-motor vehicle, or other motor vehicle drivers. Selling or transferring these types of motor vehicles is illegal already; driving these vehicles on the road is even more dangerous. Thus, the law increased the punishment on these activities, specifying that the no-fault liability imputation principle applies for these cases, no legal defense exists, and the transferee and transferor bear joint and several liability.

Article 52 specifies the scenario where a motor vehicle is stolen, converted, or looted, the thief, converter, or looter shall be liable for damage caused by said vehicle in a traffic accident. This provision is easy to understand. When a motor vehicle is stolen, the owner is already a victim. Even if he was negligent for not maintaining the motor vehicle in a safe condition, he was not the cause and should not be responsible for whatever traffic accident occurred after he lost control of the vehicle. To hold him liable for the accident would be too strict. Thus, the perpetrator who stole the motor vehicle, not the owner, should be held liable.

The last part is Article 53, which specifies the hit- and run-scenario. According to the relevant traffic regulations, a motor vehicle driver should stop the vehicle immediately after he is involved in a traffic accident, protect the scene of the accident, report the accident to police, and rescue injured people. But in reality, there are many hit-and-run occurrences, causing irreparable harm to people's lives and properties and creating a serious threat to society. To this type of tortious activities, the "Tort Law" specifies: if the vehicle is subject to compulsory insurance, compensation shall be covered by the insurance company within the compensation limit under the compulsory insurance procured for the said vehicle. If the vehicle is unknown or if the vehicle is not subject to compulsory insurance, the costs paid for rescuing or burying the injured party and other relevant costs shall be paid out of the Social Assistance Fund for Road Traffic Accidents on behalf of the liable party. The administrative organ for the Fund may, after paying compensation, claim the same from the liable party.

Medical Malpractice Liability

Medical malpractice liability refers to tort cases where medical professionals did not exercise the necessary cares specified by relevant laws, regulations, and diagnostic procedures during their medical practices and as a result caused injuries or damages to patients. Previously, China's laws and regulations on medical malpractice were not only complicated but also confusing. Medical malpractices were treated as either medical accidents or medical errors. Not only the governing rules for the two types of medical malpractices were different, but also the remedy standards were not unified, causing a lot of errors. Articles 54–64 of the "Tort Law" specified the medical malpractice liability, abolished the differences between medical accidents and medical errors, and combined the two into medical malpractice liability so that the same standard would be applied to protect patients' rights.

The medical malpractice liability referred in the "Tort Law" has three different types: the first type is called medical technique malpractice liability—medical institutes or professionals failed to perform their diagnosis and treatment obligations according to current standards, thereby caused injuries or damages to patients; this is negligence or error on medical techniques; the second is called medical ethics liability—medical institutes or professionals violated the requirements of medical ethics or breached their duty to keep confidential patients' records and therefore caused damage to patients; as can be seen, this is in nature a violation of professional ethics; and the third type is called medical product liability—medical institutes used defective medicines, infected medical devices, or substandard bloods and therefore caused injuries or damages to patients; the medical institutes, the manufacturer of the defective medicines or other medical products, or the sellers shall bear liability, which is similar to product liability.

Which liability imputation principle should be applied to medical malpractice cases is always a difficult question to answer. On the one hand, victim patients' rights should be protected. On the other hand, medical institutes' rights should also be considered. And lastly, we should also consider the overall patient group's interest. If we have protected the victim patients' interests too broadly, medical institutes would bear more liabilities, and that could be counterproductive in that the medical institutes would transfer the cost to patients in general. In light of these concerns, the "Tort Law" chose fault-based liability imputation principle as the basic rule for medical malpractice liabilities.

There are two major reasons for applying fault liability as the imputation principle for medical malpractice cases. First, medical practice in nature carries certain risks. Medical treatment, while helping to cure a patient, may cause damage to the patient. If no-fault liability or presumed fault liability is applied, medical institutes would bear too much burden and that would affect their normal medical activities and impede the development of medical research. Second, there is uncertainty in any kind of medical treatment. The same treatment may have different results on different people because of their different physiological conditions. In light of these particular concerns, many countries use the fault-based imputation principle and apply other rules only in certain specific situations.

Of course, different types of medical malpractice liabilities should be governed by different liability imputation principles: (1) Fault liability imputation principle is applied to medical technique malpractice liabilities—Article 54 explicitly specifies that "[i]f a medical institution or its medical staff members are at fault for damage inflicted on a patient during the course of diagnosis and treatment, the medical institution shall be liable for compensation." It clearly refers to the fault liability imputation principle. (2) Presumed fault liability imputation principle is applied to medical ethics liabilities, in cases where the medical professional or institute has not met its duty to inform. (3) No-fault liability applies to medical product liabilities. Because it is also a product liability issue, no-fault liability imputation principle should be applied to protect patients' rights.

Doctor-patient conflict is one of the major conflicts in today's China. The "Tort Law" devotes 11 provisions to specify medical malpractice liabilities. These provisions cover every detail of medical practice, e.g., protection on patient's privacy, duty to keep medical records confidential, prohibition on excessive medical exam, etc. Notably, Article 60 specifies three scenarios, under which medical institutes do not bear any liability:

First scenario: A patient or his close relatives do not cooperate with the medical institute on treatment that complies with medial regulation or norm. If the medical institute has exercised its duty of care and any damage suffered by the patient was caused by the noncooperation of the patient or his close relatives, the medical institute does not bear any liability.

Second scenario: Medical professionals have exercised reasonable care to save the patient's life under emergency situations; here, the term "reasonable" means that the diagnosis on the patient was accurate and the treatment was expected to be able to control the patient's condition to a reasonable degree; and the medical professionals have met other legal duties as well.

Third scenario: Treatment of the patient's illness or condition is limited by the current level of medical and treatment standard. Whether the medical professionals have met their duty of care is determined based on the current level of medical and treatment standard, i.e., whether the medical professionals have exercised the kind of care deemed reasonable under the current level of medical and treatment standard. If so, they are not at fault and bear no liability.

Environmental Pollution Liability

Environmental pollution refers to negative chemical, physical, or biological changes to the environment caused by human activities, which, in return, affect people's health, production, and life. If the pollution causes any damage, the polluter shall bear corresponding liability for the damage. This is the so-called environmental pollution liability. The provisions (Articles 65–68) governing this liability in "Tort Law" are very simple. But this does not mean that the Chinese government does not care much about environmental protection. On the contrary, China had enacted a large number of regulations or rules on environmental protection early on, including "Environmental Protection Law," "Ocean Environmental Protection Law," "Air Pollution Prevention Law," "Water Pollution Prevention Law," etc., which include quite a few infringement liability provisions.

Article 65 is the general provision for environmental pollution liabilities. For damage caused by environmental pollution, the polluter shall bear tortious liability. This indicates that the no-fault liability imputation principle applies to environmental pollution cases. According to this principle, if a victim suffers damage and there is causation relationship between the polluter's act and the damage, the polluter is held liable whether or not it is at fault. The no-fault liability imputation principle is beneficial for holding polluters accountable and encouraging people to protect the environment and reduce pollution. It should be noted that the pollution discharge limit or standard specified by state or local government is the basis for determining whether the pollution discharge entity should pay pollution discharge fees or should be regulated, not the standard or limit for determining whether the polluter shall bear any tortious liability. Even though an entity's pollution discharge amount is less than the level, it still needs to bear liability for damage caused by pollution it discharged. The elements for environmental pollution liability include the following: the polluter has committed environmental pollution activities, the victim suffered damage, and there is causation relationship between the victim's damage and the polluter's polluting activities.

Article 66 specifies that in the event of a dispute over environmental pollution, the polluter shall bear the burden of proof regarding any exemption from or mitigation of liability and the causal relationship between his conduct and the damage. The shift of burden of proof to the polluters is also for providing more protections over victims of environmental pollutions. According to this provision, if the polluter cannot meet the burden of proof, it shall be held liable for the corresponding liability. Because environmental pollution cases are often complicated and highly professional and the causation link is very complex, it is difficult for the victims to bear the burden of proof. Thus, to shift the burden of proof helps to protect the rights of those victims who are at a disadvantage.

Article 67 specifies that where there are two or more polluters, the proportion of damage for which each is liable shall be determined according to the type of pollutant, the volume of emissions, and other factors. And Article 68 is related to third party liabilities, specifying that where any damage caused by environmental pollution is attributable to a third party, the injured party may seek compensation from either the polluter or the third party and the polluter may, after paying compensation, claim the same from the third party.

It should be noted that no-fault liability is not absolute liability. Defendants can raise certain defenses recognized by law to discharge or reduce its liability. For different types of environmental pollutions, the rules regarding discharging or reducing liabilities are different. Situations recognized by Chinese law include force majeure, the victim's intent, and third party's liability. For example, Article 90 of the "Ocean Environmental Protection Law" specifies: "a party that causes ocean environmental pollution should be responsible for removing the pollution or danger as well as any damage caused". Where ocean environmental pollution is completely caused by a third party, the third party bears the responsibility to remove the danger and compensate for any damage caused.

Liability for Ultrahazardous Activities

Ultrahazardous activity (high-risk operation) liability refers to the kind of liability associated with injury or damage caused by ultrahazardous activities. Articles 69–77 of the "Tort Law" specify the ultrahazardous activity liabilities. The so-called ultrahazardous activities include civil nuclear facilities; high-speed railways; activities involving high-pressure, high-altitude, and underground operations; as well as the possession or use of flammable, explosive, poisonous, radioactive, or other high-risk materials. In sum, this is an open-ended concept, including all forms of activities that cause high risk to the surrounding environment.

To be considered an ultrahazardous activity, a specific act needs to have the following three conditions: First, the operation itself has high risk. In other words, the probability that the risk will turn into actual harm is high and exceeds people's normal sense of prevention. Second, even after reasonable prevention measures and corresponding cares were taken, damage caused by high-risk operations still could not be prevented. In everyday life, any act may cause injury or damage to people within the surrounding area. But ultrahazardous activities carry the kind of risks that cannot be completely controlled and would be difficult to be controlled by people. Third, ultrahazardous activities are legal activities; at least, they are not prohibited by law.

Article 69 is the general specification of ultrahazardous activities. It explicitly states the application of no-fault liability imputation principle—anyone who causes damage to another person by engaging in ultrahazardous activities shall bear tortious liability. In fact, applying no-fault liability imputation principle to ultrahazardous activities is commonly accepted in majority of the countries. And China's "Railway Law," "Civil Aviation Law," and "Electric Power Law" all apply this principle. Thus, Article 69 is consistent not only with existing laws of China but also with other countries' choices. It is helpful on quickly resolving disputes and providing remedies to victims.

Article 70 specifies the civil nuclear facility tortious liability. The law clearly specifies that where any damage is caused by a civil nuclear facility, the operator of the said civil nuclear facility (e.g., a legal person that operates a nuclear power plant, civil nuclear research reaction heap, civil engineering experimental reaction heap, or an entity that manufactures, transports, or stores nuclear fuel) shall bear tortious liability. It should be noted that not all force majeure defenses can be used to avoid liability. Only when the defendant can prove that the damage was caused by war or that the victim deliberately incurred the damage, liability can be discharged.

According to Article 71, where any damage is caused by a civil aircraft, the operator of the said civil aircraft shall bear tortious liability unless he can prove that the victim deliberately incurred the damage. Although this statute lists only one defense, the "Civil Aviation Law" specifies several other defenses that apply to civil aircraft tortious liability, e.g., a passenger's death or injury was completely caused by his own health condition and the carrier does not bear liability, etc.

Article 72 specifies tortious liabilities related to high-risk materials. High-risk materials are materials that are highly dangerous in nature or can cause high dangerous conditions, including flammable materials, explosives, poisonous materials, radioactive materials, or highly erosive materials. The possessor or user shall bear the liability unless he can prove that the victim deliberately incurred the damage or that the damage was caused by a force majeure event. The burden of proof is on the possessor or user. Also, if the victim is at major fault in causing the damage, the liability of the person in possession or use of the materials may be reduced.

Article 73 specifies that where any damage is caused by high-altitude operations, high-pressure operations, underground mining activities, or the use of high-speed rail, the operator shall bear tortious liability. Like Article 72, if the defendant can prove that the victim deliberately incurred the damage or that the damage was caused by a force majeure event, it will not bear liability. But unlike Article 72, which requires that the injured party must be at major fault, liability of the operator may be reduced. Article 73 only requires that the injured party be at fault for the same liability reduction treatment.

Article 74 specifies liabilities associated with discarding or abandoning high-risk materials. Because high-risk materials carry high level of danger, the owner or manager of such materials should strictly follow the rules in using, storing, or processing them in production. But in reality, some entities that store or use high-risk materials randomly dispose these materials or do not follow the safety rules in handling them, therefore threat the lives and properties of the surrounding populations. As such, the law explicitly specifies: where any damage is caused by losing or abandoning high-risk materials, the owner shall bear tortious liability; if the high-risk materials are managed by a custodian authorized by the owner, the custodian shall bear the tortious liability; if the owner is at fault, he shall be jointly and severally liable.

Article 75 specifies the liabilities related to illegally possessing high-risk materials. It is clear—where any damage is caused by the unlawful possession of high-risk materials, the party in unlawful possession shall bear tortious liability. In cases where these materials were stolen or robbed by criminals, the criminals shall bear the liability. But the owner shall exercise due care to provide safety measures on guarding against such risks. If the owner or custodian cannot prove that they exercised due care to prevent others from unlawfully possessing the same, they shall be jointly and severally liable.

Article 76 specifies the liabilities related to high-risk operation areas—where any damage is caused by unauthorized access to high-risk operation areas or storage areas for high-risk materials, if the custodian has taken security measures and fulfilled his obligation to provide warnings, his liability may be mitigated or exempted. Article 77 relates to the limit of remedy, specifying that if any law provides for a limited amount of compensation regarding high-risk operation liability, such provisions shall apply.

Liability for Damage Caused by Domestic Animals

Articles 78 through 84 of the "Tort Law" specify the liabilities for damages caused by domestic animals. Please note that these provisions are not necessarily applicable to all cases where people were hurt by animals. They are only applicable to cases where damage was caused by domestically raised animals. Generally speaking, domestic animals have the following features: they are owned or possessed by certain people; the owner or manager has certain level of control over these animals; the nature of these animals is that they are likely to cause harm or damage to people; these animals may be livestock, poultries, pets, tamed wild animals, reptiles, etc. The reason that the law specifies such a special tortious liability is that animals have unpredictable behaviors, which carry the potential risk of causing harm or damage to people. Thus, the owners or managers shall take full liabilities for all damages caused by their raised animals.

The characteristics of this special tortious liability are as follows: First, such liability is created for damage caused by domestic animals, not human. Second, it is a liability for an "object," i.e., because an object controlled by its owner or manager caused damage, the law requires the owner or manager to bear the vicarious liability for the damage-causing object. Third, no-fault liability imputation principle applies to such cases, and the purpose for that is to encourage domestic animal owners and managers to exercise higher level of care to prevent harm or damage that could be caused by such animals and to protect people's health and safety. According to this imputation principle, elements for liability for damage caused by domestic animals include damage or injury to a victim, the damage or injury that was caused by a domestic animal, and causation relationship between the damage or injury and the harmful act from the animal.

According to the law, an owner or manager does not need to bear liability for all damages caused by a domestic animal he owns or manages. For damage caused for the victim's own intent or gross negligence, the owner or manager does not bear liability or such liability should be reduced. Also, if a third party was responsible for such damage (e.g., the third party deliberately provoked, fed, or induced the animals), the victim has the right to sue and seek remedy from either the third party or the owner or manager. The law endows the victim such a right of choice for at least two reasons. First, it increases the likelihood that the victim would receive any remedy; second, it will push the owners or managers to exercise more care to control their domestic animals to reduce the chances that these animals would hurt anyone. Such design provides more protection to injured parties. Of course, after the owner or manager has made compensation to the injured party, he can seek recovery from the third party.

In our everyday life, the most common occasion where a domestic animal causes harm or damage to people is that no safety measure has been taken. For example, a dog owner walks his dog into an elevator. Because the dog is not wearing any mask, it attacks and bites another person in the elevator. In this case, the owner is liable for all damages caused by the dog. Under such situation, even the injured party is at fault for the damage or injury, the animal owner or manager's liability cannot be mitigated or discharged completely.

It should also be noted that certain animals have an abnormally high propensity to cause harm or damage and the law prohibits raising these animals domestically. For example, many cities outlaw raising large or vicious dogs within the city limit. Breaking the law by raising prohibited dangerous animals is itself a condemnable and punishable act. Thus, as long as a person has broken the law and raised large or vicious dogs or any other dangerous animals, the person shall be held liable for all damages caused by these animals and no defense is applicable.

According to the law, where any damage is caused by a zoo animal, the zoo shall bear tortious liability unless it can prove that due diligence has been exercised in managing the said animal, and in that case the zoo shall not be liable. As can be seen, what is applied here is the presumed fault liability imputation principle. Events of zoo animals attacking or harming people frequently occur. In some cases, it was because of the mismanagement or oversights by the zoos; in other cases, it was the victims' fault or negligence, e.g., stepping over fences or protection railings to feed the animals, provoking the animals, trying to take photos with the animals, or committing other harassing activities. In these situations, if the zoo can prove that it has exercised reasonable care and was not at fault, then it will not be held liable. Specifically, if the zoo can prove that the enclosure or other equipment was in good condition, there was warning sign, and the management tried to stop those dangerous or provoking activities, it is deemed that it has exercised due care.

The "Tort Law" has another special rule which relates to cases where damage is caused by an animal that is abandoned or at large after being abandoned or escaping. Whether the animal was abandoned by the owner or manager or escaped because the owner or manager has not exercised due care to prevent the escape, the owner or manager's act increased the risk the animal posed to the society. And the damage was caused because the animal was not controlled by the owner or manager and was free to wander at large. Thus, to uphold social justice and protect victims' rights, an owner or manager who has abandoned an animal or has not exercised reasonable care to prevent the animal to escape shall bear the liability for damage caused by the animal.

Liability for Damage Caused by Objects

Where a person is responsible for managing or controlling an object but fails to exercise due care, the person shall bear liability for damage caused by the object. As specified in the "Tort Law," liabilities for damages caused by objects include liability for damage caused by a building, structure, or other facility and objects that are stored therein or attached thereto; liability for damage caused by a collapsing building, structure, or other facility; liability for damage caused by an object thrown or falling from a building; liability for damage caused by the collapsing of piled materials; liability for damage caused by obstacles piled, dumped, or scattered on a public road; liability for damage caused by a falling tree; and liability for damage caused by a road digging or underground repair operation without clear signs and safety measures.

Article 85 specifies liability for any damage caused by a building, structure, or other facility and objects that are stored therein or attached thereto. Simply put, it does not matter whether it is a building, structure, an object stored therein or an object attached thereto; as long as something falls from it and causes damage, the owner or manager shall bear liability if he cannot prove his innocence. As can be seen, what is applied here is the presumed fault liability imputation principle. If your building, structure, or other facility and objects stored therein or attached thereto causes damage, you are presumed at fault and shall bear liability. Of course, after the owner, manager, or user has made compensation, he can pursue other liable party or parties (if any) for damage.

Article 86 specifies liability for any damage caused by the collapsing of a building, structure, or other facility. Here, the owner and the construction company shall bear joint and several liability. According to the law, the order in which relevant parties should be held liable for damage caused by the collapsing of a building, structure, or other facility is the owner and construction company shall bear joint and several liability first. That is, after such damage occurred, the injured party has the right to pursue either the owner or the construction company in court for the whole damage. Second, if the collapsing is not caused by the fault of the owner or the construction company but caused by a third party, after the owner or the construction company made the compensation, it can pursue the third party for the whole damage.

Article 87 specifies liability for any damage caused by an object thrown or falling from a building. This is a very controversial provision. It specifies that where any damage is caused by an object thrown or falling from a building, if it is difficult to identify the infringing party, the user of the building who is the potential infringing party shall pay compensation unless he can prove that he was not the infringing party. We should understand that the determination of this type of liability is based on fairness not fault. The liability is not an infringement liability, but majorly for compensation purposes. The purpose of this provision is to prevent such damage and deter people throwing objects from a building. It is generally recognized that the legal significance of creating such a special tortious liability is to compensate the injured party's damage, achieve social justice and fairness, reasonably distribute damage, improve social harmony, and maintain social order and stability.

Article 88 specifies liability for any damage caused by the collapsing of piled materials, e.g., rolling down, sliding down, or collapsing of piled materials. Here, piled materials refer to those materials that are piled on the ground or other places, not fixed on other objects, like the piled logs in a logging mill. Collapsing include the falling, sliding down, or rolling down of the whole or part of a pile. People who has piled the materials there can be either an owner or a manager. Defenses against this liability include force majeure, third party's fault and the victim's fault, etc.

Article 89 specifies liability for any damage caused by obstacles piled, dumped, or scattered on a public road. The characteristics of this liability are the following: (1) An obstacle was piled, dumped, or scattered on a public road and the obstacle hinders traffic. Here, a public road refers to a road for public passage and use, including a road for motor vehicles as well as sidewalks. And the dumping, piling, or scattering of an obstacle interferes with the normal and reasonable use by the public. (2) The act to dump, pile, or scatter an obstacle on a public road has caused damage, which includes both bodily injury and property damage. (3) The liable party is the relevant entity or individual, including manager of the public road, the entity or individual who set the obstacle. (4) Remedies include monetary compensation, stopping the infringement act, and removal of obstacles.

Article 90 specifies liability for any damage caused by a falling or damaged tree. Here, the damage caused by a falling or damaged tree includes not only damage or injury caused to people by a falling branch or twig but also damage caused by the falling of a fruit (e.g., injury caused by a falling coconut) or a whole tree (e.g., damage on a car by a falling trunk). Generally speaking, elements for this liability include the following: (1) There must be wrong done by a falling tree or damaged tree. Here, it can be any tree, not necessarily a tree on a roadside. And the damage can be caused by the tilting of the tree, not necessarily a complete fall, or by the breakage of the whole tree or only part of it (e.g., a branch). (2) There must be injury or damage. If the falling or damaged tree causes injury or damage to people, this element is established. Such injury can be minor injury, serious injury, or even death; and the damage includes all property damages. (3) There must be causation relationship between the falling or damaged tree and the damage.

Article 91 has two provisions, which address two different situations. The first provision specifies that if any damage is caused by a road digging or underground repair operation without clear signs and safety measures, the construction operator shall bear tortious liability. First, a permit is needed to conduct such an operation in public space or on a road, and there must be clear warning signs and necessary safety measures need to be taken. Specifically, the warning signs must be clear enough to raise people's attention to the construction or operation area; the constructor should make sure that the warning signs are stable and should maintain the signs so that they are visible during the whole construction or operation period; and if the warning signs are not enough to ensure safety, the constructor shall take extra necessary safety measures. The liable parties in such cases are usually the constructors, which are usually contractors to work on other parties' projects.

The second provision specifies that if any damage is caused by a manhole or other underground facilities, the manager shall bear tortious liability unless he can prove that he has exercised due care. Manhole is a well-like structure used in a sewage or underground pipeline system for easy access or inspection purposes. Other underground facilities include cellar, well, sewer, and underground tunnels. Managers for these underground facilities refer to those entities or individuals who are in charge of maintaining and managing these facilities. Urban underground facilities are very complicated—there are water pipelines, oil pipelines, gas pipelines, electricity wirings, etc. Different facilities may be managed and maintained by different entities. When damage occurs, the specific manager for the underground facility should be identified and should bear liability if found liable.

Chapter 10
Form of Tortious Liability

Overview

In a tort-based legal relationship, the distribution of tort liability among different perpetrators according to the type of the tortious act is called the form of tortious liability. In other words, the form of tortious liability is the basic form of distributing liabilities among the perpetrators in a tort-based legal relationship according to the corresponding liability distribution rule. That is, after determining which side should bear the liability, how should the liability be further distributed among multiple perpetrators?

The form of tortious liability has the following legal features:

First, it concerns the consequence of a tortious act—after a tortious act has occurred and all elements for tortious liability have met, the perpetrator(s) shall be held liable. It is different from the type of a tortious act in that the type of a tortious act concerns the study of the tortious act, whereas the form of tortious liability concerns the study of the consequence of the tortious act, which is the issue of who should be liable for the legal consequence of the tortious act. Also, it is different from the formation of tortious liability, which concerns the study of the rules and conditions for establishing such liability.

Second, the form of tortious liability expresses the different forms in which a perpetrator in a tortious legal relationship bears the liability. Different from the method of assuming liability, the form of tortious liability does not refer to the specific method of assuming liability, but the issue of who should bear the liability, i.e., the actor himself, his employer, etc.

Third, the form of tortious liability is not randomly chosen, but must be confirmed by law. At the same time, it is the basic form of bearing tortious liability, but not the specific method of assuming the liability. It only specifies whether a perpetrator shall bear liability by himself or through someone else and whether the liability is joint and several or distributed by share. As to what type of liability and to what degree a perpetrator should be responsible for, the form of tortious liability does not care. Those are issues concerned by the method of assuming liability and the specific content of tortious liability.

X. Li and J. Jin, *Concise Chinese Tort Laws*, China-EU Law Series 1,
DOI 10.1007/978-3-642-41024-6_10, © Springer-Verlag Berlin Heidelberg 2014

The "Tort Law" specifies ten different forms of tortious liability, including the following:

1. Self-liability, i.e., a person is ultimately liable for any damage caused by his own tortious act. This is the most central, the most important, and the most mainstream liability form, which is specified by Paragraph 1, Article 6 of the "Tort Law."
2. Vicarious liability, i.e., damage caused by a person's tortious act is not borne by the person himself, but by another person or entity. Simply put, the party committing the tortious act and the party assuming the liability are two different entities. The "Tort Law" specifies several vicarious liabilities, such as the guardian's liability specified in Article 32, employer liability specified in Article 34, and medical malpractice liability specified in Article 54.
3. Joint and several liability, i.e., multiple perpetrators shall be jointly liable for any damage caused to a victim, the victim can sue anyone of the perpetrators for full remedy and that perpetrator can pursue others for reasonable repayment. Articles 13–14 of the "Tort Law" specify the general rule for joint and several liability. Joint and several liability applies not only in joint tort cases but also in certain special tort cases, e.g., network service provider's joint and several liability specified in Article 36, illegally sell or buy a motor vehicle specified in Article 51, illegal possession of highly risk materials, etc.
4. Liability by share, i.e., each one of two or more perpetrators should bear corresponding liability to the extent he is responsible for. Three scenarios relating to liability by share are specified in the "Tort Law," and they are the tort by multiple tortfeasors without conscious cooperation specified in Article 12, multiple polluters' liability specified in Article 67, and liability for damage caused by an object thrown or falling from a building and it is difficult to determine who the real perpetrator is.
5. Quasi joint and several liability, i.e., where multiple perpetrators have caused the same damage to a victim by different tortious acts, each perpetrator is liable for the full damage; the victim may in its own convenience choose a perpetrator to sue for damage; and once that perpetrator has compensated for the victim's damage, the victim has no further claim against other perpetrators. Quasi joint and several liability also has wide applications in the "Tort Law," for example, product liability specified in Article 43, medical product liability specified in Article 59, environmental pollution caused by a third party specified in Article 68, etc.
6. Supplemental liability, i.e., two or more perpetrators are held liable to a victim in a sequence of order, and only when a perpetrator in the front of the sequence is not able to cover the full damage, a follow-up perpetrator in the sequence is required to cover the rest of the damage. Scenarios where supplemental liability applies in the "Tort Law" include the following: Article 37—damage caused by a third party's act and a manager or organizer has not exercised due care; Article 40—where a person who lacks or has limited civil capacity, while studying or living in a kindergarten, school, or any other educational

institution, suffers a bodily injury caused by a person not associated with the kindergarten, school, or educational institution, the infringing party shall bear tortious liability; and where the kindergarten, school, or educational institution fails to fulfill its management duties, it shall bear supplementary liability.

7. Corresponding liability, i.e., liability is commensurate with a perpetrator's degree of fault and contribution to damage. Corresponding liability appears frequently in the "Tort Law." It mostly occurs in cases where joint and several liability or contributory negligence applies, such as the situations specified in Article 9, where a guardian of a person who lacks or has limited capacity shall bear corresponding liability for any damage caused by the person's tortious act as a result of someone else's incitement or assistance in the event the guardian fails to fulfill his duty as a guardian; and Article 35—where a labor relationship has formed between individuals and the party providing labor causes an injury or damage to another person as a result of his labor services, the party to whom labor is provided shall bear tortious liability; and where the party providing labor causes injury or damage to himself as a result of his labor services, liability shall be borne by both parties in light of their respective degree of fault.
8. Equitable liability, i.e., a party who is not at fault is required to bear liability according to equitable principle. Articles of the "Tort Law" where equitable liability are applied include Article 32, a guardian's liability may be mitigated if he has exercised his duty as a guardian; Article 33, a person with full civil capacity shall bear tortious liability for damage done to another person for which he is at fault due to his conduct during a temporary loss of consciousness or control; where there is no fault, the said person shall, in light of his financial status, pay reasonable compensation to the victim; and Article 76, liability may be mitigated if a manager of highly risk materials has exercised reasonable care and taken adequate warning and safety measures.
9. Appropriate liability, i.e., liability that is proportional to the damage caused to a victim. The "Tort Law" has only two provisions applying appropriate liability, and they are Article 30 (excessive force used in self-defense) and Article 31 (unreasonable or excessive measures for necessity).
10. Liability to advance compensation, i.e., a non-liable party advances compensation first and then pursues the liable party for payment. The "Tort Law" specifies two forms of liability to advance compensation, which are Article 52 (where a motor vehicle is stolen and damage is caused by said vehicle in a traffic accident, the insurance company shall advance rescue cost to the victim) and Article 53 (where a motor vehicle driver flees after a traffic accident, the costs paid for rescuing or burying the injured party and other relevant costs shall be paid out of the Social Assistance Fund for Road Traffic Accidents on behalf of the liable party).

It is not difficult to see that although the "Tort Law" provides many forms of liability, these forms can be summarized into three major and basic forms: self-liability vs. vicarious liability, one-side liability vs. both-side liability, and individual liability vs. joint liability. Below, let us discuss these three forms.

Self-Liability Versus Substitution Liability

Self-liability and vicarious liability are the most common forms of liability. Their main difference is whether liability is borne by an actor himself or by a party having a certain relationship with the actor (or by a manager or custodian of a damage-causing object). If an actor is liable for his own act, the liability is self-liability or direct liability; if another party (i.e., a responsible party) is liable for the actor's act, the liability is vicarious liability or indirect liability. Self-liability is the normal form and is applied to general torts, whereas vicarious liability is an exception and is applied to special torts.

The concept of self-liability is easy to understand and fits the moral norm of our society—a person shall be responsible for his own deed. The characteristics of self-liability are the following: (1) it is an act from the perpetrator itself, (2) the act infringes on another person's legitimate right and interest, and (3) the perpetrator is liable for any damage caused by the act—the liable party and the perpetrator are the same entity.

Self-liability is the most common liability form and is applied to majority of the tort cases. In a general tort case, a perpetrator is the liable party. If not specifically specified by law, self-liability should be generally applied.

Vicarious liability means that a party is held liable for any damage caused by an actor because of its special relationship with the actor. In other words, after an actor has committed a tortious act, the actor is not held liable for any damage caused, but a party that is in a certain special relationship with the actor is. Here, there is a separation between the actor and the liable party. Vicarious liability is applied only where the law specifically specifies so. In practice, vicarious liability has been widely applied in special tort cases, such as guardian liability, liability due to temporary loss of consciousness or control, employer liability, etc.

Thus, it can be seen that vicarious liability is a rule that essentially asks someone else to assume liability for the perpetrator. Once this rule is applied in a case, the result is that the liable party is held liable not for its own tortious act but for the tortious act of someone else with whom it has a certain special relationship. In other words, the liable defendant in vicarious liability is a different person from the one who actually committed the tortious act.

At first glance, it seems unfair to hold someone liable for damage caused by tortious act not committed by him. But looking more closely, we can find that the vicarious liability rule has its social significance. Taking the employer liability as an example, the benefits of the vicarious liability rule are clear: first, an employer usually has more financial resources than an employee, and this ensures that a victim has better chance to fully compensated for damage; second, an employee works for the interest of an employer, and therefore it is not unfair to hold the employer liable for the employee's act during the course of his work for the employer; third, an employer is more capable of shifting the cost to the whole society, such as through raising price or purchasing an insurance policy; and last, an employee's error may be attributed to an employer's wrongful choice of hiring or selecting the employee; therefore, the employer is not completely innocent. In sum, vicarious liability achieves a more substantive fairness and can help us to shape a better society.

Vicarious liability in principle concerns substituting liability for a human being, i.e., the separation of an actor and a liable party. However, scholars disagree whether it also covers substituting liability for an object, i.e., a party is liable for any damage caused by an object it possessed or managed. Many scholars consider bearing liability resulted from an object as self-liability because there is no separation between an actor and a natural person. But other scholars consider it vicarious liability because all liabilities caused by special tortious acts can be covered by vicarious liability. According to the latter theory, the scope of liable party in vicarious liability covers two categories: the first is a party that is liable for an actor who has caused damage; the second is an owner, possessor, or manager of an object that has caused damage. Similarly, according to the latter theory, legal characteristics of vicarious liability include the following:

1. The separation of the liable party and the actor or object that has caused damage. In a general tort case, a liable party is the perpetrator who has caused damage. When there is only one perpetrator, the liability is borne by him alone. When there are multiple perpetrators, they shall jointly bear the liability. But vicarious liability is different. The liable party is a different entity from the perpetrator and has no direct relation with the tortious act or the damage-causing object. It has no intent to cause damage to others. The separation of the liable party from the perpetrator or damage-causing object is the objective basis for transferring liability to the liable party.
2. There must be a certain special relationship between the liable party and the perpetrator or the damage-causing object so that the perpetrator's act or the object is under custody or control of the liable party. This special relationship, between a liable party and a perpetrator, may be membership, employment relationship, guardianship, agency relationship, etc. And between a liable party and a damage-causing object, this special relationship may be ownership, possession, custodial relationship, etc. Without this special relationship, there is no basis for vicarious liability.
3. The liable party bears responsibility to make compensation for the obligated entity. In a general tort case, a victim's claim is targeted towards a perpetrator, who is the obligated entity. In vicarious liability, whether damage is caused by a perpetrator or a damage-causing object, a victim's claim is targeted towards a party that is in a special relationship with the perpetrator or the object. When an animal, an object, or a building has caused damage, its owner, possessor, or manager is the obligated entity. When a perpetrator has caused damage, his employer, guardian, or agent is the obligated entity. A victim's claim is not directed to the damage-causing object or perpetrator, but to the liable party.

The legal consequence of applying vicarious liability is that a liable party bears liability for any damage caused by a perpetrator and the perpetrator is no longer held liable for the damage. Generally, a liable party is liable alone and does not have the ability to pursue a perpetrator for repayment. Only when the perpetrator has committed gross negligence or intentional tort, the liable party may pursue the perpetrator for certain amount of repayment.

One-Side Liability Versus Both-Side Liability

According to whether liability is borne by one side or both sides of the parties of a lawsuit, a tortious liability may be categorized as one-side liability and both-side liability. One-side liability is the more frequent form, and usually it is a defendant who bears the liability. But in a few cases where damage is caused by a victim's own fault, the victim is the only party bearing the liability. Both-side liability is a form under which both a perpetrator and a victim bear the liability because, in most cases, the perpetrator has raised contributory negligence as a defense. One-side liability and both-side liability can be either self-liability or vicarious liability.

As its name indicates, one-side liability is a form in which only one side of the parties of a lawsuit is bearing liability. It can be further categorized as perpetrator one-side liability or victim one-side liability. As to perpetrator one-side liability, only the perpetrator is bearing liability and the victim does not. It mainly applies in a case where any damage is caused completely by a perpetrator and the victim is not at fault. Perpetrator one-side liability may be applied in fault liability, presumed fault liability, or no-fault liability imputation principle. Thus, the legal consequence of applying perpetrator one-side liability is that a perpetrator bears the full liability for damage caused to a victim.

Victim one-side liability is a liability form according to which a victim of tort is bearing the full liability. In certain situations, although damage is caused by a perpetrator's act, he is not at fault. Because it is entirely the victim's fault in causing the damage, the victim shall bear full liability. The precondition of applying victim one-side liability is that the victim is at fault, i.e., any damage is caused by the victim's own negligence of intentional act. The standard for determining whether a victim is at fault is not difficult to understand. Generally, it can be achieved by determining whether the victim has exercised reasonable care to protect his life safety and property. If the victim has not exercised reasonable care, and as a result puts himself in a dangerous situation and also puts the perpetrator in a situation where the perpetrator is facing legal liability for doing nothing wrong, it can be determined that the victim is at fault. Thus, the legal consequence of applying victim one-side liability is that the victim bears all liability and the perpetrator bears none.

Both-side liability is also called mixed liability, according to which both sides of the parties of a lawsuit bear liability. In such a case, both a perpetrator and a victim are liable and they share the liability. In other words, the whole liability is borne by the perpetrator and the victim, respectively. And the sum of their shares is the total damage caused thereof. Both-side liability can be either contributory liability or equitable liability.

Contributory liability is a liability form where both a perpetrator and a victim are at fault in causing damage and both should share the liability. That is, the damage is caused because of not only a perpetrator's fault but also a victim's fault. Their faults contributed to the damage jointly. The legal consequence of applying contributory liability is that the rule of contributory negligence is applied—the share of liability of each party is determined by comparing both sides' faults and contributions to the damage caused. If certain conditions are met, the court can mitigate a perpetrator's liability directly even if the perpetrator has not raised any defense.

Equitable liability is also called balanced liability. It refers to a situation where neither a perpetrator nor a victim is at fault and the damage is shared by both parties. In other words, after damage has occurred, and by applying equitable principles, liability to the damage is reasonably distributed between both parties according to each party's actual situation. Here, the actual situation refers to the degree of damage suffered by a victim as well as each party's financial capability. Also, social and media effects are considered sometimes to make sure the distribution of liability between the parties is fair and reasonable. It should be noted that the application of equitable liability should be limited to cases where neither parties are at fault and that neither presumed fault liability nor no-fault liability is applicable.

It is worth to note that there is a special both-side liability specified in China's Tort Law regarding motor vehicle traffic accidents. As specified in Article 76 of the "Road Traffic Safety Law," even if a motor vehicle driver is 100 % innocent and the whole damage is caused by a non-motor vehicle driver or pedestrian, the motor vehicle driver should still bear certain amount of liability. Generally speaking, since the motor vehicle driver has done nothing wrong or illegal, he should be released of any liability. But because a motor vehicle is at a more powerful position compared with a pedestrian or a non-motor vehicle and has better maneuverability in avoiding a traffic accident, it should still bear certain amount of liability from a moral perspective. This is essentially requiring a plaintiff to bear certain amount of liability when it is the victim not the plaintiff who is at fault. This is not only different from contributory negligence but also different from equitable liability. Its reasonableness is questionable.

Joint Liability Versus Individual Liability

Depending on whether there is just one perpetrator or multiple perpetrators, we can categorize the forms of liability into individual liability and joint liability. After it is determined that the defendant side is bearing liability, such liability can be categorized as one of the two forms depending on the number of perpetrators and the nature of the tortious act. Thus, the standard is quite straightforward—if only one perpetrator is involved, the liability is individual liability; and if multiple perpetrators are involved, the liability is then joint liability.

Specially, individual liability is a single person's liability. In other words, it is a liability form in which a single tortfeasor is held responsible for any damage it has caused. Here, the tortfeasor may be a natural person or a legal person, and it does not matter whether there is just one victim or multiple victims. The most typical individual liability is being liable for someone's own tortious act, which is also individual liability for general tortious act. In a special tort case where liability is for damage caused by someone else's tortious act or an object, as long as there is just one perpetrator, the liability is individual liability.

In contrast, joint liability occurs where multiple perpetrators are involved and they should jointly bear liability for damage caused. The purpose for us to study joint liability is to understand how to distribute liability among the multiple tortfeasors. Joint liability may be further categorized as joint and several liability, liability by share, or supplemental liability. If the act of a number of perpetrators constitutes joint tortious act or joint dangerous act, they should bear joint and several liability. If there is no fault connection among the acts of multiple perpetrators, and any damage caused by these acts is a result of pure coincidence, these perpetrators should bear liability by share. Also, under certain special specifications of law, multiple perpetrators' acts may lead to quasi joint and several liability or supplemental liability. We will discuss them below:

1. Liability by share is a liability form according to which two or more perpetrators each bear a certain share of tortious liability to a victim or creditor. The general rule of liability by share specified in Article 12 of the "Tort Law" is where two or more persons commit torts respectively, resulting in the same damage, if the seriousness of liability of each tortfeasor can be determined, the tortfeasors shall assume corresponding liabilities respectively; or if the seriousness of liability of each tortfeasor is difficult to be determined, the tortfeasors shall assume the compensatory liability evenly. Because each perpetrator is only liable for any damage caused by his own tortious act, each perpetrator's liability is separate and partial. Liability by share reflects the principle of being liable for one's own tortious act. After performing its obligation, a perpetrator cannot pursue others for repayment. In this sense, liability by share embodies fairness.

   The tortious act on which liability by share is founded is indirectly combined tortious acts from multiple perpetrators. That is, these perpetrators who did not have conscious cooperation or joint fault caused a same damage result because their acts are objectively connected. In a case where multiple perpetrators' tortious acts were indirectly combined, each perpetrator's tortious act affected the victim in different time and caused different degree of damage. Because of the aggregation or accumulation of the damages caused by each perpetrator, the final damage is more serious than the damage contributed by each perpetrator. Because there was no conscious cooperation among these perpetrators, and they could not have foreseen the possibility that their acts may be combined to cause the same damage, there was no joint intent or negligence. Thus, there is no subjective joint fault to be served as the basis for imposing joint and several liability here. As such, the law requires liability by share, according to which each perpetrator is liable for the damage caused by itself.

The legal characteristics of liability by share include the following: first, the share of liability borne by each perpetrator is part of the whole damage suffered by the victim; second, each perpetrator is liable to the victim without any sequence of order; third, each perpetrator is only liable for his own share and is not liable for other perpetrators' shares; fourth, even a perpetrator bears more than the share he should be liable, the perpetrator cannot pursue repayment from other perpetrators. In sum, the consequence of applying liability by share is that each perpetrator is individually and separately liable for his own share of liability to the victim. One perpetrator's delay or incapability of performance does not affect another perpetrator's obligation, and one perpetrator's performance does not release other perpetrators from their shares of the liability. Thus, if a victim wants to get full compensation for his damage, all perpetrators must be able to perform their obligation and fulfill their liability. As such, the protection to a victim offered by liability by share is relatively weak.

2. Joint and several liability is a form according to which a victim has the right to sue any one or more parties from joint tortfeasors or joint actors of a dangerous act for full damage, and any joint tortfeasor or joint actors of a dangerous act has the obligation to bear liability for the full damage; if one or more joint tortfeasors or joint actors of a dangerous act have made full compensation, other tortfeasors or actors are released from liability to the victim. Joint and several liability is widely applied in the Tort Law. Besides in Articles 8 through 11 of the "Tort Law," other special regulations and laws specify joint and several liability for certain situations.

The legal characteristics of joint and several liability include the following: First, each perpetrator is liable to the victim for a certain share of liability. Each perpetrator's share of liability is determined according to the perpetrator's fault and contribution to the victim's damage, and if it is difficult to determine the share, the perpetrators bear the liability equally. Second, there is no first and second in terms of order for the perpetrators to bear liability for the damage caused. Third, each perpetrator is liable for not only his own share but also other perpetrators' shares. After a perpetrator has compensated for his share, he is not released from liability yet. If other perpetrators have no capability to make compensation, the former perpetrator is required to fulfill their obligations owed to the victim. Thus, each perpetrator's liability is not limited to his own share. And the law provides the victim the right of choice to request for relief from all or part of the joint tortfeasors. Fourth, if a perpetrator has borne more than his share of liability, he can pursue other perpetrators for repayment.

The legal consequence of applying joint and several liability is that all perpetrators are jointly liable for the full damage suffered by a victim. The legal relationship of joint and several liability includes an internal aspect and external aspect. With respect to the external aspect of the legal relationship, all perpetrators are treated as a unified entity for bearing liability to the victim—it does not matter whether the victim sues one, some, or all perpetrators from the whole group, each sued perpetrator bears full liability to the victim. With respect to the internal aspect of the legal relationship, each perpetrator must bear liability to his share, and if a perpetrator has borne more than his share, he can pursue other perpetrators for repayment. Because each perpetrator is responsible for what is beyond his own share of liability, joint and several liability provides an extra safety layer for a victim's right and interest.

3. Quasi joint and several liability is a liability form according to which two or more perpetrators are each liable to the full damage suffered by a victim for different reasons, and once a perpetrator has fulfilled the liability, all others are released from the liability. Quasi joint and several liability is only applicable to certain special situations where a perpetrator's tortious act is considered not only his own act but also an act of another party who has a certain special relationship with the victim, and whether or not that party is at fault in causing the damage is not considered. In other words, when two or more perpetrators have legal obligations to a civil subject, one perpetrator's tortious act is considered all perpetrators' act, and the civil subject has the right to pursue damage from each perpetrator.

   The most typical quasi joint and several liability appears in the product liability area. For example, according Article 43 of the "Tort Law," where any damage is caused by a product defect, a victim may seek compensation from either the product manufacturer or the seller. Thus, it does not matter whether the defect was created by the manufacturer or the seller, and it does not matter whether the victim sued the manufacturer or the seller. As long as the damage was caused by the product defect, the defendant sued by the victim should bear full liability. Of course, if the product defect was created by the manufacturer, the seller may pursue repayment from the manufacturer once it has borne the liability.

   The legal characteristics of quasi joint and several liability include the following: first, liability is not distributed among the perpetrators by share, and each perpetrator bears full liability to a victim; second, there is no sequence of order among the perpetrators in terms of bearing the liability; third, there is no joint relationship among the perpetrators, and after the victim has sought compensation from one perpetrator, all other perpetrators are released from the liability to the victim; and fourth, once a perpetrator has borne the liability, whether or not he can pursue others for repayment should be determined by the actual cause of the damage.

   The reason why quasi joint and several liability forcefully imposes liability to a party having special relationship with a victim when the tortious act was actually committed by another party is to provide better protection over the victim's right and interest. Under such a situation, a victim has multiple options to seek relief, but can only choose one of them. Once the victim has sought relief through one of the options, his right to seek relief through other options is gone. Thus, in practice, a victim may choose a party that is more legally close to him or a party that is more financially capable in order to enforce his right to remedy.

4. Supplemental liability is that when any damage is caused by multiple factors, and as a result a victim can sue multiple parties for remedy, liability to the damage should be borne by the direct liable party first, and only when that party cannot fully compensate the damage, a supplementary liable party is required to

compensate the uncovered damage. In that case, the supplementary liable party has the right to pursue the direct liable party for repayment. The situations where supplemental liability is applied are very special. For example, in a case where two or more perpetrators have committed tortious act against a victim, one perpetrator committed active act and the others did not meet their duty to protect the victim, such as the scenario specified in Article 37 of the "Tort Law," where a manager or organizer has failed to fulfill its safety obligation, supplemental liability applies.

Legal characteristics of supplemental liability include the following: first, there are direct liable party and supplementary liable party (or parties)—the former party bears full liability to a victim and the latter party (or parties) bears only supplemental liability; second, the sequence of order for each perpetrator to bear the liability is different—direct liable party first and supplementary liable party second; and third, supplementary liable party has its own share of liability and shall be liable to both its own share and the damage uncovered by the direct liable party.

Thus, when supplemental liability is applied, the sequence of order is important: First, a victim should directly seek compensation from a direct liable party. If the direct liable party makes full compensation, a supplementary liable party is released of any liability to the victim, and the victim cannot seek compensation from the supplementary liable party any more. Neither can the direct liable party seek repayment from the supplementary liable party. Second, when a victim seeks compensation from a direct liable party and the direct liable party cannot cover the whole damage, the victim can seek compensation from a supplementary liable party.

It should be noted that the supplemental liability specified in the "Tort Law" is not full supplemental liability but limited supplemental liability. In other words, a supplementary liable party is held liable only for the damage that can be attributed to his fault, not the full amount of damage uncovered by the direct liable party.

Chapter 11
Methods for Assuming Liability

Overview

A method for assuming tortious liability is a concrete form in which a perpetrator is required to bear civil liability for any damage he has caused. The study of the method for assuming tortious liability focuses on determining how a perpetrator should bear liability for any damage he has caused to a victim. That a perpetrator is required by law to bear liability through a certain method reflects the law's punishment on the perpetrator's tortious act and protection over a victim's legitimate right.

As can be seen, once a perpetrator has committed a tortious act, he must assume liability proportional to his wrong through a method that is necessary for providing the right relief to a victim. Thus, a method for assuming liability is a specific means for fulfilling liability. It is also a concrete embodiment of a tortious liability form and possesses the basic features of the same.

Firstly, a method for assuming tortious liability embodies a relationship between equal entities. Tort liability is an abstract concept. To force a perpetrator to assume liability, the law must provide a form of liability first. And that is the function of the methods for assuming tort liability. Since tortious liability is a kind of civil liability in nature, fulfilling such liability must be through a civil means. The most significant characteristic of tortious liability is that such liability belongs to a relationship between equal entities. Thus, it is not difficult to understand why civil sanctions such as admonition, fine, confiscation, or detention are not methods for assuming tortious liability. The fundamental reason for a court to take such punitive measures is for punishment not compensation purposes, reflecting the unequal relationship between a judicial body and a private entity.

Secondly, a method for assuming tortious liability is both a legal obligation and a compensation obligation. As a legal obligation, a method for assuming liability is enforced by a court pursuant to its judicial power. Thus, the scope and conditions for applying a method for assuming liability have legal force. However, such method also embodies a perpetrator's obligation to compensate a victim for damage—the ultimate value of a method for assuming liability, i.e., to restore the damaged interest

X. Li and J. Jin, *Concise Chinese Tort Laws*, China-EU Law Series 1,
DOI 10.1007/978-3-642-41024-6_11, © Springer-Verlag Berlin Heidelberg 2014

of a victim in whatever way. Thus, when determining a method for a perpetrator to assume tortious liability, we should make sure that the method is appropriate by considering the perpetrator's actual tortious act and whether a victim's damage may be adequately compensated.

Lastly, the most important and frequently used method for assuming liability is damage compensation. Traditionally, with respect to civil law, the two legal systems all emphasize the importance and leading position of damage compensation. Some countries' Tort Laws are even called the "tort damage compensation law." Damage compensation is the most basic method for assuming liability because the major function of the Tort Law is to compensate a victim for any damage he has suffered as a result of a tortious act. In most cases, no matter what it is, a tortious act always causes damage to a victim in the form of bodily injury, property damage, or mental distress, each of which can be calculated into monetary damage according to some legal formula and can be covered by means of damage compensation.

However, we cannot ignore other methods for assuming liability because of the damage compensation method's leading position. With further development of our society, people's needs are becoming more and more diversified. Thus, the methods for assuming liability should be adapted to fulfill such needs. Damage compensation is useful for protecting against property damage, but is not very effective in providing sufficient protection over personality right and intellectual property right. For example, because an apology can comfort a victim who suffers mental distress to a certain degree, it can be a very effective remedy under certain situations. Also, different forms of tortious acts demand different methods for assuming liability. Take Internet-based tortious activities as examples; they are usually fast and widespread. In order to prevent the harm from spreading further, cease and desist of the infringing activities is necessary. Thus, a very important developing trend of the Tort Law is the diversification of methods for assuming liability. This not only fits the needs of ever broadening protection scope provided by the Tort Law but also provides remedies in all different aspects.

To follow the trend of modern Tort Law, the "Tort Law" of China specified eight different methods for assuming liability, including cessation of the infringement, removal of obstacles, elimination of danger, returning property, restoration to the original state, compensation for losses, making an apology, and eliminating adverse impacts and restoring the injured party's reputation. Among them, compensation for losses, returning property, and restoration to the original state are property-related liabilities and are the major methods for assuming liability. Cessation of infringement, making an apology, eliminating adverse impacts, and restoring the injured party's reputation are non-property-related liabilities and are minor methods for assuming liability. As to removal of obstacles and elimination of danger, they have both property and non-property features under certain situations. Also, Article 15 specifies that these methods can be applied either individually or in combination.

It should be noted that these eight methods were not created by the "Tort Law," but were adopted from Paragraph 1, Article 134 of the "General Principles of Civil Law," which specifies ten different methods for assuming civil liability. The "Tort

Law" does not include payment of liquidated damage and repair, remake, or exchange, because payment of liquidated damage is a breach of contract liability and is not related to tort, and repair, remake, or exchange are essential the same as restoration to the original state, which does not need to be repeated. The benefit of specifying these methods in a centralized place (or provision) is that it makes the rules clear and easy to understand. On the one hand, a victim would find it helpful as a guideline to exercise his right and to understand what method he can request a perpetrator to assume liability for damage caused. On the other hand, a court would find it easy to adjudicate a case and choose the correct method. In sum, Article 15 of the "Tort Law" includes all possible methods for assuming liability in real life and should be able to meet the needs of all types of tort cases.

When applying the methods for assuming liability specified in Article 15 of the "Tort Law," a few guiding principles should be followed: (1) the ultimate goal is to restore a victim's position from damage he has suffered; therefore, the method most appropriate for achieving that goal should be chosen; (2) multiple methods may be applied in combination so that a victim is afforded the best protection when a single method is not enough to provide adequate relief; and (3) a victim has certain level of right and freedom to choose what method or methods (e.g., monetary compensation, restoration to the original state, etc.) he requests from a perpetrator to fulfill liability. However, this right or freedom is limited so that a perpetrator's right is also considered in a balanced way. For example, if restoration is clearly impossible or too expensive, a victim must choose monetary damage.

Besides the above, Article 21 of the "Tort Law" specifies that where a tortious act injures another person physically or damages his property, the injured party may request that the infringing party assume tortious liability and cease the infringement, remove the relevant obstacles, eliminate danger, etc. It shows that when a court faces a tort case, it may exercise its power to enjoin a perpetrator's act if it is necessary to stop the escalation of any damage. Of course, the court should be cautious in determining whether to enjoin the perpetrator's act. The conditions a court should consider include the following: the tortious act is ongoing and continuing without any indication that it will stop; the tortious act endangers a victim's life and property right, and if it is not stopped, any damage or injury will become worse and worse.

Method for assuming liability and tortious liability form are two easily confused concepts. The latter refers to a form of distributing liability among perpetrators after their tortious liability has been established, such as direct liability, vicarious liability, individual liability, joint and several liability, as well as liability by share. Method for assuming liability has some connections with liability form. Every liability form requires the determination of method for assuming liability, but the differences between the two are clear. Liability form is a concept that is only relevant to multi-perpetrator torts and solves the issue of how to distribute liability among these multiple perpetrators. In contrast, a method for assuming liability applies to all types of torts and solves the issue of how a perpetrator should bear his liability.

Below, we will go over the specific content of each method for assuming tortious liability. Because of the dominant status of the damage compensation method, we will separately discuss it in the next chapter.

Cessation of the Infringement

Cessation of the infringement is a very traditional method for assuming liability under the civil law. It applies to all types of civil liabilities, particularly tortious liabilities. As its name indicates, cessation of the infringement means that a victim has the right to request a perpetrator to stop his tortious act targeted towards the victim according to law. This concerns a tortious act that is still ongoing. Once a court grants such request from a victim, any ongoing tortious act against the victim must be stopped without condition. Thus, cessation of the infringement is essentially a request to ask a perpetrator not to act.

When applying this method, we should grasp its basic legal characteristics: (1) It must be applied to an ongoing infringing activity. When a perpetrator is committing a tortious act, an injured party can request by law that the tortious act be stopped. Cessation of infringement applies to various types of ongoing tortious activities, but not to activities that already stopped or have not started yet. (2) The purpose of this method is to stop an infringement immediately so that any harm caused is not aggravated. In order to achieve this goal, a court should quickly adjudicate a victim's such request based on the specific facts of the case and issue an order even before the trial of the case (or issue the order during trial or include the order in the final judgment or verdict).

The most typical type of cases for applying cessation of infringement is intellectual property-related litigations. On the one hand, intellectual property litigations are usually more complicated in nature and last longer; on the other hand, protection of intellectual property in a timely manner is critical in such cases. Thus, any legal remedy after trial is finished would be too late in such situations. As such, Article 1 of the "Several Provisions of the Supreme People's Court for the Application of Law to Pre-trial Cessation of Infringement of Patent Right" specifies: "Any patentee or interested party may file an application with the people's court for ordering the party against whom the application is filed to cease, before the court trial, its or his act of infringement of the patent right in accordance with the provision of Article 61 of the Patent Law." This is a typical example of cessation of infringement, which effectively protects an injured party's right and interest. It should be noted that although cessation of infringement can be executed before an adjudication of a case, an applicant of this remedy should be required to offer bond if possible to avoid causing unnecessary damage to a respondent.

Removal of Obstacles

Removal of obstacles is a remedy that requires a perpetrator to remove any obstacle that prevents an injured party from exercising its legitimate personal or property rights. For example, parking a car in front of an entrance or exit way of other people's house to obstruct the entering or exiting the house, the owner of the house may require the car's owner to drive the car away to restore the pathway to the house. Thus, the crux of determining whether a party has the right to request for removal of obstacles is whether any obstacle exists. The obstacle discussed here must be illegal or inappropriate. If an obstacle is caused by a party exercising its legitimate right, even the obstacle has caused inconvenience to another party, the latter party cannot request for removal of the obstacle. Certainly, whether an obstacle exists is determined according to an objective standard, not according to any subjective standard or foreseeability. In other words, an obstacle must be actually happening and ongoing, and any obstacle in the past does not need removal.

The legal characteristics of removal of obstacles are as follows: (1) a perpetrator's act has caused an obstacle for someone to exercise his legitimate personal or property right; (2) assuming such liability is not preconditioned on fault; (3) assuming such liability is not preconditioned on the fact that any actual damage has occurred; and (4) the purpose of this remedy is to insure the proper exercise of a legitimate right. In reality, an obstructed object is usually real property. An obstacle can be either personal property or real property. And personal property may be either tangible or intangible such as gas, smoke, noise, etc.

A victim has the right to request a perpetrator to remove an obstacle. If the perpetrator does not act, the victim can request a court to order the perpetrator to act. Of course, the condition is that the obstacle was created by the perpetrator's illegal act. If the perpetrator's act is legitimate, he can refuse the victim's request. The victim can also act to remove the obstacle by himself, but any cost related to removing the obstacle should be borne by the perpetrator. A typical example of application of this remedy is removal of pollutants from a river by a polluter as requested by a victim of the pollution. Article 41 of the "Environmental Protection Law" specifies: any party that has caused environmental pollution has the obligation to remove the pollutants and compensate for any damage suffered by any person or entity as a result of the pollution.

Elimination of Danger

Elimination of danger is a remedy that demands a perpetrator to eliminate any danger caused by his act or any object controlled or managed by him to a victim's body or property. As a simple example, if an owner or manager of a house has not exercised due care to maintain and repair his house so that it may collapse at any given moment, a neighbor who is under the threat of being injured by the potential collapsing of the house may request the owner of the house to perform necessary repair to eliminate the danger of collapsing. Obviously, this remedy may effectively prevent any possible harm and damage from occurring and fully protect people's rights and interests.

As a remedy emphasizing preventions, elimination of danger has the following legal characteristics: (1) there must be an actual danger that threats people's personal or property safety, (2) no actual damage has occurred yet, (3) assuming the liability is not preconditioned on fault, and (4) the purpose of this remedy is to prevent legitimate right or interest from being harmed. Thus, the standard to determine what constitutes danger is the crux of applying this remedy in actual cases. The danger discussed here is not an actual occurrence of any harm or damage but a reasonably foreseeable occurrence according to probability.

The possibility of threat from any harm or damage that has not occurred yet does exist in real life. As to such a possible threat, a party that may potentially be injured has the right to request a perpetrator to act or not act to eliminate the danger and prevent any harm from happening. If the perpetrator does not take necessary measure to eliminate the danger, the party being threatened by the danger may request the court to order the perpetrator to bear the liability. For example, if the branches or trunk of a tree in a residential community appears to be broken and falling and therefore may cause harm to people, a party that is responsible for managing the trees in the community may be requested to eliminate this danger to prevent any harm from occurring.

Returning Property

Returning property is a remedy allowing a victim whose property has been illegally possessed or encroached to request the wrongful possessor to return the property. In other words, a party that has illegally possessed another party's property should return the property at issue. The right to request a perpetrator to return property usually exists because the perpetrator has illegally possessed someone's property. For example, a tenant refuses to move out after his lease expires or a person robs another person's property on a street. These acts can all lead to illegal possession of other people's properties. The legitimate owners of these properties have the rights to request the return of the properties.

The basic legal characteristics of this remedy include the following: (1) It generally applies to infringement on property right. As such, Article 117 of the "General Principles of Civil Law" specifies that anyone who illegally possesses the property of the state, a collective, or another person shall return the property, and Article 34 of the "Property Right Law" specifies that an owner of a personal property or real property has the right to request the return of such property illegally possessed by another one. (2) The possession must be illegal. Possessing another person's property without any legal or contractual basis is illegal possession. It can either be holding over or encroachment. An owner cannot request the return of a property that is legally possessed. (3) The property still exists. If the property has been lost or destroyed, this remedy does not apply. If the property has been damaged, the owner has the option to request for its return, damage, or restoration to its original state. (4) The purpose of this remedy is to protect the right of a property's legitimate owner, possessor, or user. Because returning property is essentially transferring the possession of the property, only when the property is transferred to the control of its original owner, possessor, or user, the property is considered as returned.

The party that has the right to request the return of a property is usually the owner of the property. But a legitimate possessor of a property (e.g., a user or renter) also has the right to request the return of the property during his possession period. When a property is jointly owned, each owner has the right to request the return of the property, but the property must be requested to be returned to the whole group of owners. If one of the owners of a jointly owned property possesses more than his share of the property, other owners have the right to request the owner to return the exceeded share. Also, returning a property must include the returning of the yield of the property because illegally possessing other people's property is a malicious possession and there is no legal basis for the illegal possessor to retain any yield earned on the property during the illegal possession. Thus, the illegal possessor must return all yields earned on the property during his illegal possession of the property and cannot request reimbursement of the cost related to returning the property to the owner.

Restoration to the Original State

Restoration to the original state means that a victim has the right to request a perpetrator to restore a property owned by the victim to its original state by repair or other means if the property was damaged by the perpetrator. In a broad sense, restoration to the original state generally refers to the restoration of a legal relationship to a state before any change, e.g., termination of a contract. In a general sense, restoration to the original state means restoring a right to a state before it is infringed or harmed, including making an apology, eliminating adverse impacts, and restoring an injured party's reputation; in a narrow sense, restoration to the original state means restoring a property to its original state if the property was wrongfully damaged. Article 15 of the "Tort Law" refers to the restoration remedy in a narrow sense—ordering a perpetrator to restore a property damaged by him by repair or other means to a state before the property was damaged.

The basic legal characteristics of restoration to the original state include the following: (1) it applies to property right infringement; (2) a victim's property was damaged because of a perpetrator's tortious act; (3) the damaged property still exists, it is necessary to restore it to the original state, and the restoration is economically feasible and reasonable; and (4) the purpose is to protect the integrity of an owner's right over the property. Thus, whether a victim's request for restoration to the original state may be granted by a court is determined by two important factors: First, there must be a possibility of restoring the damaged property to its original state. If the property is destroyed or it is impossible to restore it, the owner can only request for damage compensation. Second, it is necessary to restore the property to its original state, i.e., the owner considers it necessary to restore the damaged property to its original state and it is economically reasonable to restore it. Otherwise, this remedy does not apply.

Restoration to the original state has advantages over other types of remedies, particularly when the damaged property cannot be replaced. In that situation, restoration not only meets the owner's subjective desire but also can avoid the difficulty of determining the amount of loss. Of course, the "original state" refers to an objective state. A victim usually provides the clear criteria for the "original state." If the perpetrator raises objections and cannot reach an agreement with the victim, certain assessment is needed to determine a restoration standard.

If a perpetrator refuses to restore a property damaged by him to the original state, the property owner has the right to seek an order from the court. For example, if a drunk driver collided to a wall and caused the wall to collapse, the owner of the wall can request the driver to restore the wall to its original state. In most cases, a perpetrator performs the restoration. But a victim can also perform the restoration himself and request reimbursement of the cost from the perpetrator. It must be realistically feasible to restore a damaged property to the original state. Otherwise, the owner can only request damage compensation. In case a property cannot be fully restored, any depreciation of the property shall be compensated by the perpetrator.

Damage Compensation

Damage compensation means that a perpetrator pays a certain amount of money to a victim for any damage caused to the victim by his tortious act. Damage compensation is the most basic method for assuming liability and is also the most widely applied one. Thus, each country has clear and detail specifications of damage compensation in its Tort Law. For example, Article 16 of the "Tort Law" specifies: any party who harms another and causes bodily injury shall pay for all reasonable expenses incurred in obtaining treatment and recovery such as medical expenses, nursing expenses, and transportation expenses, as well as lost income resulted from absence from work; where the victim is disabled, such party shall pay for assistance with daily life and disablement allowance; where such party's conduct results in death, he shall pay all funeral expenses and compensation for the death.

The core of damage compensation is the existence of damage. Without damage, there shall be no compensation. The purpose of damage compensation is to provide compensatory relief to a victim so that he can recover to a state before being infringed or harmed. Thus, the general principle of damage compensation is that a perpetrator is held liable for whatever amount of damage suffered by a victim. As can be seen, damage compensation in the usual sense is not punitive. But in certain situations, if the perpetrator's act is too bad or if the perpetrator has committed the same again and again, the law may demand the perpetrator to compensate more than the actual damage. This is called punitive damage, which is an exception to methods for assuming liability.

When it is difficult or impossible to restore a victim's damaged property, damage compensation is applicable. There are three major rules in the "Tort Law," and they are the rule for compensation for property damage, the rule for compensation for infringement on material personality right, and the rule for compensation for infringement on bodily right and compensation for mental distress related to damage on property with personality interest attached. With respect to how to determine the scope and amount of damage, the next chapter of this book will have more detailed discussions.

Making an Apology

Making an apology is a method that a perpetrator orally, in writing, or by other means apologizes to a victim for forgiveness. As a method for assuming liability, making an apology emphasizes on providing psychological comfort to a victim. On the one hand, a perpetrator expresses his respect and acknowledgement of his victim's rights. On the other hand, the victim can restore his damaged or debased social status or reputation and express his anger. Therefore, in practice, making an apology is often used in cases involving infringement on the honorary rights, privacy rights, name rights, portrait rights, and other personality rights.

The basic legal characteristics of making an apology include the following: (1) it is a non-property-based remedy; (2) it majorly provides relief for infringement on personality rights; and (3) the purpose is to provide psychological comfort for a victim whose personality has suffered damage or harm. A perpetrator usually needs to personally make the apology. Firstly, he needs to acknowledge that his act is illegal and has caused damage or harm to the victim. Secondly, he needs to indicate to the victim that he will be responsible for all damages caused by his act and needs to express his sorry for causing any trouble to the victim. Lastly, he needs to promise to the victim that he will restrain his behavior so that such act will not happen again in the future.

Making an apology can be in public or in private, orally, or in writing. A judge is to make the decision on the specific manner of making an apology. Oral apology is usually directly made by a perpetrator to a victim; therefore, it is usually in private. An apology in writing can be published in newspaper or posted in public area. If a perpetrator refuses to make an apology, a court may order the perpetrator to do so and all costs related shall be borne by the perpetrator.

Eliminating Adverse Impacts and Restoring the Injured Party's Reputation

Eliminating adverse impact and restoring reputation means that when a victim's personality rights have been harmed, the victim has the right to request the perpetrator to take appropriate measures within a reasonable range to eliminate the adverse impacts on the victim's reputation so that the victim's reputation may be restored. Specifically, when a perpetrator commits a tortious act that damages a person or legal person's reputation, the perpetrator should take necessary measures within the range affected by his tortious act to restore the person's or legal person's reputation to a state before the harm or damage occurred. Thus, eliminating adverse impacts and restoring reputation are complementary to each other. Eliminating adverse impacts is the means for restoring reputation, and restoring reputation is the goal of eliminating adverse impacts.

The basic legal characteristics of these two methods are the following: (1) they are non-property-based remedies; (2) they mainly provide relief for infringement on personality rights; and (3) their purpose is to restore a victim's reputation that has been wrongfully damaged or harmed. When applying these two remedies, the impacts of the specific tortious act and the consequence of a victim's reputation damage should be considered. The general principle is as follows: a perpetrator should take corresponding measures to eliminate the adverse impacts according to the scope and degree of the adverse impacts. For example, if an article on Internet is the source of harming someone's reputation, corrected content or a notice should be posted on the relevant website(s).

In sum, each method for assuming liability specified in the "Tort Law" has its own characteristics. Under the general goal of providing relief to a victim, an appropriate method should be chosen according to the need. The victim can raise the specific type and number of remedy he desires and the judge should make the determination. From a victim's perspective, he has the right to request a remedy and can dispose this right at his own will. If the remedy request is appropriate and does not impose inappropriate burden on a perpetrator, the judge should support the request in principle. If a victim voluntarily gives up a remedy, the judge should not interfere with the victim's decision either.

Chapter 12
Damage Compensation

The Concept and Principles of Damage Compensation

Damage compensation is a tort liability based on damage suffered by a victim as a result of a perpetrator's tortious act, and the perpetrator is required to make necessary and adequate compensation for the victim's damage to fulfill the liability. Damage compensation is an important tool for a victim to achieve his civil rights. As for a perpetrator, it is an important method for assuming liability. Once a tortious liability including damage compensation is established, there exists a legal relationship on compensation payment between the perpetrator and the victim. Pursuant to this relationship, the victim has the right to receive such compensation payment, and the perpetrator has the obligation to make such compensation payment.

In determining the scope of a damage compensation-based liability, we should make sure a victim is adequately compensated for his damage on the one hand and a perpetrator is not unreasonably burdened on the other hand. Thus, we should follow some basic principles while applying this remedy in practice:

1. Using money as compensatory means. Whether a victim suffers bodily harm, property damage, or mental stress, such damage or harm should be converted into monetary damage and any compensation should be made in money. In the early histories of human beings, civil liabilities were borne and performed by a perpetrator in person. For example, under Roman law, if a person committed a tortious act and caused injury to a victim, that person would be forced to be enslaved by the victim. Many countries had changed such barbarous laws lately and had adopted the monetary compensation means generally, i.e., any damage or injury is converted into monetary damage based on fairness and reasonableness.
2. Making full compensation. A perpetrator shall be liable for all damage or injury suffered by a victim as a result of the perpetrator's tortious act. In other words, the compensation made by the perpetrator should be equal to the damage or injury suffered by the victim. Such damage is the so-called actual damage, which

X. Li and J. Jin, *Concise Chinese Tort Laws*, China-EU Law Series 1,
DOI 10.1007/978-3-642-41024-6_12,

includes not only direct damage in terms of property loss at present time but also indirect damage on property loss that would be suffered by the victim in the future as long as it is within a reasonable scope—if so, the victim can claim such damage and whether or not the perpetrator is at fault has no bearing on the outcome. Of course, the victim has a duty to mitigate the loss. That is, the victim must take active measures to prevent the damage from becoming larger. Otherwise, the perpetrator does not bear liability to that part of the loss that could have been mitigated.

Punitive damage is a breakthrough of the principles of damage compensation, but also a very controversial topic. When a perpetrator acts in indifference, intent, fraud, or other egregious nature, a judge can order the perpetrator to make extra payment to a victim on top of the victim's damage to punish the perpetrator, discourage such egregious act in general, and provide comfort to the victim. To a victim, punitive damage can provide supplementary relief in case damage compensation is not enough. To a perpetrator, punitive damage has a very strong punishment significance, which is aimed at subduing the perpetrator's impulse of recommitting such act in the future by means of reducing his properties. Punitive damage is widely used in Anglo-American legal systems, but it is difficult for civil law systems to adopt it. It is specified as a provision in principle in Article 47 of the "Tort Law" (the product liability provision) and therefore should be applied in caution in practice.

3. The principle of deduction of collateral benefits. If a victim both suffered damage and received benefit, such benefit should be accounted in calculating his damage. Here, such benefit only includes economic interests or property interests that can be valued in money, but not mental or spiritual interests. If such benefit is de minimis, it is generally not considered. In any event, the purpose of damage compensation is to provide necessary relief to a victim to restore him to a state before infringement, not a windfall. This principle requires not only that a victim should be fully compensated for his damage but also that any benefit received by the victim as a result of the infringement should be deducted.
4. Contributory negligence. If a victim is at fault, a perpetrator's liability should be reduced or eliminated according to the degree of the victim's fault. This is essentially an application of the fault liability imputation principle—a perpetrator is liable for whatever damage he has caused and a victim is liable for damage attributed to his fault or failure to mitigate. The consequence of contributory negligence is that a perpetrator's liability is partially or completely released if the victim's fault is too serious and is the major or whole reason that has caused the damage.
5. Other principles. Other principles in civil law such as balance of interests, act in good faith, prohibition of abuse of power, public order and good custom, etc., should also be considered and applied in actual tort cases so that a judge is able to adjudicate a case with a fair and reasonable result. One of the most common principles is the consideration of both parties' economic situations, e.g., if a perpetrator's financial capability is much weaker compared with his victim's financial capability, the perpetrator's liability may be reasonably reduced after receiving the victim's consideration and approval.

Damage compensation can be categorized according to different standards. According to the type of infringed right, damage compensation can be categorized as bodily injury compensation, property damage compensation, or mental stress compensation. According to the nature of the compensated damage, it can be categorized as general damage compensation or special damage compensation. According to the form of damage suffered, it can be categorized as property damage compensation or non-property damage compensation, etc.

Property vs. non-property damage is the most common and important categorization in the continental law system. Property damage compensation and non-property damage compensation constitute the most typical damage compensation rules in modern Tort Law. Property damage includes all monetary- and property-related damage, e.g., loss of commercial interest or cost for medical treatment. Non-property damage includes all damages that are not based on monetary or property loss, e.g., physical or mental suffering. Property damage can be evaluated in terms of money, although sometimes it may be rough or difficult without sufficient evidence. However, physical or mental suffering cannot be evaluated in terms of money. Although we have to use money as a compensatory means, it is just a substitution of more valuable things by money and so far the best approach a court can take.

Calculation of Property Damage Compensation

Property damage is damage that can be measured in money. This kind of damage can be resulted from infringement on people's property rights (e.g., property damage occurs because a person violates the traffic law and damages another person's car) or from infringement on people's bodily rights (e.g., medical cost incurred for infringement on the right to health). Thus, damage compensation means that when a perpetrator infringes on a victim's legitimate rights and therefore causes property damage, the victim has the right to request the perpetrator to make monetary compensation.

The legal characteristics of property damage compensation include the following: damage can be measured and calculated in money; the basis for compensation is not limited to infringement on property rights (besides infringement on property rights, intellectual property rights, equities, or other property rights such as virtual interests, infringement on personal rights can also lead to property damage compensation); it is the most basic method for assuming tort liability and the purpose is to provide economic relief to victims.

Regarding calculating the amount of property damage, it should be noted that property damage usually refers to direct damage as a result of the infringement, i.e., property loss. Besides direct damage, there may be also indirect damage, i.e., loss of income, which refers to a victim's loss of future interest related to a property that has been damaged because of a perpetrator's infringement. Indirect damage is not the loss of present property, but the possible loss of owner's future interest derived from his property. It is the loss of the possible interest that could be gained by the victim. Compared with direct damage, indirect damage has the following characteristics: what is lost is a future interest—not present interest—which may be gained as property if infringement has not occurred; it is very likely that the lost future interest can be reduced to actual property interest; this future interest would be generated from the property, damaged as a result of the infringement, and has a certain scope; it is not a false interest totally unrelated to the damaged property.

Infringement on other people's property right is the major and most basic form of property damage. It includes destroying other people's personal or real property to cause damage or complete loss of the property's external form and internal substance. To avoid inconsistencies among the damage-calculating rules in judicial practice, the law expressly specified the standard for calculating property damage—damage should be calculated on the basis of when the damage occurred, which is usually when the tortious act occurred. Thus, where any property is damaged by a tortious act, the damage should be calculated based on the market value when such damage occurred. Specifically, if a property was totally destroyed or lost, the damage should be its market value; if such type of property has never been on the market and therefore does not have a corresponding market value as a reference, other means should be applied for calculating its value, including using professional assessment services in the relevant field.

Infringement on other people's personal right also falls into the scope of property damage. A citizen's personal rights are the basic rights endowed by law, including the right to life, the right to health, bodily right, name right, honorary right, the right to portrait, the right of reputation, privacy right, custody right and the right to personal freedom, and other personal related rights. Infringing on other people's personal rights carries the consequence of bearing tortious liability. The "Tort Law" has specified particular rules regarding how to calculate damage for infringement on personal rights. Property damage due to infringement on a person's personal right can be different based on the particular tortious act and the substance of the infringed personal right, and the scope of the damage can be different as well.

The first type of damage is caused by infringement on other people's right to life, right to health, bodily right, and other material personal rights, and it generally includes active property damage and the loss of obtainable interest. According to the law, if a perpetrator commits tortious act and causes injury to a victim, the perpetrator should compensate for all medical costs, care expenses, transportation fees, and other reasonable costs or expenses related to the victim's medical treatment as well as the loss of income due to the loss of working time. If any disability is caused, the perpetrator should also compensate for disability living allowance and disability compensation. If death is resulted, the perpetrator should be liable for death compensation and any funeral cost. Active property damage includes medical costs, care expenses, transportation fees, lodging expenses, expenses for necessary nutritional supplements, and other reasonable costs and expenses for continuous medical treatment; funeral costs, expenses related to transportation, lodging, and other reasonable fees for the funeral; any disability equipment; etc. Obtainable interests include loss of income because of a victim's loss of working time; if death occurred, the victim's relatives' loss of income for participating or handling the victim's funeral; loss of expected income because of a victim's complete or partial loss of working capability; and loss of expected income in a certain future period because of a victim's death.

The second type of damage is caused by infringement on other people's right to reputation, honorary right, right to name, right to portrait, privacy right, and other nonmaterial personal rights. Although China's Supreme Court has published judicial interpretations, explaining that compensation for the above nonmaterial personal rights should be spiritual in nature, such infringement sometimes can actually lead to property damage that can be measured in money. Therefore, the perpetrator should make necessary compensation following the path of property damage compensation. For example, many celebrities' portraits can produce commercial interests and if used in advertisements or for other commercial purposes, they can produce significant economic interests. But if their portraits are used without permission, these celebrities are deprived of any economic interests they deserve. Since these economic interests can be calculated into money, such infringements on personal rights lead to property damages. Cases regarding property damages caused by infringements on nonmaterial personal rights can be handled and determined based on the different tortious acts and relevant damages. If there is actual damage in such a case, the victim should be compensated for such damage. If there is no actual damage, the amount of compensation can be determined based on the interest gained by the perpetrator or according to other calculating means.

Article 20 of the "Tort Law" specifies the principles regarding remedies on property damage caused by infringements on personal rights: first, when it is easy to determine a victim's damage or loss, the victim should be compensated for such damage or loss; second, when it is difficult to determine the damage or loss caused by an infringement on personal rights, particularly when a victim's reputation is damaged, privacy right is violated, or any other nonmaterial personal right is infringed, and it is difficult to calculate the amount of damage, and the amount of compensation should be determined based on the interest gained by the perpetrator; last, where the interest gained by the perpetrator is difficult to determine, and the victim and the perpetrator cannot reach an agreement on the amount of compensation to be paid through negotiation, the court shall determine the amount of compensation payable according to the circumstances.

Infringing on other's intellectual property right can also lead to liability for property damage, because intellectual property right is a legitimate right obtained as the fruit of undertaking intellectually creative activities and is an intangible asset based on value. Thus, intellectual property right is a combination of property right and personal right. It is not only a spiritual right such as the right of authorship but also a property right—obtaining monetary interests from such right. A perpetrator should bear liability for making compensation on property damage caused by infringement on copyright, trademark right, or patent right (the core of intellectual property right).

The compensation principle regarding intellectual property right has no big difference from the one regarding general property right. Because China's intellectual property laws have already included detailed provisions on civil liabilities, the "Tort Law" avoided repeating them. Since the general principle of "Tort Law" is to follow the relevant provisions or rules if they already exist in other laws, the specific intellectual property laws should be applied when calculating damages caused by infringements on such rights. For example, Article 48 of the "Copyright Law" specifies: where a perpetrator infringes on a party's copyright or rights related to so, the perpetrator should compensate for the party's actual damage; if it is difficult to determine the actual damage, the amount of compensation should be based on the unlawful gains obtained through the infringement. Also, Article 56 of the "Trademark Law" specifies: the amount of compensation for infringing on a party's trademark right is the gain obtained by the perpetrator via the infringement or the loss of the trademark owner because of the infringement, including the cost and expenses related to stopping such infringement. These damage-calculating rules did not change because of the enactment of the "Tort Law" and are still being used as usual.

Other common property damages include damage caused by infringement on other's stock right. Stock right is obtained through a person's investment in a corporation and is a transferable property right enjoyed by the person, who has the right to participate in certain activities of the corporation according to the law or the corporation's bylaw. Whoever infringes on other's stock right should bear corresponding civil liability for the damage caused according to the relevant laws. Also, with the development of the Internet and electronic technologies, the meaning of property is becoming broader. For example, virtual money used on Internet gaming is considered a property because an owner usually needs to contribute certain amount of money and time to gain it. If an owner's such right is infringed, he deserves monetary compensation from the infringer. The "Tort Law" has no specific provision regarding damage compensation on such type of properties. If infringement occurs, relevant regulations and judicial interpretations should be relied upon for determining the amount of compensation for such property damage.

Non-property (Spiritual) Damage Compensation Calculation

As the counterpart for the concept of property damage compensation, non-property damage compensation is a form of damage that has nothing to do with property change and cannot be measured by or calculated into money. In other words, non-property damage refers to damage that has no direct property content or loss of property value and cannot be measured by money. With respect to the scope of non-property damage, there are general view and specific view.

According to the general view, all forms of damages other than property damage, including physiological, psychological, or other spiritual damage, are non-property damages, which are not conditioned on whether the civil subject has a biological form or spiritual sense. According to the specific view, non-property damage, being a concrete damage result, firstly refers to mental anguish such as worry, despair, anger, frustration, sadness, lack of interest, as well as physical pain.

As can be seen, the general view puts legal person or other organizations into the civil subject's scope and is inconsistent with China's current laws. Article 5 of the Supreme Court's "Judicial Interpretation on Mental Stress Compensation" specifies: when a legal person or organization requests damage on mental stress based on infringement on its personal rights, the court should reject such request. Since the "Tort Law" does not disagree with this rule, it should be considered as acquiescence. However, the specific view limits non-property damage to the scenarios where infringement on a person's personal rights has led to mental stress and physical pain, which do not include abstract spiritual interest or a natural person's loss of sense or mind. Thus, the specific view is too narrow and conservative. The best approach is probably to adopt the general view but limit the civil subject to only natural person.

Whoever infringes on other's rights and causes non-property damage must bear liability to compensate for the non-property damage. According to China's legislative tradition, non-property damage has long been called "mental distress compensation" or "solatium compensation." Although the names are different, they actual refer to the same concept and they are views of the same issue from different angles. Therefore, it is unnecessary to strictly distinguish them. The reason why "non-property damage compensation" and "mental distress compensation" may be used interchangeably is because non-property damage itself refers to the loss of interest (such as mental distress or the complete or partial loss of spiritual interest) that is closely related to a victim and cannot be measured by money.

An example can help us to understand it more clearly that non-property damage compensation and mental distress compensation are essentially the same: when the right to life, the right to health, bodily right, or other material personal right is infringed, both property damage (such as medical cost, funeral cost, etc.) and non-property damage (such as physical pain or mental distress) can be caused at the same time. Thus, two different methods for damage compensation should be established: one method is for compensating property damage caused by infringement on the rights to life, health, etc., and the other method is for compensating non-property damage caused by infringement on such rights. In this sense, non-property damage compensation is to provide monetary relief to a victim for his loss of spiritual interest and suffering of mental distress.

As can be seen, non-property damage compensation is not different from mental distress compensation in essence, and its name is more scientific because the term "mental" may create philosophical impression between "mental" and "property" as well as the wrong idea that the opposite of "property damage" is mental distress and that mental distress compensation has nothing to do with property. However, following China's legislative tradition, we will continue using the term “mental distress compensation” below. Article 22 of the “Tort Law” specifies: “[w]here any harm caused by a tort to a personal right or interest of another person inflicts a serious mental distress on the victim, the victim may seek compensation for the infliction of mental distress.” This provision is the first legislation regarding mental distress compensation under Chinese law. It is like a milestone, having tremendous historical significance.

According to the mainstream view among China’s legal scholars, mental distress compensation is a mechanism allowing a victim to receive monetary compensation as a relief or comfort for damage on personal or identity rights or for suffering mental distress. The “compensation” discussed here is different from the compensation in the context of property damage, where equal value is provided for equal loss. Because it is difficult to measure mental distress with money, such “compensation” is not simply using property to compensate for a victim’s loss, but a condolence to the victim for his mental suffering or a compensation for his loss in spiritual rights. As a remedy for infringement on civil right, mental distress compensation is also punitive in nature and can punish or warn those infringers, to better protect victims’ legitimate civil rights.

Mental distress compensation must be based on the existence of mental distress, which is a victim’s suffering on mental distress or loss on spiritual interests because of a perpetrator’s infringing act. Generally speaking, mental distress has two sources: first, infringement on a victim’s physiological activities, i.e., the infringing act harmed a person’s physical body, health, life, or other material personal rights, and second, infringement on a victim’s spiritual activities, such as mood, thinking, mind, or other nonmaterial personal interests, and it causes the victim to be angry, worried, scared, sad, etc. Also, when certain personal rights are infringed, a person’s spiritual interest may be adversely affected. For example, when a person’s reputation is damaged, the direct consequence is the drop of the public’s evaluation on the person.

However, it should be noted that no matter what the source of infringement is, a victim must provide reasonable proof of the actual existence of mental distress if the victim requests compensation for it. In other words, although spiritual interests are intangible, such mental distress on which damage compensation is requested must be objective in form and factually specific. That is, compensable mental distress should not be just a startle, but must be a recognizable bodily or mental injury. In sum, recognizability of mental distress is significant in that it can help to determine whether mental distress really occurred—an important factual basis for determining whether a perpetrator should bear relevant liability.

Determining the amount of compensation for mental distress is even more important. However, it is difficult to establish such a standard, and no country has a clear rule on this issue to this date. As such, the “Tort Law” adopted the same evasive attitude, and we can only rely on judicial interpretation to make determinations. For example, Article 10 of the Supreme Court’s “Judicial Interpretation on Mental Stress Compensation” lists six factors for consideration in determining the amount of compensation for mental distress, including the degree of the perpetrator’s fault, consequences of the infringing act, interests gained by the perpetrator, the perpetrator's financial capability, and the average living condition in the area of the judicial district. Also, many local courts have specified detailed amounts (usually between 1 k and 100 k) according to their local conditions.

In sum, the amount of compensation for mental distress cannot be expressed by a simple math formula. In practice, we are relying more on judicial discretion under some rough legal principles. The many characteristics of mental distress provide theoretical possibility and realistic necessity for judicial discretion. Achieving justice in these cases depends on the free application of discretion by the judges. Because spiritual interests are intangible, the consequences of mental distress are subjectively sensed by human beings, and it is difficult to estimate damage related to mental distress, the fact that different adjudications may be reached on cases that are essentially the same does not seem unjustifiable. Thus, a judge is given broad discretion in this type of cases. However, it is not to say that a judge has unlimited discretion. That means there should be a limit to the amount of damage awarded based on mental distress so that frivolous lawsuits aimed only at economic gains are not encouraged. It should be noted that no lawsuit should be a source for economic interests. The purpose of bringing a lawsuit based on mental distress is to protect one's personal rights, not to obtain extra money income.

Making Payment on Damage Compensation

One of the most important functions of Tort Law is to provide relief to a victim for his loss. That is, a perpetrator should timely and adequately bear liability for a victim's property or non-property damage. Thus, the method for making payment on damage compensation is an important aspect of protecting a victim's right. According to the specification of Article 25 of the "Tort Law", after damage occurs, the parties concerned may discuss the method for paying compensation; where no agreement is reached through negotiation, compensation shall be paid in a lump sum; where paying compensation in a lump sum is practicable, it may be paid by installment provided a corresponding guarantee is given. As can be seen, there are two methods for paying compensation: in a lump sum, which requires a perpetrator to pay all compensation to a victim in one lump sum, and installment, according to which the perpetrator makes installment payments to the victim until the total is paid off.

Specifically, according to the above provision, the parties have the right to negotiate a method for paying the compensation, either in a lump sum or by installment. The reason to let the parties to freely negotiate a method for paying compensation is that it allows the parties to have an opportunity to express their needs, requirements, difficulties, etc., and reach an agreement based on mutual respect and agreement so that any potential problem with making such payment can be avoided or minimized. During negotiation, the major factors the parties should consider are the amount of payment, the degree of the victim's dependence on such payment, the perpetrator's capability of making such payment, etc. According to these factors, the parties may reach a reasonable and feasible agreement and payment schedule.

Of course, given a victim's loss should be adequately and timely compensated after the infringement's occurrence, if the victim does not agree payment by installment, the perpetrator should pay the compensation in a lump sum. However, if the perpetrator has real difficulty to make a lump sum payment, payment by installment should be considered or allowed. Whether there is such a difficulty and what the difficulty is should all be proved by evidence by the perpetrator, based on which the court may make its determination. Even if payment by installment is allowed, the perpetrator should provide a guarantee, which may be in the form of a sponsor's promise or the perpetrator's own property used as collateral.

Part II
Tort Law of the People's Republic of China—Rules, Explanation and Examples

Chapter 13
General Provisions

Article 1

Rule This Law is enacted to protect the legitimate rights and interests of parties in civil law relationships, clarify the tort liability, prevent and punish torts, and promote social harmony and stability.

Explanation This article articulates the purpose of the People's Republic of China's Tort Law (the "Tort Law" or "Law"), which includes four parts. First, the Tort Law protects civil parties' legal interests. Civil parties in China include natural person, legal person, and organizations that are not legal persons. The law in China grants civil parties various personal and property rights. The Tort Law protects the civil parties' legal interests by imposing civil liability on tortfeasors. Second, the Tort Law clarifies tort liability. The Tort Law specifies the identification of the tortfeasor, the constituent elements, remedies, and exemptions or reduction of liability. Thus, the Law clearly identifies the liability and possible exemptions. Third, the Tort Law prevents and sanctions tort actions. The Tort Law not only punishes the tortfeasors but also focuses on the prevention of future violations. The guiding concept behind the Tort Law is to prevent and sanction violations. Finally, the Tort Law promotes social harmony and stability. The Tort Law establishes and imposes liability for tortfeasors, and provides legal protection for the tort victims. In sum, the functions of the Tort Law demonstrated by this article are "To recover from damages" and "To prevent future harm."

Example The plaintiff was burned during a bath due to a sudden gas explosion. The Plaintiff's gas water heater was produced by a gas water heater appliance company ("the Company"). The Company removed the water heater soon after the accident. After the removal, the water heater and related products were not tested, nor did authorities identify the cause of the accident. Later, the plaintiff's family entered into a preliminary agreement with the Company. The Company paid a total of ¥50,000 in advance. After the accident, the Company paid plaintiff twice for medical expenses totaling ¥30,000. Since the two payments, the two sides could

X. Li and J. Jin, *Concise Chinese Tort Laws*, China-EU Law Series 1,
DOI 10.1007/978-3-642-41024-6_13, © Springer-Verlag Berlin Heidelberg 2014

not agree on the cause of the accident and the amount of compensation owed. The plaintiff then sued the Company. The court found that the plaintiff's burns were caused by the explosion of the water heater defendant manufacturer. The defendant, as the manufacturer of the water heater, bears the burden of proof that there was no defect in the water heater, or to provide statutory exemptions for liability. If the defendant failed to carry its burden of proof, it should bear the consequence of its failure. The defendant could not provide valid evidence to prove that the water heater had no defects or that it had any statutory exemption for liability. Therefore, the defendant should be held fully liable for the damages caused by its defective product. Although the plaintiff allowed the defendant to remove the water heater, it is the defendant who actually removed the water heater. Thus, the liability of failing to produce the water heater as evidence falls on the defendant not the plaintiff. There is no basis for the plaintiff to bear adverse consequences for defendant's removal of the water heater. Consequently, the defendant should compensate the plaintiff for all of the losses of ¥50,000.

Article 2

Rule One shall be liable for his tortious acts, in accordance with this Law, that infringe the civil rights and interests of others.

"Civil rights and interests" mentioned in this Law shall include the rights to life, health, name, reputation, honor, self-image, privacy, marital autonomy, guardianship, ownership, usufruct, security interest, copyright, patent, exclusive use of a trademark, discovery, equities, succession, and other personal and property rights and interests.

Explanation This article focuses on the object of Tort Law protection. According to the theory and practice of China's civil law, the objects protected by the Tort Law cover not only civil rights but also legitimate interests beyond civil rights. Any infringement on civil rights or legitimate interests beyond the civil rights may constitute a tort liability. Article 1 of this law states that the Tort Law protects civil rights. Article 2 defines the scope of civil rights by enumerating various rights. In light of the listed 19 civil rights, the civil rights protected by the Tort Law are absolute rights. The legitimate interests beyond the civil rights are generally considered to include personal interests (e.g., the deceased right of reputation) and property interests (e.g., pure economic loss).

Example A newspaper published a special report, which disclosed some information of the victim (deceased), the plaintiffs' daughter, and included the real name, age, and birthplace of the victim. The newspaper professed that the plaintiffs' daughter lived with one suspect as lovers and had sexual relations with another suspect. At the time when this report was published, the plaintiffs' daughter murder was still under investigation. The plaintiffs claimed that the report reveals their daughter's real name and the news randomly published distorted depictions of their daughter's private life that was irrelevant to the case or investigation. They further claimed that the report made many locals aware of the case and generated gossip, which caused plaintiffs' and their family's severe mental anguish. Thus, the plaintiffs sued the newspaper. The defendant claimed that its report was based on a correspondent's report covering the murder of the plaintiffs' daughter. The newspaper argued that its report merely made an objective coverage of the case. The newspaper argued that its report was neither inaccurate nor slander against the plaintiffs or their daughter. Therefore, the newspaper claimed that its conduct did not constitute infringement. The court held that while the murder case was still under investigation, the defendant disclosed in its report the victim's real name, age, privacy, and other facts that were irrelevant to the case. This information was sufficient to enable readers to know the true identity of the figure in the report, thus the newspaper disclosed the plaintiffs' daughter's privacy. As a result, the defendant violated the plaintiffs' daughter's right to her reputation, rendering plaintiffs and their family suffered psychological and mental pain after the loss of their loved one. Therefore, the defendant should stop the infringement, apologize, and compensate the plaintiffs' loss.

Article 3

Rule The victim of a tort is entitled to require the tortfeasor to assume the tort liability.

Explanation This article is about who bears the liability of the tort and who has the right to request for compensation. After the tort has been committed, the injured parties have the right to hold the perpetrators liable for their tort. People or natural forces can cause a tort. With respect to the former, the perpetrator is the tortfeasor; with respect to the latter, although there is no general concept of natural forces as a perpetrator, due to the law's imposition on people certain duties to act—e.g., keeping one's pet under control or maintaining proper working conditions—the person who fails to perform his/her duty will be deemed as the perpetrator. The tortious activity causes damages to social resources, which could be personal or property damages. The victim is the person who suffers personal or property damages. There may be multiple victims, the individual among the victims who has the right to request or hold the perpetrator liable is the "requester." The perpetrator bears the tort liability. Right to compensation can be vested in direct or indirect victims. Indirect victims include dependents and close relatives. Obligation to compensate can be imposed on the direct perpetrator, the person who has vicarious liability, or the person who has supplemental responsibility.

Example Zhang, a driver for a corporation, while driving a bus shifted lanes and collided with another bus in front of his. Zhang's failure to maintain sufficient distance from this other bus caused the collision. This collision caused the other driver to lose control of his bus and the death of four passengers on the other bus, including Wang. Under the liability confirmation delivered by the traffic police,

Zhang bore full responsibility for the accident. Wang's family sued Zhang's employer, seeking compensation for funeral expenses, dependent's living expenses, and death compensation. After accepting the case, Wang's wife gave birth to a baby boy. The wife, as the baby's legal agent, sued on behalf of the dependent baby the defendant corporation for living expenses. The court found that Zhang, during his driving of the motor vehicle, violated relevant provisions of the "Highway Traffic Regulations," which resulted in the accident, thus he should bear full responsibility for the accident. Zhang caused this accident within the scope of his employment. Therefore, the defendant corporation, under the theory of respondeat superior, bears the liability for compensation. Wang's parents were 48 and 47 years old at the time of the accident. Although ill, they cannot be regarded as lacking labor capacity. Consequently, their claim for living expenses was denied. Wang's baby boy, not yet born at the time of the accident, should be regarded as being actually raised by Wang had he been alive; thus, his claim for living expenses should be allowed.

Article 4

Rule Even if a tortfeasor is required to assume administrative or criminal liability for certain conduct; those liabilities shall not preclude the tortfeasor's tort liability.

Where a tortfeasor's assets are inadequate to cover the tort liability and administrative liability or criminal liability for the same conduct, the tortfeasor shall first satisfy the tort liability.

Explanation This article regulates concurrent liabilities. In accordance with the first rule of the article, if the tortious conduct imposes tort, administrative, or criminal liability, the tortfeasor bears both tort and administrative liabilities or both tort and criminal liabilities. This is called concurrent liabilities: tort liability and criminal or administrative liability may apply concurrently and are not mutually exclusive. The reason for allowing concurrent liabilities is that each liability has its own purposes—the purpose of imposing administrative liability is to maintain social order, the purpose of imposing criminal liability is to punish perpetrators and prevent future harms, the purpose of imposing civil liability is to make the victim whole again—the three purposes can coexist. According to the second rule of the article, if the tortfeasor's assets are sufficient to satisfy all concurrent legal liabilities, then there is no issue of priority (which liability should be given the priority for satisfaction); if the tortfeasor's assets are insufficient to satisfy all legal liabilities, the tort liability will get the priority. This establishes the principle of giving priority to civil liability.

Example Yue, a traffic patrolman, and Bai, a traffic warden, noticed that defendant Li did not wear a safety helmet while riding a motorcycle. Yue stopped Li and walked towards the road with Bai. Defendant Li, in fear of being caught driving without a license and that the motorcycle had a fake license plate, accelerated in order to escape the inspection. Yue immediately avoided the collision. Bai was standing behind Yue and was unable to get out of the way. Li's motorcycle hit Bai and dragged him approximately 4.5 m. Li fled, but was subsequently arrested by the traffic Patrol Squadron. The city prosecuted Li. Additionally, Bai sued Li for monetary compensation for bodily injury caused by Li, including economic loss, medical expenses, dental expenses, lost income, hospital food subsidies, caring expenses, nutrition expenses, disability compensation, and traveling expenses. The court found that Li intentionally accelerated when Yue notified Li to stop for inspection knowing that driving at high speed might cause bodily injury to others. Li deliberately ignored this consequence. Moreover, Li continued to flee and caused serious injuries to Bai after the collision. The court held that Li was guilty of intentional assaults. Li's intentional assaults caused economic loss to the plaintiff; thus, Li should be held liable.

Article 5

Rule Where other laws provide for any specific tort liability, such special provisions shall prevail.

Explanation This article articulates the principle of giving priority to other special Tort Laws and the compatibility of Tort Law with other laws. According to this tort liability article, if special Tort Laws dictate, special provisions should apply; when there is no special Tort Law, the general provisions of the Tort Law apply. In other words, special Tort Laws are for particular special interests, such as trademark rights. Special Tort Laws are adopted as a special way to find infringement or composition of elements. Liability attribution is also different from those in ordinary tort principles. Therefore, due to special Tort Laws' effect on subject matter and personal jurisdictions, it should prevail. When there is no applicable provision of special Tort Laws, the complementary effect of the general provisions in Tort Law comes into play.

Example Hu registered a company to trade local special products. Additionally, he registered the "Yellow River" trademark. During his company's operation, another company engaged in illegal counterfeiting, used the Yellow River trademark, and made more than ¥30,000 in profit. Hu sued the defendant for damages. The court found that the defendant company's conduct clearly infringed. In the application of the laws—due the "Trademark Law of People's Republic of China" has more detailed requirements than the Tort Law—the trademark law should apply.

standing behind. Yue and was unable to get out of the way. Li's ... pale but did ... [illegible]

Chapter 14
Constituting Liability and Methods of Assuming Liability

Article 6

Rule One who is at fault for infringement of others' civil rights or interests of shall be subject to tort liability.

One who is at fault, per statutory provisions, and cannot prove otherwise shall be subject to tort liability.

Explanation Rule 1 of this article is about the principle of fault liability, and Rule 2 relates to the principle of presumption of fault, which is part of the principle of fault liability. The relationship between the principle of fault liability and the principle of presumption of fault is about fairness and justice. Although the principle of presumption of fault has the same four elements as the principle of fault liability, in some cases, it is inherently difficult for the victim to prove those elements. In those cases, it is clearly unfair to let the tortfeasors avoid liability simply due to the victim's inability to prove the fault; therefore, under certain circumstances, the principle of presumption of fault should be applied instead of the principle of fault liability. The party with the burden of proof is different under the principle of fault liability and the principle of presumption of fault: under the former, the burden of proof is on the victim; under the latter, the burden of proof shifts to the tortfeasor. Because the fault is presumed, the burden to negate this presumption is on the tortfeasor. For the tortfeasor to prove that she has no liability, she has to prove that she is not at fault subjectively. The principle of presumption of fault applies to specific torts that are prescribed by law, it cannot be arbitrarily applied. The general principle of fault liability applies to torts, unless the law specifically states otherwise.

Example Wen, a self-employed businessman, went to a bank to deposit money. While Wen was filling out some paperwork in the hall, the suspect noticed him and decided to rob him. After completing the paperwork, Wen went to the counter to deposit the money. The suspect went up to Wen and stood very closely, which was a clear violation of the rule requiring customers to keep a minimum distance from

X. Li and J. Jin, *Concise Chinese Tort Laws*, China-EU Law Series 1,
DOI 10.1007/978-3-642-41024-6_14,

each other. However, this obvious violation was not caught by either the security guards or other bank employees. When Wen put the cash bag on the counter, and handed some of the cash to the bank teller, the suspect attempted to snatch the bag. During the ensuing fight, the suspect shot Wen twice in his chest to force Wen to give up the cash. Wen died from the gunshot wounds. The suspect fled the scene without any of Wen's cash, and successfully avoided being caught by the security guards. The suspect has been listed as wanted since the murder and attempted robbery but has not been brought to justice. Wen's family sued the bank. The court held that the direct cause of Wen's death was the suspect's criminal act. The defendant bank did not commit any intentional tort. However, the bank failed to perform its duty to protect the customers' safety within a reasonable standard, because it failed to provide proper security facilities and mechanism to maintain order in transactions. Therefore, the bank was at fault and should bear supplemental liability.

Article 7

Rule When the law provides that one shall assume the tort liability for infringing others' civil rights or interests, regardless of fault, he shall be subject to such statutory provisions.

Explanation This article stipulates the principle of strict liability (literally translated, "no-fault liability"). "General Principles of Civil Law of the People's Republic of China" ("Civil Law") established the principle of strict liability. In Article 106, Clause 3 of the Civil Law, it stipulates: "Citizens and legal persons who breach a contract or fail to fulfill other obligations shall bear civil liability. Citizens and legal persons who through their fault encroach upon state or collective property or the property or person of other people shall bear civil liability. Civil liability shall still be borne even in the absence of fault, if the law so stipulates." Meanwhile, Article 123 of the Civil Law provides details regarding strict liability. The purposes of establishing the principle of strict liability is, on one hand, to impose strict responsibility on people who engage in high-risk operations and encourage them to take extreme care during their operations in order to minimize potential personal and property damage to third parties. On the other hand, strict liability's purpose is to allocate the risk of potential damages to parties who engage in high-risk operations and protect the victim's interests. Due to great contributions of the principle of strict liability on the allocation of responsibilities and the resolution of disputes, the Tort Law inherits the relevant stipulation from the Civil Law, to further clarify the meaning of strict liability within the Tort Law.

Example A high school arranged for its students to attend an army unit military camp. One of the activities for the students was shooting practice. On the day of the shooting practice, the plaintiff Wang and his family were visiting their ancestors' grave which was about 400 m away from the shooting range. A student's stray bullet hit and wounded Wang, leaving him with ninth degree disability. Wang sued the high school and army unit for damages, claiming the two defendants failed to take appropriate warning and protective measures for the students' shooting training. The court held that the army unit established the shooting range within its boundaries, put up warning signs within the range, and engaged in shooting practice that complied with military regulations. The army unit and the high school had no subjective intent to injure the plaintiff. However, Wang was in fact shot and wounded. According to the relevant law, the two defendants should be held liable under the strict liability doctrine. Since Wang was injured by students that were engaged in a school-arranged activity, the school should bear the direct (main) responsibility, while the army unit should bear supplemental liability.

Article 8

Rule Where two or more persons jointly commit a tort, resulting in damage to another, they shall be jointly and severally liable.

Explanation This article is about joint tort liability. The concept of joint tort liability has two versions: general and specific. General joint tort liabilities include joint intentional tort, joint reckless conduct, joint tort without conspiracy, etc. Specific joint tort liability only applies to joint intentional tort. This article focuses on specific joint tort liability. Article 130 of the Civil Law provides: "If two or more persons jointly infringe upon another person's rights and cause him damage, they shall bear joint liability." This Civil Law article is almost identical with the article we are discussing here, with some slight textual variation. Joint tort liability is a general tort liability; this tort liability also uses the principle of fault liability and has the same four elements: conduct that violates the law, damages, causation, and fault. The difference between joint tort liability and general tort liability is the requirement of two or more perpetrators under joint tort liability.

Example Jiang, a petrochemical company's employee, was responsible for selling the company's products to a transformer company. One day, Jiang received a bank draft from the transformer company. Jiang forged the petrochemical company's seal and used it to make the bank draft payable to any third party. Then he took the forged bank draft to Wu, an officer at a tool company, and explained to Wu that he needed money for his personal business. Jiang asked Wu to indorse the bank draft on the tool company's behalf and withdraw the money for him. Wu, a good friend of Jiang, did what his friend asked him to do. Jiang's conduct constituted embezzlement and fraud and was subsequently discovered and prosecuted. On the civil liability side, the court held that the tool company was liable for the petrochemical company's losses. The tool company accepted the bank draft and cashed it for Jiang when it had no transaction with the petrochemical company. The tool company should have been aware that its conduct was a violation of the Law of Negotiable Instruments and financial regulations. Although the tool company was unaware of the fact that Jiang forged the seal, it failed to take reasonable care to review the legality of Jiang's possession of the bank draft. The tool company's lack of reasonable care was in violation of the law and its duty of care to avoid infringement on others' legitimate interests. Thus, subjectively, the tool company was negligent due to their violation of the duty of care owed to the petrochemical company. Objectively, the tool company cashed the bank draft and handed the money to Jiang. The tool company's conduct played a supporting role to Jiang's fraud and embezzlement of the petrochemical company money, as such the tool company contributed to the petrochemical company's losses. Therefore, Jiang and the tool company should be jointly and severally liable for the petrochemical company's damages.

Article 9

Rule One shall be jointly and severally liable when abetting or assisting another person in committing a tort.

One who abets or assists a person who does not have civil capacity or only has limited civil capacity in committing a tort shall assume the tort liability; the guardian of such a person without civil capacity or with limited civil capacity shall assume the relevant liability due to failing to fulfill his guardian duties.

Explanation This article imposes joint and several liabilities on parties who incite or assist others to engage in tortious conducts. The inciting/assisting party is considered as a co-tortfeasor. Although objectively, the inciting/assisting party does not engage in tortious conduct, but merely has the intention to do so. It would be unfair to the incited or assisted tortfeasor to impose the liability solely on him. Thus, the Tort Law treats both the inciting/assisting party and the tortfeasor as co-tortfeasors. The Civil Law has no provisions regarding this type of tortious conduct. However, Section 148 of Opinions of the Supreme People's Court on Several Issues concerning the Implementation of the General Principles of the Civil Law of the People's Republic of China (For Trial Implementation) suggests, "a person who abets or helps others to engage in tortious conduct is a joint tortfeasor, and shall bear joint and several civil liability." Obviously, this article is a specification on the Opinions. The Tort Law should have priority over the Opinions.

Example Cheng, a 29-year-old, was unemployed. He found that during the night at a construction site in his residential district some copper wires were left unattended. He intended to steal those wires, but was not willing to do it himself. So he abetted two minors to steal the wires, which were worth more than 3,000 RMB. Cheng quickly squandered the money. After the matter was brought to light, Cheng was prosecuted. Regarding the civil compensation, the court held Cheng liable for abetting juveniles to infringe other's interests. Additionally, the court held that the two minors' parents were negligent and, as guardians of the children, should bear the corresponding supplemental liability.

Article 10

Rule Where two or more persons engage in conduct that endangers the safety or property of another and the specific tortfeasor cannot be determined, all of them shall be jointly and severally liable. If the specific tortfeasor, whose conduct caused the damage, can be determined, then the tortfeasor shall be liable.

Explanation This article is about joint risky conduct. Civil Law does not provide provisions on joint risky conduct. Article 4 of Interpretation of the Supreme People's Court of Some Issues concerning the Application of Law for the Trial of Cases on Compensation for Personal Injury suggests, "when two or more persons jointly engaged in conducts that endanger others' personal safety and caused damages, if the actual perpetrator cannot be identified, all the persons shall bear joint and several liability in accordance with Article 130 of the Civil Law. If any of the persons could prove the damages are not caused by themselves, he or she shall not be held liable." This article on Tort Law divides the cases where two or more people engaged in conducts that endanger other people's body or property into two types: (1) When the perpetrator(s) could be identified, the perpetrator(s) should bear the liability. (2) When the perpetrator(s) cannot be identified, all the persons who engage in the risky conduct should be held jointly and severally liable. Obviously, this article's stipulation on joint risk conduct is more reasonable.

Example When three elementary students Gu, Xie, and Zheng were swimming in a river, they suddenly found Zhou was washing his shoes across the river. Gu convinced the others to throw stones at Zhou. The three children then threw stones at Zhou, one of which hit Zhou's left eye. Zhou was hospitalized immediately and diagnosed with a rupture in the left eyeball. Zhou sued the three children for damages. The court found that the three defendants threw the stones at Zhou, as a result he suffered damages. The three defendants were held jointly and severally liable. Because none of the parties could prove who threw the actual stone that injured the plaintiff, none of the defendants should be excused from liability. Moreover, the three defendants had limited civil capacity; thus, the guardians of the three defendants should bear the obligation for compensation, jointly and severally.

Article 11

Rule Where two or more individuals commit torts resulting in the same damage, but each one's act is sufficient to cause the entire damage, the tortfeasors shall be held jointly and severally liable.

Explanation This article is about joint tort liability without conspiracy. Although the Civil Law does not give specific provisions regarding such conduct, Article 3 of Interpretation of the Supreme People's Court of Some Issues concerning the

Application of Law for the Trial of Cases on Compensation for Personal Injury suggests that two or more people who jointly caused harm to others, with or without joint intent or contributory negligence, shall bear joint and several liability in accordance with Civil Law Article 130. Under this judicial interpretation, joint tort liability without conspiracy is divided into two categories: (1) Two or more people, without joint intent or contributory negligence, whose infringement jointly and directly caused the same harm, should be held liable for a joint tort and shall bear joint and several liability in accordance with Civil Law Article 130. (2) Two or more people, without joint intent or contributory negligence, whose infringement jointly but indirectly caused the same harm, should be held liable separately in proportion to their faults or contributions to the damage. For the first type, the judicial interpretation identified it as a joint tort. The second type is not considered a joint tort. In applying laws, the Tort Law should have priority.

Example While the defendant Zhu was driving a bus he owned, he collided with a truck driven by Ding, an auto manufacturer's employee. The collision resulted in the death of the plaintiffs' daughters, passengers on Zhu's bus. Traffic police divided the liability equally between Zhu and Ding, while the deceased bore no liability. The two defendants, Zhu and the auto manufacturer, reached a compensation agreement, stipulating that each would pay 50 % of the plaintiffs' compensation. After the agreement was made, the auto manufacturer made full payment to the plaintiffs, but Zhu did not. Subsequently, the plaintiffs sued Zhu to collect the judgment payment from him and sued the auto manufacturer, stating it should be held liable for the unpaid compensation on the ground that the two defendants were jointly liable. The court held that the two drivers did not have joint subjective intentions; the perpetrators' conducts were independent from each other; thus, this was not a joint tort. If the two tortfeasors were held jointly and severally liable because an unpredictable condition resulted the two unrelated tortious conducts causing the same harm, the consequences would be too harsh and contrary to the basic rules of Tort Law. Therefore, the plaintiffs' claim to hold the auto manufacturer jointly liable had no legal basis and was rejected, but Zhu should make the compensation payment within a specified time.

Article 12

Rule Where two or more persons commit torts resulting in the same damage and the seriousness of each tortfeasor's liability can be determined, then the tortfeasors shall assume corresponding liabilities respectively. If the seriousness of each tortfeasor's liability is difficult to determine, the tortfeasors shall assume the compensatory liability evenly.

Explanation This Article is about non-joint tort by multiple perpetrators without conspiracy. This article differs from Article 11 in that each perpetrator's own conduct is insufficient to cause the whole damage even though all the perpetrator's tortious conducts caused the same damage. Therefore, any perpetrator's misconduct is a necessary condition for the damages. This article differs from Article 8 in that it is complimentary to the scope of joint tort liability prescribed by Article 8. Article 8 applies to situations where the tort is committed jointly by several perpetrators. This article, however, applies to situations where the tort is committed by perpetrators separately. In cases that have multiple tortfeasors, we should first attempt to apply Article 8. If Article 8 does not apply, then we should then turn to Article 11. And, if Article 11 also does not apply, we should see whether this article applies.

Example Li and Liu both held a grudge against Zhang. One day, due to the deep grudge, both Li and Liu planned to kill Zhang. Without any conspiracy, Li and Liu both planned to ambush Zhang on his way home from work and kill him with a dagger. Liu first saw Zhang in a remote alley, attacked Zhang with a dagger, and fled the scene. Li then saw Zhang with several wounds, Li then stabbed Zhang several times and Zhang eventually dies. Zhang's family, in a collateral civil action, sued Liu and Li for damages. The court held that Liu and Li committed the crime without any conspiracy, but the autopsy report was unable to determine who made the fatal stab. Therefore, the two defendants were held equally liable.

Article 13

Rule Where, in accordance with the law, the tortfeasors assume joint and several liability, the victim is entitled to require some or all of the tortfeasors to assume the liability.

Explanation This article is about the responsibility for joint and several liabilities. Joint and several liabilities are generally derived from joint torts or torts prescribed by special provisions, which are similar to property rights and debts. After one or more tortfeasors have compensated the victim, proportional liability may be allocated among the tortfeasors. This ensures the tort victims receive compensation, which is in line with the Tort Law's nature to make the victim whole. Specifically, the joint debt refers to the situation where there are multiple debtors; the debt could be satisfied by the payment made by any debtors. Similarly, the concept "joint credit" refers to the situation involving multiple creditors, when the debtors made full payments to any creditor, the debtor's obligation will be deemed satisfied. This article is about the joint debt. The significance of joint and several liability is that all the judgment debtors have obligations to satisfy the full amount of the judgment debt, which makes it easier to compensate the judgment creditor.

Example Yu purchased the latest iPhone 4. One day, Yu had some disagreements with two colleagues, one of which incited the other to secretly break Yu's new phone. Yu found out and sued the two colleagues for damages. The court held both defendants jointly and severally liable. When Yu sought to enforce the ¥5,000 judgment, one defendant was financially unable to satisfy this judgment. Yu promptly sought to enforce the judgment against the other colleague. In accordance with Article 13 of the Tort Law, the court enforced the judgment against the colleague who was financially capable to satisfy the full judgment.

Article 14

Rule The amount of compensation to be incurred by the jointly and severally liable tortfeasors shall be determined according to their respective liabilities. If the degree of their respective liabilities is difficult to determine, the liability for compensation shall be divided evenly.

A tortfeasor who paid an amount of compensation exceeding his contribution is entitled to be reimbursed by other tortfeasors who are jointly and severally liable.

Explanation This article is about the division of the joint and several liabilities among the tortfeasors. Two related issues are involved: the conditions of the division and the determination of joint and several liabilities. In joint debt, when one debtor made payments that are more than his share of the debt, the debtor has the right to claim against other debtors. Claims should meet the following conditions: first, the debtor has satisfied the debt; second, the debtor has reduced or completely eliminated other debtors' debts; and third, the debtor has paid more than his share in the joint debt. In a joint debt, the share of each debtor may or may not be clear. The court could decide the percentage among the debtors, especially regarding the debt associated with joint tort liability. Courts apply the principle of fault liability to determine the percentage of each tortfeasor's responsibility in joint and several liability claims. An essential element of the principle of fault liability is that tortfeasors' responsibility should be consistent with their degrees of fault, provided that their faults can be appropriately divided and apportioned to determine the scope of their tort liabilities. Assigning liability in accordance with the degree of fault attributable to jointly and severally liable tortfeasors is a sign of maturity of the principle of fault liability, which becomes more rigorous and reasonable. One thing should be noted, the ultimate purpose of the Tort Law is to make the tort victims whole again. Thus, if individual's responsibility cannot be determined among the tortfeasors, assigning liabilities equally is a more equitable remedy. The identification of joint and several liability is in accordance with the tortfeasors' fault. In most cases, the court should decide liability based on the degree of faults to reflect principles of fairness. There is another way to determine the size of responsibility in a joint tort: comparison of the cause and effects. The cause and effect measures the specific contribution of each cause resulting in damages. In determining the percentage of joint and several liabilities based on the cause and effect, the larger the role a cause plays, the larger percentage assigned to the tortfeasor who is attributed with that cause, and vice versa. When the cause and effect cannot be determined, the liability should be assigned among tortfeasors equally. However, this article should be resorted to only when the previous two articles cannot be applied.

Example Qian, who was intoxicated, gave Li a ride home. Qian was driving the car on a road under construction and collided with some construction materials. Both Qian and Li were injured, Qian survived but Li died on his way to the hospital. The accident investigation concluded that Qian was driving while intoxicated and speeding at the time of the accident. Additionally, it concluded that the construction company did not set up warning signs. The faults were divided as 60 % for Qian and 40 % for the construction company. The court held Qian and the construction company are jointly and severally liable. It also held that the total compensation for Li's family was one million RMB, of which Qian was responsible for ¥600,000 and the construction company for ¥400,000. Thereafter, the construction company made a one-time payment of 1 million RMB to Li's family, Qian did not pay. The construction company brought Qian to court and petitioned for payment of ¥600,000. The court ruled that Qian should pay the construction company ¥600,000 plus reasonable interests.

Article 15

Rule The main methods of compensation for tort liabilities include the following:

1. Cessation of infringement
2. Removal of obstruction
3. Elimination of danger
4. Return of property
5. Restoration to the original status
6. Compensation for losses
7. Formal apology
8. Elimination of adverse impacts and restoration of reputation

These methods of compensation may be adopted individually or in any combination.

Explanation This article prescribes remedies for tort liability claims. Some tort remedies are similar to the remedies for property and debt claims, such as restoration to the original state or cessation of the infringement. Other remedies are on mental levels, such as making an apology and restoring the injured party's reputation. People are legally entitled to remedies for mental damages when their rights such as right to dignity, identity, or property are violated. The specific legal remedies prescribed by the Tort Law are more flexible and more direct, in comparison to the Civil Law, and will also be improved in practice. The eight specific remedies prescribed by this article have different characteristics and can be applied individually or in any combination, depending on the case.

Example Zhang is a civil servant. At a friend's gathering, Zhang offended a local newspaper reporter, Sun, due to drunkenness. Sun held a grudge against Zhang ever since and was waiting for an opportunity to retaliate. One day, Sun finally had an opportunity to do so—he made up a story of Zhang and his fictitious mistress, printed this story on posters, and pasted the posters around Zhang's work place. Sun's conduct caused considerable harm to Zhang's reputation. Thereafter, Zhang sued Sun. The court held Sun to make an apology statement in the newspaper he worked at, take down the posters, and pay Zhang ¥3,000 as compensation for mental damages.

Article 16

Rule Where a tort causes any personal injury to another person, the tortfeasor shall compensate the victim for the reasonable costs and expenses for treatment and rehabilitation, such as medical expenses, nursing fees, travel expenses, as well as lost wages. If the victim suffers any disability, the tortfeasor shall also pay the costs of disability assistance equipment for the life of the victim and a disability indemnity. In the event that a tort causes the death of the victim, the tortfeasor shall pay the funeral service fees and death compensation.

Explanation This article articulates the scope of compensation with regard to different consequences caused by a personal injury. The Tort Law is not orientated to punish acts causing damage, nor to educate and stop people who commit wrongful acts, nor simply to compensate for the damage of victims. It is designed to balance competing social interests and eventually guarantee balanced development of different social interests without sacrificing other social interests. The relationship between the parties' interest and the social interests should be taken into consideration to achieve balance between social and individual interests. Duty and its breach is the key of fault liability in modern Tort Law. How shall the defendant assume liability and what liability shall be assumed? Basic rules for application are specifically provided in provisions of the Tort Law. The form of expenses that liability can give rise to is relatively specific, such as medical expenses, nursing expenses, transportation expenses, disability compensation, and so on. The expenses mentioned above shall be definite and within specific standards and references. It is provided in the previous Interpretation of the Supreme People's Court of Some Issues concerning the Application of Law for the Trial of Cases on Compensation for Personal Injury that compensation for bodily injury and death is based on the standard of per capita disposable income of urban residents or per capita net income of rural residents. The rationality for the standard of compensation should be constantly improved in practice. Yet this article draws a bright line on items that shall be compensated, which contributes to concrete implementation.

Example Feng was hit and injured by a Benz while walking. Feng was taken to the hospital where he died. Feng's wife Li just delivered a daughter 1 month ago and Feng's parents were getting old, ill, and unattended. The four plaintiffs sued the driver and prayed for funeral expenses, compensation for death, family members' property loss caused by dealing with the accident, and the daughter and parents' living expenses. The court ruled that the driver shall pay compensation for relevant costs totaling ¥800,000.

Article 17

Rule Where the same tort causes the deaths of multiple people, an equal amount of death compensation may be determined.

Explanation There are prerequisites for the application of this article. Firstly, it must be a major security or traffic accident. Secondly, more than one person dies as a result of the tort. Disputes would be difficult to settle if the amount of compensation for death is determined on the decedents' age, income, or other attributes. Nowadays, major traffic accidents, mining accidents, and major labor safety accidents occur frequently. The number of victims is increasing and usually becomes a group or class. A universal compensation standard reflects the principle of justice and promotes the efficiency of problem resolution. It is inconsistent with respect for the value of life and after reform and opening up China's practice to apply different compensation standards to different people. Money can be calculated but life and health are priceless. Maybe a farmer earns less than a businessman, but their lives shall be given the same respect. Lives are of same value, which is a principle in accordance with the trend.

Example A university is located in a downtown area with chaotic traffic. One day, three students went out for food and while in the street crossing were hit by a driver. The driver fled in fear. The three students died at the scene of the accident. The driver was convicted of causing traffic casualties, a crime in China. In the resulting civil action, the driver argued that two of the victims were from rural areas; damages should be less accordingly. The court held that lives are of same value and the students who lost their lives in the same accident should not be treated differently because they were from different places. Consequently, the court ruled that compensation of ¥600,000 shall be paid to each of their next of kin in accordance with the Tort Law.

Article 18

Rule When a tort results in the victim's death, the victim's relative is entitled to hold the tortfeasor accountable. When the victim of a tort is an entity and the entity splits or merges, the entity succeeding to the rights of the victim is entitled to hold the tortfeasor accountable.

When a tort results in the victim's death, those who have paid the medical expenses, funeral fees, and other reasonable expenses for the victim are entitled to compensation from the tortfeasor, unless the tortfeasor already paid such costs and expenses.

Explanation This article articulates who can step into the shoes of the victim, if the victim dies. This article classifies who has the right to make claims into two categories. One is that the infringed party is a person; if the person dies, his/her close relatives shall have the right to claim for compensation. The other is that the infringed party is an entity; when the entity has been merged or divided, the successor entity, as a consequence of merger or separation, has the right to claim for compensation. The third party who loses living expenses because of the death of the direct victim as a supporter thereof has the right of claim for compensation for the loss. In principle, the compensability of the loss is accepted by all the law systems today. The compensation for the loss of living expenses of a dependent is a compensatory system of the Tort Law. The basis of this principle is that the infringer unlawfully deprived the victim's right to life or infringed the victim's right to health, which resulted in the loss of earning potential. This loss of earning potential causes the dependent's premature loss of living resources, in which case the infringer shall compensate the dependent for support according to the law.

Example One day Fei was hit by a falling brick while passing by a construction site and was immediately sent to the hospital for medical treatment by a Good Samaritan, Su. Su advanced the medical fees of ¥3,000 for Fei, but Fei was severely injured and died. Su later asked the developer of the site to reimburse the medical fees paid, but the developer refused asserting that Su was not a relative of the decedent. Su was angry and then sued the developer. The court ruled that the developer shall pay Su the medical fees and additional interest at the bank rate over the same period.

Article 19

Rule Where a tort causes any loss to the property of another person, the amount of loss to the property shall be calculated based on the market price at the time of occurrence of the loss.

Explanation This article deals with the calculation of lost value when the infringed party suffers property damage in the case of property infringement. Determining the damage is the key to resolving the case. After determining the damage, determining how to compensate the victim, how much compensation is required, and how to calculate property loss are necessary. In a competitive market, price is jointly determined by supply and demand. To protect the utmost interest of the victim, the compensation should be paid according to the market price when the loss occurred.

Example Liquid waste discharged by A company polluted Lu's fishpond and caused the death of a large number of chubs. At that time, A company agreed that Lu should sell chubs that died from the pollution at a lower price and A company would make up the difference between the lower sale price and the market price. Lu then sold 600 catty chubs for ¥2 per catty while the market price then was ¥2.6–2.7 per catty. Afterwards, A company refused to pay. Lu sued the company and claimed compensation for price difference and replacement of polluted water. The court confirmed the facts alleged by the plaintiff and held that there was causation between the defendant's act and the death of the fish and shrimps. Thus, the defendant bears the consequence that was the death of the fish and shrimps in the plaintiff's pond. The market retail price of chubs was 2.6–2.7 per catty; thus, the proper price difference should be ¥0.65. As for replacement of polluted water, it was nearly 1 year from the pollution to the time of the suit and the condition of pond could not be identified so the court did not support this claim. The court ruled that the defendant compensate the plaintiff in the sum of ¥390, but overruled plaintiff's other claims.

Article 20

Rule Where infringement of personal rights and interests results in property loss, the compensation shall be made according to the loss suffered by the victim as the result of the tort. If the loss suffered by the victim is difficult to determine and the tortfeasor gains any benefit from the tort, the tortfeasor shall compensate the victim according to the benefit gained by the tort. If the benefit gained by the tortfeasor from the tort is difficult to determine, the victim and the tortfeasor disagree to the amount of compensation after consultation, and an action is brought to a people's court, the people's court shall determine the amount of compensation based on the situation.

Explanation This article is a regulation of how to determine the compensation where property loss is incurred by infringement of personal rights and interests. Where infringement of personal rights and interests caused property loss, the infringing party shall first of all pay compensation according to the loss incurred therefrom which require the victim to prove not only the fact that his rights and interest were infringed but also the amount of property loss caused by the infringement of the rights and interests thereof. In many circumstances, the victim usually cannot prove the amount of property loss; if the amount of loss is difficult to determine and the infringing party gains interest therefrom, the infringing party shall pay compensation according to the benefits gained; in the case where the benefit gained by the infringing party is difficult to determine, the people's court shall determine the amount of compensation payable according to the circumstances. This article establishes three occasions that progress in depth.

Example Han and Luo are high school classmates. Luo failed the preliminary exam of the technical secondary school and did not qualify to be consigned to schools.

Han passed the exams and got admitted to a commercial school. But the school did not notify Han of his universal exam results and the passing mark to be consigned. With the help of his father, Luo attended the commercial school under Han's name. Luo did not carry the admission card for entrance examination when enrolling. His student files at the commercial school was still the candidate materials formed in the high school entrance exam, which included two physical examination forms with Han's pictures, semester remarks, Han's papers in the universal exam, and other relevant materials. Han did not receive the admission information and went back to school during this period and later entered a technical labor school and eventually was allocated to a factory job. In addition, Han was unemployed for more than 1 year. When Han learned that Luo falsely used his name to attend the school, he instantly sued Luo, Luo's father, the commercial school, the middle school, and the city's Education Commission for infringing his right to name, his right to education, and other relevant rights and sought compensation for property loss and mental damage. The court held that Luo's father and others took unlawful measures to have Luo attend the school in the name of Han, in which Luo, Luo's father, the middle school, and the Education Commission all are at fault. This infringement of the right to name essentially infringed Han's right to education as a citizen based on the constitution. Due to Luo's infringement of Han's right to name and right to education, Han went back to school, paid for city population increment to become an urban resident in order to receive higher education, and paid lawyer's fee for the suit. All the fees are direct property loss caused by infringement of the right to education thus shall be compensated. The tuition fees paid to the laboring technical school by Han was normal expenditure for education but still property loss caused by infringement. Luo's vested interest during the infringement, namely, the earnings drawn in the name of Han except for essential living expenses, shall be ruled to be owned by Han to punish the unlawful act. The severe mental damage was caused by the defendant's infringement of Han's right to name and right to education so the defendants shall pay compensation to Han for mental damage according to the highest compensation standard for mental damage provided by the higher people's court of the province.

Article 21

Rule Where a tort endangers the personal or property safety of others, the victim of the tort may require the tortfeasor to assume the tort liabilities, including but not limited to, cession of infringement, removal of obstruction, and elimination of danger.

Explanation This provision articulates types of tortious liability that the injured party may request when a tortious act injures another person physically or damages her property. This article is somewhat similar to Article 15 of the Tort Law; both provide means of assuming tortious liability, but differ in range. We may say in the

Tort Law the scope of Article 21 is narrower than that of Article 15, for Article 21 barely provides types of tortious liability that the injured party may request where a person is injured or her property is damaged, while Article 15 covers additional situations of tortious liability such as the case of loss compensation. Compared with other tortious liability, ceasing infringement, removing relevant obstacles, and eliminating danger are rather special. This article helps to play the preventive function of Tort Law, meaning preventing infringement from occurring. The key point of Tort Law lies in preventing possible infringing parties from conducting such acts which are unexpected by the society. This prevention belongs to the type of preliminary prevention. This article applies ceasing infringement, removing relevant obstacles, and eliminating danger to all the tortious acts. It not only helps to protect the lawful interests of civil subjects but also performs its preventive function of Tort Law.

Example Qiu and Wei are neighbors. Qiu's house adjoins the wall which Wei wants to remodel. Wei needs to pull down his wall to rebuild a new one. But as the construction progresses, Qiu's house suffers foundation settlement damage and a large crack in the main structure. Unable to reach an agreement, Qiu sues Wei, requesting him to cease the remodel and compensate for the loss of ¥2,000. After hearing the case, the court thought that Wei's remodel was the direct reason for the damages to Qiu's house, and if the construction continued, more damages would occur, and the house could possibly collapse. So the court held that Wei cease the construction and compensate Qiu ¥2,000 to strengthen and repair the damaged part.

Article 22

Rule Where any harm caused by a tort to a personal right or interest inflicts a serious mental distress on the victim, the victim may seek compensation for the infliction of mental distress.

Explanation This article provides compensation liability for mental distress in tort liability. The Tort Law defines the amount and calculating method of mental distress compensation. Provision about compensation liability for mental distress in the Tort Law defines the character of such liability as tortious liability. This is the first time China's current law defines mental distress compensation. Mental distress means harm to spiritual activities of civil subjects. The laws and explanations of China about applicable scope of mental distress compensation mainly lie in the Civil Law enacted in 1986. The Article 120 of this general rule articulates that if a citizen's right of personal name, portrait, reputation or honor is infringed upon, he shall have the right to demand that the infringement be stopped, his reputation be rehabilitated, the ill effects be eliminated, and an apology be made; he may also demand compensation for losses. Obviously, it is inappropriate for the Civil Law to regard only part of personal rights as under the scope of mental distress compensation. While in the Tort Law, to take all the personal rights into the scope of mental distress compensation reflects the progress of law in China. Furthermore, this article does not limit the application of mental distress compensation merely to fault liability of tortious act. That is to say, whether it is the application of fault liability, presumptive fault liability, or no-fault liability, as long as a person's personal rights are damaged and serious mental distress is caused, liability for mental distress compensation arises.

Example For a long time, Jin has held a grudge against Yang. On several occasions, Yang has accused Jin of misconducts at work. One day, the two quarreled with each other because of some disagreement. Jin cursed at Yang with evil words. Jin revealed Yang's adultery with a married woman and her abortions. Meanwhile, Jin scratched Yang's face, which led to a permanent scar. Afterwards, Yang suffered great mental pressure, fell ill for a long time, and could not go to work or live a normal life. Therefore, Yang sued Jin and request compensation for medical expenses, mental distress, and loss of work of ¥100,000 in total. After finding out the facts, the court thought that Jin's assaults led to serious damages to Yang's mental status and reputation, so the defendant shall bear tortious liability and compensate for the loss of property and mental distress of ¥80,000.

Article 23

Rule When one suffers any damage as the result of preventing or stopping the infringement upon the civil right or interest of another person, the tortfeasor shall be liable for the damage. If the tortfeasor flees or is unable to assume the liability, and the victim of the tort seeks compensation, the beneficiary shall properly make compensation.

Explanation This provision articulates the principle that the beneficiary shall compensate the injured party appropriately. The Article 23 of the Tort Law defines that when a party suffers an injury while seeking to prevent or stop another party's civil rights and interest from being injured, if the infringing party avoids liability or lacks capacity to bear liability and the injured party claims compensation, the beneficiary "shall" pay appropriate compensation. This differs from Article 109 of the Civil Law and Article 142 of Opinions of the Supreme People's Court on Several Issues concerning the Implementation of the General Principles of the Civil Law of the People's Republic of China (For Trial Implementation), which suggest that the beneficiary "may" pay appropriate compensation to the injured party. Obviously, the Tort Law is intended to encourage people to promote social morality through caring for each other, helping each other in the name of justice, and deterring the offenders in the whole society. However, the compensation for the injured party does not contain compensation for mental distress. If the helper dies, his relatives are likely to suffer mental distress. But such mental damage is not caused by the beneficiary's act. As a result, it is impossible for the beneficiary to assume supplemental liability for the mental distress; in a situation where the infringer is in hand, it is less likely for the beneficiary to assume supplementary liability for the personal liability which should be assumed by the infringer. So, under the scope of the principle of "beneficiary compensating," the beneficiary will not and should not assume the liability for mental distress. What the beneficiary bears is not the compensation liability for the Good Samaritan, so it is impossible for the beneficiary to undertake all the damages according to the "all compensation principle." In addition, the range of compensation cannot be determined completely by the range of damage. In most cases, compensation is aimed at loss which the Good Samaritan suffers. To surmise, whether the compensation is appropriate should be determined by the extent of beneficiary's interests which the Good Samaritan protected, the economic status of the beneficiary, and the degree of damage that the Good Samaritan suffered, among other factors.

Example Xue is a university student. One day, he passed by an isolated section of road and saw an outlaw was trying to rape a woman. Xue dashed ahead regardless of his safety to stop the outlaw. Seeing Xue coming forwards, the outlaw immediately took out a fruit knife and stabbed Xue three times. Xue's lung was injured and the medical expenses cost more than ¥30,000. Although the suspect has been brought to justice, he cannot afford the medical fees because of his family's poor financial status. So, Xue asked the rescued female to compensate his loss appropriately. They failed to reach an agreement, so Xue filed a lawsuit against the woman. The court held that the rescued woman shall compensate Xue's loss appropriately. But considering the financial status of the rescued woman is not well, the court decided the rescued woman shall compensate Xue's medical fees ¥10,000.

Article 24

Rule Where neither the victim nor the actor is at fault for the occurrence of damages, the loss may be borne by both parties based on the actual situations.

Explanation This provision articulates the concept of fair loss sharing. Fair liability was regarded as one of the criterions of liability before the concept of fair loss sharing was proposed. Fair liability is the practice of fair principle in the field of civil liability. Fair liability should not be considered as a criterion of liability. The Article 132 of the Civil Law provides as follows: "If none of the parties is at fault in causing damage, they may share civil liability according to the actual circumstances." This provision is the principle set from the fair position, with both party's detailed situation taken into consideration and should be applied after the compensation liability has been decided. Fair liability itself does not have the function to determine the imputation of liability. The Tort Law uses the direct statement "bear the loss" to replace the statement "bear the civil liability" in the Civil Law. This change also reflects this viewpoint. When considering the extent of loss to determine how to fairly share the loss, attention should be paid to several aspects. First, the extent of loss should be first combined with the affordability and then considered. Second, the extent of damage to the helper should be considered in combination with the situation of benefits that the beneficiary gained. Third, the extent of damage should be considered in combination with the situation of the injured party. It is notable that what the law provides is how to fairly share the loss, not how to equally share the loss. The court should think over the parties' characters, financial status, extent of damage, and the future influence on the victim's life and then decide who will undertake part or most of the compensation liability.

Example Yan and Li played badminton together. Li hit the ball back and the ball injured Yan's eyes and caused Yan 9th degree disability. Medical expenses cost Yan about ¥30,000. Yan sued Li, requesting Li to compensate his medical expenses and mental distress. The court thought that the plaintiff and the defendant both have certain knowledge of the possible dangers in the motion process and consent to such risks by participating in the game. Subjectively, the defendant did not have any intention or negligence of injuring the plaintiff. What is more, no action violates the sports rules. There is a lack of tortious liability elements. So it is completely a coincidence. But it will be obviously unfair for the plaintiff himself to undertake the total consequence of damage, for there is causation between the defendant's behavior and the plaintiff's injury. So the court held that the plaintiff himself bear 60 % of the liability, with the other 40 % undertaken by the defendant. As to the compensation for mental distress, the defendant has no fault in this case; therefore, the claim is not supported.

Article 25

Rule Upon the occurrence of any damage, the parties may consult each other about the methods to pay for compensations. If the consultation fails, the compensations shall be paid in a lump sum. If it is genuinely hard to make the payment in a lump sum, the payment may be made in installments, provided that a corresponding security is given.

Explanation This provision articulated the method for paying compensation for tortious liability, focusing on whether a lump sum or installment payment is more appropriate. The Civil Law does not require corresponding guarantee for installment. While in practice, many cases cannot be enforced due to the lack of requirement. So, the Tort Law articulates as follows: "the payment may be made in installments, provided that a corresponding security is given." Such articulation is in favor of the creditor's safety and on time compensation, which will protect the interests of creditor for the better. The so-called guarantee may be both property guarantee (such as mortgage and pledge) and personal guarantee. Additional methods which have the function of a guarantee may also be accepted. For example, escrow of a bank or bank paying for the compensation is also used frequently.

Example Corporation A infringed trademark rights of corporation B. Upon mediation, corporation A agreed to compensate corporation B the loss totaling ¥100,000. But no agreement on the method for paying the compensation was made. Corporation A's working capital is insufficient, so it proposed for corporation B to use corporation A's production equipment at a discount, while corporation B insisted on cash payment. At last, under mediations by the court, corporation A agreed to pay the compensation within 10 months in ten ¥10,000 monthly installments and meanwhile pledge its workshop to corporation B.

Chapter 15
Circumstances to Waive Liability and Mitigate Liability

Article 26

Rule If the victim's fault also contributes to the occurrence of damage, the liability of the tortfeasor may be mitigated.

Explanation This article is the provision about fault offsetting. The victim's fault, also known as "fault of their own," is when the victim fails to exercise the proper due care of their property or personal safety, and the victim is at fault, deliberately or negligently, in the injury or damage. In terms of the victim's fault, the victim should have been able to foresee and take measures to avoid the occurrence of damage, but because of the negligence or other reasons, the victim did not foresee and take appropriate measures, so as to facilitate the damage. Therefore, the victim shall bear the liability for their own fault. The fault of victim has basically two forms: first, the victim's fault on the occurrence of damage, which means that the victim is at fault in the initial occurrence of damage, and, second, the victim's fault on the additional injury or damage, which means that the victim is at fault in the additional damage caused by the infringer. This article articulates that, where the victim is at fault, the liability of only the infringing party "may be mitigated," rather than be exempted completely. As for determining how much and whether to mitigate, the court still needs to estimate according to specific circumstances.

Example Gao went to a wild animal zoo. He found a big hole in the Tiger Hill safeguard and went into the Hill ignoring the "KEEP DISTANCE" warning sign. As a result, he was injured by a tiger and died. Gao's parents sued the zoo for entire liability, totaling ¥500,000. The court found that though the zoo failed to fulfill its security duty, Gao, as an adult who should know that the Tiger Hill is dangerous, disregarded caution and commonsense, so he also had liability for his death. As a result, the court held that the zoo should compensate Gao's parents the total losses of ¥300,000.

X. Li and J. Jin, *Concise Chinese Tort Laws*, China-EU Law Series 1,
DOI 10.1007/978-3-642-41024-6_15,

Article 27

Rule If the damage is caused intentionally by the victim, the actor is not liable.

Explanation This article is the provision that exempts an actor where the injury or damage is intentionally caused by the injured party. The accused shall be exempted, where the entire damage is intentionally caused by the victim, or where the victim's intentional conduct is the only reason for the damage. If there is evidence to prove that the damage is caused by the victim and evidence to prove the actor deliberately or negligently incurred the damage, then Article 26 in this chapter shall apply. The victim's intentional fault is one of the exemptions of the accused; it implies the circumstance that the damage is caused by the victim's own intentional fault and the accused themselves have no intentional act or negligence. Where the fault or damage of the accused is to a large extent, though the victim is at fault deliberately, it cannot be completely exempted.

Example Xu was driving his Mercedes to visit his customers. On the way he encountered Pan, who planned to commit suicide. Pan not only wanted to die but also hoped to get some compensation payments for his family, so he rushed into the closed highway. When Pan saw Xu, he ran to hit Xu's car directly and Xu's reaction was too late to avoid the collision. As a result, Pan was killed on spot. Later, Pan's family sued Xu for tortious liability. However, the video from the traffic police showed that Pan was obviously bent to die by hitting Xu in violation of the traffic rules and Xu was not at fault deliberately or negligently. Therefore, claims of Pan's family were dismissed.

Article 28

Rule If the damage is caused by a third party, the third party shall assume the tort liability.

Explanation This article is a provision about the injury or damage caused by a third party. In addition of the plaintiff and defendant, the third party in this situation causes the occurrence or addition of damage, so the third party bears some tortious liability. That is to say, after the tortfeasor engaged in tortious conduct, a third party's conduct breaks the causal relationship between the tortfeasor and the victim, which excuses the tortfeasor.

Example Nie renovated his house and he hired Ge to assist. Li, Nie's neighbor, also helped with the renovation. During the renovation, Li accidentally hit Ge's head with a brick. Ge's injury cost him ¥2,000 in medical expenses. Ge sued Nie for compensation. Nie applied to list Li as a third party and asserted that Ge's loss was caused by Li, so Li should bear the loss. The court agreed with Nie's argument and found that while Ge was Nie's employee, his loss was directly caused by Li, a third party; therefore, Li should bear the liability.

Article 29

Rule If any damage to another person is caused as a result of force majeure, no liability shall be assumed. Where the law provides otherwise, such provisions shall prevail.

Explanation This article articulates force majeure. Force majeure can fully eliminate general tort liability, except in absolute and fairness liabilities situations. Force majeure must be the only reason for the damage for the defendant to claim full exemption. That is to say, no causal relationship between the defendant and the damage exists and the damage is caused entirely by force majeure; thus, the defendant is not at fault and should be exempted. Where force majeure is part of the reason for the damage and the defendant is also at fault, i.e., in the circumstance that force majeure and the defendant's fault jointly caused the damage, claiming force majeure can only mitigate the defendant's liability.

Example Shi is a college student. One day, when he passed a crossroad, there is a sudden earthquake, the earthquake caused the billboard of an advertising company to fall and hurt Shi, resulting in ninth degree disabilities. Later, Shi sued the advertising company for tortious liability. The court found the advertising company's billboard met safety requirements and regarded the earthquake as force majeure, which could not be foreseen and prevented. The advertising company was not at fault and should not bear the liability.

Article 30

Rule Anyone who harms another in self-defense shall not be subject to tort liability. If the self-defense is disproportionate in force, causing any undue harm, the person exercising self-defense shall assume appropriate liability.

Explanation This article articulates reasonable self-defense and excessive self-defense. In fact, the Tort Law follows the criminal law approach on reasonable self-defense, and the principles are basically the same. In the Tort Law, where action taken in self-defense is disproportionate to the threat, such disproportionate action will give rise to liability for any unnecessary damage. The liability and compensation could be calculated in two ways: (1) compensation consistent with the consequences of the damage caused by excessive defense, but not all of the damage, and (2) according to the specific circumstances of each case, parties' mental state, legitimacy of the action, and other elements when the defendant is taking precautions should be considered; the defendant will not be asked to bear full responsibilities.

Example Kong is a vagrant. One day, he came to Xi's watermelon booth and after drinking caused a disturbance. He asked Xi for a watermelon as round as the Earth and that weighs exactly 22 lb. Xi begged on his knees, but Kong still thought Xi was being disrespectful, so he threatened to teach Xi a lesson. Xi, fearful of Kong, tried to help him find a watermelon, but none satisfied the specifications. Irritated, Kong took out a knife to stab Xi. Xi picked up a knife to block the attack but somehow injured Kong's eyes. Kong paid more than ¥10,000 for medical expense. Then Kong sued Xi. The court found that Xi's conduct was reasonable self-defense, whereas Kong's attack with knife threatened Xi' life and safety. Xi's self-defense was not excessive in force; therefore, Kong's civil claims were dismissed.

Article 31

Rule Where damage is caused by necessity, the person giving rise to the danger will be liable. If a natural phenomenon causes the danger, the person causing the damage out of necessity shall not be liable nor shall make appropriate compensation. If improper measures out of necessity are taken or a minimum threshold is exceeded, causing any undue damage, the person causing the damage out of necessity shall assume appropriate liability.

Explanation This article is related to identification of avoiding danger. In the Tort Law, avoiding danger also follows the criminal law approach on relative theory. Here, what needs to be explained is the question of "appropriate compensation." If there is no fault from the third party, or from the person who tried to avoid the danger, and the victim and the beneficiary are not the same person, then the beneficiary shall pay a reasonable amount of compensation to the victim. The reasoning for this principle is that the preservation of interest or reduction of loss of the beneficiary was realized by the sacrifice of the victim's interest. This provision represents the demand of fairness, which is the pursuit of the civil law.

Example Plaintiff A is an eel farming company. Defendant B is a hydroelectricity station, which is the administrator of reservoir B, and makes use of reservoir B by generating electricity. The plaintiff's farm is located in the northeastern side of the entrance of defendant's office space, about 100 m from the reservoir B's floodway. During a typhoon heavy rainfalls resulted in the water level rising. Because the defendant opened three sluices directly without informing anyone downstream, together with excessive, fast floodwater, the water escaped from the floodway to the defendant's office space. The water washed away eels worth ¥300,000 from the plaintiff's farm. In addition, before the typhoon, the defendant increased the height by 1 m of a substation's small dam in the floodway, which slowed the speed of the water's flow. The plaintiff claimed that the defendant underestimated the hazards caused by the typhoon and flood: the defendant did not discharge the flood in advance of the typhoon to store up the largest hydropower generating capacity. The defendant failed to fulfill his duty to inform and opened three sluices to discharge the floodwaters, while the dam slowed down the discharging speed causing the water to spill over the floodway and submerge the plaintiff's eel pond. As a result, the plaintiff suffered heavy losses and the defendant should bear the fault liability. The plaintiff sued the defendant for his loss of eels and interests. The court found that the typhoon and the rainfall resulted in the reservoir's water level rising, which is managed by the hydroelectricity station. It is true that there were some factors of a natural disaster. However, the hydroelectricity station had not discharged the floodwaters in advance and did not open one of the sluices to discharge the flood until the water level was about 1 m over the warning line. When the water level went over the warning line for 2 m, the defendant opened three sluices to discharge the flood without properly informing those downstream. Because of the excessive, fast floodwater, together with the 1 m increase in height of a substation's dam, the rising water level, and the slow discharging speed, the flood rushed into the eel company's farm. As a result, the farming company suffered heavy losses. The hydroelectricity station was at fault and bears the appropriate civil liability. However, the farming company's claim that the defendant should bear all the fault liability could not be sustained. There were natural factors in this case, so relative laws and judicial interpretations apply, and the court judged the defendants liability at 70 %.

Chapter 16
Special Provisions on Tortfeasors

Article 32

Rule If a person with limited or no civil capacity causes any damage to other persons, the guardian shall assume the tort liability. If the guardian has fulfilled his duty of care, his tort liability may be mitigated.

If a person, who owns property, with limited or no civil conduct capacity, causes any damage to another, the compensations shall be paid out of his property. The guardian shall make up any shortfall in compensations.

Explanation The first part of Article 32, Clause 1, articulates one's guardianship duty to a person with limited or no civil capacity. And the second part of Article 32, Clause 1, articulates the restriction of the guardians' duty. To constitute liability for the guardian, four conditions should be met: (1) the actor must be a person with limited or no civil capacity, (2) the actor must commit the tortious act, (3) the behavior conducted by the person with limited or no civil capacity must have caused damage or injury, and (4) the subject who bears liability must be the guardian of a person with limited or no civil capacity. What the guardian shall bear is not her own tort liability, but a vicarious liability. So, when certain conditions are met, the guardian's liability may be mitigated. Restrictions of a guardian's vicarious liability include two aspects. First, the guardian is not at fault. A person under guardianship has certain freedom of action. If the guardian fulfills her guardianship duty but still bear full liability, it will cause unfairness to her. Therefore, as long as the guardian fulfills her guardian duty, the tort liability she bears for the person under guardianship may be mitigated. Second, compensation can be paid from the person under guardianship's property. If the person under guardianship has his own property, the damages shall be paid out of his own property first. The shortfall, if any, will be paid by his guardian. The second clause of this article disaccords with what is provided in the civil law. Article 133, Clause 2, of the civil law articulates that if the property of a person under guardianship is insufficient to pay for damages, the guardian, who is not an institution, shall pay the shortfall. However, Article 32, Clause 2, of the Tort Law deleted the phrase "who is

X. Li and J. Jin, *Concise Chinese Tort Laws*, China-EU Law Series 1,
DOI 10.1007/978-3-642-41024-6_16, © Springer-Verlag Berlin Heidelberg 2014

not an institution" on theory that when, as a guardian, an institution has equal legal status with a natural person, they shall bear tort liability for the shortfall.

Example Cui and Dai are both in first grade. On their way home from school, they played the toy pistol which Cui's parents bought for him. Unexpectedly, Cui aimed the pistol at Dai's eyes and pulled the trigger, which shot a toy projectile. As a result, Dai's eyes were damaged and his eyesight was severely impaired. The medical expenses totaled ¥8,000. As legal agents, Dai's parents sue Cui, requesting him to bear the liability for Dai's injuries. The court held that the negligence of Cui's parents led to Cui's tortious act, and, as a result, they should bear the tort liability. Moreover, through investigation, we knew that Cui possesses personal property of ¥30,000, bequeathed from his grandfather. So the court finally decided that Cui shall pay Dai's medical expenses with his inheritance, while the shortfall, if any, be paid by his parents.

Article 33

Rule Where a person with full civil capacity causes damage, as the result of temporary loss of consciousness or control, to another, if he is at fault, he shall assume the tort liability; or if he is not at fault, the victim shall be appropriately compensated according to the actor's economic status.

Where a person with full civil capacity causes damage, as the result of temporary loss of consciousness or control due to alcohol intoxication or abuse of narcotic or psychoactive drug, to another, he shall assume the tort liability.

Explanation Article 33, Clause 1, articulates the tort liability of a person with full civil capacity during a temporary loss of consciousness. To constitute tort liability of a person with full civil capacity under a temporary episode of unawareness, three conditions should be met: (1) the actor must be a person with full civil capacity, (2) the tortious act conducted by the actor must be during a temporary loss of consciousness, and (3) the tortious act conducted by the actor during a temporary loss of consciousness must have caused injury or damage. According to the provision of Article 33, Clause 1, even if the tort happened during a temporary loss of consciousness, the actor still bears liability. But the liability should be categorized as one of two kinds. The first category the actor is at fault. On account of the fact that the actor is at a temporary loss of consciousness, it is difficult to judge whether he is at fault. As a result, when judging whether the actor is at fault, it means to judge whether he is at fault with the cause of action, in other words, whether the actor is at fault with cause of the temporary loss of consciousness. The second category the actor is not at fault, which means the actor is not at fault on temporarily losing consciousness. If the temporary loss of consciousness is caused by some other reasons instead of the actor himself, the actor may not bear the full tort liability. But based on the fairness doctrine, the actor shall pay appropriate compensation in light of his financial status. This is equitable liability, and what the actor shall bear is the equitable liability. The second clause of this article addresses an actor with full civil capacity causing injury or damage to another during a temporary loss of consciousness or control due to inebriation or abuse of a narcotic or psychotropic drug. Such situation is a variation on the first clause where the actor is at fault. But a temporary loss of consciousness or control due to inebriation or abuse of a narcotic or psychotropic drug has certain illegality, so the circumstance is treated more severely and the liability for the injury or damage caused is greater. As a result, such situation is listed separately to stress its tort liability.

Example Xia is a somnambulist who regularly sleepwalks once a month. Generally, he sleepwalks in his own yard for several rounds and sometimes cuts wood or draws water. However, he himself does not know it at all. One day at midnight, Xia's friend Deng quarreled with his wife and came to Xia's house, intending to spend the night there. Unexpectedly, the moment Xia heard the knock and opened the door, he was in state of sleepwalking. Unconsciously, Xia picked up a brick and hit Deng's head, causing a concussion and Deng's eye to bleed; these injuries led to medical expenses in excess of ¥5,000. Deng sued Xia requesting him to bear the tort liability for the injuries. The court held that Xia was unconscious at that time and thus without fault. But considering the financial status of both sides, the court decided that Xia should compensate Deng ¥1,000.

Article 34

Rule If an employee causes damage to another person while acting within the scope of his employment, the employer is vicariously liable and shall assume the tort liability.

If, during the period of labor services dispatch, a dispatched employee causes damage to another while acting within the scope of his employment, the employer accepting the dispatched employee shall assume the tort liability; and the employer dispatching the employee, if at fault, shall assume the corresponding supplementary liability.

Explanation Clause 1 of this article is a general provision about the employer's liability. To constitute the employer's tort liability, three conditions must be met: (1) the actor must be a worker of an employer, (2) the act conducted by the actor is within the scope of his employment, and (3) the act of the worker must constitute a tort. The party liable for injury or damage done by a worker is the employer. What the employer bears is liability without fault. Clause 2 of this article articulates the employer's liability under special circumstances. The difference between the two clauses lies in who the liable party is. Although Clause 2 insists that the employer shall bear liability, it still allocates the liability between two different types of employers, based on the fact that the employer who accepted the labor dispatch supervises the workers directly. Thus, the employer who accepted the labor dispatch bears tort liability. Meanwhile, the dispatching agency manages the workers indirectly. So if the dispatching agency is at fault, it also bears the corresponding supplementary liability.

Example Fu is a worker at a chemical factory. One day after work, Fu went to a restaurant with some friends. While drinking, Fu injured a waitress Lu due to a trifle, which costs Lu more than ¥2,000 in medical expenses. Lu brought a lawsuit soon thereafter and listed the chemical factory as the defendant (a deep pocket) in order to gain more compensation. Through investigation, the court held that although Fu is a worker of the chemical factory, his conduct was as an individual instead of as an employee. So, the court dismissed Lu's claim because the chemical factory was the wrong defendant.

Article 35

Rule In a labor relationship formed between individuals, if the party providing labor services causes damage to others due to the labor services, the party receiving the labor services assumes the tort liability. If the party providing labor services suffers damage to herself due to her own labor services, both parties shall assume corresponding liabilities according to their respective faults.

Explanation The first sentence of this article articulates the liability of the party who provides service which caused injury or damage to another due to performance of the said service. To have this article applied, three conditions should be met: (1) there is a labor service relationship between individuals; (2) the tort occurs within the scope of the work, with injury or damage caused due to performance of the service; and (3) action of the party providing service has constituted a tort and actually caused injury or damage to another. The party receiving the service bears tort liability for the injury or damage caused by the party providing service, and such liability is the final liability and no-fault liability. The second sentence articulates the liability of the party receiving service for the injury or damage to the party providing service due to performance of the service. The applicable conditions of the second sentence are the same with those of the first, but attention should be paid that this clause generally articulates that the liability of the party receiving service for the injury or damage to the party providing service is liability with fault, for it does not separate different reasons of the injury or damage to the party providing service due to provision of the service.

Example Tang invited some of his fellow villagers, including Li, to help build three tile-roofed houses in preparation for his son's wedding. Under construction, a piece of tile dropped from Li's hand carelessly and hit Du, a passerby. Du suffered injuries costing more than ¥3,000 in medical expenses. Du brought Tang and Li to court, requesting them to bear tort liability for his injuries. The court held that there is a service relationship between Tang and Li, so the tort liability for the injury caused by Li should be borne by Tang who accepted Li's service. So judgment is in favor of Du for the more than ¥3,000 in medical expenses.

Article 36

Rule Where network users or Internet service providers utilize the network to commit a tort to individuals' civil rights and interests, they shall be subject to tort liability.

Where a network user commits a tort through the Internet services, the victim of the tort is entitled to request the Internet service provider to take necessary measures such as deletion, blocking, or disconnection. If, after being notified, the Internet service provider fails to take necessary measures in a timely manner, it shall be jointly and severally liable for any additional damage, together with the said network user.

Where an Internet service provider knows that a network user is infringing upon the civil rights and interests of others through its services and fails to take necessary measures, it shall be jointly and severally liable, together with the said network user.

Explanation Clause 1 articulates the direct tort liability of the network subscriber and the Internet service provider. To determine whether the network subscriber or the Internet service provider constitutes a tort depends on related provisions in the Tort Law, the Copyright Law, and other related areas of law. Clauses 2 and 3 of this article articulate the joint and several liability of the Internet service provider for the tortious act committed by the network subscriber using the network. There are two ways for an Internet service provider to be joint and several liability. First, already knowing the fact that the network subscriber used the network to commit tortious act, the Internet service provider took no necessary corrective measures. When it comes to this point, we should pay particular attention to two problems: (1) knowledge in this article is not limited to actual knowledge but includes what the Internet service provider should have known, and (2) judging standards of knowledge depend on specific circumstances. Second, if the network subscriber used the network to commit a tort, and the injured party notified the network provider to take necessary measures, Internet service provider failed to take necessary measures in a timely manner after receipt of the notice. We should pay attention to the point that the network subscriber is the direct tortfeasor. So the Internet service provider shall bear joint and several liability for the additional damage caused. If the Internet service provider has taken necessary measures after receipt of the notice, it shall not bear liability for the damage incurred before the receipt of the notice.

Example Yin and Hua hated each other. Yin was always seeking for revenge against Hua. One day after learning Photoshop, Yin joined a photo of Hua's head with a spoof picture from the Internet, creating an illusion that the picture was taken while Hua was naked with another person at the hotel. Moreover, Yin made up scandalous gossips on certain forums. Knowing this, Hua contacted related websites in time, requesting them to delete such contents and trace the tortfeasor. The websites noticed this situation upon the post appearance but thought it would attract more traffic. As a result, they refused Hua's requests time after time, which subsequently increased traffic volume by millions within only 3 days. Someone got Hua's address through a "human flesh" search and caused great damage to Hua's reputation and daily life. Hua initiated a lawsuit, asking the related websites to delete the post immediately, extend a formal apology on a conspicuous position, eliminate ill effects, bear joint and several liability with the tortfeasor who had not been determined yet, and compensate for a loss of more than ¥10,000. Subject to Article 36 of the Tort Law, the court held that these websites immediately stop the infringement, offer an apology, eliminate adverse effects, and bear joint and several liabilities for the loss caused by the tortious act.

Article 37

Rule If managers of a hotel, shopping mall, bank, station, recreation spot, or other public amenities or organizers of mass activities fail to fulfill their duty of safety and protection and cause damage to others, they shall be subject to tort liability.

If damage to others is caused by a third party, the third party shall assume the tort liability; and the manager or organizer, if failing to meet his duty of safety and protection, shall assume the corresponding supplemental liability.

Explanation Clause 1 of this article articulates the safety obligation of preventing others from having their safety jeopardized. The safeguard's obligation is to prevent his behavior from causing personal injury or property damage to another. If this happens, the obligator shall bear liability himself. Clause 2 articulates the safeguard's obligation of preventing a third party from jeopardizing the safety of others. In other words, if the direct tortfeasor is the third party, the liability shall be allocated between the individual safeguarding others and the third party. We can divide it into two situations: (1) if the injury is caused by the third party and the safeguard has fulfilled his safety obligation, we may decide that it is the third party that separately committed the tortious act and shall bear independent liability, while the safeguard is not liable, and (2) if the injury is caused by the third party but the safeguard has not fulfilled his safety obligation, then both of them shall bear liability. Regardless of being in the second situation, the safeguard's liability is neither joint and several liability caused by contributory infringement nor the shared liability, which results from plural causes of one damage. Instead, the safeguard bears supplemental liability, based on a combination of the third party's infringement and the safeguard's omission. As to the victim, the third party is the person directly liable, while the safeguard is the person indirectly liable. The supplementary liability of the safeguard under circumstances of the second situation of Article 37, Clause 2, has two characteristics: (1) such liability is the liability by order and (2) such liability is respective liability. There is an order between the third party's tort liability and the safeguard's supplementary liability. Only when the third party cannot bear the tort liability should the safeguard bear supplemental liability. Even if the third party fails to bear liability, the safeguard needs not bear all liability. Instead, the safeguard shall bear his part of liability according to the degree of his failure to satisfy his duty.

Example Yan went on a business trip and checked in at a five-star hotel. One day when Yan was out, his property in the room was stolen, resulting in losses of more than ¥10,000. Later, the thief was arrested, but the stolen property was not recovered. In the collateral civil action, Yan requested the hotel to compensate him for his loss on account of not having fulfilled its duty of safety/care. Through investigation, the court found that the theft happened during the daytime and was recorded by hotel cameras; however, the hotel failed to detect or restrain the theft in time. The hotel promised Yan that their security guard system is so strong that such accidents would never happen. Consequently, the court held that the hotel undertake the supplemental liability and pay compensation of ¥3,000.

Article 38

Rule When a person without civil capacity suffers a personal injury while studying or attending a kindergarten, school, or any other educational institution, then the kindergarten, school, or other educational institutions will be liable, unless it can prove that it fulfilled its duty of care.

Explanation This article articulates the criteria for allocating liability to kindergartens, schools, or other educational institutions specifically when dealing with a person who has no civil capacity and is injured at school. According to the provision, educational institutions have a duty of care that includes safety obligations combined with a form of contractual. If a person with no civil capacity sustains a physical injury while studying or attending a school, the school shall bear compensatory liability for the injury or damage incurred according to the fault doctrine. It is worth discussing the principle of presumptive fault at this point. Under the presumption of fault, the law presumes that the defendant is at fault and shall bear civil liability if the plaintiff can prove the defendant caused the injury and the defendant cannot prove otherwise. Presumption of fault reverses the burden of proof. If the kindergarten, school, or other educational institution cannot prove that it has met its duty of care, such as fulfilling its educational and management duties, then the law presumes that it is at fault and assigns it the liability. The law sets a higher standard of obligations for educational institutions in regard to individuals with no civil capacity because they lack cognitive ability. This article provides that such educational institutions shall bear this liability but remains silent as to the scope of such liability. According to Article 7, Clause 1, of Interpretation of the Supreme People's Court of Some Issues concerning the Application of Law for the Trial of Cases on Compensation for Personal Injury, if kindergartens, schools, and other educational institutions, which carry educational, management, and protective obligations, fail to fulfill duties and cause injury to minors or the minors attending a kindergarten, school, or other educational institution cause an injury to another, then the kindergarten, school, or other educational institution will bear the compensatory liability corresponding with its fault. Although this article makes a distinction between a person with no civil capacity and a person with limited civil capacity through assigning liability to kindergartens, schools, and other educational institutions, it does not specify the scope of liability assigned. So, we may refer to the old provision that kindergartens, schools, or other educational institutions shall bear compensatory liability corresponding with its fault.

Example Jian sent his 3-year-old son, Xiao Jian, to a private full-time kindergarten. One day while playing, Xiao Jian fell and hit the corner of a raw iron crib. The corner was quite sharp and led to a wound one centimeter deep and five centimeters long on Xiao Jian's head. The kindergarten sent Xiao Jian to the hospital for medical treatment, and Xiao Jian's medical care totaled ¥10,000. Jian sued the kindergarten, requesting the kindergarten bear the liability for injury. The court held that the kindergarten had not considered the obvious potential safety hazard of the dangerous baby crib and that the kindergarten was at fault for there was inadequate supervision when Xiao Jian was playing. Consequently, the court decided that the kindergarten should pay Xiao Jian ¥6,000 for medical expenses.

Article 39

Rule When a person with limited civil capacity suffers a personal injury while studying or attending a school or any other educational institution, the school or other educational institution shall be liable if it failed to meet its duty of care, including its duties of education and management.

Explanation This article articulates the criteria for allocating liability to kindergartens, schools, or other educational institutions with respect to a person with limited civil capacity injured at school. This article is closely related to the previous article, Article 38. In this article, the duty of care is mostly the same as with that in Article 38. The only difference is that the victim to whom this article applies is a person with limited civil capacity instead of a person with no civil capacity. Compared with a person with no civil capacity, a person with limited civil capacity is mentally mature, has certain cognitive ability and discernment, and can fully recognize those behaviors that easily may cause injury or damage to others. This article is specific to injury caused by a kindergarten, school, or other educational institution and the liability it shall bear for a person with limited civil capacity. Compared with Article 38, the criteria for liability in this article are different. This article adopts the fault liability principle for kindergartens, schools, or other educational institutions. It is unfair to the kindergarten, school, or other educational institution if they carry too heavy a burden of proof, especially because a person with limited civil capacity is mentally mature and can participate in many activities. Additionally, imposing a heavy burden of proof would urge such educational institutions to restrict certain activities, which for a person with limited civil capacity is unfavorable to their life and development. As to the personal injury caused by a person with limited civil capacity, the kindergarten, school, or other educational institution bears fault liability. Fault liability is the civil liability that the tortfeasor assumes intentionally or negligently causing injury and the corresponding damage suffered determines the scope of compensation. In particular, the articles differ in their burden of proofs. In this article, the principle of "who advocates, who proves," the kindergarten, school, or other educational institution bears no initial burden of proof, while the victim bears the burden to prove that the educational institution failed to fulfill its educational and management duties.

Example Huang is a 12-year-old fifth grader at the village primary school. During the school's spring cleaning, Huang fell from the second floor, which left him with high-level quadriplegia and permanent paralysis of the lower limb. As guardians, Huang's parents took the school to court, claiming that the school failed to meet its duty of care because no teachers were supervising when the school organized the students to clean windows high-up, and requested the school to compensate for Huang's injury. Through investigation, the court found that the school required students of every grade to clean the windows which caused the students on the second floor to face an extremely hazardous risk to their safety. What is more, there was no special person to supervise or instruct; consequently, the school was held liable for Huang's injury. The final judgment was that the school should pay Huang's future medical expenses and disability benefits totaling ¥600,000.

Article 40

Rule If, while studying or attending a kindergarten, school, or any other educational institution, a person without civil capacity or with limited civil capacity suffers a personal injury caused by a person not related to or attending the kindergarten, school, or other education institution, then the infringing person shall assume the tort liability. The kindergarten, school, or other educational institution shall assume the corresponding supplemental liability if it failed to fulfill its duty of care.

Explanation This article articulates the allocation of liability between educational institutions and third parties for the tortious conduct of a third party when the victim is a person with limited or no civil capacity in the school's care. If a person other than the personnel of the kindergarten, school, or other educational institution causes the injury, he shall bear the tort liability according to the requirements of the Tort Law. In other words, the liability the third party shall bear is the general tort liability. The kindergarten, school, or other educational institutions shall bear supplemental liability under these circumstances if they failed to meet their duty of care. Only when the third party cannot compensate for the victim's injury does the kindergarten, school, or other educational institutions need to bear the supplementary liability. Additionally, the kindergarten, school, or other educational institution only bears supplemental liability when it fails to fulfill its duty of care and the victim proves that the kindergarten, school, or other educational institution failed to meet its duty of care. Conversely, if the kindergarten, school, or other educational institution meets it duty of care or other legal obligations, they may not bear any liability. Another point to pay attention to is how the duty of care is determined. Courts determine the appropriate duty of care on the practical conditions, mainly the safety and supervision provided, security measures taken, and the facilities.

Example Mao studied at a kindergarten in downtown. One day, a homeless guy rushed into the kindergarten, because he wanted to take revenge on society. Worried about their own safety, the kindergarten security guards did not attempt to stop him, instead they called the police. The guy attacked the kindergarten facilities and hit Mao knocking him to the ground. As a result, Mao suffered a concussion. Mao was unconscious by the time the police has control of the situation. Mao's medical expenses totaled ¥8,000. Because the outlaw had no ability to pay compensation for Mao's medical expenses, Mao's parents sued the kindergarten requesting it to assume the tort liability for the injury and pay for the medical expenses. The court held that the kindergarten did not meet its duty of care, particularly its duty to provide a safe environment, and should bear supplemental liability in the form of ¥5,000.

Chapter 17
Product Liability

Article 41

Rule A producer assumes tort liability if its product causes damage to others due to a defect.

Explanation This article articulates the tort product liability of the producer. Product liability is a kind of civil liability that producers and sellers bear when damage results from the defective product and in violation of the duty of care that infringes other's person or property. The "producer" in product liability refers to the following: (1) the manufacturer of the product; (2) the one who deems itself a producer, by placing its name, labeled name, trade name, trademark, or other marks on the products; or (3) the natural or legal person considered the virtual producer of products according to its involvement in the process of manufacturing, distributing, selling, or other matters of the products. In modern production, although components are generally sourced from multiple factories, the producer in product liability shall be the product's final manufacturer. The producers of the defective parts or raw materials are not producers for product liability. The producer bears no-fault liability, which means that it shall bear product liability to victims regardless of whether or not it is at fault, as long as the above three elements are established and there is no exemption.

Example Lin bought an electric pressure cooker which was defectively designed by a factory and was prone to explosion after repeated use. While Lin was using the pressure cooker, it exploded. As a result, he suffered fifth degree disability. The court found that Lin's damage was caused by a defective product; thus, the producer bears all liability. Consequently, the court held the factory shall compensate Lin for ¥200,000.

X. Li and J. Jin, *Concise Chinese Tort Laws*, China-EU Law Series 1,
DOI 10.1007/978-3-642-41024-6_17,

Article 42

Rule If the seller is at fault for the product's defect that results in damages to others, the seller shall assume the tort liability.

If a seller fails to specify the producer of a defective product or the supplier of the defective product, the seller shall assume the tort liability.

Explanation This article articulates the tort product liability of a seller. The first clause of this article articulates the fault liability of sellers for product liability. Note that the fault liability of sellers only applies to the internal apportionment of liability among sellers and producers. In external liability, the seller still bears no-fault liability. In other words, regardless of the seller's fault resulting in the damage caused by the products, it shall bear the liability to pay compensation in accordance with no-fault liability first. After bearing the external liability, if the seller is not at fault for defective products, it can claim indemnity from the producer, the transporter, the warehouse, or another third party. If the seller is at fault for the product defect, it has no right to recover from other liable parties. If the producer bears the external liability first, it may, after paying compensation, recover the same from the seller who is at fault. The second clause of this article articulates particular circumstances where the sellers shall bear no-fault liability. The circumstances where the seller is unable to identify either the producer or the supplier of defective products include the following: (1) when defective products identifications do not reference the factory's name or factory's address and the seller did not strictly enforce the check and acceptance system to identify the products during purchasing, (2) when the seller is unable to find the defective product's producers or suppliers, and (3) when the producer of defective products makes forgery or infringes the factory's name or factory's address and after checking sellers have failed to identify such forgeries. Where the seller is unable to identify either the producer or supplier of defective products, the seller shall be deemed as the products' producer and will bear no-fault liability. This provision, on the one hand, protects the victim of defective products and ensures they gain timely compensation; on the other hand, it urges the seller to strengthen the checks and acceptance of products, thus preventing danger to the consumer's body and property from the defective products put into market.

Example A second-hand car trading company bought a 2001s old Santana at a low price from an owner and then prepared to resale it for a profit. Before the sale, Shang, the company manager, took the good gearbox, battery, and brake away from the car down and replaced with worn ones. A few days later, Ye bought the car, because of Shang's promise that the car was in good condition. One day, Ye drove this car to a friend's meeting but the brake failed causing a traffic accident. Ye suffered multiple rib fractures. After testing, it was determined that the replaced parts were the cause of the accident. The court found that the second-hand car trading company's repairs made the car defective, which was the cause of accident. Therefore, the court ruled in favor of Ye and that the company should compensate Ye ¥10,000.

Article 43

Rule If damage arises from a defective product, the victim may request compensation from the producer of the product or the seller of the product.

If the product defect is caused by the producer and the seller has compensated the victim, the seller is entitled to seek reimbursement from the producer.

If the defect of the product is caused by the seller and the producer has compensated the victim, the producer is entitled to seek reimbursement from the seller.

Explanation This article articulates product liability between the producer and the seller. The system of liability can be divided into internal and external aspects. The first clause of this article articulates external product liability between the producer and the seller. External liability is the liability which the producer and the seller bear towards the injured party. This is the no-fault liability principle. As long as the product's use caused the user damage and there is a casual relationship between the damage and the defective product, regardless of who is at fault, the injured party has the right to seek compensation from either the producer or seller. Only a producer or seller, who can prove it has an exemption for liability, can be exempted. A producer or seller may claim, as an exemption, that it did not put the product into circulation or that when putting the product into circulation, the defect could not be found by existing technology. The second and third clauses of this article articulate the internal product liability assignment between the producer and the seller. After bearing external liability, the producer and the seller shall claim an internal compensation from each other. Under this circumstance, the producer still bears no-fault liability and the seller bears the fault liability. After the producer bears external liability, if the product's defect is caused by the seller's fault, then the producer may claim the same from the seller and vice versa.

Example Long bought tainted food from a store; after eating he vomited and had diarrhea caused by food poisoning. Long paid ¥500 for medical expenses. Then, Long negotiated with the store for compensation. The store believing the defect was caused by the factory refused to pay compensation. Long sued the store. The court found the food problem was not caused by the store. But, according to Article 43 of the Tort Law, the court ruled that the store shall compensate Long and it can later sue the factory for reimbursement.

Article 44

Rule If damage is caused to a person by a defective product and the defect is the fault of a transporter, warehouseman, or other third party, the producer or seller who has paid the compensation is entitled to seek reimbursement from the third party.

Explanation This article articulates the tort product liability of the transporter, the warehouseman, or other third parties. According to Article 43, the user of a defective product, whose body or property is damaged because of the product, may claim compensation not only from the seller but also from the producer. However, the victim may not claim compensation directly from liable transporters, warehousemen, or other third parties. In other words, even if the third party is at fault for the product's defects, they would not bear liability directly. After the producer or the seller of the defective product has assumed external liability, they may claim internal compensation from the transporter, the warehouseman, or other third parties at fault. As a matter of procedure, Article 153, Clause 2, of Opinions of the Supreme People's Court on Several Issues concerning the Implementation of the General Principles of the Civil Law of the People's Republic of China (For Trial Implementation) prescribes: "Where the transporter and the warehouse is liable for product quality, the producer or the seller who claims compensation, may bring a new lawsuit, or list the transporter and the warehouse as third party and handle jointly."

Example Niu was responsible for delivering milk to stores. In order to save transportation costs, the air conditioner was turned off, which resulted in the milk spoiling. The seller only noted the milk was within the warranty period and sold the milk. As a result, a consumer was poisoned and the seller compensated the consumer for losses exceeding ¥2,000. The seller sued Niu for the compensation paid. The court ruled according to Article 44 of the Tort Law, Niu shall compensate the seller.

Article 45

Rule If the defect of a product endangers the personal or property safety of an individual, the victim may require the producer or seller to assume the tort liability and remove the obstruction or eliminate the danger.

Explanation This article articulates methods for assuming product liability, such as removal of obstacles and elimination of danger. Generally speaking, actual damage must be one of the elements of tort liability. However, this simple remedy is only the relief after damage and to some extent has its own limitation. In order to achieve the precaution function of the Tort Law and adequate protection of the person or property of the product user and the other third parties, the law provides for the removal of obstacles and elimination of danger as a proactive remedy. This allows that protection of person or property in advance will be realized. Removal of obstacles is a kind of method for civil liability where the injured party shall take some legal action to remove the obstacles, thereby making sure that the legal interests of victim are exercised. Elimination of danger is required when a product's defects may cause damage; the potential victim has the right to ask that the court require the liable party to take effective action to remove the danger or possibility of infringement. The danger here is a real threat that may occur at any time. The danger here shall refer to an objectively existed danger, not a subjectively imagined danger.

Example Su bought an off-road vehicle from a car dealer, and he found the vehicle brake system often experienced intermittent failures. Su asked the dealer to repair the breaks and the dealer told Su it was a quick fix. However, Su found out the dealer had only replaced a second-hand brake device and the break failures continued. In order to avoid the danger, he asked for a new replacement brake device. But the dealer refused this request because it is not within the repair, replacement, return, service plan. Su then sued the dealer for the brake replacement, which would eliminate the danger. The court found that the previous repair had not completely solved the safety problems and held that the dealer shall replace the brake device until the danger is completely eliminated.

Article 46

Rule If a product's defect is found after the product is put into circulation, the producer or seller shall take such remedial measures as necessary, such as issuing warnings and recalls in a timely manner. The producer or seller who fails to take remedial measures in a timely manner or take insufficient and ineffective measures shall be tortuously liability, if the defect results in damages.

Explanation This article articulates obligation of producers and sellers to provide after-sales warnings and issue product recalls. In product liability, "when putting into circulation the defect had not been existed" and "when putting into circulation the defect cannot be found according to existing technology standards" are two exemptions that provide a defense. However, after putting the products into circulation, if the producer or the seller learns the product was defective, they cannot willfully allow the defective products continued circulation and possible damages by virtue of these exemptions. They must take remedial measures proactively to avoid the damage; otherwise, they bear the tortious liability. Consequently, this article, to a certain extent, limits the exemptions to product liability. In 2004, the State Administration of Quality Supervision, Inspection, and Quarantine; the National Development and Reform Commission; the Ministry of Commerce; and the Customs General Administration jointly formulated Provisions on the Administration of Recall of Defective Auto Products, the first officially established product recall systems in China. Subsequently, in July 2007, the State Council formulated Special Rules of the State Council on Strengthening the Supervision and Management of the Safety of Food and Other Products and once again established a product recall system, this time for food, edible agricultural products, drugs, and other products related to human health and safety. In August 2007, the General Administration of Quality Supervision, Inspection and Quarantine promulgated the "The Administrative Provisions on the Recall of Children's Toys" and

"The Provisions on the Administration of Food Recall," which expanded the scope of the recall system. In 2009 the Food Safety Law was promulgated and came into force, and it established the food recall system in the legal context. Thus product liability law's application continues expanding, which is of great significance in the protection of consumers' rights.

Example A company produced a laptop battery with an unknown technical flaw; after continuous usage, the battery may spontaneously combust. Unfortunately, the battery was circulated heavily in the market. The manufacturer learns of this situation but remains silent in fear that its reputation and economic interests could be affected. As a result, Gao's computer combusted and caused an indoor fire resulting in damages in excess of ¥10,000. After the cause of the fire was identified, Gao sued the battery manufacturer. The court held the manufacturer liable for Gao's losses. In subsequent years, the defective battery caused a few accidents and made injured some consumers. These victims also received compensation on a case-by-case basis.

Article 47

Rule If the producer or seller continues to manufacture or sell a product after learning of the existence of a defect in the product and the defect results in the death or serious injury to a person, the victim is entitled to punitive compensation.

Explanation This article articulates product liability's punitive compensations principle for the producer and seller. The function of the Tort Law mainly embodies in recovering or preventing damages. However, as the economy develops and the gap to information widens, the economic strength between producers and sellers becomes wider. In product's liability cases, vulnerable consumers often find it difficult to obtain full compensation, because of some obstacles, such as litigation costs and the burden of proof. As a result, consumers cannot regulate, via the Tort Law, the operator in a dominant position. Therefore, in accordance with substantive fairness principles and in order to protect vulnerable consumers, the rules of punitive compensations for the malicious tortious acts of producers and operators have been gradually adopted by legislation. Punitive compensations are exceptional compensation damages and must meet certain conditions before applying. According to this article, the first requirement is the subjective knowledge of producer and seller, which means producers and sellers knew or should have known of the potential risks. Second, it requires the defective product actually causes personal damage, such as death or serious bodily injury. Property damage caused by a defective product does not qualify for punitive damages. Moreover, punitive compensations have no upper limit. This means that a judge may use her judicial discretion in determining the monetary penalty, using such factors as the victim's injury, the severity of risk for damages, the degree of subjective malice by the producers and consumers, and other social influences. Finally, the nature of liability for punitive compensation is a kind of private law liability rather than a mandatory public law liability, thereby claiming punitive damages is up to the victim.

Example Tian was diagnosed with rectal cancer by a hospital and checked himself into the hospital for surgery with Dr. Du. On a private occasion, Dr. Du took two chemotherapy pumps—one domestic, the other imported—from his briefcase and told Tian's wife that the chemotherapy pump is for local chemotherapy, which is comparatively harmless but effective. While priced more expensively, Dr. Du stated the imported pump is better. Tian's wife purchased the imported chemotherapy pump for ¥3,300. Dr. Du performed the surgery on Tian, removed the section of the rectum with cancer, and installed the imported chemotherapy pump. When the hospital started Tian's chemotherapy, they found medicinal liquid had spilled out from the chemotherapy pump and the vicinity of wound cannot healed due to infection. As a result, the chemotherapy was stopped. The hospital determined that the chemotherapy pump had failed and consequently removed the chemotherapy pump from Tian's body. And Tian was transferred to another hospital because he now needed internal radiotherapy. Subsequently, Tian condition deteriorated and he soon died. Tian's wife discovered that Dr. Du's chemotherapy pump was not registered at the Drug Administration Department, but was missing its product certificate of competency and description, meaning it was an adulterated product prohibited for sale. In the lawsuit against Dr. Du, Tian's wife claimed damages for economic loss and mental distress. The court found that the plaintiff had not consented to Dr. Du's treatment that caused Tian's death but that she sued because of the substandard quality of the chemotherapy pump. Therefore, the court reclassified the case as a product liability dispute rather than medical accident. After an investigation Dr. Du's imported chemotherapy pump proved to be an adulterated product. Under the punitive damage provision of the Tort Law, Dr. Du bears liability of ¥6,600 for the defective pump and ¥10,000 for other losses, including medical expenses and loss resulted from absence from work. Meanwhile, plaintiff's claim for mental distress was denied, because Tian's death was not the inevitable consequence of the adulterated chemotherapy pump.

Chapter 18
Liability for Motor Vehicle Traffic Accident

Article 48

Rule Where a motor vehicle traffic accident causes any damage, liability shall be assumed according to the relevant provisions of the Road Traffic Safety Law.

Explanation This article is a general provision for automobile traffic accident liability. Unless the Road Traffic Safety Law provides a specific provision, this law shall apply. The imputation principle of automobile traffic accident liability does not directly follow fault or no-fault principle; however, it is a system which considers various factors to establish liability. The current trend in Tort Law legislation is that specific principles apply in specific situations; this reflects the specialization of legislation techniques. The PRC's Road Traffic Safety Law specifies the imputation principle of automobile traffic accident liability that the insurance company shall bear no-fault liability, within the scope of compulsory third party liability insurance, for the motor vehicle. Where a motor vehicle is involved in a traffic accident and causes personal injury, death, or property loss, the insurance company shall indemnify the victim within the scope of the third party's liability insurance coverage. The Social Assistance Fund for Road Traffic Accidents pays the costs of rescuing liable party's victim; thus, it applies no-fault liability. The administrative organization of the fund may claim compensation from the liable party. Fault liability applies to traffic accidents between motor vehicles. The party at fault in a traffic accident shall bear the liability; if both parties are at fault, they each bear their share of the liability. No fault liability applies for traffic accidents where the driver injures a passenger or a pedestrian. Where a traffic accident injures a passenger or a pedestrian, the driver shall bear the liability; where the passenger or pedestrian intentionally or negligently cause the accident, the driver shall bear no liabilities or mitigated liabilities.

Example Jia drove his Nissan to a relative's house and hit Li, who was crossing an intersection. The police assigned 70 % of the liability to Jia and 30 % of the liability to Li. The two parties went to court due to disputes over the exact amount of

X. Li and J. Jin, *Concise Chinese Tort Laws*, China-EU Law Series 1,
DOI 10.1007/978-3-642-41024-6_18, © Springer-Verlag Berlin Heidelberg 2014

compensation. Li claimed for 70 % of his medical fees and lost wages from Jia and the insurance company, which totaled ¥10,000. The court held that the Road Traffic Safety Law required the insurance company to pay Li up to the limit of the insurance policy. The amount in excess of the insurance policy is up to Jia to pay. Because of the insurance clause in this case, the insurance company paid ¥5,000 and Jia paid the remaining ¥2,000.

Article 49

Rule Where the owner and the driver of a motor vehicle are not the same person—due to rental, leasing, or any other reason—the liability of a traffic accident lies on the owner. The owner's insurance company shall pay compensation within the limits of the owner's insurance. The driver shall make up any shortfall in compensation; and if the owner is at fault for causing damages, he shall assume the corresponding compensatory liability.

Explanation This article articulates who shall bear the traffic accident liability when the owner and the user of a car are not the same person. Compulsory insurance is required for all vehicles in case of an accident. So in circumstances such as a lease, lending, etc., if the driver is involved in an accident and liability arises from the accident, then the owner's insurance company may cover damages up to the limit covered in the car's policy. Compensation paid by the insurance company is limited by the terms of the insurance policy. However, the driver may be liable for any damages that exceed the insurance policy limits. The driver not only includes the lessee but also the borrower, the pledgee during the period of pledge, the repairer during the repair period, the depository when the vehicle is kept by others, or anyone who actually drives the vehicle. It should be clarified that this article only applies to owners and drivers in a lease, lending, or other similar relationship. When the driver is an employee, acting within the scope of their work, or someone with whom the drivers formed a labor relationship, Article 33 or Article 34 of the Tort Law shall apply. Thus the employer or the person who hires the labor shall assume liability, not the driver. If the owner of the vehicle is at fault in causing the damage, then he shall assume the corresponding liability. The standard of care applied to the owner refers to the owner's obligation to make sure the driver has a license and maintaining the vehicle up to the appropriate safety requirements. Once this duty of care is breached, the owner of the vehicle shall bear corresponding liability in respect to his fault.

Example Lou rented a car for a business trip from a car rental company. In a suburban area, he hit a pedestrian causing a thigh fracture and several soft tissue contusions totaling ¥1,000 in medical fees. The traffic police concluded that Lou was fully liable for the accident. The victim asked the insurance company to accord to the insurance policy, which the insurance company refused because it believed Lou should pay the compensation. Finally, the court heard this case and ruled that the insurance company should compensate the victim the ¥1,000, according to the insurance policy. If the car rental company wanted Lou to indemnify them, it could bring a lawsuit against Lou.

Article 50

Rule Where a motor vehicle has been transferred and delivered from one party to another, through sale or other transaction, but the transfer in ownership has yet to be registered and the liability of a traffic accident lies on the side of the motor vehicle, then the insurance company shall pay compensation within the scope of the insurance policy. The transferee of the motor vehicle shall make up any shortfall in compensation.

Explanation This article articulates traffic accident liability for motor vehicles in the process of an ownership transfer. When a traffic accident involved a vehicle, where the ownership has not been transferred and the driver is liable, the liability shall be borne by the insurance company according to the vehicle's insurance policy. It is provided by this article that where a motor vehicle covered by insurance is at fault for an accident, the insurance company shall compensate within the limits under the insurance policy, regardless of ownership name change or who procured the policy. Where a traffic accident involves a motor vehicle, where the ownership has not been transferred and the driver is liable, the shortfall after the insurance company's compensation shall be borne by the transferee. Although the name of the owner has not been changed, the transferee is in actual control of the vehicle and thus shall be liable. Due to the relatively high price of motor vehicles, many people sell cars using installments. The seller commonly contracts to keep the ownership to ensure that all the payments are paid. And the buyer assumes liability because the buyer has actual control over the vehicle for use and profit. It is provided by the "Supreme People's Court's Reply on that the Seller Who Keeps the Ownership of Vehicles Should Not Assume Civil Liability Where the Buyer Uses a Vehicle Paid by Installments for Transportation And Causes Damages on Others' Property Due to Traffic Accidents" that where vehicles are purchased by installments and the seller keeps the ownership of vehicles before the buyer pays all the installments, the seller shall not be civilly liable when the buyer contracts for cargo transportation with others and uses the vehicle for transportation during which others' property is damaged due to traffic accidents. These two provisions are consistent with each other.

Example Song and Ji reached an agreement to transfer Song's Passat to Ji. Ji drove the car with Song to the DMV to finish the transaction. On the way to the registration agency, Ji hit and killed an 8-year-old child, Ma, who was crossing the road. The traffic police found Ji fully liable. Ma's parents claimed compensation totaling ¥360,000. Immediately, the insurance company paid ¥200,000, the maximum under the policy, and who should be held liable for the shortfall was in dispute. Ma's parents sued both Song and Ji. The court held that Article 50 of the Tort Law provided that the car was actually transferred to Ji who thus should be held liable. Therefore, Ji was liable for the shortfall totaling ¥160,000.

Article 51

Rule Where an illegally assembled motor vehicle or a motor vehicle reaching the scrapping standards, which has been transferred through sale or other transfer method, causes a traffic accident that results in damages, the transferor and the transferee shall be jointly and severally liable.

Explanation This article articulates traffic accident liability in the event that the vehicle or motor vehicle that is due to be scrapped is sold or transferred. In accordance with Measures for Administration of Recycling of Scrapped Motor Vehicles, "assemble motor vehicles" thereof are motor vehicles fabricated with engines, steering wheels, transmissions, front and rear axles, and frames (commonly referred to "the five major units") from discarded vehicles and other spare or accessory parts. "Due to be scrapped" means vehicles which have reached the state discarded standard or, although they have not reached the state discarded standard, the engine or chassis is severely damaged and thus does not conform to the state safety specifications for motor vehicles operating on roads, or cannot meet the state motor vehicle pollutant emission standard for inspection. The transferor is at fault, provided that an assembled motor vehicle or a motor vehicle that is due to be scrapped is sold or transferred. The transferor is fully aware that the vehicle lacks technical safety features and may severely endanger people's lives or safety or property yet still sells the vehicles. Subjectively the transferor possesses indirect intention and constitutes joint infringement with the transferee of the motor vehicle. Accordingly, the Tort Law provides that the transferor and the transferee shall be held jointly and severally liable. It is noteworthy that this article is the only automobile traffic accident article in the Tort Law which provides joint and several liabilities.

Example Lai wanted to purchase a car but he did not have enough money. He heard that Qiu owned an old Santana that was due to be scrapped. One day, Lai met Qiu and expressed that he wanted to buy this car. Qiu considered that Lai offered ¥8,000, while only ¥6,000 could be obtained if scrapped. Qiu also believed that Lai would drive the car in the countryside, thus reducing the risk of any accident. As a result, Qiu sold Lai the car and told Lai that he neither took the car for its annual technical safety inspections nor paid the compulsory motor vehicle insurance fee. The next day, Lai drove the car and hit Wang at the entrance of the village due to an ineffective brake. Wang sued both Lai and Qiu. The court held Lai and Qiu jointly and severally liable for the compensation.

Article 52

Rule If a traffic accident is caused by a motor vehicle that has been stolen, looted, or robbed, then the person who commits the stealing, looting, or robbing shall be liable for any damages. If the insurance company paid any rescue expenses within the limits of the insurance policy, then it is entitled to seek reimbursement from the party culpable for the accident.

Explanation This article articulates traffic accident liability of stolen, robbed, or looted motor vehicles. Where a motor vehicle is stolen, robbed, or looted, the perpetrator shall be liable for damages caused by the accident. This is because the subject liable for traffic accidents should be the one who uses the motor vehicle and assumes the risk. In respect with the compulsory insurance for motor vehicles, the insurance company covers the liability of traffic accidents that occur when the owner of the vehicle drives normally and where the owner allows others to drive. The insurance company has no obligation to compensate for the liability caused by the thief, robber, or looter driving the vehicle. "Paying on behalf of" concept in this article refers to circumstances where the driver flees after the accident; thus, no one can reimburse the costs of rescuing the injured or burying the decedent. To avoid delay in rescuing the injured or burying the decedent, the law states that the insurance company shall pay the costs in advance. This is a legal obligation of social assistance borne by the insurance company rather than a contractual obligation originated from the insurance contract. Provided that the cost to rescue and treat the injured is paid after the services are provided, i.e., the victim or his family did not pay in advance for the rescue or hospital treatment, there is no urgent need for "paying in advance." The legal obligation for the insurance company to pay in advance is based on the urgent nature of the situation. The legal obligation of paying in advance does not exist without the objective condition of urgency.

Example Pei owned a Jetta, which was stolen at 10 a.m. Pei reported the stolen car to the police. The police soon found the car; the thief while driving hit a pedestrian, Huang, in a crosswalk and fled the scene on foot abandoning the car. The insurance company paid the medical fees ¥10,000 for Huang. A few days later, the thief was caught and sued by Huang and the insurance company. The court combined the two cases and ruled that the thief compensate Huang for the medical fees; he paid out of ¥20,000 and reimbursed the insurance company for the ¥10,000.

Article 53

Rule When the driver flees after an accident occurs and if the vehicle is covered by the compulsory insurance, the insurance company shall make compensation within the limits of the insurance policy. If the motor vehicle cannot be identified or is not covered by the compulsory insurance and the expenses for the victim's injury or death—such as rescue, medical treatment, and funeral fees—need to be paid, the Social Assistance Fund for Road Traffic Accidents shall advance the payment. After advances are made out of the Social Assistance Fund for Road Traffic Accidents, the governing body of the fund is entitled to seek reimbursement from the party culpable for the accident.

Explanation This article articulates the Social Assistance Fund for Road Traffic Accidents obligation to pay costs on behalf of the liable party. Where a driver flees after a traffic accident, the vehicle is identifiable and the vehicle is covered by compulsory insurance, then compensation shall be covered by the insurance company within the limits under the compulsory insurance procured for the vehicle. Fleeing includes both driving away from the scene of the accident and abandoning the motor vehicle at the scene of the accident to evade legal liabilities. If the vehicle is unknown or if the vehicle is not subject to compulsory insurance, the costs for rescuing or burying the victim, along with other relevant costs, shall be paid out of the Social Assistance Fund for Road Traffic Accidents. It is provided by Article 17 of the Road Traffic Safety Law that the State will establish social assistance funds for road traffic accidents. These funds improve the protection of victims' rights and interests in traffic accidents. In addition, where the costs paid for rescuing the injured parties exceed the insurance policy limits, the Road Traffic Safety Law, not this article, provides that the amount in excess shall be paid by the Social Assistance Fund for Road Traffic Accidents. The administrative body for the fund may, after paying compensation, seek compensation from the liable party. The person liable for the traffic accident can still require the insurance company to pay compensation within the scope of the compulsory third party liability insurance policy for the motor vehicle.

Example He, the plaintiff, purchased the compulsory motor vehicle insurance for his car from the defendant insurance company. The coverage for death and disability compensation under the compulsory insurance was ¥110,000. While covered by the insurance, the plaintiff drove the car and caused the death of a victim. He fled after the accident. One month later, the plaintiff paid ¥270,000 to the relatives of the deceased by way of mediation. After fulfilling his obligation of compensation, the plaintiff asked the insurance company to pay him ¥110,000 according to the compulsory insurance policy. The defendant argued that because of Regulation on Compulsory Traffic Accident Liability Insurance for Motor Vehicles, where a driver flees after an accident, it is the Social Assistance Fund for Road Traffic Accidents that should pay the costs for rescuing or burying, along with other relevant expenses, the victim on behalf of the culpable party, not the insurance company. So, the defendant refused to pay because the plaintiff fled after the accident. Subsequently, the plaintiff filed a lawsuit and claimed the benefits under the compulsory insurance of ¥110,000 from the defendant. The court held that, as was provided by law, the State applies a compulsory third party liability insurance system to motor vehicles and established a social assistance funds for road traffic accidents—the specific measures are formulated by the State Council. It was also provided by law that where a vehicle was involved in a traffic accident that caused personal injury, death, or property loss, the insurance company shall indemnify the fund within the limits of the compulsory third party liability insurance policy for the vehicle. As a result, even if the culpable party fled, the insurance company was obliged to compensate the victim.

Chapter 19
Liability for Medical Malpractice

Article 54

Rule If a medical institution or its medical staff members are at fault for damages inflicted on a patient during the course of diagnosis and treatment, the medical institution shall be liable for compensation.

Explanation This article provides the doctrine of liability fixation and the subject of liability in the case of medical malpractice. The doctrine of liability fixation in a medical malpractice context is liability for fault, i.e., during the diagnosis and treatment. The liability for damages to the patient caused by the misconducts of the medical institution or its medical professionals should be borne by the medical institution. Liability for fault in a general tort applies here. Although medical malpractice has its distinctiveness, it is wrong to say that all the distinctive torts should not apply the liability for fault. Instead they have some distinctiveness in the burden of proof and the distribution of liabilities. So in a medical malpractice situation, a medical institution is liable only if its professionals performed misconducts; if not, they would not be held liable. This article specifies that the subject of liability in a medical malpractice is the medical institution whose professionals are blamed; the reasoning is that the legal person is a social organization and its conducts are performed by its members. Regardless of how the damage is caused, be it by its members under the instruction of the institution or by unintended negligence when its members or agents are carrying out their duties, the fault should be presented as a conduct of a specified legal person. It is not that the medical professional who performs misconducts is not liable, but instead after the medical institution has compensated the victim, the medical professional should, inside the organization, compensate the organization he affiliates with. What is more, if the medical professional intentionally causes the damage, the act is not professional misconduct and is not the organization's fault, but is a general tort, in which the doctrine of direct liability applies, i.e., the medical professional should bare the tortious liability individually.

X. Li and J. Jin, *Concise Chinese Tort Laws*, China-EU Law Series 1,

DOI 10.1007/978-3-642-41024-6_19,

Example During a surgery, the surgeon negligently left medical gauze inside Huo's abdomen. Huo experienced tremendous pain after the operation and had to have a second surgery to remove the gauze. Several of Huo's abdominal organs were impaired due to the injuries caused by the gauze. Huo sued the hospital for compensation. The court held that Huo's damage was due to the negligence of the surgeon, so the hospital should bear the tortious liability and Huo won the case.

Article 55

Rule The medical staff shall explain to the patient the situation regarding his illness, the options for medical treatment, and the measures they will take for diagnosis and treatment. If any operation, special examination, or special treatment is needed, the medical staff shall explain the medical risks, alternate medical treatment plans, and other relevant information to the patient in a timely manner, and obtain the patient's written consent; or, when it is not proper or possible to explain the information to the patient, then explain the information to a close relative of the patient, and obtain a written consent from the relative.

If a medical person fails to fulfill her obligations stated in the preceding paragraph and causes damage to her patient, the medical institution shall be liable for compensation.

Explanation This article provides the obligation of medical professionals to inform and explain and the tortious liability borne by medical professionals in cases when they fail to fulfill their obligations. During the course of medical treatment, a patient has the right to know and learn all the information about his treatments and to choose what he considers to be the best. This right has the nature of a personal right and is part of the patients' health rights in the medical sphere. A patient's right to know includes, inter alia, two aspects: (1) the right to know his health condition and (2) the right to know and choose his treatment options. Obviously, the medical professional's obligation to inform is mainly a safeguard to assure the patient's right to know. The medical professional's obligation to inform includes, inter alia, three aspects: (1) the obligation to effectively explain diagnosis and treatment (if the medical professional fails to truthfully inform about the treatment, the acceptance of the patient should be void); (2) the obligation to inform about inevitable risks for each treatment option (the patient or close relatives should be informed of the risks which cannot be precluded even if the duty of care has been met; otherwise, the medical professional cannot be exempted from liability for unexpected results), and (3) the obligation to report. The medical professional should not conceal any of the patient's health conditions or the treatment's effectiveness from the patient or his close relatives.

Example A hospital has recently developed a new treatment measure. When Pi came for treatments, his doctor found that his symptom fitted the new treatment measure very well and he was a best sample to test the effectiveness of this measure.

So, the doctor encouraged Pi to take this measure. When Pi inquired about the risks of this measure, the doctor concealed the possible negative effects. As a result, Pi took the measure, but he incurred brain death from an allergy. Pi's wife sued the hospital and asserted the hospital failed to inform Pi of the possible risks of the treatment. The court ruled that the patient's right to informed consent must be protected, so the hospital should bear tortious liability for giving insufficient information to Pi.

Article 56

Rule In the event of an emergency, if the consent of a patient or his immediate relative is unable to be obtained, such as rescue of a patient in critical condition, then with the approval of the person in charge of the medical institution or an authorized person in charge, the corresponding medical measures may be taken immediately.

Explanation This article provides the hospital the right to administer appropriate medical treatment in a life-threatening situation. In a life-threatening situation, when opinion from the patient or his close relatives cannot be obtained, the medical professionals have the right to administer appropriate medical treatment under the authorization of the responsible person for the medical institution. This right can be named the exempted right to save. The application essentials include the following points: (1) it needs to be a life-threatening situation, i.e., situations when the patient's condition is so critical that there may be danger to life or damage to the organs beyond saving; (2) the medical professional is unable to obtain consent from the patient and his close relatives; and (3) the decision-maker is specified. "Unable" can be caused by objective factors, i.e., the patient is unconscious and not able to communicate expressed intentions, while his close relatives are not present and cannot be contacted in time. It also can be caused by subjective factors, i.e., the patient is unconscious and his close relatives refuse to make their expressed intentions. The decision-maker should be the responsible person or the authorized person for the medical institution; however, judicial interpretation should be formulated on which persons should be deemed as the responsible persons.

Example This case happened before the Tort Law was enacted. Zhang's wife was pregnant for 8 months. One day she felt pain in her abdomen and her husband sent her to the hospital. Although it was just a minor pain in her abdomen, the doctors performed a medical check-up and found the condition to be very serious and that a Caesarean operation needed to be done immediately. However, Zhang refused to sign on the notification of the operation, and nobody could, including the doctors, relatives of Zhang's wife, and even the police, persuade him to sign the notification. Zhang's wife passed away because of late treatments. Such tragedy would not have happened had the Tort Law been enacted earlier, because the hospital is now authorized to take medical measures without Zhang's consent.

Article 57

Rule If a medical staff fails to fulfill her obligations of diagnosis and treatment corresponding to the current medical treatment level and causes damage to a patient, the medical institution shall assume the compensatory liability.

Explanation This article provides the tortious liability of medical professional who failed to perform diagnosis and treatment obligations. Since the diagnosis and treatment performed by the medical professional concern people's life and health, which is special in nature and of great importance, this article sets an expert's duty of care for medical professionals. That is to say the medical professional shall perform the duty of care which is appropriate according to the medical standards of the time and place. Article 55 mentioned the identification of fault; this article is one of the criteria for that identification: whether or not duty of care in the diagnosis and treatment has been performed.

Article 57 is the source of the medical professional's duty of care. There are two doctrines regarding this duty of care. The first doctrine is the duty of care in the medical treatment contract context; it refers to the legal nexus formed by the doctor performing the diagnosis and treatment entrusted by the patient or for some other reasons as the medical treatment contract specifies. The medical professional's duty of care is one of the obligations regulated by the medical treatment contract. Second is the duty of care in medical tortious acts. The diagnosis and treatment resulted in the undesirable and sometimes vicious consequences that share a commonality with the tortious act. Fault is one of the constitutive requirements for tort. An ordinary tortfeasor can be deemed as faulty when she fails to reach the general standard of a reasonable person. However, in the case of the medical professional, higher standards and the expert's duty of care shall be reached in the diagnosis and treatment, since the medical professional is an expert in the area of medical care. What Article 57 of the Tort Law provides is the latter duty of care, which, when broken, can be used as the basis for the identification of fault on the side of the medical professional.

Example Qu's wife had renal failure; the hospital's diagnosis was that her left kidney needed to be removed. However, surgeon Ye reviewed the CT photo upside down and mistakenly removed the right kidney, which caused her death. Qu sued the hospital for damages. The court held that the negligence of the doctor caused the death of Qu's wife. Thus, Qu won the case.

Article 58

Rule Under any of the following circumstances, a medical institution shall be presumed to be at fault for any damage caused to a patient:

1. Violating laws, administrative regulations or rules, or any other provision on the procedures and standards for diagnosis and treatment

2. Concealing or refusing to provide the medical history data related to a dispute
3. Forging, tampering, or destroying any medical history data

Explanation This article provides the fault assumption liability of medical institutions. The medical institution shall in its diagnosis and treatment produce evidence on the nonexistence of the three circumstances provided in this article, i.e., violating laws, administrative regulations or rules, and other relevant requirements on diagnostic and treatment practices; concealing or refusing to provide medical records relating to the dispute; and forging, tampering, or destroying medical records. If the medical institution cannot provide sufficient evidence on the nonexistence of the three circumstances, the medical institution shall bear the tortious liability. If the medical institution can provide sufficient evidence to prove that it has no fault, it does not bear tortious liability for the damage on the patients according to the principle of fault liability. This article is also a further illustration of the "fault" mentioned in Article 54, providing the criterion for fault on the medical institution by giving three specific conducts, while Article 57 provides the criterion by judging upon whether or not it fulfills the medical professional's duty of care. Article 57 is abstract, and Article 58 is specific, but they are not overlapping. In practice, Article 58 pays more attention on the allocation of the burden of proof.

Example Chai was hospitalized because of an operation on his rectum. During recovery, Chai felt sick and informed the hospital several times expressing his doubts about the transfusion he had received. However, the attending doctor considered it a normal side effect of the operation; the doctor persisted in the transfusion and promised Chai that he was not in any danger. On the fifth day after the operation, Chai showed symptoms of cardiac failure and died. His relatives asked the hospital for medical records, and the hospital refused. His relatives then brought a lawsuit against the hospital. The hospital argued that the medical records were lost during a removal to the warehouse, so they could not produce them. The court held that the hospital's act was in conformity with the circumstances provided in Article 58; thus, the hospital was deemed at fault, and the plaintiff won the case.

Article 59

Rule If a patient suffers damage due to defective drugs, disinfectants, and medical devices or transfusion of blood that do not meet the standards, she may seek compensation from the producer or blood-supplying organization as well as from the medical institution. If the said patient seeks compensation from the medical institution, the medical institution is entitled to, after paying compensation, seek reimbursement from the producer or blood-supplying organization liable for the damage.

Explanation This article provides the tortious liability on damages caused by defective drugs, infected medical devices, or substandard blood. To understand the term "defective" in this article, we can refer to Article 46 of the Product Quality Law: "'defective' means the product can unjustifiably endanger one's body or property; when national or industrial standard has been made to protect human body and health, and the safety of one's property, it means below that standard." Patients harmed by defective drugs, infected medical devices, or substandard blood are entitled to seek compensation from the producer, the blood supplier. If the patient selects to seek compensation from the medical institution, the medical institution may, after paying compensation, claim the same from the liable producer or blood supplier. They are jointly and severally liable.

Example Bian suffered a massive hemorrhage while giving birth. The hospital gave her a blood transfusion. However, after the transfusion, Bian was diagnosed with HIV, and the cause was identified to be the blood transfusion. Bian sued the hospital for damages. The hospital argued that the damages were caused by the blood supplier, which the hospital has no obligation to test. The court held that the hospital was liable according to this article, so it cannot refuse to compensate Bian. But the hospital can claim the same from the culpable blood supplier after paying compensation.

Article 60

Rule Under any of the following circumstances, a medical institution shall not assume compensatory liability for any damage caused to a patient:

1. The patient or his immediate relative does not cooperate with the medical institution in the diagnosis and treatment that comply with therapeutic standards.
2. The medical staff has fulfilled the duty of reasonable diagnosis and treatment in the case of an emergency such as rescue of a patient in critical condition.
3. Diagnosis and treatment of the patient are difficult given the limitation of prevailing medical standards.

Under the circumstance in item one of the preceding paragraph, if the medical institution or any of its medical staff is also at fault, the medical institution shall assume the corresponding compensatory liability.

Explanation This article provides the grounds of relief for medical institutions. If the patient or any of his close relatives fails to cooperate with the medical institution in the course of qualified medical treatment, the medical institution shall not be liable to pay compensation. To apply it appropriately, we should combine it with the second clause. The circumstances when the patient or any of his immediate relatives fails to cooperate with the medical institution in the course of qualified medical treatment vary greatly; sometimes it is merely the fault of the patient or any of his close relatives. For example, when the medical professional fulfilled the duty of informing and of diagnosis and treatment, but the patient or any of his close relatives does not cooperate with the diagnosis and treatment. Sometimes it is a mixed fault, i.e., both sides are at fault, under which circumstances the medical institution shall bare corresponding responsibility. For damages caused by medical measures used to save the patient in a life-threatening situation in which reasonable obligation has been meet, the medical institution shall not be held liable for compensation. Two essential factors have to be met under these circumstances. First, it must be a life-threatening situation for the patients. Second, the medical professionals have satisfied their reasonable obligation. According to recent diagnosis and treatment standard, reasonable obligation includes four criteria. First, the medical institutions accurately diagnose the patient's condition. If the situation is emergent, reasonable control of the condition has to be performed before further diagnosis and treatment. Second, the treatment measures and the medicines used shall be proper and reasonable. Third, cautiously fulfill the obligation to inform. Fourth, the damage to the patients caused by the emergency treatment shall be controlled within a reasonable amount of time given the patient's condition. For the third ground of relief mentioned, the medical institution shall prove that in the medical and scientific condition of that time, the disease is hard to diagnose and treat, or the diagnosis and treatment of the disease can cause unexpected and unpredictable risks. Notice that the medical institution and its medical professionals do not bear the obligation to guarantee a cure. If, the disease is difficult to cure, and damages rather than cure were the result of the treatment in which the medical professional fulfilled his obligation according to the medical standard of the time, the medical institution shall not be liable to pay compensation.

Example Working in a factory, Gong was hit on his head by a paper box that fell from above, but Gong insisted that he was fine and a paper box could not stop him from going back to work. His workmates forced him to go to the hospital for a check-up. The doctor suggested a CT, because the corner of the paper box may cause brain damage, a similar occurrence had once caused a patient to die of rupture of blood vessel in the brain. Gong considered the suggestion as ridiculous and refused to comply. He was actually annoyed and thought the doctor was trying to rip him off. The doctor and his workmates could not persuade him to do a CT. A few hours after he left the hospital, Gong started vomiting, he was sent back to the hospital, but nothing could be done to save him. The legal medical expert identified the cause of death to be rupture of a blood vessel in the brain, and it could have been cured if timely treated. Gong's family members sued the hospital, claiming that the hospital failed to fulfill its obligations and indulged Gong to leave and die. The court held that it was Gong who refused to be treated even after the hospital informed him about the consequences. The court dismissed the case.

Article 61

Rule The medical institution and its medical staff shall record and properly maintain the hospital admission logs, medical treatment order slips, test reports, operation and anesthesia records, pathology records, nurse care records, medical expenses sheets, and other medical history data according to the relevant provisions.

If a patient files a request for inspecting or copying the medical history data in the preceding paragraph, the medical institution shall provide the data.

Explanation This article provides the obligation which should be fulfilled by the medical institution and its medical professionals. The first clause provides that medical institutions and their medical professionals shall complete and properly maintain medical records. Medical institutions and their medical professionals shall complete and properly maintain medical records according to requirements of the medical administration department of the State Council. The basic requirements for the completeness of the medical records are objective, genuine, accurate, timely, and complete. Medical records which are not completed because of emergency treatments shall be completed within 6 h after the emergency treatment, and the delay in recording be annotated. The falsification, forgery, concealment, and robbery of medical records are forbidden. The second clause of this article provides the patient's right to access and make copy of the medical records. According to this article, the subject of this right shall be the patient himself. Whether someone other than the patient can request access to or make copies of the records is regulated in the regulations issued by related departments. According to Regulations on the Management of Medical Records in Medical Institutions issued by the Health Department and the State Pharmaceutical Administration combined, medical institutions shall grant the request to check or make a copy of the medical records of the following persons and institutions: the patient and his agent, the close relatives or agent of the deceased patient, and the insurance companies.

Example While riding a motorcycle, Hou collided with a mini car driven by Yang. Hou was injured and hospitalized. After he left the hospital, the disability appraising committee for traffic accidents identified Hou as 5-degree maim in the brain and 8-degree maim in the eyes. Yang made a motion for reidentification. The provincial disability appraising committee for traffic accidents required him to provide medical records, CT, and the original expert report for reidentification. When the plaintiff asked the defendant for his medical records, the defendant told him that his medical records were lost. The plaintiff argued that because the defendant lost his medical records, he could not reidentify his maim and should be compensated for the loss from the damages received if the reidentification came out. Therefore, the defendant should compensate him for his medical care expenses, future medical care expenses, allowance for disability, traveling costs, etc. The court held that since the plaintiff was hospitalized in the accused hospital and had paid off the fees, the contract between the plaintiff and the defendant was established, so the plaintiff has the right to acquire sufficient information in law. The defendant should pay for the traveling cost due to failing to fulfill its duty. Because the plaintiff cannot produce enough proof to show the damages arising from the lost of the medical records, his claim was not supported by the court. In the end, the court ruled that the hospital only had to pay for Hou's traveling cost.

Article 62

Rule The medical institution and its medical staff shall ensure the privacy of a patient is kept confidential. If any private data of a patient is divulged or any of the medical history data of a patient is open to the public without the patient's consent, causing any damage to the patient, the medial institution shall assume the tort liability.

Explanation This article provides the tortious liability for the infringing of the patients' privacy. The tort action has to be an unauthorized disclosure of the patient's private or medical records. The privacy of the patient means the patient's mental or physical secrets that the patient does not want to disclose in circumstances that do not contradict the interests of others or society. The patient's privacy includes physical characteristics; reproductive system diseases; physical defects; special diseases that may affect the patient's social image, status, and professional practice; the patient's history of diseases, life, and marriage; the history of disease in the patient's family; the patient's social circle, property, and other economic conditions; etc. For the protection of the patient's privacy, three clinical aspects have to be paid attention. Except when the law or regulations dictate otherwise, the patient or his close relatives' consent is needed for a third party or organization to read a patient's medical records. The clinical medical report or research, without the patient's consent, shall not be published using real name and real medical records and shall not be reported as a literature. The use of the photographic data requires the patient's consent. Pictures that can reveal the identity or characteristic of the patient cannot be taken freely and shall not be published as photographic art. The live broadcast or TV broadcast of the patient's operation requires a letter of attorney from the patient or his close relatives and shall try to avoid the revealing of the patient's identity or private parts.

Example Chi caught a kind of sexually transmitted disease and was cured in the accused hospital. The hospital advertised Chi's case in the local newspaper without his consent, and it was broadcasted by the local TV station several times. This had been widely gossiped among Chi's colleague, and Chi was under pressure that he could not go to work normally. As a result, Chi sued the hospital and claimed that it should bear tortious liability. In his complaint, Chi asked the hospital to compensate him ¥50,000 for mental distress, stop the tortious act immediately, and withdraw the TV advertisement. The court held that the hospital violated Article 62 of the

Tort Law and caused great damage to Chi's normal life. So, the hospital should immediately stop the infringement and compensate Chi for his mental distress.

Article 63

Rule The medical institution and its medical staff shall not perform unnecessary examinations in violation of the norms and standards for diagnosis and treatment.

Explanation This article prohibits unnecessary checks carried out by medical institutions and their medical professionals. According to this article, two standards are listed defining unnecessary checks. First, whether or not they are in accordance with clinical norms. The clinical norms are norms which come from clinical experiences in the medical profession. Second, although not being specified by clinical norms, according to general judgment of medical professionals, the checks exceed the basic requirements of the diagnosis of the disease and do not comply with the characteristics and discipline of the disease.

Example Rong wrenched his ankle while playing basketball. With the help of his classmates, the doctor gave him an MRI. Meanwhile, the doctor also prescribed a routine blood test, a routine urine test, etc., and told him that an overall check would help him recover sooner. In the end, Rong was diagnosed as slightly wrenched in his ankle. The doctor prescribed him two bottles of Yunnan Baiyao and required him to have complete rest. Rong thought that a simple wrench did not need to be given an MRI, and an overall check was far more than necessary, so he sued the hospital. The court held that the MRI was a scientific check for him, and there was no evidence that it was unnecessary. But an overall check was not necessary because it was unrelated to the diagnosis. Thus, the hospital should return fees for Rong's overall check.

Article 64

Rule The legitimate rights and interests of the medical institution and its medical staff are protected by law. Anyone who interferes with the order of the medical system or obstructs the work and life of medical staff shall be subject to legal liability.

Explanation This article provides that the legitimate rights and interests of medical institutions and their medical professionals are protected by law. Medical institutions and their medical professionals have legitimate rights and interests according to law. According to "Medical Professional Law and the Regulation on the Administration of Nurses" ("Medical Professional Law"), medical care providers shall in there clinical practice have legitimate rights and interests. Persons who disturb the clinical order and obstruct the work and life of the medical professional shall be liable. Article 21 of the Medical Professional Law provides that there are seven rights in the practice of medicine, among them the fifth right is that “in the clinical practice, the personal dignity and safety shall not be offended.” At the same time it provides that persons who hinder the clinical practice, insult, libel, threaten, beat up the professional or infringe on the personal freedom of the professional, and interfere with the normal life and work of the professional shall be punished according to the Security Administration Punishment Law. If the person violates the criminal law, he shall also be liable for his crime.

Example A kid hit by a car was sent to a hospital. Without being paid, the hospital performed expertise emergency treatment for him, but the kid still passed away. His family members could not accept the fact that the child’s injuries were too serious and thought that the child’s death was due to the bad performance of the doctor. Consequently, the family members mauled the doctor collectively. Later, they gathered dozens of armed people, surrounded the doctor, forced him to kowtow to the child, and beat him again and again until the police came. The doctor was later identified as third degree disabled, with skull fracture and spine dislocation. What is more, he was almost caught in high paraplegia. The court held that the defendant organized, planned, conducted, and participated in gathering a crowd to disturb the social order. The activity was of a serious nature, which not only halted the routine work of the hospital but caused great damages. The defendants’ behavior has already constituted the crime of collectively disturbing social order. Thus, the two defendants were sentenced to 6-month detention under the criminal law and to pay jointly and severally to the doctor ¥300,000 as compensation.

Chapter 20
Liability for Environmental Pollution

Article 65

Rule Where any damage is caused by environmental pollution, the polluter shall assume the tort liability.

Explanation This article articulates general regulations of damage caused by environmental pollution and specifies the scope regulated by this chapter. For the purpose of this article, tortious liability of damage caused by environmental pollution contains three constituent elements that are the existing of environment-polluting conduct, the existing of damage, and causality between conduct and damage. Considering the variety of polluting forms, this article adopts polluter rather than emitter. The concept of pollution comprehends not only environmental pollution to the living environment, such as air, water, ocean, and land, but also pollution to the ecological environment, such as the destruction of biological diversity, water loss, and soil erosion, caused by destruction of ecological natural resources. And the forms of environmental pollution include not only traditional pollution forms, such as water pollution, atmospheric pollution, noise pollution, etc., but also new forms like light pollution, radiation pollution, and so on. Domestic pollution between residents adopts fault liability, and it is mainly resolved by contiguous relationship provided by Property Law of the People's Republic of China rather than this chapter. However, environmental pollution caused by enterprises and manufacturers should be applied with no-fault liability, which is regulated by Tort Law, Environmental Protection Law, Law on the Prevention and Control of Atmospheric Pollution, Law on the Prevention and Control of Water Pollution, and other related laws. Environment-polluting conduct contains act and omission.

Example A chemical factory was located at the entrance of a village. Its chemical waste was discharged without treatment into the local river, which polluted not only the water supply in the lower reaches but hundreds of acres of local farmland, resulting in failed harvests. The villagers filed a collective action against the chemical factory. After investigation and evidence collection, the court ruled that

X. Li and J. Jin, *Concise Chinese Tort Laws*, China-EU Law Series 1,
DOI 10.1007/978-3-642-41024-6_20, © Springer-Verlag Berlin Heidelberg 2014

the chemical factory had to stop discharging waste, clean the river channels, and compensate all the villagers' losses.

Article 66

Rule Where any dispute arises over environmental pollution, the polluter assumes the burden of proof that it should not be liable or that its liability should be mitigated under certain circumstances provided by law. Additionally, the polluter has the burden of proof that there is no causation between its conduct and damages.

Explanation This article assigns the burden of proof regarding excuses or exemptions from liability and causation. Environmental pollution liability is special tortious conduct, and it applies the principle of no-fault liability. Firstly, the principle of no-fault liability is applied to prompt the person controlling the polluting factors to perform his obligation against environmental pollution and take positive measures to prevent environmental pollution. Secondly, no-fault liability is applied to strengthen the protection of victims. In environmental pollution actions, the polluter cannot be exempted from liability by proving no fault of his own. He can merely prove the existence of excuses or exemptions from liability provided by law to eliminate or mitigate liability. Environmental pollution liability inverts the burden of proof for causation; a presumption of causation is noteworthy because it is a partial transference of proof obligations from the plaintiff to the defendant. The defendant shall bear the consequence of incapability of producing evidence. Although the plaintiff bears no burden of proof for the existence of causation, he bears the burden of proof for damages and polluting conduct.

Example Women in a village constantly delivered infants with malformations. The prescription of the specialists in a university hospital indicated that mercury content inside the infants which could be caused by excessive discharge of waste by a local chemical works severely exceeds the limits. The subsequent investigation carried out by the environmental protection department shows that the mercury discharge of the chemical works exceeded the standard by more than 1,000 times and that there is no other source of mercury in the village. The victim sued the chemical works claiming tortious conduct. The chemical works argued that the plaintiff could not prove the existence of causality and thus cannot win the lawsuit. The court held that the defendant shall bear the burden of proof, but the defendant failed to produce evidence and therefore the court ruled against the defendant.

Article 67

Rule If the environmental pollution is caused by two or more polluters, the degree of liability of each polluter shall be determined according to the type of pollutant, volume of emissions, and other factors as deemed appropriate.

Explanation This article regulates who bears environmental pollution liability when shared by several people who have no communication of intention. Where plural tort cases arise out of the same nucleus of facts resulting in one or more damages, the acts of several people are treated separately, to varying degrees, rather than combined as an integral whole to determine the damage. Each act acts differently on the damage and its causative potency varies. Causative potency is the effect of each cause, among the several causes that result in the same damage, has on the occurrence or expansion of the damage. The theory of causative potency applies to what proportion of tortious liability each actor assumes or to the share of damage between the tortfeasor and the victim. Generally speaking, the greater the causative potency, the more liability shall be borne, and in turn, the weaker causative potency, the less liability. The comparison of causative potency and the comparison of fault of the parties involved are comprehensively applied to decide the distribution of liability. The proportion for which each is liable is mainly based on the proportion, which a polluter's conduct takes, of causative potency in inducing the damage. It is quite complicated to decide the causative potency in environmental pollution. When the proportion of liability is specified, the type and volume of waste discharged by polluters should be considered. The calculation of the volume of discharge is the product of the total volume of liquid waste discharged multiplied by the discharge concentration rather than simply the total volume of liquid waste discharged. The amount of discharge of an emergency can refer to monitoring data, and the amount of accumulative waste discharged can be measured by the volume reported by the discharging bodies, daily monitoring data, monitoring data from the environmental protection department, etc. In addition, besides the two factors (the type of pollutant and the volume of discharge), other factors such as distance from the place where pollutant is discharged, how long the discharge lasts, perniciousness of pollutant, etc., should be taken into account. Polluters are liable for their own proportion, though not jointly and severally liable, nor liable for all the compensation. Thus, one polluter shall have no claim for compensation from the other polluters thereof internally.

Example There were two paper mills in a city which abut each other and discharge liquid waste into the same river. As the liquid waste did not reach the dischargeable standard, the local river was polluted and a ¥5 million loss was caused. The environmental protection department established a special investigation team to carry out the investigation and found out that the two mills discharged liquid waste that exceeded the standard by 100 times but the volumes of discharge differed largely. Mill A discharged an accumulative total of 600 tons, and Mill B discharged 200 tons. Finally, the court ruled that Mill A was liable for the compensation of ¥4 million and Mill B was liable for compensation of ¥1 million.

Article 68

Rule If any damage is caused by environmental pollution due to the fault of a third party, the victim may seek compensation from either the polluter or the third party. After making compensation, the polluter is entitled to seek reimbursement from the third party.

Explanation This article articulates how liability is assumed where any damage is caused by environmental pollution attributable to a third party. There are two premises for the application of this article. First, the polluter has no fault in the occurrence of the damage or the faults of the polluter and that of the third party will not constitute joint infringement based on the oneness of content of fault while the polluter has fault. Second, causation between polluter and damage is required; otherwise, the polluter would be exempted from liability because no causation exists between him and the damage which makes the third party at fault liable for all damages, so as to produce the foundation to lose nontypical joint and several liability. The third party and the defendant do not share joint intent and negligence, namely, no communication of intention. The acts of both do not constitute as a coordinated act, so joint infringement does not exist between the third party and the polluter. Fault of the third party mentioned in this article is separate and interventional. For the purpose of this article, the polluter cannot be exempted from environmental liability, regardless of the third party's act being intentional or negligent, a general negligence or a major one. In addition, the polluter cannot be exempted from liability regardless of the relationship between the third party's act and the damage, even if the third party's act is the only cause of the damage. In other words, the third party's act is absolutely no excuse or defense for the polluter to assume no or mitigated liability. Environmental tortious acts attributable to the third party are not acts polluting the environment directly. It is not different from general tortious acts. The third party at fault is not the direct actor resulting in environmental pollution. It is the acts of the polluter that actually result in damages caused by environmental pollution. However, the acts of the polluter do not simply cause damages from environmental pollution. Under that circumstance, the polluter generally has no fault or the fault does not constitute joint environmental infringement of no communication of intention with the fault of the third party. Where any compensation for damage caused by environmental pollution is attributable to a third party, the burden-allocation principle of "he who is affirming must prove" is adopted in respect of third party, and inversion of burden of proof is adopted with regard to the polluter.

Example Due to intoxication, Geng's car bumped into a chemical raw material warehouse owned by a chemical factory. Hazardous substances spread and resulted in losses of ¥8 million to nearby residents. The victims sued the chemical factory and claimed compensation. The chemical factory argued that the accident was caused by the third party and it had no fault. Based on Article 68 of the Tort Law, the court ruled that the chemical factory was liable and must pay compensation in advance. However, the chemical factory could seek reimbursement from Geng to which the fault belonged afterwards.

Chapter 21
Liability for Ultrahazardous Activity

Article 69

Rule One who causes any damage to another while engaging in an ultrahazardous operation shall assume the tort liability.

Explanation This article is the provision on tort liability incurred by causing damages by someone who is engaging in ultrahazardous activities. According to this article, the person who engaged in ultrahazardous operation will be strictly liable for injuries caused to others. Strict liability for ultrahazardous operations allows the victim to accuse the perpetrator of a tort, and the victim does not have to prove that the perpetrator is at fault, as long as the victim's harm is caused by perpetrator's engaging in ultrahazardous operations. To be liable for damages caused by ultrahazardous activities, four elements must be met: (1) the perpetrator is engaging in an ultrahazardous operation, which is legal or at least not forbidden by the law, that could cause danger to its surroundings; (2) the inherent danger of this operation to its surroundings and the possible damages this operation may cause are foreseeable; (3) the ultrahazardous activity has caused harm; and (4) there is a relation of causation between the ultrahazardous activity and the harm.

Example A Power Company is fixing high-voltage wire poles. Due to the operation error of workers, the high-voltage wire was cut and shocked the victim that resulted in severe burns and multiple organ failures. After 1 day of emergency treatment, the victim died. The victim's family members sued the Power Company. According to Article 69 of the Tort Law, judgment was entered for the plaintiff.

Article 70

Rule If a nuclear accident occurs at a civil nuclear facility and causes any damage to other persons, the operator of the civil nuclear facility shall be tortiously liable,

X. Li and J. Jin, *Concise Chinese Tort Laws*, China-EU Law Series 1,
DOI 10.1007/978-3-642-41024-6_21, © Springer-Verlag Berlin Heidelberg 2014

unless it can prove that the damage is caused by a situation such as war or by the victim intentionally.

Explanation This article is the provision on tort liability incurred by harm caused by a civil nuclear facility. The principle of no-fault liability applies in this case. Nuclear activities performed by humans are a type of ultrahazardous operation which is dangerous to the surroundings. Because of the conditions of the existing nuclear industry, although people take extreme caution towards each aspect of operations, dangerous accidents could cause harm to surrounding persons and properties and the environment. For the purposes of protecting the safety of people and property, the Tort Law provides that where any harm is caused by a nuclear operation, the operator shall assume tort liability, even if the operator is not at fault. There are two exemptions from liability for a civil nuclear facility. First, if the harm caused by a civil nuclear facility is caused by war or other similar situation, the operator of that civil nuclear facility shall not be liable. According to Article 6 of the "Official Reply of State Council on the Issue concerning Liability incurred by Harms caused by Nuclear Accident," when a nuclear accident is directly caused by armed conflict, an act of hostility, war, or riot, the operator of the nuclear facility shall not be liable for the harm caused by the nuclear accident. Second, the operator of the civil nuclear facility shall not be liable if the victim intentionally incurred the harm caused by the nuclear accident.

Example An accidental nuclear leak occurred at a nuclear power plant, polluting a large area of the local fields and causing the local peasants a loss of more than ¥10 million. It was proved in the subsequent investigation that the accident was caused by the nuclear facility's decrepit equipment. There was no evidence of sabotage. The two sides disputed over the amount of the compensation the plaintiff sued for. According to the investigation, the court determined the amount of loss and held that the nuclear power plant shall indemnify the local peasants for the actual losses.

Article 71

Rule If a civil aircraft causes any damage to persons, the operator of the civil aircraft shall assume the tort liability unless it can prove that the damage was caused by the victim intentionally.

Explanation This article is the provision on tort liability incurred by harm caused by a civil aircraft. According to this article, the principle of no-fault liability shall apply in this case. Aviation is a profession which requires both high professionalism and high technical skill, because most of the accidents happen in the air; sometimes it is impossible for the victims to prove subjective fault. Even if they could prove this, the cost for victims to prove such fault is often extremely high. Moreover, damage prevention in this field solely depends upon the perpetrator, the proprietor of the aircraft. The victim is incapable of preventing such harm from happening.

Also, because aviation risks exist and the technology to prevent it is less developed, the reduction of aviation accident costs must depend on whether the proprietor of the aircraft takes every possible precaution and is willing to bear high prevention costs for more developed preventive measures. Therefore, only no-fault liability provides an aircraft proprietor with greater motivation to develop new measure which can reduce accident costs. And only no-fault liability can provide the perpetrator with greater motivation to prevent the harm from happening. The exemption from liability incurred by harm caused by an aircraft only applies if the victim intentionally caused the harm. The proprietor of the aircraft shall not assume tort liability in this situation.

Example The plaintiff took defendant's flight (an international airline company) to travel abroad. When the plane took off, the left engine malfunctioned and the passenger instantly evacuated from the plane. During the emergency evacuation, due to the bumpiness in the aircraft and the smoky environment, the plaintiff was injured. The plaintiff sued and claimed that the defendant should compensate for his loss. After an investigation, the court confirmed the injury and plaintiff's actual loss and ruled that the defendant shall be liable for plaintiff's actual loss.

Article 72

Rule The possessor or user of inflammable, explosive, acutely toxic, radioactive, or any other ultrahazardous materials shall assume tort liability of damage to another, unless the damage is intentionally caused by the victim or by force majeure. If the victim is grossly negligent during the occurrence of the harm, the liability of the possessor or user may be mitigated.

Explanation This article is the provision on tort liability incurred by causing harm to another by the possession or use of ultrahazardous materials. According to this article, the possessor or the user of flammable, explosive, acutely toxic, radioactive, or other ultrahazardous materials will be held strictly liable for harm these materials cause to another person. The liability incurred by possessing or using ultrahazardous materials has three constitutive requirements: (1) possessing or using flammable, explosive, acutely toxic, radioactive, or other ultrahazardous contents; (2) harm was caused; and (3) causation between the possession or use of the ultrahazardous materials and the harm. There are two exemptions from such liability: (1) the victim intentionally caused the harm, and (2) the harm was caused by force majeure. This article also provides that, if the aggrieved party is grossly negligent, the liability of the possessor or user of the ultrahazardous materials may be mitigated. This provision means that during the occurrence of the harm, if the aggrieved party was ordinarily negligent, his liability cannot be mitigated. This provision also means that in the case of no-fault liability, the fault is used to mitigate the perpetrator's liability.

Example The defendant (Xiao) operated a fireworks factory outside a village close to Zhong's field. Before the spring festival, the factory speeds up its production. Due to working continuously, the workers were exhausted. Because production was dangerous, an explosion occurred in the factory. This explosion killed five workers and Zhong, who was working in the field at the time. The families of the workers were indemnified by the defendant. However, the defendant and Zhong's family failed to reach an agreement on compensation, which resulted in a lawsuit. The plaintiff (Zhong's family) claimed that the defendant should compensate ¥500,000. The defendant argued that because Zhong worked in the field during the slow season, he was grossly negligent for his death. The court ruled that Zhong working in his field was absolutely proper. Therefore, Xiao's argument was not supported, and judgment was entered for the plaintiff.

Article 73

Rule If damage is caused to another by an aerial, high-pressure, or underground excavation activity or by the use of high-speed rail transport vehicle, the operator shall assume tort liability unless it can prove that the damage was caused by the victim intentionally or by force majeure. If the victim was negligent for the occurrence of the harm, the liability of the operator may be mitigated.

Explanation This article is the provision on tort liability incurred by harm caused by an aerial, high-pressure, or underground excavation activity or by the use of a high-speed rail transport vehicle. According to this article, where any harm is caused to another by an aerial, high-pressure, or underground excavation activity or by the use of a high-speed rail transport vehicle, the operator shall assume tort liability. To be noted, in this article, the concept of "high-speed rail transport vehicle" is used. However, in "General Principles of Civil Law of the People's Republic of China," the concept of "high-speed means of transport" is used. Because Chapter six of the Tort Law has specific provisions on liability for motor vehicle traffic accidents, liability for ultrahazardous activity rules out the liability for motor vehicle traffic accidents. Also, because Chapter nine of the Tort Law has a specific provision on civil aircrafts, a "high-speed rail transport vehicle" includes a train and a subway. According to this article, where any harm is caused to another, the perpetrator will be held strictly liable. There are three element requirements for such tort liability: (1) the operator engaged in aerial, high-pressure, or underground excavation activity or used a high-speed rail transport vehicle; (2) the operator's actions caused harm to another; and (3) there is causation between the operator's actions and the harm. The perpetrator's liability may be mitigated when the harm is caused by the victim intentionally or by force majeure. If the aggrieved party has general fault in the occurrence of the harm, the operator's liability may be mitigated.

Example The defendant was the contractor of a city's government subway construction project. During the company's tunneling, the construction caused a massive collapse. A Passat was driving on the road and fell when the collapse happened. The driver suffered cervical vertebra and high paraplegia. The victim sued the company for compensation. The company claimed that they should not be liable because the collapse related to the design of the subway line which was done by another company and that the collapse was force majeure and was difficult to foresee. The court ruled that the collapse is a type of engineering accident, so defendant's argument was ignored and judgment was entered for the plaintiff.

Article 74

Rule If any damage is caused to another by the loss or abandonment of ultrahazardous materials, the owner shall assume tort liability. If the owner handed the ultrahazardous materials to a third party for management, the manager shall assume tort liability; and if the owner is at fault, he/she shall be jointly and severally liable with the manager.

Explanation This article is the provision on tort liability incurred by harm caused by the loss or abandonment of ultrahazardous materials. According to this article, where any harm is caused to another by the loss or abandonment of ultrahazardous materials, the owner of such materials shall assume tort liability and will be held strictly liable for the harm. There are three elements required for such liability: (1) the act of losing or abandoning the ultrahazardous materials, (2) harm, and (3) causation between the act and the harm. If the harm is caused when the owner delivered the ultrahazardous materials to another for management, the person who assumes the tort liability shall be the managing person. If the owner is at fault, he/she shall be jointly and severally liable with the person who manages the materials. If the owner is not at fault, he/she shall not assume tort liability.

Example A company's production involved using radioactive material. Even after the production ended, the material can still cause extremely strong radioactive harm. The company usually kept this material safely in its warehouse. However, when the company's factory relocated, it decided to abandon the no-longer-available radioactive material to a deserted mountain located 100 km away from the factory. Wang and two loggers found the abandoned material and took it home not knowing the material was hazardous. The material later caused these three persons and their family great physical harm. The court ruled that the company understood the hazard of the radioactive material, but still intentionally abandoned the material, neglecting the safety of others. Therefore, the company was liable. Judgment was entered for the plaintiff and the defendant was compensated a total of over ¥3 million.

Article 75

Rule If damage to another is caused by the illegal possession of ultrahazardous materials, the illegal possessor shall be liable. If the owner and the managing person cannot prove that it has fulfilled its duty of a high degree of care in preventing others from illegal possession, they shall be jointly and severally liable with the illegal possessor.

Explanation This article is the provision on tort liability incurred by harm caused by the illegal possession of ultrahazardous materials. According to this article, when ultrahazardous materials are illegally possessed and cause harm to another, the illegal possessor shall assume tort liability. Due to another person's illegal possession of the ultrahazardous materials, the owner and the managing person lost control over the material and did not actually operate ultrahazardous operation. However, because their right to engage in ultrahazardous operation still remains, their obligation to keep the ultrahazardous material is not eliminated. Therefore, if the owner and the managing person cannot prove that they fulfilled their duty of a high degree of care in preventing others from illegal possession, they shall be jointly and severally liable with the illegal possessor. The owner and the managing person shall assume the liability incurred by the negligence so that it will objectively encourage them to fulfill their duty of care to prevent losing the ultrahazardous materials. If the owner and the managing person can prove that they are not at fault for the illegal possession of the ultrahazardous materials, they shall not assume tort liability.

Example The victim (Jiao) and his coworker Yin were both security guards of a property management company. One day, as Yin patrolled the residential area, he stole a green-bottled smart brand drink which he later poured into the victim's cup. After the victim drank the drink, he felt a great pain in his stomach. The victim's coworkers immediately sent him to the hospital. The victim was treated and hospitalized for 13 days. The medical care and the transportation cost the victim ¥25,000 in total. The subsequent investigation proved that the drink Yin stole contained hydrochloric acid and sulfuric acid which caused chemical burns on the victim's esophagus and gastric mucosa. According to forensic examination, these were minor injuries. During hospitalization, the property management company paid ¥7,700 in advance for Jiao's medical expenses. However, both Yin and the property management company refused to pay the rest of the victim's expenses. The court ruled that Jiao's harm was caused by Yin's act of pouring the stolen drink into Jiao's cup, so Yin shall assume the majority of the liability. However, the property management company was careless in keeping the liquid containing hydrochloric acid and sulfuric acid in drink bottles, so as to allow Yin to possess the liquid so easily. Therefore, the company was at fault and shall also assume tort liability. The court held that Yin shall compensate Jiao and that the company shall be held jointly and severally liable with Jiao.

Article 76

Rule Where any damage is caused by entering an area of ultrahazardous activities or an area storing ultrahazardous materials, if the managing person took safety measures and fulfilled its duty to warn, its liability may be mitigated or it may assume no liability.

Explanation This article is the provision on special occasions where tort liability can be exempt. Because of the danger ultrahazardous activities and ultrahazardous materials can bring, to protect the interests of victims, the law requires that the perpetrator be held strictly liable. However, ultrahazardous activities or operations that involve ultrahazardous materials are legally authorized or, at least, not forbidden by law. Also such activities utilize modern technology to serve society, benefiting people's standards of living and the greater good of humankind. So such activities are not only authorized by law but also encouraged. The provision of law that provides assuming liability for ultrahazardous activities should not be so harsh and should allow people involved in ultrahazardous activities to have some freedom to develop technologies. Otherwise, the law might interfere with societal development. The core problem is to determine whether the managing person took safety measures and fulfilled its duty of warning. Generally speaking, safety measures included setting isolated areas and taking protecting measures like radiation proof or insulation. The duty of warning includes setting up prominent signs to provide security. The specific safety measure requirements and the duty of warming are provided by different laws. For example, Article 11 of "Regulations on the Protection of Power Facilities" provides that "Power administrative departments at and above the county level shall take following measures to protect power facilities: (1) put up marks on the boundaries of overhead power line protection zones, specifying the width of the protection zone and the rules for protection; (2) put up marks in major roads or navigation sections where power lines cross, specifying the safe distance between the conducting wires and the objects to cross; (3) put up permanent markers for underground cables after their completion and notify related departments in writing of the position of the underground cables; (4) put up permanent markers for under-water cables after their completion and notify related departments in writing of the positions of the under-water cables." And Article 10 of "Regulations on the protection of railway transport safety" provides that a "Safe protection zone should be set up on both sides of the railway. The width of the safe protection zone, which spreads out from the embankment of the railway, the slope's bottom or top, the railway cutting or the outer side of a railroad bridge, should be determined as follows: (1) in urban areas, not less than 8 meters; (2) in the urban and suburb residential areas, not less than 10 meters; (3) in rural residential areas or towns, not less than 12 meters; and (4) in other areas, not less than 15 meters. Railway transport enterprises should set up marking stakes on the boundary of the safe protection zone. Other protection methods, such as walls and fences, should also be set up according to specific requirements of different occasions."

Example A nuclear power plant stored raw uranium in a separate and stable warehouse with security facilities. Special guards were hired to guard the warehouse and safety warnings were set up. Liu and some other pupils were curious about why there were so many guards around the warehouse. They cooperated in leading the guards away and stole the key to the warehouse. They ended up being radiated and seriously hurt. Their families sued the nuclear power plant for tort liability. The court ruled that the nuclear power plant had provided sufficient safety protection measures, but the parents of the victims failed to fulfill their obligation of custody. Therefore, the nuclear power plant was not liable. As the result of court mediation, the nuclear power plant compensated each victim ¥10,000 for humanitarianism concerns.

Article 77

Rule If the law provides a compensation limit for an ultrahazardous activity, such provision shall govern.

Explanation This article is the provision on compensation for liability for ultrahazardous activities. The limit on compensation for liability for ultrahazardous activities shows the law's balance in the interests of victims and operators. As a theory of responsibility allocation, the real function of no-fault liability is not to settle the subject of who should assume liability but to settle the division of loss. Legislation under no-fault liability is aimed not to sanction against antisocial behaviors but to reasonably allocate the harm. The no-fault liability determines that assuming liability is based on protecting the victims' interests. Its main goal is to compensate the economic loss of the victim. However, the law limits such compensation, usually providing provisions on maximum indemnity or limiting the range of compensation. Such limits are set up because no-fault liability without fault is to compensate the economic loss of the victim. However, if protecting the victim's right is being stressed excessively, it might result in imbalance of interests and cause unfairness to the perpetrator. This article refers to the law in a narrow sense, only the laws which are approved by the NPC and its Standing Committee. This compensation limitation applies only when it is prescribed by law. The compensation limitation prescribed in administrative regulations, local regulations, rules, and other regulatory documents shall not be the basis of issuing a compensation limit.

Example A malfunction occurred to the break of a train, which caused the victim hurt seriously. The victim suffered a total of about ¥200,000 in losses. The plaintiff sued the defendant. The parties could not reach a settlement on the amount of compensation. The defendant claimed that the compensation should be ¥40,000, because Article 5 of "Provisions on the Compensation for Harm to Passengers during Railway Transport" provided that "to any railway transport enterprise which should assume compensation according to 'Provisions on the Compensation for Harm to Passenger during Railway Transport', the maximum indemnity for death or injury of a passenger shall be ¥40,000 per person, and the maximum indemnity for the loss of the passengers' luggage shall be ¥800 per person." The plaintiff claimed that an implied railway passenger transport contract existed between the defendant and him. As the transporter, the defendant should have fulfilled its obligation to transport the plaintiff safely to his destination without delay. In addition, defendant's argument did not correspond with the provisions of the contract law. Also, before the plaintiff sued, close relatives of other passengers already brought a lawsuit. In that suit, the court decided the standard of compensation based on the "Explanation of the Supreme People's Court of Some Issues Concerning the Application of Law for the Trial of Cases on Compensation for Personal Injury." In this case, if the court approved ¥40,000 limit in compensation, a breach of contract suit would result in a compensation of less than 1/5 of the compensation of a victim in a tort suit. Obviously, it was not fair that the same case could have different results. Also, "Provisions on the Compensation for Harm to Passenger during Railway Transport" is not the law in the narrow sense, and its authority in the legal hierarchy is very low. Therefore, the court ruled that the compensation for the plaintiff shall be ¥200,000.

Chapter 22
Liability for Harm Caused by Domestic Animal

Article 78

Rule Where a domestic animal causes any damage to another, the keeper or manager of the animal shall be subject to tort liability, but may assume no liability or assume mitigated liability if it proves that the harm is caused by the victim intentionally or by the gross negligence of the victim.

Explanation This article is a general regulation for damage caused by a domestic animal. It specifies that, in general situation, the strict liability or liability without fault shall be applied when damages are caused by a domestic animal. Although it seems the keeper or manager is responsible for his pets' conduct, his own carelessness in keeping or managing pets is the source of liability. Where the danger resulted in damages, the keeper or manager shall assume civil liability. Liability cannot be mitigated or reduced, but a legal defense is possible if the infringed was intentional or had major fault. And this article adopts the reverse burden of proof, which conforms to Clause 5 of Article 4 of Some Provisions of the Supreme People's Court on Evidence in Civil Procedures. In the article, the keeper or manager would not be liable or be able to mitigate liability if he/she can prove that the damage was incurred by the injured party deliberately or the injured party was at major fault for the damage. If the keeper or manager fails to provide sufficient evidence, he/she shall be liable. Obviously, the purpose of this article is to help the injured party get compensation in an easier way.

Example Tan raised a large dog at home. He did not have it chained and let it run freely in the yard. One day Tan sent for a rag collector to collect waste paper boxes. When the victim entered the yard, the dog pounced on him and bit a piece of flesh off his leg. The attack also gave the victim a concussion. The dog did not stop biting and pouncing until Tan held it back. In court, Tan asserted that the dog possessed a gentle character and that the victim provoked the dog, which was the main cause of the accident. The Court required Tan to submit evidence showing the victim's fault, and Tan failed to do so. So, the Court ruled that Tan was liable and should compensate the victim ¥10,000.

X. Li and J. Jin, *Concise Chinese Tort Laws*, China-EU Law Series 1,
DOI 10.1007/978-3-642-41024-6_22, © Springer-Verlag Berlin Heidelberg 2014

Article 79

Rule If any damage is caused to another person by an animal keeper or manager's failure to take safety measures in violation of management rules, they shall be subject to tort liability.

Explanation This article articulates the liability where damage is caused by a failure to take security measures for an animal. The exemptions in Article 78 do not apply to tort cases and apply when there is a failure to take security measures for an animal in violation of regulations. The civil liability where any damage is caused by a domestic animal is a no-fault liability. That is to say, when demanding compensation, there is no need to consider whether or not the keeper or manager is at fault. As long as the victim can prove the actual loss and causation, liability can be attributed to the other side. However, if the victim was negligent in incurring damage, his liability may be mitigated or exempted. But where damage is caused by a failure to take security measures for an animal in violation of regulations, the exemption does not apply to the keeper or manager of the animals. The regulation of animal domestication and management shall not be violated under any circumstances. Where any damage is caused by the violation of regulations, the tort liability cannot be exempted due to the victim's fault (e.g., intentionally beating, provoking, feeding animals, or ignoring warning signs). In China, the number of animals, especially dogs, biting people is rising year by year. The purpose of this article is to protect personal safety and property. It aligns with social fairness and justice that the keeper or manager shall bear more liability and more risk of animal domestication, which is in accordance with the legislative purpose of the Tort Law.

Example Miao raised a large dog. The city in which he lived had promulgated a local regulation which required large dogs domesticated in a residential community must be leashed or kept in the cage. Miao's dog was very large but Miao never put it into the cage. One day, Miao's friend came to visit. He found the breed of Miao's dog was relatively rare and then played with it. While playing with the dog, he was bitten by the dog, resulting in a loss of ¥5,000. The victim sued Miao for tortious liability. But Miao argued the victim was bitten because he intentionally provoked the dog and therefore should be exempted. The court found that Miao's possession of a large dog violated local regulations and he should not be exempted. Therefore, the judgment was entered for the plaintiff.

Article 80

Rule If any damage to another person is caused by a dangerous animal such as a violent dog, whose possession is banned, the keeper or manger of the animal shall be subject to tort liability.

Explanation This article articulates the liability of damage caused by dangerous and domestication prohibited animals. A number of cities in China have developed their own "Dog Domestication Management Measures" and some similar regulations. These regulations, which strictly and amply regulate local domestication of dogs while accompanied by implementation of standards, detail the prohibited breeds of dog. For example, in "The Rules of the Jining Stockbreeding and Veterinary Administrative Department on Jining City Prohibited Breeds and Standards," mastiff, St. Bernard dog, Great Dane, Great Pyrenees, bloodhound, and other 37 kinds of fierce dogs were listed as prohibited breeds. In addition, the police and the Stockbreeding and Veterinary Administrative Department also prescribe a body height (shoulder height) and body length limit. A large dog exceeding this limit is prohibited. Where any damage is caused by prohibited animals, the keeper shall bear risk liability. In view of the high risk of prohibited animals, even if victims were deliberate or negligent, the keeper cannot be exempted. Especially where normative law has prohibited, but the keeper ignores the law on purpose, it is in accordance with jurisprudence that it bears aggravated liability.

Example Chai regards a dog as his life, especially Tibetan mastiff. One day, he got a purebred Tibetan mastiff from his friend. He muzzled the mastiff at night and showed it off by tying it to the entrance of the hutong. Neighbors all kept away from it in fear. Fang from another village came to visit his relatives. When he was passing Chai's entrance of the hutong, the mastiff savagely broke its chains and muzzle and mauled Fang to death. Fang's wife sued Chai for tortious liability. Chai asserted that the amount of damages should be reduced because he had taken security measures. The court found that local regulations prohibited domestication of fierce dogs such as the Tibetan mastiff. Even though Chai had taken security measures, it was clearly not enough for a Tibetan mastiff. Chai shall bear tortious liability. The court ruled that Chai shall compensate Fang's family for a total loss of ¥300,000.

Article 81

Rule If a zoo animal causes damage to another person, the zoo shall assume the tort liability unless it can prove that it has fulfilled its duties of management.

Explanation The article is about the liability of the zoo whose animals have injured someone. The article intended to reduce the liability of state-owned zoos which render services for the people. Therefore, the zoo mentioned in this article shall refer to state-owned zoos. For private zoos, Articles 78, 79, and 80 shall apply. The article states that the liability of the zoo depends on the doctrine of presumption when referring to the injuries from animals. However, if the zoo can prove that either the animal sheds or cages were working properly, obvious warning signs were set up, or the administrators had dissuaded visitors from teasing and throwing objects at the animals or climbing over the railings without authorization, it can then be concluded that due diligence in management was exercised. If due diligence was exercised, the zoo shall not be liable. The liability of the zoo is based on the doctrine of presumption that the zoo exists for public welfare and is open to the general public. If the zoo bears too much liability, it may cause an increase in admission prices, which is against the public's expectation. Also, in order to balance the interests between the victim and the zoo, the liability of the zoo shall be mitigated or exempted when the victim is grossly negligent.

Example Mr. Lei went to the city zoo on Sunday. When he came to the cage of the black bear, he felt excited even as a grown-up. While he was leaning close to the cage to watch the bear, the bear suddenly rushed at him. Because the cage had been in repair for many years, which make it fragile, it could not contain the force of the bear. As a result, the cage ruptured, the bear broke out of the cage and beat Mr. Lei on the ground. Mr. Lei's face had been badly mauled and his ribs were broken. The medical fee was ¥2,000. Mr. Lei filed suit for the zoo to compensate for the medical expenses. The zoo alleged that they should not be held liable since they exercised due diligence to lock the bear in its cage. After the inquisition, the judge ruled that was the zoo was liable for neglecting the upkeep of the cage, allowing the bear an opportunity to break out of it.

Article 82

Rule If an abandoned or fleeing animal causes any damage to another person during the time of its abandonment or fleeing, the original keeper or manager of the animal shall be subject to tort liability.

Explanation This article is the provision about tortious liability for damage caused by animals that are out of control. The act of abandoning an animal is deemed that the owner of a property abandons his property. Hence, abandoning an animal is indeed abandoning the ownership of the animal. However, an abandoned animal is not managed and is very likely to cause damage. The original keeper or manager of an abandoned animal shall bear tort liability for damage, because although the original owner abandoned their ownership, it is the abandonment that caused an unmanaged animal to bring about damages. Therefore, the keeper or manager is considered the liable party for damage and compensation. The owner does not give up its ownership of an escaped domestic animal. The animal's escape means the owner temporarily lost possession and control of the animal. There is no change of ownership. Once the escaped animal causes damages to another, the original keeper or manager still bears tort liability. The escape of an animal due to improper management or abandonment aggravates the degree of danger the animal causes an individual and vice versa. Therefore, to protect public welfare, the original keeper or manager should bear tort liability for abandoning and the mismanagement of his animal.

Example Mu raised a big German shepherd. Due to a move to another province with his whole family, he abandoned it in the village. The abandoned dog became a stray dog. No one wanted to adopt it because the dog was very fierce. One day, it bit Weng in the village. Weng stayed in the hospital for more than a month and brought a lawsuit against Mu. But, Mu argued that he was no longer the owner of the dog. According to this article, the court held that Mu shall be liable.

Article 83

Rule If any damage is caused to another person by an animal through the fault of a third party, the victim may seek compensation from the keeper or manager of the animal or from the third party. After compensating the victim, the keeper or manager of the animal is entitled to seek reimbursement from the third party.

Explanation The article prescribes the burden of tortious liability when a third party is at fault for damage caused by an animal. Elements of the keeper's liability for damage caused by an animal where the third party is at fault include the following: (1) The third party who executes conduct is at fault. The fault includes intention and negligence, both of which are wrongful, and the conduct includes an act and omission. (2) The fault of the third party and danger caused by the animal are considered to be combined. If there is only the fault of the third party, without being combined with the danger of the animal, the keeper does not bear any liability. (3) A victim suffered damage caused by realization of the danger of the animal. (4) Another is the existence of causation. Only after the victim proves the existence of causation, can he require the keeper to bear liability. If the third party's fault resulted in a suspension of causation, the keeper bears no liability. From the perspective of this article, the third party bears fault liability and the victim is required to bear the burden of proof. The keeper of the animal bears liability without fault. Consequently, from a procedural perspective, it will be more expedient if the victim requires the keeper to be liable for his damage because the victim does not have to prove the keeper's fault.

Example Cao raised a Satsuma in his house. One day, Lu and Zhu paid a visit to Cao's house. The Satsuma, willing to play with people, wanted to lick Lu. However, Lu hated close contact with animals so he kept frightening the Satsuma. Cao did not mind this because he thought it was amusing. But, the Satsuma thought Lu was playing with it and pounced on Lu. Lu got angry, pushed the dog away, and then chased and hit the dog with a stick. The Satsuma was provoked and began to bite Lu. Zhu was unexpectedly injured by the Satsuma, which cost Zhu more than ¥1,000 in medical care. The three parties did not reach an agreement on compensation after Zhu's recovery. Zhu then took Cao to court, requiring him to compensate. But Cao thought it was Lu who caused the accident, so he should not bear any liability. The court heard the case and, following Article 83, ruled against Cao. So, Cao paid Zhu ¥1,000 as compensation. At the same time, Cao sued Lu for reimbursement for his compensation. Finally, Cao won the case.

Article 84

Rule Animals shall be kept in compliance with the law, in a manner that respects the social morals, and without interference with the life of others.

Explanation This article is a regulation requiring animal keepers to abide by laws, and its main aim is to expect people to raise animals civilly. It is an encouraging rule and not a basis for judgment. This article mainly relates to the morality and justice which should be abided by when raising animals. In accordance with regulations, raising animals is a right of keepers; however, exercise of these rights should have its boundaries and restrictions, namely, to refrain from hindering others' exercise of rights. Raising animals must be in accord with legal compulsory regulations and also show respect for the universal social value. Refraining from hindering the lives of others is the basic behavioral standard of raising animals. Following this standard is the way can we ensure the normal order of lives, which is the legislative purpose of Tort Law. This article is a part of legal principles and is an encouraging item rather than a legal norm, which must consist of constitutive elements and legal consequences. Consequently, this article cannot be used as the foundation for judgments.

Example Xiang, who lives in the top story of a building, is an enthusiast of pigeons. He built some pigeons' cages to raise pigeons on the top floor of the building. But this behavior caused annoyances to his neighbors. The adjoining residents' windowsills were piled with pigeons' feces, and the downstairs residents could not open windows, or else their houses would be full of odor and pigeons feathers. The noise of the pigeons in the early morning also made it difficult for the neighbors to sleep well. Negotiations between neighbors and Xiang were not successful, because Xiang insisted that it was his individual right to raise pigeons. Eventually, with the mediation of the commission of residents, Xiang recognized his error and promised to bring the pigeons back to his rural hometown and raised them there. Meanwhile, he would compensate the neighbors who were affected ¥50 per door for cleaning.

Chapter 23
Liability for Harm Caused by an Object

Article 85

Rule Where any building, structure or facility, or any object that is stored therein or attached thereto drops or falls down, causing damage to another person, if the owner, manager, or user cannot prove that he is not at fault, he shall assume tortious liability. After providing compensation, the owner, manager, or user is entitled to seek reimbursement from other liable persons.

Explanation This article articulates the tortious liability for damage caused by a collapsing building, structure, or other facility, or by falling objects that are stored therein or attached thereto. The alleged "buildings" are facilities constructed on land for residential purposes, production, or storage, such as housing; the alleged "structures or other facilities" are facilities other than buildings constructed on land, such as bridges. The alleged "objects that are stored therein or attached thereto" are objects that are stored in or attached to the building, structure, or other facility, but are not a part of it, such as a billboard on a wall. Where any damage is caused by a collapsing building, structure, or other facility or by falling objects that are stored therein or attached thereto, the owner, manager, or user shall bear tortious liability. This liability is based on the principle of fault liability, but the method of proof is an inverted burden of proof, namely, the owner, manager, or user of a collapsing building, structure, or other facility or falling objects that are stored therein or attached thereto shall bear the burden to prove that there is no subject fault. If it is unable to prove there is no subject fault, it shall bear tortious liability. In other words, it is presumed by law to be at fault, but the law allows it to prove there is no subject fault. If it is unable to meet its burden to prove, it shall bear tortious liability.

Example An advertising company erected a billboard about 5 m tall with six large decorative lights on the top front of its store. One day, Gu came to the company to print some advertising materials. When he came out of the door, a large light fell and hit him in the head, immediately resulting in syncope. After being sent to the hospital, Gu paid ¥50,000 for medical expenses. Gu sued the advertising company for tort liability.

X. Li and J. Jin, *Concise Chinese Tort Laws*, China-EU Law Series 1,
DOI 10.1007/978-3-642-41024-6_23, © Springer-Verlag Berlin Heidelberg 2014

The advertising company argued that Gu's damage was caused by an upstairs resident who pushed the light down because he was unhappy with the strong light but cannot prove that. Finally, the court judgment was that the company shall bear tort liability.

Article 86

Rule If any building, structure, or facility collapses, causing any damage to other persons, the construction employer and contractor shall be jointly and severally liable. After providing compensation, the construction employer or contractor is entitled to seek reimbursement from other liable persons.

If the collapse of any building, structure, or facility, which causes any damage to other persons, is attributed to any other liable persons, such persons shall assume the tort liability.

Explanation This article is a stipulation on the tort liability caused by a collapsing building, structure, and other facility and is mainly directed to collapsing due to quality issues. The building owner and construction organization cannot defend itself by claiming there is no subjective fault. This article adopts a strict liability doctrine, namely, a doctrine of no-fault liability. Because a collapsed building, which is different from a falling object that is stored in or attached to a building, victimizes non-specified persons and may bring personal injury or pecuniary damage to anyone, strict liability is stipulated in this article. According to strict liability, the building owner and construction organization cannot argue to exclude liability by claiming there is no subjective fault but can argue that they acted legitimately.

Example A real estate developer assigned the construction work of his estate to a construction team. When it was close to capping, a brick fell from the 12th floor and hit Mai; a passerby Mai was afterwards verified to have a second-degree disability. Mai sued the real estate developer and the construction team requiring them to assume tort liability. The real estate developer argued that it was the construction team that did the constructing work, not the developer. However, the court ruled that the real estate developer and the construction team assume joint liability.

Article 87

Rule If an object is thrown out of or falls down from a building, causes any damage to another person, and there is difficulty determining the specific tortfeasor, all the users of the building who could possibly commit the tort shall be liable, except for those who can prove that they were not the tortfeasor.

Explanation This article provides assumptions for tort liabilities where any damage is caused by an object thrown or falling from a high-rise building and the tortfeasor is yet to be found. It applies only in circumstances in which any damage is caused by an object thrown or falling from a high-rise building or building of partitioned ownership and the tortfeasor's identity is not clear. And if the damage occurred, not due to an object thrown or falling from a building, but by several people's joint wrongful acts, the article shall not be applied. This is the main difference between this article and joint danger. The user of the building, as mentioned in this article, shall be the person in actual control, possession, or management of the building. He may be the owner of the building or the user in circumstances such as a lease or lending. The reason to find them as liable parties is that they are actually controlling the building. On one hand, because they gain advantages from using the building, bearing potential liability is in accordance with the concept of fairness; on the other hand, it can also encourage them to exercise due care in the management and control of the building. Compared to the tortious circumstances in which damage is caused by the building facilities, this article makes the user of building bear more responsibility of due care. Where damage is caused by the building facilities, the principle of fault liability shall be applied, and only the subjective fault is presumed. However, this article not only presumes subjective fault but also presumes the causal relationship in the elements of liability. Therefore, the law also gives potential liable parties the right to defend. That is to say, where there are several users in the high-rise building, if one or more can prove it was impossible for them to engage in infringing conduct, they can refuse to take liability. The provision, to some extent, balances the interests of the parties. Because this provision has the characteristic of "double presumption of fault," in order to balance the interests of the parties, the law uses the term "compensation restitution" rather than general tortious liabilities of "compensation." And therefore, the amount of specific compensation should be decided by a judge within the scope of his discretion in specific cases.

Example Ni went home late at night. While he was passing the building of Unit 5, he was injured by a trash can falling from the building. Even though Ni is out of danger after 10 h of rescue at the hospital, he is still diagnosed as 3rd degree disabled and suffers permanent blindness of his left eye. Medical expenses were ¥50,000, and posttreatment costs of ¥90,000 are still needed. After investigating, the police did not find the culprit. Ni filed a lawsuit against ten householders residing above the first floor of Unit 2, requesting them to pay compensation. The householder of room 302 on the 3rd floor proved that the whole family was traveling in another city at the time; the other nine householders could not prove that they did not throw the trash can. Finally, the court made a judgment that the nine householders each compensate Ni for ¥5,000.

Article 88

Rule If stacked objects collapse and cause any damage to another, the person stacking the objects shall assume the tort liability if he/she cannot prove that he/she is not at fault.

Explanation The purpose of Article 88 is to fix the tort liability for any damage caused by a collapsing pile of materials. The "stack" means stuffs that are piled up on land or somewhere else, and "collapse" means the piled stuff tumbled, fell back, or dropped, causing damages to the victim. For any damage caused by a collapsing pile of materials, the party responsible for the stacking shall bear the fault for tort liability, unless he/she can prove that he/she was not at fault. And from the aspect of the burden of proof, an inverse burden of proof is available. If the person responsible for the stacking can prove that he/she was not at fault, he/she has already paid attention to their management obligation and duty; accordingly, he/she shall not bear tort liability. The person responsible for the stacking can also make a demurrer that the damage is caused by natural events or force majeure.

Example Yuan set up a decorations store and stocked a batch of decoration materials. However, because he lacked a storehouse to keep the materials, Yuan piled the materials up in a public square. Unfortunately, the 2.5-m-tall piled materials were flipped over by fierce winds in the middle of the night and hit Qi's car, which was parked beside the road. Qi paid ¥3,000 to repair the car. Qi sued Yuan, but Yuan claimed that he should not be liable for damages because the square is a public place and the damage was attributed to the wind—a kind of natural event that constitutes force majeure. The court held that the accused piled up the materials in the public square before obtaining permission from the property management company and neglected his obligation to watch and bind those dangerous materials together while the bad weather conditions were not totally unforeseeable. All those factors contributed to the damages, so Yuan shall bear tortious liability and compensate Qi for ¥3,000.

Article 89

Rule If any damage is caused to other persons by objects piled, dumped, or scattered on a public road, which obstruct passage, the relevant entity or individual shall assume tortious liability.

Explanation This article stipulates tort liability for the harm caused by the objects piled, dumped, or scattered on a public road. It mainly applies to situations where the harm is caused by objects piled, dumped, or scattered on a public road, with its public character particularly emphasized. Public roads include but are not limited to roads as defined in Highway Law, Highway Management Regulation, and Law on Road Traffic Safety. For the purposes of this law, public roads include roads for the passage of both vehicles and pedestrians. Strict liability principle, also known as the no-fault liability, applies to this article. That is to say, no tortfeasor may exercise the right of defense on the grounds of no fault. Liability without fault is prescribed by law for harm caused by objects piled on a public road, in that the act is in itself tortious. While public roads are intended for public passing, no unit or individual shall cause harm to others by piling, dumping, or scattering objects on the road.

Example Mi is a lorry owner and helps others to transport architectural crude wood. When carried by the lorry to some section of the highway, the wood rolled down to the road. The vehicles behind the lorry, with no time to dodge the wood, collided with the wood and fell into the subgrade. This resulted in the tragic death of one and the injuries of two. The family of the victims then brought a lawsuit against Mi. The court, after hearing the case, ruled that the crude wood fallen from Mi's high-speeding lorry was the proximate cause of the accident and rendered a judgment against Mi for tort liability and compensation of over ¥2,000,000 to the victims.

Article 90

Rule If any damage is caused to other persons by a broken tree, the owner or manager of the tree shall assume the tort liability if he/she cannot prove that he/she is not at fault.

Explanation This article is the provision on tort liability incurred by the damage caused by a damage tree. For the purposes of this article, "tree" refers to a tree which is planted or naturally grows. As there is no restriction in this article on the range of the tree, the "tree" should have a broad interpretation, which would include trees that grow in woodland, in public places, and in the territory of private house. For the purposes of this article, "owner" refers to the entity or individual who has ownership rights to the tree according to the provisions provided by property law, and "manager" refers to the entity or individual who actually possesses, cultivates, or utilizes the tree. The owner or the manager of the tree has the duty of care to manage the tree and shall be subject to tort liability where damage is caused by a damaged tree due to the defect of management. This article is the provision on fault liability, with an inverse burden of proof, that is referred to when damage caused by a damage tree happens. The owner or manager of the tree shall bear the burden of proof to prove that he is not at fault. If the owner or the manager proves that he is not at fault, he shall not bear tort liability.

Example When the storm came, the plaintiff with his wife and son was driving in the natural landscape area that the defendant (a tourism development services company) utilized for a tourism program. The plaintiff found it difficult to continue the tour and began to turn around. On the way back, a mason pine broke and fell, causing a fracture of the plaintiff's son's leg and left arm. It also caused a brain concussion of the plaintiff's wife and punched a big hole in the back of their car. The plaintiff sued the Tourism Development and Services Co., Ltd., for tort liability. The plaintiff argued that the defendant should have known that the weather and woodland were important elements attributing to the safety of tourists, but there were not any security measures. In addition, when the accident happened, the defendant could not provide first aid, resulting in treatment delay. The defendant, as manager of the trees, claimed that the accident was a result of force majeure and that the broken mason pine was growing well. The defendant claimed that the management of the mason pine was proper, so it was not at fault. The court ruled that the defendant operated the tourism program with a business purpose in the woodland, is the operator of the tourism program, and is the manager of the trees in the landscape area. Therefore, the defendant had the obligation to ensure the safety of the tourists, to pay more attention to and be more cautious with managing the trees in the landscape area. According to the photo that the plaintiff provided, the broken mason pine's top was bare and started to rot from the pine's center to its outside, indicating that the defendant was negligent in the management of the mason pine. Therefore, the defendant's counterargument that the accident was a result of force majeure was held inadmissible, as the defendant also could not prove that the plaintiff was at fault. The defendant's counterargument of waiving liability was not accepted. The defendant bore corresponding civil liability for the damage caused by the damaged mason pine, which was under their management. Judgment was entered for the plaintiff.

Article 91

Rule If anyone digs a pit, repairs, or installs any underground facility, etc., at a public venue or on a public road, but fails to set up any obvious warning signs or take any safety measures and causes any damage to other persons, he/she shall assume the tort liability.

If a manhole or any other underground facility causes any damage to other persons, the manager of the manhole or the facility shall assume tort liability if he/she cannot prove that he/she has fulfilled the duties of management.

Explanation This article is about tort liability damage caused by construction on or under the ground. The tort liability in this article is generally applied to construction in public places, roads, and channels because of a certain degree of risk each contains. This kind of risk is not unavoidable if the construction operator or manager performs with a reasonable duty of care. But they have to bear tort liability in situations where they violate, fail to perform, or insufficiently perform their attention obligations to either serve as a warning or secure the safety of others. The subject responsible for tort liability is the construction operator instead of the owner, manager, or the specific labor, because it is the construction operator that realistically occupies, manages, and controls the construction site. Moreover, it can urge the operator to take positive measures to prevent the danger with more cautious attention. There are two situations in this article, and the imputation principles are also different. According to Clause 1, when the damage is caused by construction on the ground, the principle of strict liability, which is also named no-fault liability, should apply. It means, even if the construction operator does not have subjective fault, their behavior should also bear the responsibility. Based on the law, even if the construction operator sets clear signs or takes safety measures but not enough to prevent the damage, they should still bear tort liability. However, according to Clause 2, when the damage is caused by underground construction, the fault liability principle should apply. In relation to the evidence, the burden of proof is shifted to the manager. If the manager can prove he/she has fulfilled his/her duties, he/she can refuse to undertake tort liability.

Example A construction team contracted a repair task in a national highway. All of a sudden, a heavy rain came when the workers were laying water stopper. So they ran to the shed without setting up any warning signs. At this time, due to poor visibility and vacancy of warning signs, a big truck passed quickly and then plunged into a deep groove, leaving a serious injured driver and a damaged car. Later the driver sued the construction team for tortious liability. The defendant pleads that when the driver was driving on the slippery road, he did not take a reasonable duty of care, so the defendant should have a reduced liability. The court held that the plaintiff was driving in a normal manner. It was the construction team's carelessness of not setting up warning signs caused the accident, so the construction team should bear tortious liability. Therefore, the court ruled against the defendant.

Chapter 24
Supplementary Provision

Article 92

Rule This law shall come into effect on July 1, 2010.

Explanation Though the Tort Law was promulgated to the public on December 26, 2009, Article 92 prescribes that "This Law shall come into effect on July 1, 2010." Therefore, the Tort Law is effective at the time the law clearly stipulates, not when the law was promulgated. This executes Article 51 of the Legislation Law, which provides that "In a law, the time for its entry into effect shall be clearly stipulated." Whereas the Tort Law is a significant law involving comprehensive matters and closely relating to daily life, it should be given a preparative window before enforcement, in order for people to become familiar with, aware of, and eventually master the statutes. The Supreme Court shall validate or construct new judicial interpretations based on the needs of judicial trial. The matter of retroactive effect is a top priority in judicial practice. According to Article 84 of the Legislation Law, "Laws, administrative regulations, local regulations, autonomous regulations, separate regulations and rules shall not be retroactive, but the regulations formulated specially for the purpose of better protecting the rights and interests of citizens, legal persons and other organizations are excepted." The Tort Law cannot be retroactive in judicial practice because there is no special stipulation on retroactive effect. In another words, tortious acts before the Tort Law's effective date cannot apply to its statutes but only to the previous relevant regulations. In situations where the tortious acts happened before the Tort Law became effective and its consequences last through the law's effective date, the Tort Law should be applied retroactively. Where the tortious acts happened before the Tort Law became effective and the tortious results arise after the law is effective, the Tort Law is also retroactive and should be applied.

Example Gu bought a box of tofu from a supermarket, made a tofu salad, and ate it on June 30, 2010. Unfortunately, Gu had a severe abdominal pain the following day and was diagnosed with food poisoning by a doctor. Gu stayed in the hospital for 3 days. After seeking the cause of the food poisoning, Gu found the tofu was a

X. Li and J. Jin, *Concise Chinese Tort Laws*, China-EU Law Series 1, DOI 10.1007/978-3-642-41024-6_24, © Springer-Verlag Berlin Heidelberg 2014

contaminated product because the amount of bacteria exceeded the standard. Therefore, Gu filed a lawsuit against the related manufacturer. Although the tortious act occurred before July 1, 2010, the tort damage arose after July 1, 2010 and for this reason the court should apply the Tort Law in this case.

Part III
Torts in Practice—100 Selected Cases

The 100 tort cases in this book are all selected from published selections from the official newspaper, website and reports of the Supreme Court of China, and have reflected the function of the tort law in settling actual legal conflicts. It represents the level of knowledge and operating skill Chinese officials have of Chinese tort law.

Readers shall be aware that China does not have a legal system of case law. Therefore, these cases can only be promoted as typical cases by the official, and there is no guarantee that other courts adjudicating on cases having similar facts and circumstances would come down with the same ruling.

Chapter 25
General Provisions

#1 The Concept of Tort; Legislative Purposes

Case: Bozhao Wang vs. Weijian Zhang et al.

Facts: Defendant and Plaintiff were screen actors in the same ancient costume movie. In the characters Plaintiff and Defendant played during the shooting of episode 34 scene 8, the Defendant struck the Plaintiff, as required by the story line, causing Plaintiff multiple bodily injuries.

Issue: Was Defendant liable for unavoidable accidental minor injuries resulting from the nature of the job?

Holding: Plaintiff's minor injuries caused by Defendant during the shooting obviously went beyond what was necessary. However, considering the specificity of action movie filming, these kinds of injuries were unavoidable. Additionally, Defendant actively apologized after the event. In sum, intentional injuries could not be proved by sufficient evidence. Defendant was not liable for the accidentally caused injuries.

Rule: Defendant is not liable due to the mere existence of injuries. Subjective intention of the actor and objective circumstances of the injury should be considered.

#2 Application Scope; Infringement upon Right of Portraiture

Case: Xiang Liu vs. Lifestyle Newspaper Office et al.

Facts: Liu, a domestic well-known athlete, filed a complaint alleging the newspaper office used his image, without his authorization, on the cover of its newspaper issue number 1003, with an advertisement of the company's shopping festival.

X. Li and J. Jin, *Concise Chinese Tort Laws*, China-EU Law Series 1,
DOI 10.1007/978-3-642-41024-6_25, © Springer-Verlag Berlin Heidelberg 2014

Issue: Did the unauthorized use of an athlete's image along with a commercial advertisement in newspaper cover constitute infringement?

Holding: The trial court held that the publishing was fair use as the newspaper office's use was retrospective reporting. The appellate court reversed and held, simultaneously showing Plaintiff's image and the commercial advertisement on the same paper made Plaintiff directly connect with the advertisement. This connection resulted in a high likelihood of public confusion of "Plaintiff [] advertising for the shopping festival." Plaintiff's personal right was infringed by the shopping festival advertisement. This was not substantially different from using Plaintiff's image as the advertisement directly. In sum, the appellate court ruled that Defendant infringed Plaintiff's right to his image and is liable for compensation.

Rule: The unauthorized use of an athlete's image along with a commercial advertisement on a newspaper cover constituted infringement of the athlete's right to his image.

#3 Cause of Action for Aggrieved Party; Product Liability

Case: Jinxing Wu vs. Wuxi No. 4 People's Hospital and Wuxi Sanaisi Trade Co.

Facts: Suffering from a fracture as the result of a traffic accident, Plaintiff was taken to the hospital and had surgery to implant a bone plate set in his body. The implanted bone plate set fractured unexpectedly. As a result, Plaintiff had to have a second surgery. Plaintiff alleged that although Defendants were not negligent for the surgery, they were still liable for the injury because they used a defective product.

Issue: If the victim of a defective product chose to sue the seller, not the manufacturer, can he/she get compensation from the seller?

Holding: Negligence liability was imposed on the sellers of the product, i.e., liability cannot be imposed without the finding of negligence. However, when a person or property is injured or damaged by a defective product, an aggrieved party can recover from the manufacturer or the seller. Hence, court ruled the hospital was liable.

Rule: The seller is liable for injury caused by a defective product and shall compensate the victim.

#4 Choice of Law; Product Liability

Case: Gansu Province Administration Bureau of Highway vs. Yokohama Rubber Company

Facts: A fatal accident was caused by the bursting of an SUV's left front tire during normal operation. According to the inspection, the tire was found to be manufactured by a Japanese corporation in its factory in Japan. Plaintiff brought a complaint against the Japanese corporation. The dispute was concerning whether to apply Chinese Tort Law or Japanese Tort Law.

Issue: Which country's law shall apply when injury was caused by an imported product?

Holding: The court held that the principle of *lex loci delicti commissi* governed this case; however, it included both the law of the place where the tortious act happened and the law of the place where the resulting injury happened. If the two places conflicted, the court could choose between either of them. In present case, the tortious act happened in Japan and the injury happened in China. So the court could apply either Japanese or Chinese Tort Law. However, according to international judicial remedy principle, in the cases of product liability from a defective product, victims were always in disadvantaged positions. To protect victims' legal rights, the court should properly consider requests from victims. In sum, the court decided to apply Japanese Product Liability Law.

Rule: When injury is caused by an imported product, with proper consideration of victims' requests, the court can choose to apply the law of the place where tortious act happened or the place where injury happened.

Chapter 26
Constituting Liability and Methods of Assuming Liability

#5 Negligence; Contributory Negligence

Case: Shuying Ren vs. Ito Yokada Shopping Mall (Shilipu Branch) of HT-Store Company Ltd.

Facts: Plaintiff, a 60-year-old woman, was injured when she participated in a sales-promotion program held by Defendant. As a result of the chaos in the mall, massive number of customers, and the mall's poor organization, Plaintiff was pushed, fell over, and suffered an innominate bone fracture.

Issue: Can the injured customer, who was at fault when the accident happened, recover damage from shopping mall?

Holding: As the operator of the sales-promotion program, Defendant should have anticipated the large number of customers and spaced apart the pedestrian flow. Here, Defendant failed to comply with his duty with due care. Conversely, as an elderly person, Plaintiff should have foreseen the potential for chaos in the shopping mall and taken proper measures to protect herself from being pushed over and getting injured. Plaintiff was partially at fault for her own injury. Therefore, Defendant's liability was diminished accordingly.

Rule: When a customer was partially at fault for her own injury, the shopping mall remains liable, but the liability shall be diminished in accordance with the degree of the customer's negligence.

X. Li and J. Jin, *Concise Chinese Tort Laws*, China-EU Law Series 1,
DOI 10.1007/978-3-642-41024-6_26, © Springer-Verlag Berlin Heidelberg 2014

#6 Negligence; Nonfeasance

Case: Lifeng Yan and Kan Xie vs. Yan Zeng, Cifu Ruan, and Jinghui Ruan

Facts: Three companions went to a bar and became intoxicated into the late evening. One of them fell down the stairs and could not get up. Unable to wake him, the other two companions asked the waiters to put him on a bunk made from combining several chairs and left him sleeping in the bar. The next morning, the waiters found the man dead.

Issue: Did the companions have the duty to take affirmative acts to help their friend in danger?

Holding: Although it was beyond the bar's scope of duty to allow the intoxicated customer to stay in the bar, the bar was negligent by not sending him to the hospital. Instead of leaving him in the bar, the two companions had a duty to call an ambulance or send their intoxicated companion to the hospital. Both parties' nonfeasance combined constituted the cause of decedent's death. In sum, the bar and the companions of the decedent were found liable, respectively.

Rule: When the decedent accidently died in the bar, the decedent's companions shall be liable for wrongful death if they failed to fulfill their duty of due care.

#7 Strict Liabilities; Damage Caused by Domesticated Animals

Case: Chengde Xiao vs. Shendong Liu

Facts: Plaintiff was greatly afraid of dogs. One day while visiting a relative, Plaintiff suddenly came upon a large dog in the yard. The dog was owned by Defendant, a deliveryman for gas canisters. In Plaintiff's attempt to escape in a hurry, he fell and was seriously injured.

Issue: If a person is injured from his lack of caution in attempting to escape an animal he feared, can he recover from the animal's owner?

Holding: Although the dog did not attack Plaintiff, who was injured because of his own fear and lameness, Defendant, as the manager of the dog, should be partly liable for Plaintiff's damages, unless he could prove either no causation exists between his dog and Plaintiff's injury or Plaintiff was grossly negligent at the moment. Due to his failure to prove either of them, Defendant was found liable for 70 % of the damage.

Rule: The keeper of the animal shall bear strict liability. Even if the victim's own fault also contributed to his injury partly, the animal's keeper shall be still strictly liable, unless he can prove there was no causation or the victim was grossly negligent.

#8 Strict Liability; Ultrahazardous Activity

Case: Tairun Guo vs. Chongqing (Dazu) Power Supply Company Ltd.

Facts: Plaintiff was killed by electric shock while harvesting corn in his own yard. The right side of Plaintiff's chest came into contact with two broken power lines of a fallen telephone pole. The pole was blown over by strong wind a few days prior.

Issue: Shall the Power Supply Company be held liable if broken power lines, blown off by wind, were the cause of a person's death?

Holding: In the instant case, the local neighborhood committee, not the Power Supply Company, had the property rights for the broken power lines. However, the Power Supply Company collected rural power line maintenance fees from the residences for many years. The Power Supply Company had the duty to maintain the power lines but failed to take reasonable measures to prevent the accident. The Power Supply Company was strictly liable for the victim's death. The court found causation between the inaction of Defendant and the death of Plaintiff. Therefore, the Defendant was liable for compensation.

Rule: The Power Supply Company has the duty to keep the power lines in a safe condition; therefore, it is liable for the injury caused by the electric shock of the broken power lines blown off by wind.

#9 Strict Liability; Ultrahazardous Activity

Case: Ronxian Ni vs. Qidong Gas, Ltd., et al.

Facts: Plaintiffs, a couple, were injured by a gas explosion in the community garage. Evidence showed that (1) the pipeline of gas dropped, so lots of gas leaked; (2) the leaked gas found its way to the garage through underground tunnels; and (3) the gas in the garage exploded finally. Plaintiffs brought a lawsuit against the gas company; Defendants argued that they should not be liable because a developer added a drainage system in the garage causing the accident.

Issue: Should the gas company or the developer be liable for the gas explosion of community garage?

Holding: The court held that supplying gas was a kind of high-risk operation and strict liability should be applied. The causal relationship between the developer's addition of the drainage system and the explosion was too remote. Additionally, the developer was reasonable in adding the drainage system in the garage and was not at fault. In sum, the developer was not liable, and the gas company shall compensate Plaintiff.

Rule: The gas company shall be liable for the gas explosion in the community, not the developer.

#10 Strict Liability; Product Liability

Case: Fengde Jiang vs. Dezhou Yafei Automobile Trading Company

Facts: Plaintiff bought an electro-tricycle from Defendant and parked it in front of his house. One night, Plaintiff noticed abnormal sounds from the tricycle and went to check it. The tricycle exploded suddenly and caused Plaintiff both injury on his body and damage to his property. Plaintiff sued Defendant for compensation.

Issue: What elements are necessary to support a product liability case?

Holding: Generally, strict liability is imposed for damage caused by defective products. To establish a product liability case, the essential elements are the following: (1) the defect of product, i.e., unreasonable danger to the safety of a person or property; (2) damages; and (3) the causation between the defect and damages. In this case, the Plaintiff's vehicle lacked a major power switch, which was a serious defect. Defendant shall be liable for the injury caused by the defect of its product.

Rule: The elements needed to establish a product liability case are the following: a defective product, damages, and causation.

#11 Joint Tort Liability; Joint and Several Liability

Case: In re Shaocong Mo's right to portraiture

Facts: A movie star entered a 1-year-term endorsement contract with a company. However, after 1-year-term, the company continued to print the image of the movie star on its products. These products were sold to tens of thousands of families through the channels of intermediaries and retailers. The movie star sued the company, intermediaries, and retailers for infringement.

Issue: Can intermediaries and retailers be jointly and severally liable with a manufacturer for infringement if they sold infringing products without the knowledge of the infringement?

Holding: The trial court held that it was clear that the manufacturer infringed Plaintiff's right to his portraiture. Although the intermediaries and retailers had no knowledge of the infringement, because of the fact they sold infringing products, they infringed Plaintiff's right and caused losses. Thereafter, although the appellate court held that the trial court did not error in finding the manufacturing company infringed, the appellate court found that the intermediaries and retailers did not intend to jointly infringe Plaintiff's right to his portraiture, nor did they actually commit infringement. In addition, the appellate court found it was against fairness if joint and several liability was imposed on the intermediaries and retailers for every potential infringement of the products they sold. Inspecting for potential infringement in their products also went beyond the intermediaries' and retailers' capability. In sum, the intermediaries and retailers should not be found liable for the infringement.

Rule: If the intermediaries and retailers sell infringing products which they have neither intent nor knowledge of infringement, they are not jointly and severally liable for the infringement with manufacturer.

#12 Joint Dangerous Liability; Joint and Several Liability

Case: Qian gan Liao vs. Qian gan Liao et al.

Facts: Plaintiff's son cut wood up on a hill with other villagers. Because the hill is very steep, and four of them were faster than the others, they are just on the top of other villagers. Obviously, two groups of villagers could not see each other. The villager's steps up the hill caused a rock to become loose. The rock fell and hit and killed Plaintiff's son at the foot of hill. Plaintiff alleged the four villagers at the top of the hill committed joint dangerous acts and sued for damages.

Issue: If several people committed joint dangerous acts, were they jointly and severally liable for a victim's damage?

Holding: The trial court believed cutting wood in the mountain happened every day and was not dangerous, so the Plaintiff shall bear the burden of proof to prove the Defendant was negligent. Because the Plaintiff cannot prove, so his claim was dismissed. The appellate court also believed no proof was submitted to prove the causation between cutting wood and rock falling. In addition, no proof suggested that the four villagers committed the dangerous act mentioned above jointly. So the appellate court's decision was against the Plaintiff. However, the court of retrial ruled that this case is a typical "joint dangerous act" case: (1) the dangerous act was committed by several persons; (2) cutting wood has inherent danger, resulting in the injury of the Plaintiff; and (3) the Plaintiff's injury was caused by one of four villagers, but we cannot identify which one is the real wrongdoer. As a result, the burden of proof to identify which one is the real wrongdoer shall be placed on the Defendants. However, the Defendants failed to identify one, so they shall be held jointly and severally liable for the Plaintiff's damages.

Rule: Several persons are jointly and severally liable for victim's damage if their acts constitute joint dangerous acts.

#13 Liabilities of Dividable Tortfeasors

Case: Xiuxiang Sun vs. Jiangsu Telecom Company Ltd. (Haian Branch) and Zhong Jin

Facts: Riding an electric bicycle to return home, Plaintiff was unseated by steel wires hanging in mid-air causing him to fall on the ground heavily. Thereafter, a truck moving towards Plaintiff failed to take timely measures to stop and hit her. Plaintiff got injured. The steel wires were found to belong to Telecom. Plaintiff sued Telecom and the truck driver.

Issue: If two tortfeasors were the cause of the victim's injury, but their tortious acts are separable, how are the liabilities divided between them?

Holding: The court held that there was no common intent or negligence between Telecom and truck driver, so they were independent tortfeasors. In the present case, two acts linked tightly together may have hurt Plaintiff independently. It was difficult to determine the damage contributed by the two acts. Consequently, Telecom and the truck driver should be held jointly and severally liable for the Plaintiff's injury. Additionally, Telecom was found to be more culpable for its failure to properly maintain the steel wires. So between Telecom and the truck driver, Telecom bears a majority of the liability and the truck driver bears a minority.

Rule: In the event that two independent tortfeasors cause the injury, they are jointly and severally liable for the damage. The apportionment of damage between them should be determined by their respective fault.

#14 Joint and Several Liability

Case: Yuangen Zheng et al. vs. Shengzhou Yanhu Real Estate Development Company

Facts: Plaintiff purchased a commercial residential apartment from Defendant. As a result of poor maintenance of the fire hydrant, Plaintiff's apartment was flooded. Evidence showed that although the property was developed by the development company, the property service company, recruited by the development company, maintained communal public facilities, including the fire hydrant.

Issue: Shall the real estate development company or the property service company be liable for the flood damage of property caused by a poorly maintained fire hydrant?

Holding: The court held that because the fire hydrant was within the unsold apartment and the real estate development company still held the title of the unsold apartment, it will be responsible for the maintenance and repair of the fire hydrant. If the fire hydrant was broken and caused damages, the real estate development company shall compensate.

So, the real estate development company shall bear the tort liability. In addition, because the real estate development company had a property services contract with the property service company, the property service company owed contractual duty to Plaintiff to properly manage the property. Therefore, the property service company was also liable for breach of contract. In sum, the two companies should bear unreal joint and several liability for Plaintiff's damage. Obtaining compensation from any one of them could eliminate the entire liability.

Rule: While the real estate development company violated tort law and the property service company violated contract law at the same time, due to the malfunction of the fire hydrant, both shall bear unreal joint and several liability for victim's damages. The victim can get compensation from any one of them.

#15 Formal Apology; Remedies

Case: Chao Meng vs. Huainan Post Office

Facts: The post office negligently delivered a court judgment to an irrelevant third party instead of the Plaintiff. As a result, Plaintiff failed to exercise his right of appeal and lost the litigation. Plaintiff sued the post office for compensation and a formal apology in the newspaper.

Issue: Was the remedy of a formal apology available when the Plaintiff did not suffer any harm to his personality?

Holding: The court held that the remedy of a formal apology was an available remedy only when a citizen or legal person's right of personality was injured. In a contract dispute, there was no legal basis for Plaintiff to claim a formal apology unless Plaintiff proved that his right of personality was harmed by Defendant. In sum, according to given facts, the post office did not need to formally apologize to Plaintiff.

Rule: The remedy of a formal apology is not available when the Plaintiff cannot prove Defendant's negligence caused any harm to his personality.

#16 Personal Injuries

Case: Xiangyu Zheng vs. Xiamen Huli Community Neighborhood Committee and Xiamen Zhuzong Property Service Company Ltd.

Facts: While exercising in the community fitness area, Plaintiff's finger was pinched off when he put his finger in the fitness equipment. The community fitness area was managed by the property service company. Plaintiff sued the property service company and the community neighborhood committee.

Issue: Shall the community neighborhood committee or the property service company be liable for the injury caused by the public fitness equipment?

Holding: The court held that the right to use the fitness equipment was transferred from nation, represented by local sport bureau, to all residences in the community. (The government built these fitness equipments and donated them to all residences in the community. So, the right to use the fitness equipment was transferred from the government to the residences.) As a result of accepting the donation from the residences, the community neighborhood committee became the supervisor of the equipment and had the duty to maintain and manage them. However, the fitness equipment was also within the management scope of the property service company. The company also had a duty to keep the equipment in good condition. Consequently, both of the Defendants were liable for the injury caused by the equipment. The only difference was that Plaintiff could choose to recover on the theory of breach of contract or tort liability. Because Plaintiff is a minor, his parents are his guardians and shall be responsible for his safety. So, Plaintiff's parents, as guardians, were also liable for the injury since they failed to fulfill their duty of guardianship. In sum, the property service company should be held liable for 70 % of the damage, the community neighborhood committees should be held liable for 10 %, and Plaintiff's parents should be liable for 20 %.

Rule: The property service company, the community neighborhood committee, and the guardians of minors were all liable for the injury caused by the public fitness equipment in community.

#17 Property Damages

Case: Linchang Jin vs. Agricultural Bank of China, Shanghai Branch (Baoshan Subbranch), et al.

Facts: Plaintiff's debit card was stuck in an Agricultural Bank of China ATM when he finished his operations and quit. He immediately went to the bank business hall, reported the situation, and completed reporting documents under bank's staff instruction. However, someone had stolen Plaintiff's password and withdrew ¥4,700 from the account before it was frozen. Plaintiff sued the bank and alleged that the property damage was a result of the bank's failure to provide a reliable service facility and their inefficiency in freezing the account.

Issue: Shall the bank be liable for the damage if a customer's bank account funds were stolen after their bank card became jammed in the ATM?

Holding: The court held that the bank fulfilled its duty to inform by posting a warning note on the ATM. It was not the bank's fault that the Plaintiff's password was stolen. The bank was liable for the ¥200 withdrawn after the account was frozen and was not liable for ¥4,500 withdrawn before the account was frozen.

Rule: If the customer's password was stolen due to his own carelessness, the bank shall not be liable for any loss before the account is frozen. However, the bank shall freeze a customer's account in a timely manner if the customer informed the bank his password was stolen. If the bank failed to do that quickly enough, it may be required to compensate the customer's losses.

#18 Emotional Distress; Right of Personality

Case: Zhengli Zhang vs. The Public Transportation Company

Facts: Plaintiff was a disabled veteran who had PRC disabled veteran credentials for free bus service. Plaintiff was publicly humiliated by bus captains twice when he tried to board two buses owned by Defendant. The bus captains alleged Plaintiff's credentials were forged and forced him to pay. Plaintiff brought suit and claimed that Defendants publicly humiliated him resulting in serious emotional distress. Plaintiff sued for a public apology and compensation.

Issue: When can people seek compensation based on emotional distress?

Holding: The court held that Defendant's employees did not have the capacity of discerning true credentials from the fake. Their announcing that Plaintiff used fake credentials and forcing him to pay in public undoubtedly seriously injured Plaintiff's reputation and personality. One can easily conclude that Plaintiff suffered emotional distress as a result. Therefore, Defendant shall be liable and compensate.

Rule: People can get compensated based on emotional distress if he was humiliated in public in the manner such that a reasonable person would find unbearable.

#19 Emotional Distress; Noise Pollution

Case: Ming Li and Jun Wang vs. Beijing Zhuangwei Real Estate Development Company Ltd.

Facts: After Plaintiffs moved into Defendant's community, they heard loud noises from the pump housing in the basement. Defendant did not deny the existence of noise but failed to resolve the problem. Plaintiffs sued for emotional distress because the noise affected their daily lives and injured their emotional and physical health.

Issue: Was the noise pollution a good cause of action to seek compensation on emotional distress?

Holding: The court held that evidence showed that the degree of the noise at night greatly exceeded the regulated maximum limit. Therefore, Defendant was found liable for noise pollution. Defendant owed a duty to take further reasonable measures to improve residents' living environment and was held liable for the emotional distress caused by the pollution.

Rule: When residents' daily lives are affected by noise pollution, their emotional distresses shall be compensated.

#20 Emotional Distress; Right to Reputation

Case: Yan Zhang vs. Beijing Times Newspaper

Facts: Plaintiff alleged that Defendant published a report and humiliated him by misrepresentation. This report had baneful influence on Plaintiff's life and caused injury to his reputation. Plaintiff sued for a formal apology in the public media, eliminating adverse impacts and restoring reputation, and recovery for emotional distress.

Issue: Can a person get compensated for emotional distress, if he believes that the anonymous character in the misrepresenting negative report is him?

Holding: The court held that although Defendant's report in which the characters were anonymous might be slightly related to Plaintiff, the public would not have reasonably associated the Plaintiff with the report. In addition, the journalist had stated in the report that due to failing to personally contact the people in the story, no definite conclusion could be made. As a result, no negative public evaluation was caused. Plaintiff's reputation was not harmed. Finally, the court rejected Plaintiff's claims.

Rule: No emotional distress occurs and no compensation is available if people cannot prove that a reasonable person can understand the anonymous character in a misrepresenting negative report is him.

#21 Allocation of Losses; Vicarious Liability

Case: Tingying Jiang et al. vs. Tao Wang and Tianjun Mou

Facts: The driver of a Dongfeng truck gave the deceased a lift. While speeding on the freeway, the right door of the truck opened suddenly for unknown reasons. The deceased fell from the truck and was crushed to death. The deceased's father sued both the driver and the owners of the truck.

Issue: Shall the owner of the vehicle or the driver be liable for the death of the passenger due to the driver's negligence?

Holding: The court held that the operator was liable for any injury caused by operating a high speeding vehicle which created high risks to the surroundings. Therefore, Defendant should compensate for the deceased's damages. Meanwhile, because the deceased did not fasten his seat belt when he was on board, he failed to fulfill his duty of due care and should be held partially liable for his injury. The driver was not held liable for damage because he acted within his scope of employment when the accident happened, and the Plaintiff failed to prove the driver was intentionally or grossly negligent. As a result, on the basis of fairly allocating losses between the owners and the passenger, the owners of the truck were held liable for 50 % of the damage.

Rule: The owners of the vehicle were liable for the death of the passenger who, for unknown reasons, fell out of the vehicle and got killed when the vehicle was speeding on the freeway. If the passenger was negligent in part, the losses shall be fairly allocated between the owners and the passenger.

#22 Allocation of Losses; Personal Injuries

Case: Lan Lu vs. Bo Pang

Facts: Plaintiff and Defendant went to gym to play badminton together. During a mixed doubles game, one of Plaintiff's eyes was struck by the shuttle hit back by Defendant. Evidence showed that the injury reached ninth-degree disability standards. Plaintiff sued for recovery.

Issue: If a person was injured purely due to an accident in a sports match, the risk of which he foresaw, can he get compensated from his opponent?

Holding: The court held that when they participated in sport, both Plaintiff and Defendant could foresee the risk of danger and should accept potential injuries. In the instant case, there was no dispute that Plaintiff's injury was caused by Defendant. However, the purpose of Defendant's activity was hitting the shuttle back into Plaintiff's field. Defendant did not intentionally or negligently injure Plaintiff. In addition, Defendant did not violate normal rules of sport and could not possibly foresee that such an ordinary act might hurt Plaintiff. As a result, Defendant had no fault for the injury and was not held liable for the harm. The event was incidental even in sport games. However, causation could be established between Defendant's act and Plaintiff's injury, and Defendant's eye injury was as serious as the ninth-degree of disability. It was also unfair to impose all the loss on Plaintiff. So, Defendant was found liable for 40 % and Plaintiff bore 60 % of the losses.

Rule: Even if a person is not at fault at all, he is sometimes liable for part of the damage he caused in a sports match because he may be required by the court to share the losses with the injured party.

Chapter 27
General Tort Liability

#23 Personal Injuries

Case: Li Gong vs. Xinjiang University

Facts: Plaintiff was a student of Xinjiang University. One day he drank and got intoxicated. After coming back to his dormitory he went, in the dark, to the toilet at 10:00 pm, fell down, and got injured. Plaintiff sued Xinjiang University for compensation. Plaintiff alleged that the cause of the injury was Defendant's failure to maintain the lights in toilet and he had to walk in the dark.

Issue: Shall the university be liable for the damages if a student fell down and got injured in an inadequately lit dormitory toilet?

Holding: The court held that as a student in the south campus of the university Plaintiff's drinking during school hours violated school regulations. And due to his intoxication, he went to the north campus dormitory nearby to rest. But since he was not familiar with the north campus dormitory, he failed to exercise ordinary caution and got injured. Therefore, Plaintiff should bear the majority of the responsibility for his injury, i.e., 70 %. Because of the university's failure to properly maintain the dormitory, it also contributed to the injury and should bear the minority of the responsibility of the loss, i.e., 30 %.

Rule: A university shall be liable for its students' damage if it fails to keep the dormitory in a good and safe condition.

#24 Personal Injuries

Case: Qing Ma vs. Xintai Securities Co., Ltd. and Grand Metro Hotel et al.

Facts: The deceased put his shoe pads on the windowsill. The shoe pads were blown down by strong winds so the deceased climbed over the window

X. Li and J. Jin, *Concise Chinese Tort Laws*, China-EU Law Series 1,
DOI 10.1007/978-3-642-41024-6_27, © Springer-Verlag Berlin Heidelberg 2014

to pick up the pads. But the bearing board of the outside air-condition condenser unit collapsed, and he fell to his death from the building. Relatives of the deceased brought a suit against the manager of the hotel and alleged that the bearing board of the outside air-condition condenser unit looked solid but was no more than a thin gypsum board which could barely bear any weight. Defendant failed to post a warning and should be held liable for the death of the deceased.

Issue: Shall the hotel be liable for a guest's injury if the guest's conduct was extremely dangerous and went beyond the imagination of a reasonable person?

Holding: The court held that the deceased stepped on the bearing board of the outside air-condition condenser unit which had very limited bearing capacity. To prevent guests from climbing over windows, protective equipment was installed on all the windows of the hotel to limit the width of the opening of the window. The deceased unscrewed the protective equipment with a screwdriver and stepped on the board, which caused his death. As an adult with full mental capacity, the deceased failed to make a proper evaluation of his own acts and should be held liable for the damage. The hotel could not have foreseen that guests would unscrew the protective equipment to climb over the window. So it was unfair to compel the hotel to set warning signs for the potential danger of the bearing board. In sum, the hotel was not liable for the deceased's death.

Rule: If the hotel fulfilled its duty of care to protect its guests, it is not liable for the victim's damage caused by his own dangerous and unforeseeable conduct.

#25 Personal Injuries

Case: Yunuan Lin vs. Jianbao Zhang et al.

Facts: Plaintiff was an old woman in poor health. One day, she witnessed her son being beaten up and falling limply to the floor with blood on his face. Plaintiff suffered serious mental distress and fainted immediately. Plaintiff was sent to the hospital and was hospitalized for 12 days. After that, Plaintiff sued the assaulter to recover her losses including medical expenses.

Issue: Can a person get compensated from an assaulter, if he/she witnessed the assaulter beating and injuring his/her immediate relative?

Holding: The court held that the Plaintiff's elderly age and valetudinarianism were the major reasons for her fainting and falling. Witnessing her son's injury was merely a contributing factor. As a result, Defendant should bear a minor part of Plaintiff's loss, i.e., 20 %.

The court expanded the scope of recovery to parties whose right to health was injured. Health rights provide injured parties with a cause of action to recover for their personal injury.

Rule: A person's right to health is indirectly harmed when she witnesses an assaulter hurt her immediate relative in a brutal manner, so she is entitled to seek compensation from the assaulter.

#26 Property Damages; Safeguard Obligation

Case: Qingguo Shi vs. Zhenhua Zhang

Facts: Plaintiff went to a bath center and put his purse containing a large sum of money in a locker. After he took a bath and returned to the locker, he discovered that his money was stolen. Plaintiff sued the bath center and alleged that the bath center failed to post warning signs or take sufficient measures to ensure the safety of guests' property. So, Defendant shall be liable for the loss.

Issue: Did the bath center have the obligation to ensure the safety of guests' property?

Holding: The trial court held that Defendant owed Plaintiff the duty to safeguard of his property when he went to the bath center. The property damage suffered by Plaintiff was a result of Defendant's failure to fulfill his obligation to safeguard. As a result, Defendant shall be held liable for the damages. The appellate court held that Plaintiff also had the duty to take reasonable care of his own money. Since the amount of money was large, Plaintiff should have deposited his purse at the front desk, which Plaintiff failed to do so. The bath center was negligent because it failed to take enough security measures to prevent the theft. In sum, Defendant and Plaintiff should both bear 50 % of the loss respectively.

Rule: The bath center owed an obligation to safeguard its guests, and guests shall also take reasonable care of their own safety.

#27 Property Damages

Case: Tonghai Yu vs. Shanghai City God Temple First Shopping Center Company et al.

Facts: Plaintiff lost his credit card after eating a meal in a restaurant. Printed on the front side of the card are the card number, bank mark, and the embossed cardholder's pinyin name. The cardholder's signature is on the back side of the card. Although Plaintiff called the police immediately, another person used the card without authorization, shopping on Defendant's POS machine in the evening. Plaintiff brought suit to recover his property damage from Defendant.

Issue: Shall the shopping center be liable for the losses suffered by a credit cardholder if it failed to check the signature on the credit card and did not find that someone was falsely using it?

Holding: The court held that as the credit cardholder, Plaintiff failed to fulfill his duty to take due care of his card. Plaintiff was liable for his negligence. However, Plaintiff's duty was limited to the due care of an ordinary customer. As a professional business organization, Defendant's duty of care was much greater and its failure to compare the signature of the false user with the signature of the cardholder was an obvious breach of its duty. Therefore, Defendant's negligence exceeded Plaintiff's negligence in degree of seriousness. Defendant shall bear a major part of the loss.

Rule: In order to protect customers, the shopping center shall take reasonable measures to ensure that the credit cards are used properly, or it may be held liable.

Chapter 28
Defenses for Tort Liability

#28 Force Majeure

Case: Xuwu Tang vs. Jing Tan

Facts: Defendant organized 34 tourists to visit an attraction in Chongqing. However, there was a flood that killed 19 of the tourists, including Plaintiff's relatives. Plaintiff alleged that what caused the accident was Defendant's lack of organization and knowledge regarding the potential danger. Defendant's failure to take reasonable measures to protect the team after the flood occurred also contributed to the tremendous number of deaths. Defendant shall be held liable for his negligence.

Issue: Is a flood regarded as a kind of force majeure which can be used as a defense for tort liability?

Holding: The court held that, in this case, tourists went on a self-service tour and entered that area without permission or reporting it to any departments. That area was not open to the public and was so dangerous that no one could have provided protection for these tourists. The disaster was caused by an incidental flood which was force majeure. Therefore, these 34 tourists should be responsible to their own safety. The Defendant was not held liable for the injury. The court dismissed Plaintiff's claims.

Rule: Flood is a kind of force majeure, which is a valid defense for tort liability.

#29 Force Majeure

Case: Xueqin Pang vs. Hanchen Wang

Facts: The deceased worked at a construction site. When a storm attacked, he was killed by the collapse of a work shed in which he took refuge from the storm. Relatives of the deceased sued the manager of the

X. Li and J. Jin, *Concise Chinese Tort Laws*, China-EU Law Series 1,
DOI 10.1007/978-3-642-41024-6_28, © Springer-Verlag Berlin Heidelberg 2014

construction site and alleged that the major cause of the deceased's death was Defendant's failure to reinforce the work shed.

Issue: Is a storm regarded as a kind of force majeure, which can be used as a defense for tort liability?

Holding: It was a reasonable person's judgment that the deceased chose the safest steel construction nearby to avoid the storm when the storm attacked. As a person with all civil capacities, the deceased was not to blame. For Defendant, since there were several possible causes for the work shed's collapse, to use force majeure as a defense, Defendant should provide sufficient evidence to eliminate the possibility that the collapse of the work shed was caused by defective construction. In this case, Defendant failed to prove that natural forces were the only cause of the collapse and that the construction satisfied safety requirements. Finally, as the owner and manager of the shed, Defendant should be held liable for the deceased's death.

Rule: A storm is a kind of force majeure, and if it can be determined as the only cause of damage, it is a valid defense for tort liability.

#30 Comparative Negligence

Case: Weiguo Yin vs. Chongqing Electric Power Co. (Yangjiaping Power Supply Bureau)

Facts: Plaintiff was shocked and injured by an electrical power wire when he parked his vehicle under the power wire and climbed on his vehicle to take down the waterproof cover. Plaintiff brought a lawsuit against Power Supply Bureau for damages.

Issue: If both parties are negligent, can the victim get compensated?

Holding: The trial court held that Plaintiff was negligent when he climbed on his vehicle and came within 2 m of the power wire. Plaintiff should bear a major part of the loss. On the other hand, as owner of the power wire, Defendant failed to take effective measures to make the land as flat as possible, which shortened the distance between the land and the power wire. As a result, Defendant should be liable for the injury with respect to its fault. The appellate court held that the Power Supply Bureau had a duty to check, maintain, and manage all the power supply equipment. Evidence showed that the height of the power wire in this case did not meet regulation requirements. Furthermore, Defendant noticed this dangerous situation for a long time. Because it failed for a long time to take reasonable measures, Defendant was grossly negligent and shall be liable for a major part of the loss, i.e., 80 %. At the same time, as an adult citizen with full civil capacity, Plaintiff's actions were negligent. Plaintiff failed to fulfill his duty of due care and caused his own injury. Defendant's liability should be reduced with respect to Plaintiff's comparative negligence.

Rule: The doctrine of comparative negligence allows a party to get compensation from the other party, albeit reduced according to his own negligent contribution to the occurrence of damages.

#31 Comparative Negligence

Case: Huang vs. Property Service Company

Facts: During the Wenchuan earthquake, Plaintiff felt a strong vibration in his city. Being extremely fearful, Plaintiff descended to an emergency stairway from the fifth floor. When Plaintiff reached the middle of second and third floor, he found the door was closed. Plaintiff mistakenly thought the emergency door was locked, ran back to the third floor, and tried to jump from a window to a nearby platform. Plaintiff missed the platform and fell from the window. Plaintiff alleged that the ambiguous signs set by Defendant (a property service company) caused his injury. Therefore, Defendant failed to fulfill his duty of due care and shall be liable for the damage.

Issue: When both parties are negligent, which one shall prevail?

Holding: The court held that both parties were negligent in this case. Plaintiff improperly reacted when he jumped from the building to avoid being injured by the earthquake. He shall be liable for a major part of the unnecessary damage. Defendant failed to set clear signs to distinguish the normal exits from the emergency exits, causing Plaintiff confusion under an emergency situation. Defendant shall be held liable for a minor part of the damage.

Rule: Even if the Plaintiff's negligence is the major cause of the damage, he is entitled to seek compensation from the Defendant, whose liability can be reduced with respect to his fault.

#32 Comparative Negligence

Case: Jintong Liang et al. vs. Tao Tao

Facts: The owner of a boat tied up his boat and left it going ashore. After he came back, he found a stranger cooking the deck of his boat. He expelled the stranger, but the stranger fell into the water and drowned. The decedent was found to be psychotic. Family members of the decedent sued the owner to seek compensation.

Issue: Who shall be liable for the death of an insane person, his family members, who did not fulfill their duty to take care of him, or the person who killed him accidentally?

Holding: The trial court held that Defendant, the owner of the boat, had no intent to harm the decedent. It was proper for Defendant to drive out the decedent when he found the decedent cooking on his boat without his consent. The decedent drowned due to his negligence and should be liable for the damage himself. However, given the facts, as justice required, Defendant shall pay the decedent's family members a little sum of money. The appellate court held that the decedent was psychotic with limited civil capacity. As his guardians, his family members failed to fulfill their duties of guardianship. They should be liable for the major part of the damage, i.e., 80 %. However, Defendant has improperly reacted, his actions making the decedent panic and caused the decedent to drown. Therefore, Defendant should be held liable for a minor part of the damage, i.e. 20 %.

Rule: When both parties are negligent, liability shall be allocated between both parties on the basis of their respective fault.

#33 Statute of Limitations

Case: Congfang He vs. Chongqing Monorail Transit Engineering Company

Facts: When Plaintiff passed a construction site, he found the gate of the warehouse open. When Plaintiff stole a barrel of waterproofing glue, he was caught by the security. When they got into a dispute, an unidentified man came out from the gate of the site and punched and injured Plaintiff's left eye. Plaintiff received medical treatment in the hospital, and his injury was evaluated to be an eighth-degree disability. Plaintiff sued the construction company for damage and alleged that the company employed the assaulter. The construction company denied the employment relationship and alleged that Plaintiff failed to file his complaint within 1 year of the injury, so the case should be dismissed under the statute of limitations.

Issue: When shall the clock start in calculating the statute of limitations in a personal injury case?

Holding: The court held that the statute of limitations had not yet run out since the Plaintiff obtained expert testimony evaluating the degree of his injury after he was discharged from the hospital. The filing of his complaint was within the 1 year of obtaining the expert testimony. However, Plaintiff failed to prove the employment relationship between the assaulter and Defendant. So, the court ruled against Plaintiff.

Rule: In personal injury cases, the statute of limitation is calculated from when the Plaintiff knows the level of severity of his injury, i.e., obtaining expert testimony evaluating the injury.

Chapter 29
Special Provisions on Tortfeasors

#34 Guardian's Liability

Case: Yuangui Tian et al. vs. Rudong No. Four People's Hospital

Facts: A schizophrenic was sent to the hospital and received first-degree nursing care. After a period of treatment, the nursing care was switched to second-degree care. However, the schizophrenic hung himself in the bathroom one day. Family members of the decedent sued the hospital for damage.

Issue: Who owed a guardian's duty to the schizophrenic: his family members or the hospital?

Holding: The trial court held that Defendant owed a duty of care to the decedent, which was based on the law that the hospital should guard its patients. Defendant was negligent because it violated nursing regulations by improperly switching the decedent from first-degree to second-degree level of nursing care. However, Defendant's negligence was not the direct cause of the decedent's death. Therefore, Defendant shall only be liable for part of the compensation for death and mental distress. The appellate court held that the duty of guardianship was not transferred from the family members of the decedent to the hospital when the decedent was hospitalized. The hospital's liability shall be determined based on the seriousness of its negligence. Considering that Defendant's fault was minor and that it is a public interest organization with low profits, the appellate court found that damages for mental distress should not be granted. The rest of the trial court's judgment was upheld.

Rule: If a patient commits suicide in the hospital, the hospital shall bear tort liability only when it is found to be negligent because the duty of guardianship is still owed by the family members of the patient.

X. Li and J. Jin, *Concise Chinese Tort Laws*, China-EU Law Series 1,
DOI 10.1007/978-3-642-41024-6_29, © Springer-Verlag Berlin Heidelberg 2014

#35 Guardian's Liability

Case: Liju Fan vs. Gaiying Wang and Xiaofei Zheng

Facts: Plaintiff was the mother of an infant. One day, she hired an 11-year-old child as a babysitter with the consent of the child's parents. The child carried the infant on her back, but she accidentally fell on her back and caused the infant's death.

Issue: When both parties breached their duty of guardianship, which shall prevail?

Holding: The court held that the mother of the infant failed to fulfill her duty of guardianship by hiring an 11-year-old child as a babysitter. The mother was held liable for 80 % of the damage. Meanwhile, the parents of the 11-year-old were also at fault by allowing their child engage in work not suitable for her age. They were held liable for 20 % of the damage.

Rule: When both parties breached their duty of guardianship, liability should be determined by evaluating and comparing each party's fault.

#36 Guardian's Liability

Case: Wang et al. vs. Mou et al.

Facts: Three minors went swimming in a pond together. When one of them drowned, the other two were scared and ran back home after searching fruitless for the other. The two minors did not inform their parents or the decedent's parents about the accident. After that, when the decedent's parents finally discovered their child drowned, they alleged that the accident occurred as a result of the two children's failure to ask for help in time.

Issue: How is liability allocated among minors who have only limited civil capacity?

Holding: The court held that all three of the minors were persons with limited civil capacity. Notwithstanding that they had the capacity to realize the danger of swimming in a pond, they went swimming together, getting into danger voluntarily. The decedent assumed the danger and the accident occurred as a result of his reckless. Therefore, he should bear the majority of the damage. Since the other two children reacted negligently, they should bear a minor part of the damage, i.e., 10 % for each.

Rule: When several children are involved in a tort situation, their liabilities shall be determined with respect to their faults, and their faults shall be evaluated according to their age.

#37 Guardian's Liability; Employer's Liability

Case: Chuanhai Cheng et al. vs. Zhumei Xu et al.

Facts: The decedent was killed by Defendants' psychotic third son when she was invited to Defendants' place to butcher pigs. The decedent's husband sued Defendants and alleged that Defendants failed to fulfill their duty of guardianship for their psychotic family member, which caused the decedent's death.

Issue: If an insane person killed others, what liability shall his family members bear?

Holding: The trial court held that Defendants knew their third son was psychotic. Their failure to fulfill their duty of guardianship when they invited the decedent to come to their house to help caused her death. Defendants should be liable for the damage. The appellate court held that Defendants' liability was not merely based on the insufficiency of guardianship but also on the grounds of employment relationship (the victim was working for them while she was killed).

Rule: If an insane person killed another, the victim's relatives can seek compensation from the psychotic family members based on the grounds of insufficiency of guardianship.

#38 Employer's Liability; Personal Injuries

Case: Jinan Wu et al. vs. Dehua Ni et al.

Facts: Plaintiff's daughter was murdered by Defendant, the driver and owner of a taxi, when she rode in his taxi. Plaintiff sued and claimed for damage.

Issue: When a passenger is murdered by a taxi driver, shall the taxi company be held vicariously liable?

Holding: The court held that three criteria were required to establish an employer's vicarious liability: (1) the wrongdoer was employed by the employer; (2) causation is found between the employee's acts and the damage; and (3) the employee's acts were within their scope of employment. The dispute in this case was whether murder by the driver was within the scope of employment. The court found the following: (1) no evidence to show that Defendant ordered the driver to commit murder or that Defendant subsequently ratified the driver's act; (2) the murder was not consistent with the driver's job requirements; and (3) the murder was not related to the driver's duty of employment. In sum, the wrongdoing was not within the scope of employment. The taxi company was not held vicariously liable.

Rule: In order to establish the employer's liability, the court must find the following: (1) the wrongdoer was employed by the employer, (2) causation between the damage and the employee's acts, and (3) the employee's acts were within the scope of employment.

#39 Employer's Liability

Case: Jianfa Wu vs. Quanzhou Fengze Shunxin Property Service Company

Facts: During the quarrel between Plaintiff and Defendant's security, Plaintiff was hit on the head with a padlock by the security. Plaintiff fainted and was sent to the hospital. Thereafter, Plaintiff brought a lawsuit against Defendant.

Issue: Shall an employer be vicariously liable for its employee's illegal acts?

Holding: The court held that Defendant owed the duty to maintain order in the community and to protect the personal safety and the property of the residents. Defendant was at fault when its employee hit and injured a resident while of carrying out his employment duties. Defendant was held vicariously liable. However, Defendant had the right to recover from the actual wrongdoer.

Rule: If the acts of its employee are illegal, but within the scope of employment, the employer shall be held vicariously liable for damages.

#40 Employer's Liability

Case: Tianli Liu vs. Chongqing Hongli Water Conservancy Counseling Company

Facts: Plaintiff, an employee of Defendant, was assigned by his boss to attend a conference. On his way back, he was injured in a traffic accident. Plaintiff claimed that attending the conference was within the scope of his employment. So, Defendant shall reimburse him the medical expense as a result of the accident.

Issue: Shall the employer be liable for an employee's injury caused during the employee's return from a business conference?

Holding: The court held that Plaintiff's injury occurred on a business trip, which was within the scope of employment. Even if the employer was not negligent, the employer shall be strictly liable for its employee's injuries occurring within the scope of employment.

Rule: The employer shall be liable for an employee's injury caused within the scope of employment, even if the employer is not at fault.

#41 Employer's Liability; Independent Contractor

Case: Yunlin Liu vs. Dingxiong Tang

Facts: The owner hired a labor contractor for a construction project, who then hired a worker to transport bricks. When operating a tractor, the worker hit and killed a pedestrian. He fled from the accident. Parents of the decedent sued the worker, labor contractor, and owner of the project for damages.

Issue: Shall the labor contractor bear an employer's liability and be vicariously liable for damage caused by his worker?

Holding: The court held that since the decedent was not comparatively negligent, all fault in the accident attributed to the worker. As the employer of the wrongdoer, the labor contractor was vicariously liable. The owner was also negligent for hiring a contractor that had no construction qualifications. So, the owner was held jointly and severally liable.

Rule: The labor contractor shall bear an employer's liability and be vicariously liable for damage caused by his worker.

#42 Employer's Liability; Independent Contractor

Case: Shouzhong Yuan et al. vs. Beijing Gaoliying Woollen Mill et al.

Facts: A driver voluntarily helped the decedent deliver goods. While transporting the goods, the driver, driving a van, got involved in an accident and the decedent was killed. Family members of the decedent sued the driver for damage.

Issue: When a person causes injury while volunteering and giving free help, who shall be liable?

Holding: The court held that when a person helping free of charge causes injury to another while helping, the beneficiary shall be liable for the damage. In this case, the driver was helping the decedent without charge and the aggrieved party was the beneficiary. So, the driver's liability should be reduced accordingly.

Rule: When a person causes injury while volunteering and providing free help, the beneficiary shall be liable. If the victim is the beneficiary, the liability of the helper can be reduced.

#43 Torts on Internet; Infringement on Copyright

Case: Baidu Inc. vs. Beijing Sanqieryi Technology Company

Facts: Both parties provided free downloadable address bar searching software. However, users found that the two softwares conflicted and actively disturbed each other: if a user installed Plaintiff's software in advance, Defendant's software could not correctly run. If a user installed Defendant's software in advance, Plaintiff's software could not be installed. Evidence showed that both companies intentionally modified each other's registry. Finally, Plaintiff sued Defendant for copyright infringement and infringing on the right to information dissemination through networks.

Issue: If the accused software intentionally prevented the other software from functioning properly, does it infringe on copyright or the right to information dissemination through networks?

Holding: The court held that because both companies modified each other's registry, and the registry was not part of the software, these acts did not constitute copyright infringement. The purpose of the right of information dissemination is to supply software to the public in wire or wireless form, so as to make sure everyone is able to obtain the software at any time he wants or at any place he chooses. In this case, although the accused software conflicted with each other, Defendant did not shield, block, or obstruct Plaintiff from freely supplying its software to the public. Therefore, Defendant did not infringe Plaintiff's right to information dissemination through networks.

Rule: Preventing an opponent's software from functioning properly by modifying its registry is not infringement on copyright or the right to information dissemination through networks.

#44 Torts on Internet; Infringement on Copyright

Case: Star Group Ltd. vs. Shanghai Tudou Network Technology Company

Facts: Plaintiff was the exclusive licensee of a video program in Mainland China. The Plaintiff exclusively owned the program's website copyright, telecast right, and the right to information dissemination through networks. Defendant was a large video sharing website which provided memory space for registered users and unlimited free access to the stored video to the public. Plaintiff found a large amount of unauthorized videos on Defendant's website. The public was able to watch and download an unlimited number of videos. Plaintiff alleged its rights were infringed by Defendant and suffered a huge amount of economic loss. Plaintiff requested that Defendant delete the videos and pay damages. Although the Defendant deleted the videos, they refused to compensate for damages.

Issue: When a video website deletes infringing videos after receiving notice of infringement from the aggrieved party, shall the website still be held liable for the infringement?

Holding: The court held that if Defendant, as an Internet service provider, knew or should have known the acts were tortious, it should be held jointly liable. In this case, because Defendant was a site specializing in sharing of films, television, and entertainment programs, it should impose a higher standard care. Although Defendant did not directly commit infringement, it was at fault for providing memory space to wrongdoers and aiding the infringement on the right to information dissemination through networks. Deleting the objectionable videos was insufficient to prove that Defendant had taken effective and necessary measures to prevent any future infringement. As a result, Defendant was held liable for damage.

Rule: The video website deleting the infringing videos after being informed of the infringement is not sufficient. The video website should take measures to prevent infringement from happening again, or it shall bear tort liability.

#45 Torts on Internet; Infringement on Copyright

Case: Sohu.com Inc. vs. Shanghai Tudou Network Technology Company

Facts: Plaintiff exclusively owned the right to information dissemination through networks, advertising rights, and other rights of a Hong Kong movie in Mainland China. Defendant was a large video sharing website which provided memory space for registered users and unlimited free public access to the video. Plaintiff found that when the name of the movie was searched, 177 results could be found available to public at Defendant's website. Plaintiff asked Defendant to delete the video and compensate the damages. Defendant refused and Plaintiff sued.

Issue: How does a court determine whether a website knew or should have known of the existence of infringing videos found on their website?

Holding: The trial court held that because the movie in this case was not released in Mainland China and only released in Hong Kong 4 years prior, Defendant did not and should not have known the existence of the infringement. So Defendant was not at fault and not jointly liable. The appellate court held that as an Internet service provider supporting memory space, Defendant organized all the videos uploaded by users. This business model brought additional risk of copyright infringement and therefore raised the standard of care to a higher level. As a result, because Defendant could foresee the high possibility of infringement but failed to prevent it, Defendant was negligent and held liable for damages.

Rule: A video-sharing website is held to a higher standard of care and shall take affirmative actions to prevent copyright infringement.

#46 Torts on Internet; Infringement on Copyright

Case: Jia Jia vs. Baidu Inc.

Facts: Plaintiff was a novel writer. He found one of his novels in Defendant's online library without his authorization. Plaintiff sent a notice of infringement to the Defendant and reported the infringement to the authorities. The Defendant deleted the novel in time, but Plaintiff filed the complaint regardless. Plaintiff alleged that Defendant was also an Internet content provider, rather than only an Internet service provider, so it shall be responsible for the novels uploaded by its users. Moreover, Defendant participated heavily in the process of infringement because users could only delete uploaded novels within a short period of time. The online library was organized according to the content of the works, and the most popular novels were listed in the front of web pages. Defendant encouraged and rewarded users to upload novels. Defendant also reserved the rights to use uploaded novels freely, permanently, and irrevocably.

Issue: Was the business model of a free online library, the contents of which were uploaded by numerous users and organized by the website, contrary to the relevant provisions of Tort Law?

Holding: The court held that the reasons listed by Plaintiff could not prove Defendant was not an Internet service provider. In addition, Plaintiff failed to prove that his novel was so popular and influential that Defendant knew or should have known of its existence in its online library. In fact, the novel was never listed on the most popular works or any other recommendation page. Accurate searching was needed to find the novel. Therefore, Defendant did not jointly infringe Plaintiff's rights and was not held liable for damage.

Rule: When the online library website is an Internet service provider and the work is not popular enough, the mere fact of its existence in the library does not indicate that the website knows or should have known of the copyright infringement.

#47 Torts on Internet; Infringement on Trademark

Case: Shanghai Yinian Fashion Trade Co., Ltd. vs. Zhejiang Taobao Network Company

Facts: Plaintiff was a fashion trade company who owned exclusive rights to a trademark. Defendant managed an Internet trade website, which provided an Internet platform for identified users. Plaintiff found a user on Defendant's website selling counterfeit products of the products sold by Plaintiff. Plaintiff alleged that the existence of counterfeit products on a profitable professional Internet trade platform may prove that the website aided in infringement, and the website should be held jointly and severally liable.

Issue: When an online store sold counterfeit products through an Internet trade platform, shall the platform company be held liable?

Holding: The court held that trade information in the platform was massive and updated all the time. It was impossible for Defendant to find all infringements from the product information provided by online stores. Therefore, Defendant was not at fault and could not be found to have aided the infringement. In addition, after receiving notice of infringement and proof of ownership from Plaintiff, Defendant provided information identifying the objectionable store and prevented it from doing business. Defendant had fulfilled its duty of care and shall not be liable for damage.

Rule: The platform company is not liable if one of its numerous users sells counterfeit products through its Internet trade platform.

#48 Safeguard Obligation

Case: Changfu Chen et al. vs. Foshan Yangguang Ceramics Company Ltd.

Facts: Two employees of Defendant lived in the same dormitory and got involved in a dispute one day. During the quarrel, one killed the other. The decedent's father sued the employer for compensation.

Issue: If an employee is injured by his fellow employee in the dormitory, shall the employer be held liable?

Holding: The court held that (1) By providing a dormitory to its employees, the employer was giving welfare rather than doing business. Therefore, the employer owed no duty of care to guarantee security. (2) Defendant did not commit tortious activity. (3) Because the case was an unexpected violent crime, Defendant could not reasonably foresee the crime. Defendant was not negligent. (4) There was no causation between the employer's acts and the death of the employee. As a result, Defendant was not liable for the victim's death.

Rule: If an employee is injured by his fellow employee in the dormitory, the employer shall not be held liable.

#49 Safeguard Obligation

Case: Yonghui Chen vs. China Construction Bank (Shuangxi Subbranch, Development Zone Subbranch, and Jinhua Branch)

Facts: Plaintiff went to Defendant bank and prepared to deposit ¥300,000 in cash. When he was waiting, someone rushed into the bank and grabbed the cash he put on the counter. Evidence showed that there was no security in the bank at that time. Plaintiff sued the bank for compensation.

Issue: Did the bank owe the duty of safeguard its depositor?

Holding: The court held that customers' property and personal safety should be protected when they receive services from the bank. When the bank failed to fulfill its reasonable duty of care and a third party causes the customers' injury, the third party should be liable for the damages. If the bank was negligent, it shall bear the supplementary tort liability to the extent it could have prevented it had reasonable care been adopted. In this case, because Defendant was negligent, it shall be held liable for 50 % of the damage.

Rule: The bank owes the duty of safeguarding to its depositor. If it fails to fulfill its duty, it shall bear the supplementary tort liability for the damage caused by a third party.

#50 Safeguard Obligation

Case: Guosheng Zhang et al. Sue Zheng He Park

Facts: Defendant is a free public park. To prevent accidents, warning signs were posted around a pond in the park and security staffs were assigned to patrol. A few years ago, a child fell into the pond but was saved by party security soon after. However, Plaintiff's son was not that lucky. He fell into the pond when playing with other children. The park security failed to notice the accident and did not rescue the boy in time. Plaintiff's son died and a lawsuit was brought against Defendant to seek compensation.

Issue: When a child drowns in a free public park, shall the park be held liable?

Holding: The trial court held that as a free public park, Defendant had fulfilled its duty of care by adopting reasonable measures. So, Defendant was not liable. The appellate court held that the duty of care concerning security included two types of safety: safety in substance and safety in procedure. Defendant fulfilled its duty of safety in substance. However, in the aspect of safety in procedure, Defendant did not fulfill its duty. For example, the park did not hire enough security to protect visitors' safety. Considering the negligence of both parties and the causation of the accident, the park was found liable for 15 % of the damage.

Rule: The free public park owes the duty of safeguarding to visitors. If the visitor gets injured due to its negligence, the park shall bear liability with respect to the seriousness of its fault.

#51 Safeguard Obligation

Case: Yiwen Chen vs. Guangzhou Huadu Jincheng Property Service Company

Facts: Plaintiff leased a store from the owner to sell jade in a shopping mall. The owner signed a property service contract with Defendant, and Plaintiff paid the management fee directly to Defendant. One morning, Plaintiff found that the store was burglarized the night before when the shopping mall was closed. He sued the property service company and claimed that the company's poor management was the cause of his loss.

Issue: When a store in shopping mall was burglarized, shall the property service company be liable?

Holding: The court held that although the property service contract was not signed between Plaintiff and Defendant, since Defendant received the management fee directly from Plaintiff, gave a receipt in return, and provided management service to Plaintiff, the property service relationship could be found between them as a matter of fact. Defendant had the duty to provide reasonable security service and adopt reasonable measures to protect Plaintiff's property. However, Defendant failed to fulfill its duty and provided the thieves the chance to enter the shopping mall and steal Plaintiff's property. Therefore, Defendant was negligent and shall be liable for the part of the damage with respect to its fault.

Rule: The property service company owes the duty to safeguard stores in the shopping mall and shall bear tort liability if it fails to take reasonable measures to prevent stores from being burglarized.

#52 Safeguard Obligation

Case: Xique Huang vs. Hongbo Hao et al.

Facts: Defendant posted an outdoor activity plan on a website. The decedent applied and got enrolled. However, when camping on a mountain at night, the decedent felt uncomfortable and died even after her companions gave her first aid and called for help immediately. Evidence showed that the decedent was killed by the low temperature. Family members of the decedent sued the organizer of the activity.

Issue: When a team member died during an outdoor activity, shall the organizer be liable?

Holding: The trial court held that the duty of safeguarding was imposed on the owner, manager, operator, or other responsible individuals for the places used for social purposes. All these individuals had control over the places. In this case, the accident occurred in a wild nature park, over which the Defendant had no control. In addition, this activity was not profitable. Therefore, Defendant had no duty to protect the safety of decedent's person or property. The appellate court held that self-help outdoor sport was not a business activity but a social activity. As a leader of the activity, the organizer had the reasonable duty to take care of the safety of the team members. In this case, Defendant proposed the application guidelines and selected team members before the activity. Considering the circumstances and Defendant's capacity, Defendant had adopted all reasonable measures to save the decedent when the accident happened. Defendant fulfilled his duty of care to the participants. Therefore, the court found Defendant was not negligent. The decedent's death was caused by natural circumstances and her physical condition. Defendant was not liable for her death.

Rule: When the organizer of an outdoor activity has taken all reasonable measures to save the life of a team member, he does not bear tort liability, even if the team member eventually dies.

#53 Safeguard Obligation

Case: Min Zheng et al. vs. Rizhao Haibin National Forest Park

Facts: A company organized a forest park tour for its employees and entered a contract with a travel agency. The agency delegated a local tour guide in the park to arrange the journey. During the tour, one employee was drowned by the ebb tide. Obviously, the employee was not good at swimming, so when the wave went back, he failed to swim towards shore and was brought into the deep sea by the wave. Family members of the decedent sued the company, the travel agency, the local guide, and the forest park for damage.

Issue: When the employee suffered injury during the tour organized by the employer, did the employer owe a duty to safeguard the employee and does it bear tort liability for the harm?

Holding: The court held that there was a contractual relationship between the decedent and the travel agency, the local guide, and the forest park. All of them owed the duty to safeguard the decedent. With full civil conduct capacity, the decedent was negligent by ignoring the guide's warning and going swimming in the sea. So, the decedent was liable for part of the damage with respect to his fault. The forest park had a duty to minimize the risk. However, the park did not give safety lessons nor provide safety equipment to tourists. In addition, when the accident happened, the monitoring equipment did not notice it at all. And when the decedent's companions called for help, no security, medical staff, or lifeguards came to help. The park was severely negligent and should be held liable for a major part of the damage. Because the travel agency and local guard lead tourists to the sea, knowing there was no swimming in the contract, and the guard only warned but did not stop the decedent when the decedent went to swim, they were negligent and shall be liable for the damage with respect to their fault. The company had no duty to safeguard its employees during the journey, and organizing the tour was not sufficient as the cause of decedent's death, so the company was not liable.

Rule: The company does not owe a duty to safeguard its employees during an outdoor tour organized by the company.

#54 Torts Towards Students

Case: Wang Yafeng vs. Xihua Lidazhuang Fengqiao Elementary School et al.

Facts: When teachers in an elementary school organized their students to pick up bricks on campus during a class break, two students got into a fight. One was hit and injured by a brick thrown by the other. The injury was appraised as a tenth-degree disability.

Issue: When an elementary student was injured by his schoolmate on campus, shall the school be liable?

Holding: The court held that the wrongdoer in this case was a person with limited civil capacity. He shall bear tort liability for part of the damage, to the extent of his capacity of control and his judgment in the light of his age and intelligence. Since the guardians of Plaintiff were negligent by not taking Plaintiff to medical treatment in time, Defendant's liability could be reduced accordingly. The school did not give safety lessons before organizing the activity nor did the school notice the injury in time when the accident happened. As a result, the school was negligent by failing to fulfill its duty of care. The school was held liable for 30 % of the damage. The guardians of the victim were held liable for 30 % of the damage. The parents of the wrongdoer were held liable for 40 % of the damage.

Rule: If the elementary school breaches its duty of care and fails to prevent fighting between students on campus, it shall be liable for the victim with respect to its fault.

#55 Torts Towards Students

Case: Ding vs. Neixiang County Kindergarten

Facts: Plaintiff is a minor in a kindergarten. One day, Plaintiff took part in an exercise class in a playground with other children in his class. A few teachers watched and supervised. However, Plaintiff fell from the slide and got injured. The injury was appraised as a tenth-degree disability.

Issue: When a minor got injured in the exercise class organized by the kindergarten, shall the kindergarten be liable for the damage?

Holding: The court held that when a school or kindergarten organizes activities, they should adopt measures to protect students' safety. As a minor without civil capacity, Plaintiff was vulnerable and had weak capacity for judgment and self-protection. The kindergarten had a duty to educate, manage, and protect Plaintiff when he was in school. In this case, the measures taken by the kindergarten was insufficient to protect the Plaintiff from getting injured. Defendant did not fulfill its duty of care and was held liable for Plaintiff's damage.

Rule: When a minor is injured in the exercise class organized by the kindergarten, the kindergarten shall be liable for the damage, if it does not take enough measures to fulfill its duty of education, management, and protection.

#56 Torts Towards Students

Case: Wu vs. Yichang City Mechanical and Electrical Engineering School

Facts: Plaintiff was a student leader. He was in charge of organizing a Teacher's Day evening party. When he went to teaching building No. 2 to meet a teacher, he was trapped in a broken stair and was injured. His calcareous was fractured and the injury was appraised as a tenth-degree disability.

Issue: When a minor student was injured at school due to the poor infrastructure of the school building, what liability shall be imposed on the school?

Holding: The court held that as an educational institute, the school had the duty of educating and managing the students. The school also owed a duty to protect students from injury by maintaining the school buildings, school yard, and other public equipment, and keeping them in a reasonable condition of safety. However, in this case, the stairs in teaching building No. 2 did not meet this reasonable standard. The poor condition of the stairs directly caused Plaintiff's injury. So, the school was negligent and shall be held liable for the damage.

Rule: The school has the duty to provide a safe campus for students. If it fails to do so, and a minor student gets injured due to poor building infrastructure, the school shall be found negligent and liable.

#57 Torts Towards Students

Case: Yannan Gao et al. vs. Miyun Xiwengzhuang Center Kindergarten

Facts: A kindergarten had a school bus to pick up and drop off students. One day, the school bus dropped a girl off at her village as usual. The driver did not find the girl's parents, but her 12-year-old sister instead. The driver turned the girl over to her sister and left. When they were crossing the street, the sisters were hit by a minibus. Both of them were seriously injured.

Issue: When the minor was hit and injured on the way home by a vehicle, shall the kindergarten be liable for the damage?

Holding: The court held that according to the decision made by the traffic police, the two girls were liable for a major part of the accident, and the driver of the minibus was liable for a minor part. The driver's employer had paid his part of the compensation. In addition, the kindergarten has the duty to educate, manage, and protect the students. If the kindergarten did not fulfill its duty and caused a student's damage, it shall be held liable for part of the damage with respect to its fault. In this case, the school bus did not send the student back into her guardians' control, thus the kindergarten had not yet fulfilled its duty. Therefore, the damage was caused while the student was within the kindergarten's control. The court ruled that the kindergarten shall be liable for any losses suffered by the student, except for the losses caused by the minibus driver's employer.

Rule: If the kindergarten provides school bus service, it shall be liable for damages for failing to fulfill its duty of care while picking up and dropping off students.

#58 Torts Towards Students

Case: Deyu Zhao vs. Wushi Tian and Liaoyang No. 20 High School

Facts: Because the playground was wet and slippery after snow, the physical education teacher dismissed the class and let the students play with each other by themselves. However, Plaintiff's left foot was injured by his classmate when they were wrestling for fun. The injury was appraised as a ninth-degree disability. Plaintiff sued the wrongdoer and the school for damage.

Issue: If a student was injured when playing with his classmate in PE class, shall the school be liable for the damage?

Holding: The court held that Plaintiff assumed the risk when he chose to wrestle during recess time. However, as a result of both parties' negligence, Plaintiff was injured. Thus, the wrongdoer should be held liable for a major part of Plaintiff's damage, in which his guardians shall compensate 50 % of the damage. As Plaintiff was comparatively negligent, his guardians shall be held liable for 10 % of the damage. The school was also negligent for failure to keep the class in order and stop the students' dangerous activity. Because the school's negligence contributed the accident, it shall be liable with respect to its fault, i.e., 40 % of the damage.

Rule: When a student gets injured when playing with his classmate in PE class because of the teacher's nonfeasance, the school shall be held liable for the damage.

Chapter 30
Product Liability

#59 Product Liability

Case: Nansheng Bao vs. Nanhua Xiang

Facts: A person bought and drank some bulk Chinese liquor when having dinner at the mess hall. Going home, he felt dizzy, limp, and nauseated. His wife immediately sent him to the hospital and he was diagnosed with alcohol poisoning. After testing, the content of formaldehyde in the bulk Chinese liquor was found to exceed standards. Therefore, he sued the mess hall for compensation. The mess hall alleged that it was not the producer of the bulk Chinese liquor, which was supplied by a third party, and it had no knowledge about the defect.

Issue: Can a victim seek compensation from the seller, which is not the producer of the defective product?

Holding: The court held that the mess hall had the duty to provide food and beverages meeting quality standards to customers. When damage was caused due to the mess hall's failure to fulfill its duty, it shall bear tort liability. Although the defective liquor was manufactured by a third party, Plaintiff had the right to choose to recover from the seller rather than the manufacturer according to the relevant provision of the Tort Law. In the instant case, after the Plaintiff filed suit against the manufacturer for compensation, the Defendant could also recover from the manufacturer in a separate suit.

Rule: The victim of a defective product can choose to sue either the seller or the manufacturer. If the seller is not at fault, he is entitled to seek reimbursement from the culpable manufacturer.

X. Li and J. Jin, *Concise Chinese Tort Laws*, China-EU Law Series 1,
DOI 10.1007/978-3-642-41024-6_30, © Springer-Verlag Berlin Heidelberg 2014

#60 Product Liability

Case: Xianghui Liang vs. Zhengzhou Parkson Retail Development Company

Facts: Although Swarovski was a well-known synthetic crystal accessories retailer, Plaintiff was not aware of that fact. He bought a few accessories from the Swarovski store in Defendant's shopping mall, which provided an invoice indicating "crystal pendant" and "crystal bracelet." When he found out the accessories were imitation crystals, he felt cheated and sued Defendant.

Issue: If the invoice did not indicate the name of the goods in detail, did it constitute fraud?

Holding: The court held that crystal included natural crystal and synthetic crystal. In this case, Plaintiff bought synthetic crystal from Defendant. Although only "crystal" was written on the invoice, it did not show that the customer bought natural crystal. In addition, Plaintiff failed to prove the salesmen defrauded him by misleading him or that he intentionally concealed facts. Therefore, no fraud was found in this case, and Plaintiff's claim was dismissed.

Rule: The incomplete description of a purchase on an invoice is not enough to constitute fraud.

#61 Product Liability

Case: Mengxuan Wu vs. Pigeon Corporation et al.

Facts: A mother did not obey the operation rules several times while using the feeding-bottle sterilization box. One time, she uncovered and exposed the box in an accessible place in the kitchen before it sufficiently cooled down. After a while, her child went into the kitchen and turned over the sterilizing box. As a result, the child was scalded on the face, neck, and chest. The mother alleged the sterilizing box had design defects. She sued the manufacturer on behalf of her child.

Issue: How is reasonable risk distinguished from defective design when the product has caused a consumer's injury?

Holding: The court held that a defect meant that the product created unreasonable safety risks to a person or their property. Heating and boiling water like a microwave oven to sterilize was the mechanism of the sterilizing box. Although the sterilizing box at high temperatures was dangerous, this danger was the reasonable side effect of its function. In addition, the product instructions clearly indicated steps of operation and notes to prevent injury from scalding. It is not difficult for users to follow these steps and notes, which, if followed, were sufficient to prevent injuries. Therefore, defective design was not found in this case. The injury was a result of the mother's violation of the operation rules and insufficient guardianship. Defendant was not held liable.

Rule: If the steps of operation and notes are clearly indicated and following them is sufficient to prevent the injury, acceptable risk relative to the design is reasonable.

#62 Product Liability

Case: Xuehua Li et al. vs. Henan Zhengzhou Hongfa Farm Machine Company

Facts: The decedent bought a wheeled tractor from a farm machine company. The tractor was manufactured by a tractor company. A few days after he began using the tractor, the steering wheel fell off and he was killed immediately. Family members of the decedent and the farm machine company settled after the accident. The farm company agreed to pay a fixed amount of compensation and, in return, family members of the decedent admitted the accident was caused by uneven ground and the decedent's noncompliance of the operational rules. However, after the settlement, family members of the decedent hired professionals to investigate the tractor and found that the steering wheel fell off as a result of weak welding between the steering shaft and hub shaft. As a result, family members of the decedent ignored the settlement and sued the farm machine company for damage.

Issue: Can the aggrieved party sue for product liability after settling with the seller and admitting that the injury was not caused by the product?

Holding: The court held that, in this case, the decedent's death was in fact caused by the defective product. Therefore, the manufacturer (the tractor company) and the seller (the farm machine company) were liable. Although family members of the decedent and the farm machine company had reached a settlement and agreed that the accident had nothing to do with the product quality, according to the investigation, the actual and direct cause of the accident was the defective product. The settlement could not deny the fact that the product was defective. Therefore, the two companies were held jointly and severally liable.

Rule: The aggrieved party can still sue for product liability even after settling with the seller and admitting that the injury was not caused by the product, if the subsequent investigation indicated otherwise.

#63 Product Liability

Case: Haibo Shi and Jianmei Cai vs. Ronggang Huang, Fuqiang Lu, and Zhongshan Jutian Bath and Kitchen Electric Company Ltd.

Facts: A man bought a water heater from a shopping mall and installed it in the bathroom of his dormitory by himself. His daughter died from carbon monoxide poisoning when she used it. According to examination, the product was not defective, but the installment violated regulations, which resulted in gaseous exhaust that could not be ventilated to the outside when the water heater was functioning.

Issue: When injury was caused by an electrical product that satisfied the national security requirement, can product liability still be found?

Holding: The trial court held that straight exhausting gas water heaters were prohibited by law. Although the water heater in this case was designed to be stove piped, the manufacturer did not provide an exhaust pipeline, so the user could only install the water heater as straight exhausting. Therefore, the product was defective, and the manufacturer shall be liable for the decedent's death. The appellate court held that obeying the statutory standard was a very basic requirement for businesses. The product could still create unreasonable risk even if it met the statutory standard. In this case, because the exhaust pipeline was not provided by the manufacturer, customers who had weak judgment capacity might install the water heater in a dangerous way. The company did not adopt all reasonable measures to minimize risks created by the product. The product was defective. Therefore, the manufacturer and the seller were jointly and severally liable. However, as Plaintiff did not follow the instruction manual of the product which required professionals to install the machine, he was comparatively negligent and shall be held liable for a major part of the damage. Meanwhile, as the product satisfied the national security requirement, the manufacturer and seller's fault was minor. They shall be held liable for a minor part of the damage.

Rule: When the injury is caused by an electrical product that satisfies the national security requirement, product liability can still be found when the manufacturer or seller is negligent in warning or instructing.

Chapter 31
Liability for Motor Vehicle Traffic Accident

#64 Traffic Accident Liability

Case: Yuehong Liu vs. Jianming Zhang et al.

Facts: When Defendant was driving his vehicle, he hit and killed Plaintiff's shepherd dog. Plaintiff sued for damage.

Issue: Shall it be regarded as a traffic accident as defined by the law of torts when a dog was hit and killed on the road by a car?

Holding: The court held that the essential elements of a traffic accident were the following: (1) the subject of the accident was an automobile, (2) the accident happened on the road, (3) the damage was caused by driver's negligence or accident, and (4) the damage included personal or property damages. In this case, the dog was not the subject of the accident, but the property of its owner. Therefore, this case satisfied elements of a traffic accident. Defendant shall be imposed with traffic accident liability according to the law of torts.

Rule: It is a traffic accident when a dog is hit and killed on the road by a car, so the culpable driver shall bear liability according to the law of torts.

#65 Traffic Accident Liability

Case: Duanying Gao et al. vs. Deyi Xu and China Continent Property and Casualty Insurance Company (Huaian Branch)

Facts: Defendant was unlicensed and intoxicated, when he operated a motor tricycle. Subsequently, he hit and killed a person on the road. The traffic police determined that Defendant's fault was the major cause of the accident. Evidence showed that Defendant bought compulsory motor vehicle insurance from an insurance company for the vehicle.

X. Li and J. Jin, *Concise Chinese Tort Laws*, China-EU Law Series 1,
DOI 10.1007/978-3-642-41024-6_31, © Springer-Verlag Berlin Heidelberg 2014

Issue: When a traffic accident was caused by an unlicensed and intoxicated driver, shall the insurance company be held liable within the limitations of the compulsory motor vehicle insurance?

Holding: The court held that the motor vehicle insurance was compulsory and aimed at promoting public welfare. The insurance company shall perform their debt service obligation as long as there was personal injury, whether or not the driver was negligent. Therefore, the insurer of the vehicle should compensate the injured party within the limitations of the compulsory motor vehicle insurance. For the exceeding parts and other parts of the damage which were not covered by the insurance, the driver shall be held liable for 70 %.

Rule: Even if the driver was unlicensed, intoxicated, and the major cause of a traffic accident, the insurance company is liable within the limitations of the compulsory motor vehicle insurance.

#66 Traffic Accident Liability

Case: Guofu Zheng et al. vs. Lei Shi et al.

Facts: The driver of a catering company drove the company's car out without permission and caused the death of a passenger. According to the traffic police's ruling, the driver was fully responsible. Evidence showed that, although the car was used by the company and the car payment was made by the general manager of the company, the car was registered under the name of his friend.

Issue: Who shall bear the liability of the traffic accident caused by the car, its nominal owner or its actual owner?

Holding: The court held that the general manager's friend was the nominal owner of the car. The car was not under his control, and he was not liable for the damage. In the interests of justice, because the general manager and the company controlled the car and enjoyed the benefits brought by the car, they had the duty of management. As they failed to fulfill the duty, they were held jointly and severally liable for the damages. The court ruled that (1) the driver was liable for the damages and (2) the general manger and the company were held jointly and severally liable.

Rule: The nominal owner of the car is not liable if he is not negligent, while the actual owner can be found liable if he fails to fulfill his duty of management.

#67 Traffic Accident Liability

Case: Deping Huang et al. vs. Liang Zhang et al.

Facts: B borrowed a Santana from the owner A, and C was the driver when the accident happened. A passenger was killed in the accident. The traffic police ruled that, because C violated the regulations, he should bear full responsibility.

Issue: How are liabilities among the driver, the party borrowing the car, and the party lending the car allocated?

Holding: The court held that C was liable for the accident as he deliberately drove without a license and failed to fulfill his duty of care. He was the direct cause of the damage and was the only wrongdoer in the car accident. B knew C for a long time, and B knew or should have known that C did not have a driver's license. In addition, he allowed C to drive the car without the owner A's permission. B was also negligent. However, as B had no common intent or negligence with C, he was not jointly and severally liable for the damage, but only liable for his own negligence. As the owner, A did not lend a defective car to B. Also, he did not cause the accident nor did he profit by doing so. Therefore, A was not held liable.

Rule: If the lender of a car is not negligent, he is not liable for the traffic accident caused by his car.

#68 Traffic Accident Liability

Case: Shanghai Xuanang Transportation Company vs. Chaojun Xiong et al.

Facts: The accident occurred when Defendant was driving a truck to transport goods. The accident caused property damage and personal injury. Evidence showed that Defendant bought the truck from the truck company with installments. Due to the fact that the last several installments had not yet been paid, the truck was still registered under the name of the truck company.

Issue: Which shall be liable for the traffic accident, the party controlling the car in fact or the party owning the car in law?

Holding: The court held that the wet road after rain, speeding, and the improper reaction of the driver caused the accident. As a result, the driver was fully responsible for the damage. Although the truck company was the nominal owner of the truck, this arrangement was only aimed to urge the payment of installments. The driver had free and complete control of the truck, so he was liable for the damage caused during his operation of the truck. The truck company was not held liable.

Rule: When the nominal owner and the actual user of the vehicle are different, and the user has free and complete control of the vehicle, the user is liable for the damage caused by him, and the nominal owner is not held liable.

#69 Traffic Accident Liability

Case: Dandan Jin vs. Zhicheng Wu, Zhijin Wu, and Dazhong insurance Company (Ningbo Branch)

Facts: Defendant rode a motorcycle without a license and hit Plaintiff, causing Plaintiff's tenth-degree disability. The traffic police determined that the motorcycle driver was fully responsible for the accident.

Issue: Shall the insurance company compensate the victim's personal injury within the limitations of the compulsory motor vehicle insurance, even if the accident was caused by an unlicensed driver of a motor vehicle?

Holding: The court held that, when personal injury was caused in automobile accident, the insurance company shall compensate within the limitations of the compulsory motor vehicle insurance. Article 22 of the Regulation on Compulsory Traffic Accident Liability Insurance for Motor Vehicles provided that, when an unlicensed wrongdoer causes property damage while operating a motor vehicle, the insurance company shall not compensate for the damage. The regulation was silent in personal injury situations. Therefore, although the damage in this case was caused by unlicensed operation, the insurance company shall compensate. The driver shall be held liable for the damage exceeding the insurance limits.

Rule: Even if the accident is caused by an unlicensed driver, the insurance company shall compensate the victim for personal injury within the limitations of the compulsory motor vehicle insurance.

#70 Traffic Accident Liability

Case: Xinlong Zhuang and Xinhai Zhuang vs. Jinhua Henghui Hot-dip Galvanizing Company and PICC (Jinhua Branch)

Facts: The collision happened at an intersection between a truck and a tricycle. The tricycle rider died in the accident. The traffic police concluded that the degree of responsibility between the two parties could not be determined.

Issue: When the traffic police cannot determine the respective responsibilities of the parties in an accident, who shall assume tort liability?

Holding: The court held that, when a motor vehicle accident causes personal injury or property damage, the insurance company should compensate the damage within the limitations of the compulsory motor vehicle insurance. In this case, since the truck driver bought the compulsory motor vehicle insurance from the insurance company, the insurance company should compensate for the tricycle rider's damage. Because the relative responsibilities could not be determined, a presumption should be made that the truck driver was liable for the damage exceeding the insurance policy coverage. Because the tricycle rider did not get off the tricycle when he crossed the road, the rider violated traffic regulations, and the driver's liability could be reduced accordingly.

Rule: When the traffic police cannot determine the respective responsibilities of the parties in the accident, the insurance company shall compensate for the damage within the limitations of the compulsory motor vehicle insurance.

#71 Traffic Accident Liability

Case: Yaping Hao vs. Xinjiang Uyghur Autonomous Region Public Security Department

Facts: A government agency official hit and injured the aggrieved party driving the agency's vehicle. The injury was appraised as a tenth-degree disability, and the driver was found fully responsible for the accident by the traffic police. The aggrieved party sued the government agency for damage.

Issue: When a government official caused the traffic accident by driving the agency's vehicle, shall the government agency be held liable for the damage?

Holding: The court held that Defendant (Public Security Department) was the owner of the vehicle. Since the wrongdoer was a formal official of the agency and controlled the vehicle, it could be inferred that the agency authorized and approved the wrongdoer's use of the vehicle when the accident happened. Therefore, Defendant shall be liable for the damage. In addition, as the manager of the wrongdoer, Defendant had the duty of management over the wrongdoer's acts. Defendant could be found negligent in managing the wrongdoer. Plaintiff's injury was caused by this negligence. This approach could also support the Court's ruling. However, since the wrongdoer's driving was not within the scope of the authority as a government official, the State Compensation Law did not apply here.

Rule: When a government official causes the traffic accident by driving the agency's vehicle, the agency shall be liable for the damage.

Chapter 32
Liability for Medical Malpractice

#72 Medical Malpractice Liability

Case: Guoqiang Yan vs. Beijing Haidian Obstetrics and Gynecology Hospital

Facts: Plaintiff was a pregnant woman who had regular examinations at Defendant's hospital. At the tenth examination, the doctor found there was too much amniotic fluid and unusual fetal movement. However, the doctor did not take the findings seriously and just arranged an oxygen uptake for Plaintiff. Lastly, the doctor asked the Plaintiff to come back the next morning. However, during her examination the next morning, Plaintiff had a stillbirth.

Issue: What level of duty of care is owed to the patient by a hospital?

Holding: Because of the importance of medical treatment for a patient's life and health, a medical professional bears a duty of care to every patient. In this case, the doctor-patient relationship had been established. When the unusual symptom was found, Defendant did not notify Plaintiff of the danger and the possibility of an accident, nor ask her to stay in hospital for observation. Therefore, the hospital, as an institution for medical professionals, was at fault for its failure to fulfill the duty of care and notification. The stillbirth might also be attributed to Plaintiff's personal reason. However, since it could not be concluded that the fetus would have died even if Plaintiff stayed in hospital, there was causation between the medical treatment and Plaintiff's damage. Therefore, Defendant was liable in this case. Given Plaintiff's personal reason and the uncertainty of stillbirth, Defendant shall bear partial liability.

Rule: Where any damage is caused to a patient during the course of medical treatment, the medical institution shall be held liable if it failed to fulfill its professional duty of care.

X. Li and J. Jin, *Concise Chinese Tort Laws*, China-EU Law Series 1,
DOI 10.1007/978-3-642-41024-6_32,

#73 Medical Malpractice Liability

Case: Delin Jiang vs. Haian Traditional Chinese Medicine Hospital

Facts: Plaintiff suffered a fracture from a car accident, and was sent to the Defendant hospital to have an open reduction and internal fixation surgery. After he was discharged, Plaintiff did not feel well. X-ray examination showed that the fixation was broken so Plaintiff had to undergo a second surgery. The reexamination results showed that the fixation fracture could be attributed to several reasons. The operation was not medical malpractice because there were no surgical errors and all the devices were licensed and certificated.

Issue: Which party shall bear the burden of proof in a medical malpractice case?

Holding: Regarding medical malpractice, the medical institution has the burden of proof to show lack of causation between the medical procedure and the damage. It was certain that Plaintiff suffered damage because the fixation from the first surgery broke and Plaintiff had to undergo another surgery. Although the test showed that there could be several reasons for the fixation fracture, the causation between the medical procedure and the fracture was not excluded. Since Defendant did not demonstrate the lack of relevance between medical procedure and the damage, the causal relationship could be presumed. Even though it was not medical malpractice, the hospital should also bear liability for breach and damage. Because Plaintiff did not return for a visit for several years after the surgery, he shall also bear a part of the liability for his damage. Here, Defendant's liability could be mitigated.

Rule: In a medical malpractice case, the medical institution shall bear the burden of proof to show the lack of causation between the medical procedure and the damage.

#74 Medical Malpractice Liability

Case: Kai Wu vs. Zhangjiawan veterinary station

Fact: Plaintiff's dog had a fever, so he sent the dog to the veterinary station. After its treatment, the dog did not feel well. In fact, its condition worsened, and the dog finally died. Plaintiff sued and claimed that Defendant did not carefully diagnose the dog and blindly treated its disease as a general fever, which resulted in the dog's death. The dog died due to an infectious disease.

Issue: What principle of liability shall be applied in treating animals?

Holding: Tort Law regarding the medical treatment of animals applies a principle of fault liability rather than a presumption of fault. The veterinary station had recommended testing the dog for canine parvovirus, but Plaintiff refused and thus delayed the diagnosis. There was no mistake in the dog's treatment. Therefore, Defendant was not at fault and not liable.

Rule: The principle of fault liability shall be applied in treating animals.

#75 Medical Malpractice Liability

Case: Qiuhong Li vs. No.154 People's Liberation Army Hospital

Facts: Plaintiff was a pregnant woman. During the fifth month of her pregnancy, she went to the Defendant hospital for vaginal bleeding. The hospital asserted that the situation was very severe and, in particular, told Plaintiff that using antibiotics was necessary, but could easily cause a miscarriage or intrauterine infection, and her unborn child would not be secured. However, Plaintiff insisted on protecting her fetus and refused to use antibiotics except penicillin. A few days later, Plaintiff's situation worsened. The hospital told Plaintiff that miscarriage was inevitable, so if she continued taking miscarriage prevention measures, stillbirth or other severe results may occur. But Plaintiff did not change her mind and just wanted to keep the fetus. She also admitted in writing that she was advised of the situation. Thereafter, the fetus was stillborn and Plaintiff suffered septic shock.

Issue: Shall the hospital be liable for any damages suffered by the patient if it fulfilled its duty to inform the patient of all available choices and the possible results?

Holding: During the entire treatment, the hospital reminded and explicitly introduced the possibility of miscarriage and uncontrollable complications, and Plaintiff also admitted her understanding in writing. Therefore, the hospital's obligation of information and highest duty of care had been fulfilled. Further, the hospital was not at fault because it did not violate the standard treatment and process. Plaintiff was an old woman and was pregnant for the first time, and she insisted on keeping the pregnancy despite the high risk, as well as the possibility of infection and complication. Finally, the infection could not be controlled with the limited antibiotics, which worsened her condition. The aforesaid situation, rather than the hospital's medical treatment, was the real reason for Plaintiff's damage. Therefore, the hospital was not held liable.

Rule: If the hospital fulfilled its duty of information, and the patient voluntarily makes a dangerous choice, the hospital is not liable for the outcome brought by the choice.

#76 Medical Malpractice Liability

Case: Guang Hu vs. Chengdu Infectious Diseases Hospital

Facts: Plaintiff was suspected of suffering rabies so he was transferred to the infectious diseases hospital. The hospital diagnosed that it might be rabies or asthma, but treated it as rabies. Plaintiff insisted on being transferred to another hospital. The other hospital diagnosed Plaintiff with asthma, but still required him to be injected with the rabies vaccine. Thereafter, Plaintiff sued the infectious diseases hospital for misdiagnosis.

Issue: If an infectious disease is difficult to be diagnosed as a matter of fact, shall the hospital be held liable for misdiagnosis?

Holding: Medical misdiagnosis is quite normal in treating patients, which cannot be always regarded as a fault. A diagnosis needs a time and a series of medical activity and might change as the disease develops. Defendant's diagnosis was made within a short period of time considering the fact that Plaintiff was bitten by a dog and transferred for suspicion of rabies. These actions should not be deemed unreasonable. Moreover, because of Plaintiff's second transfer in a short period of time, Defendant had no opportunity to test and modify the diagnosis. After the transfer, the other hospital also demanded Plaintiff take the rabies vaccine, which showed that rabies was not completely excluded. In addition, when Plaintiff was in the hospital, Defendant made a treatment plan for rabies according to the understood information and took necessary anti-infectious disease measures. When Plaintiff's guardian asked to transfer the Plaintiff, Defendant explained the possible adverse result of the Plaintiff leaving the hospital. Defendant then arranged the transportation, and doctors took fluids and oxygen readings on the way, making sure Plaintiff was transferred safely. Therefore, Defendant had fulfilled its duty of care and took reasonable measures for Plaintiff's treatment, so it was not liable.

Rule: The medical institution is not liable for medical misdiagnosis, if it fulfills its duty of care and is not at fault.

#77 Medical Malpractice Liability

Case: Ruichang Wu vs. Jiangsu Renmin Hospital

Facts: Plaintiff went to the accused hospital for treatment of diarrhea. The doctor asked about his kidney condition and recorded "blood sugar and kidney function are normal" according to Plaintiff's own statements. After that, the patient was diagnosed with intestinal infection and injected intravenously with gentamicin. However, during the injection, the patient showed symptoms of acute renal failure and had to be hospitalized. However, this incident was not identified as medical malpractice.

Issue: Could the hospital be exempt if the patient did not disclose his medical history fully and truthfully?

Holding: Plaintiff's condition was renal failure caused by gentamicin. Although the treatment process was not identified as medical malpractice, the expert conclusion was not clear on whether Defendant had medical fault. The expert conclusion was unclear on whether the doctor carried out the obligation for paying attention to Plaintiff's potential renal insufficiency due to long-term hypertension and the high probability that gentamicin would cause acute renal failure under this condition. Accordingly, Defendant could be held as failing to satisfy the burden of proof. The judicial evaluation conclusion confirmed that, before and during the gentamicin injection, Defendant failed to check the patient's renal function according to his actual symptoms and make sure there were no adverse reactions to gentamicin. Thus, Defendant did not satisfy his duty of care and was at fault for the damage. Therefore, Defendant shall be held liable. Defendant claimed that medical history should be provided truthfully and properly by the patient. This assertion would exempt a medical institution's duty of care and duty of inquiry and thus impose the duty of professional judgment on patients, which diverges from medical regulation.

Rule: If a medical professional fails to perform his diagnosis and treatment obligations according to current standards, thereby resulting in damage to the patient, the medical institution concerned shall be held liable. The failure to disclose the precise medical history cannot exempt liability.

#78 Medical Malpractice Liability

Case: Junjun Zhong and Jinguo Wang vs. Ningbo Zhenhai District Zhuangshi Peizhen Hospital

Facts: A patient went to the hospital for a sore throat and fever. After a routine examination, he was diagnosed as having an upper respiratory tract infection with high fever and was prescribed an infusion and oral medication. He went home after the infusion, but suffered a sudden physical abnormality during the night and died after being sent to the hospital. An autopsy identified it as a sudden cardiac death.

Issue: Shall the hospital be liable when the patient did not die from the disease diagnosed and the treatment?

Holding: The primary cause of the patient's death is cardiodynia. The upper respiratory tract infection with high fever resulted in pulmonary congestion, edema, and severe oxygen deficiency, which ultimately caused the sudden cardiac death. However, the patient's cardiodynia was not caused by Defendant's treatment, and this disease is hard to diagnose. Thus, Defendant was not at fault for both the occurrence and diagnosis of cardiodynia. And there was no fault in the Defendant's diagnosis for the patient's upper respiratory tract infection with high fever, which was consistent with Defendant's allegation. Plaintiff said concurrent use of penicillin with roxithromycin and aspirin may have increased the toxicity of penicillin. However, the patient did not die from penicillin poisoning, so there was no causal relationship between Defendant's treatment and the patient's death. Because the patient was responsible for keeping his medical records, Plaintiff should bear the burden of proof. Since the medical malpractice identification was not carried out due to the insufficiency of records, Plaintiff shall assume disadvantageous litigation results. Given that Defendant demonstrated that there is neither fault nor causal relationship shown by presenting autopsy reports, medical prescriptions, and other evidence, Plaintiff's claim could not be supported by the court.

Rule: Where the damage is not caused by medical treatment and the medical institution is also not at fault in other aspects, there is no medical malpractice liability.

Chapter 33
Liability for Environmental Pollution

#79 Environmental Pollution Liability

Case: The Fisheries Management Office of Yahekou Reservoir vs. Nanyang Yahekou Power Generation Company Ltd.

Facts: Plaintiff was a contractor of a reservoir for fish farming. The local power plant used this reservoir for cooling water. The power plant extracted water from this reservoir, and during the extraction, many fish are absorbed into the tube and heated to death. The power plant also discharged sewage into this reservoir, poisoning many fish. Plaintiff suffered great losses from that, so it sued the power plant and asked for compensation.

Issue: How is the burden of proof in an environmental pollution case allocated?

Holding: Plaintiff possessed fish farming license issued by the government, thus, was lawfully using the reservoir. The damage caused by Defendant existed as a matter of fact. The damaging actions were continuous, the consequence was harmful, and there was causation between the actions and the damage. According to related legislation, environmental pollution Tort Law applies strict liability and the Defendant shall bear the burden of proof. In this case, Defendant cannot provide evidence of exemption or against causal relationship, so it should bear the tort liability for Plaintiff's damage.

Rule: In the event of a dispute over environmental pollution, the polluter shall bear the burden of proof regarding any exemption from or mitigation of liability and the causal relationship between his conduct and the damage.

X. Li and J. Jin, *Concise Chinese Tort Laws*, China-EU Law Series 1,
DOI 10.1007/978-3-642-41024-6_33,

#80 Environmental Pollution Liability

Case: Zhao Mou vs. Shanghai Zhongji Yuandong Cargo Container Ltd.

Facts: Plaintiff was a pregnant woman whose apartment was across the street from Defendant's work place. Defendant was working on painting and drying cargo containers which emitted benzene, methylbenzene, dimethylbenzene, dust, and noise. In a report by the environmental monitoring department from 2003 to 2004, the density of pollutants and speed of emission seriously exceeded the allowable amount, which polluted the environment in the residential area and threatened the residents' health. Plaintiff required Defendant to stop polluting and take protective methods, but Defendant never responded to the requisition. Then, Plaintiff had to terminate her pregnancy because of a chromosomal abnormality in the fetus. Plaintiff believed it was caused by the pollution and brought a lawsuit against Defendant.

Issue: How can the Plaintiff shift of burden of proof in an environmental pollution case?

Holding: The pollution caused by Defendant's work was demonstrated by the monitoring report, so the court supported Plaintiff's claim of stopping Defendant's pollution. But, there was no proof that could establish the connection between pollution and the chromosome abnormality of the fetus. Therefore, Plaintiff failed to provide enough evidence to establish a prima facie case and was not successful in shifting the burden of proof. Because causation could not be proved, Defendant was not liable for Plaintiff's abortion.

Rule: In order to trigger a shift in the burden of proof, the Plaintiff must establish a prima facie case in advance, by proving the connection between pollution and the specific damage.

#81 Liability Allocation Among Multiple Polluters

Case: Weirong Qu vs. Shanghai Hanyin Medicine Company

Facts: Plaintiff was a contractor of a 14-acre pond for shrimp breeding, which was surrounded by three companies, A, B, and C. One day, Plaintiff found many of the shrimp in his pond were dead and obvious acts of water pollution. The report of a local environmental monitoring department showed that the main reason for the water pollution was that A exceedingly poured sewage into this area. Furthermore, B's sewage was discharged into the sea through C's tube while the tube was leaky, also polluting the water in this area.

Issue: How are liabilities among multiple polluters allocated?

Holding: The discharged sewage resulted in the shrimps' death and caused Plaintiff to suffer great loss. Plaintiff's loss was partially attributed to the leakage of B's sewage from the tube. So both A and B should bear joint liability. C did not manage its tube well, which resulted in the pollution, so C should bear residual liability in addition to B's liability. Besides, Plaintiff did not mitigate his loss by raising additional shrimp, so he should bear the part of the loss caused by his own fault.

Rule: Where there are two or more polluters, the proportion of damage each is liable for shall be determined according to the type of pollution, the amount of emissions, and many other factors.

#82 Environmental Pollution Liability

Case: Ling Yang vs. The City Development Company of Beijing, Beijing Shouchuang Company Ltd., Beijing Municipal Engineering Administration Department, Beijing Subway Company Ltd., and Chenkai Company

Facts: Plaintiff moved into a residential community and found there was serious noise disturbing his normal daily activities. An investigational report showed that the noise came from Jingtong Road (run by Beijing Shouchuang Ltd.), Jianguo Road (run by Beijing Municipal Engineering Administration Department), and the Fuxingmen-Bawangfen Subway (run by Beijing Subway Ltd). In addition, Chenkai Company, as the developer of the residential community, did not keep the buildings a reasonable distance away from the roads and installed completely ineffective soundproof windows.

Issue: Can public interest be an exemption for environmental pollution liability?

Holding: The three roads and subway at issue were for public interest. The residential building where Plaintiff lived was built much later than the roads and subway. Therefore, the court did not support Plaintiff's claim against the managers of the roads and subway for the noise. However, the developer, Chenkai Company, shall be liable because there was not enough distance between the building and the roads and the effectiveness of the soundproof windows did not meet acceptable standards.

Rule: Public interest could be an exemption for environmental pollution liability.

#83 Environmental Pollution Liability

Case: Fujin Li vs. Xuzhou Tongli Casting Company Ltd.

Facts: Plaintiff planted peach trees, but suffered great losses because Defendant emitted a lot of dust which killed these trees. The local agriculture department indicated that the dust emitted by Defendant disrupted the pollination, fertilization, and leaf photosynthesis and respiration causing the trees to stop growing and die. Defendant challenged the credibility of the appraiser hired by Plaintiff because the agriculture department was not as professional as the environmental monitoring department. However, Plaintiff could not afford the high costs of the environmental monitoring department.

Issue: Was it necessary to obtain a report from the professional environmental monitoring department in order to demonstrate causation?

Holding: Because the examination expense was much higher than the amount of possible compensation, mandatory examination will lead to unreasonably high litigation fees which did not fit the economic interests of both parties. So the court turned to common sense and logic and decided that there was causal relationship between Defendant's acts and Plaintiff's damage. So, Defendant shall be held liable for Plaintiff's damage.

Rule: Causation could be established by common sense.

#84 Environmental Pollution Liability

Case: Xiaodong Lu vs. Yongda Company

Facts: Defendant had an exhibition hall next to the residential community where the Plaintiff lived. There were three road lamps turned on between 7 p.m. and 5 a.m. the next day. The strong light of the three lamps shined into Plaintiff's bedroom which made him sleepless.

Issue: Might strong light incur environmental pollution liability?

Holding: Defendant's strongly lit lamps were too close to the residence community, and there was no shelter at all, so the light shined directly into Plaintiff's bedroom. The light was so strong that it changed the dark environment, which residents got used to, and amounted to a heavy light pollution as defined by the Regulation of Urban Environmental Lighting. Defendant shall bear tort liability and compensate Plaintiff's actual damage caused by the light pollution.

Rule: Strong light could be identified as a kind of environmental pollution and may cause tort liability.

Chapter 34
Liability for Ultrahazardous Activity

#85 Ultrahazardous Liability

Case: Weixing Shi vs. Shengli Oil Management Company

Facts: Plaintiff was an employee of a restaurant. One day Plaintiff climbed the roof in order to change the flag, but he touched a power line and was injured by electricity. The 35 KV power line on the restaurant's roof, managed by the local power company, was very dangerous.

Issue: What principle of liability shall be applied in an ultrahazardous liability case?

Holding: The power company cannot demonstrate that Plaintiff's injury was none of its business, so according to the shifting of the burden of proof, Plaintiff's damage was caused by the power company. Based on the principle applying strict liability in an ultrahazardous liability case, the power company shall be held liable for Plaintiff's damage even if it had no fault at all. However, Plaintiff should have expected that it was very risky to approach a power line, but he went to the roof without any protection. Thus, Plaintiff was also held partly liable for his own damage.

Rule: The principle of strict liability shall apply in an ultrahazardous liability case.

#86 Ultrahazardous Liability

Case: Liangxian Yin vs. Datang Guoji Lixian River Power Company

Facts: A three-member family had to cross a river during their trip. The water was very shallow and flowed slowly, so they decided to walk across the river. However, when the riverbank measured just 6 m, flooding came

X. Li and J. Jin, *Concise Chinese Tort Laws*, China-EU Law Series 1,
DOI 10.1007/978-3-642-41024-6_34, © Springer-Verlag Berlin Heidelberg 2014

suddenly and swept the wife and the child away. Several days later, their two bodies were found at 7 km away from the site of the accident. The flood was caused by the power company's opening of the sluice gate.

Issue: Is giving sufficient warning a valid defense?

Holding: The power company was operating according to the relevant regulation when the accident happened. They made the warning by blowing horns 50 min before opening the gate as well as putting warning signs downstream and training villagers nearby on how to avoid harm. So the company had met the reasonable standard of care. The site of the accident in this case was more than 4 km away from the sluice gate. This location was beyond the scope of warning. Therefore, the power company was not held liable.

Rule: For ultrahazardous torts, if all necessary security measures have been taken and sufficient warnings have been given, the liability may be mitigated or even exempted.

#87 Ultrahazardous Liability

Case: Taitan Chen and Wencui Chen vs. Railway Bureau of Zhengzhou and Railway Bureau of Chengdu

Facts: Plaintiff took a train to Shanghai. When the train passed Zhengzhou Station, she got off and went to the restroom. However, when she came back, the train had started to leave. So she ran and tried to catch the train along the railroad but was struck and killed by another train.

Issue: What level of duty of care shall the Railway Bureau owe to the passenger?

Holding: The Defendant Railway Bureau of Chengdu was the carrier and bore the obligation to ensure passengers' safety until their arrival at their destination. Hence, it shall be held liable for a passenger's death during the passenger's travel. In addition, when Plaintiff was chasing the train, Defendant Railway Bureau of Zhengzhou failed to fulfill its regulatory obligation to warn of hazards and ensure the safety of passengers and other people. Thus, it was also liable for Plaintiff's death. Therefore, the two Railway Bureaus shall bear joint liability.

Rule: The operator shall bear tort liability for damage caused by the high-speed rail, unless it can prove that the victim deliberately incurred the damage or that the damage was caused by force majeure.

#88 Ultrahazardous Liability

Case: Aiyin Ruan vs. Xinchang Railway Company and Ruiping Hong et al.

Facts: The victim went to a pond in the suburbs to fish. When he cast the fishing line into the water, the line touched a power line. The victim died from electronic shock. The power line belonged to a railway company.

Issue: If no laws or regulations were violated, can tort liability based on ultrahazardous activities still be found?

Holding: Defendant Company managed the power line with acceptable standards, but this could not exempt its liability. The law of ultrahazardous torts applies strict liability rule. Defendant Company did not have any statutory exemptions, so it should bear liability. Plaintiff failed to show causation between the fishpond contractor and the death, so Plaintiff's claim against the contractor was not upheld by the court. The victim should have been given reasonable standard of duty of care, but death was partially caused by his own negligence. Therefore, Defendant Company's liability could be mitigated by the victim's negligence.

Rule: Anyone who causes damage to another person by engaging in ultrahazardous activity shall bear tort liability. The liability can be mitigated or exempted if he can prove that the victim deliberately incurred the damage.

#89 Ultrahazardous Liability

Case: Shuangxi Pan vs. the 150 Division of the No.8 Army Corps of Agriculture

Facts: Plaintiff changed his job and his new employer let him live in a warehouse that was used to store highly toxic pesticides for a long time. Several years later, he and his family suffered peripheral nerve inflammation.

Issue: What principle of liability shall be applied when bodily harm was caused by ultrahazardous materials?

Holding: Plaintiff was damaged by living in a warehouse where highly toxic pesticides were stored; this was an ultrahazardous tort. Defendant was not exempt from liability because Defendant could not show that Plaintiff intentionally caused the damage. The warehouse manager employed by Defendant knew that pesticides were stored where Plaintiff lived over 4 years, but the manager did not take any measures to prevent the harm. Therefore, the court held that there was a causal relationship between Defendant's behavior and Plaintiff's damage. Defendant shall be held liable.

Rule: When ultrahazardous materials cause damage, the principle of strict liability shall apply, and the person in possession or use thereof shall bear the tort liability.

#90 Ultrahazardous Liability

Case: Yunping Liu vs. Beijign Gas Group Company Ltd.

Facts: Plaintiff went home after work and found a strong smell of gas in the apartment. Before he could take any measures, there was a sudden explosion. Plaintiff suffered very serious injuries because of the explosion. Even before the accident happened, other residents in the building smelled the gas and reported it to the Beijing Gas Group Company Ltd. However, the person working for the gas company just checked the reporter's apartment and left without examining the real cause of the gas leak.

Issue: Does gas amount to an ultrahazardous material?

Holding: Although gas is flammable and explosive, it is commonly used and not highly dangerous because accidents can be avoided during normal use. Furthermore, the accident in issue did not happened during the gas company's operating process. Hence, this case was a regular tort rather than an ultrahazardous tort that applies strict liability. Plaintiff could not demonstrate Defendant's fault, and evidence before the court showed that the service call at the other resident's apartment was not negligent. Thus, no causation was established between Plaintiff's damage and Defendant's act. Therefore, the court did not support Plaintiff's claim of damage against Defendant.

Rule: Gas is commonly and easily used without accidents, so it does not constitute an ultrahazardous material.

Chapter 35
Liability for Harm Caused by Domestic Animals

#91 Liability for Harm Caused by Domestic Animals

Case: Wei Peng vs. Tongmei Xue

Fact: Plaintiff was a minor. He lived next door to Defendant and was bitten by Defendant's dog when he was playing in his own yard. Defendant denied that the dog bit the Plaintiff, so Plaintiff brought a lawsuit against Defendant claiming compensation.

Issue: When a dog bites a minor, what liability shall the dog owner bear?

Holding: According to the evidence presented and common sense, Plaintiff's complaint was more plausible because the two parties were neighbors who had prior disputes over the owner's insufficient control of his dog. Therefore, the court held that Plaintiff was injured by Defendant's dog. Defendant was held liable for Plaintiff's damage because of his carelessness in raising the dog. But Plaintiff's parents shall also bear partial liability because they were negligent in supervising the minor.

Rule: The owner of a domestic animal shall be liable for damage caused by the animal unless sufficient compelling evidence shows otherwise.

#92 Liability for Harm Caused by Domestic Animals

Case: Zhao Zhang vs. Jian Gong

Facts: Plaintiff was stung by a bee when he passed Defendant's house. The next day, Plaintiff's face was swollen and painful. Although he did not have convincing evidence, he believed the bee was raised by Defendant. So, he brought a lawsuit against Defendant.

Issue: How can a victim prove the ownership of an animal that caused damages?

X. Li and J. Jin, *Concise Chinese Tort Laws*, China-EU Law Series 1,
DOI 10.1007/978-3-642-41024-6_35, © Springer-Verlag Berlin Heidelberg 2014

Holding: It can be assured that the Defendant owned the bee because Plaintiff was stung just outside Defendant's house. Furthermore, Defendant's visit to Plaintiff in hospital was also evidence showing Defendant's owned the bee. Therefore, Defendant shall be held liable unless he can demonstrate he did not own the bee or that Plaintiff's negligence contributed to his damage.

Rule: The ownership of a domestic animal can be established with a series of circumstantial evidence.

#93 Liability for Harm Caused by Domestic Animals

Case: Mr. Li vs. Mr. Tang

Facts: Plaintiff and Defendant are both old men. When they walked around with their dogs, their dogs fought with each other. Plaintiff worried that his dog might be hurt by Defendant's dog, which is much bigger. So, he tugged on the dog's leash, but stumbled and suffered a comminuted fracture.

Issue: Is the victim entitled to seek compensation if his own negligence contributed to the accident?

Holding: The court found that Plaintiff's damage was caused by his own action of tugging the leash. On one hand, as an old man, Defendant's ability to manage a big dog was diminished, and he did not take any effective measures to prevent potential danger when the dogs were fighting. Defendant had no excuse, so he shall be held liable for Plaintiff's damage. On the other hand, Plaintiff was 77 years old and lacked sufficient capability of managing an animal and self-defense, so he was also partly negligent. Therefore, the court held that the damages shall be divided equally between Plaintiff and Defendant.

Rule: If the Plaintiff's negligence also contributed to the accident, the Defendant's liability can be reduced accordingly.

#94 Liability for Harm Caused by Domestic Animals

Case: Tianxin Xu vs. Rui Yin et al.

Facts: Defendants A, B, and C were contractors of a chicken farm. A raised a big watchdog in the farm. One day, the dog bit Plaintiff when A and B brought the dog with them to buy water at Plaintiff's home.

Issue: If a domestic animal has several owners, how is the tort liability shared among them?

Holding: A was the keeper and manager of the dog, so he was liable for the damage caused by the animal. B and C had a partnership with A, so they shall bear the joint liability. Plaintiff was 5 years old when the tort happened, so his parents shall also bear 5 % of the liability due to their negligent supervision.

Rule: When there is more than one keeper or manager of a domestic animal, all keepers shall bear joint liability for any damage caused by the animal.

Chapter 36
Liability for Harm Caused by Objects

#95 Liability for Harm Caused by Objects

Case: Fangyuan Chen vs. Mr. Xu

Facts: The owner of a house leased the third floor to a tenant. The lease did not have an agreement regarding maintenance. About half a year later, a pedestrian was hit by a piece of falling glass window and died.

Issue: Who shall be liable for the victim's damage: lessor or lessee?

Holding: The decedent's death was caused by the fallen window of the rented house. According to related provisions of the Tort Law, the owner or manager of the house shall bear tort liability, unless he can prove he was not at fault. The lessee, as the user, had direct control over the house, so he had the obligation of proper use and management of the house. At the same time, the lessor shall also take the responsibility for basic repairs of the house. Therefore, both the lessor and the lessee are liable to the decedent. Based on the court's holding, the lessor shall bear 40 % of the liability and the lessee 60 %.

Rule: Where any damage is caused by falling objects from a rented house, both the lessor and the lessee shall bear tort liability unless he can prove he was not at fault.

#96 Liability for Harm Caused by Objects

Case: Falling Ashtray Hitting a Pedestrian in Chongqing

Facts: Plaintiff was chatting with his friend outside a residential building but was suddenly hit by a falling ashtray from the building. Although Plaintiff did not die, it resulted in serious aftereffects in Plaintiff. However, the police could not determine who threw the ashtray.

X. Li and J. Jin, *Concise Chinese Tort Laws*, China-EU Law Series 1,
DOI 10.1007/978-3-642-41024-6_36, © Springer-Verlag Berlin Heidelberg 2014

Issue: Shall all of the residents be liable for damage caused by the falling ashtray?

Holding: It is too difficult to determine the tortfeasor. Except for the two families who were not home that day, anyone living in the building might be at fault. Based on the principle of constructive tort liability, the damage shall be shared by every resident in the building.

Rule: Where any damage is caused by an object thrown from a building, if it is difficult to identify the person throwing the object, everyone in the building at that time who is potentially the perpetrator shall pay compensation, unless he can prove it was impossible for him to have thrown the object.

#97 Liabilities for Damage Caused by Damaged Tree

Case: Wenjing Wu, Kaiyi Zhang, and Caijuan Wu vs. Health Travel Agency of Xiamen and Yongchun Niumulin Traveling Company Ltd. of Fujian

Facts: Plaintiff took part in a 2-day trip hosted by two travel companies and a local company. During the trip, it suddenly began to rain, but the tour guide asked the travelers to keep walking rather than staying sheltered from the rain. As a result, Plaintiff was struck from a falling pine tree on the way and died.

Issue: Who shall bear the liability of damage caused by a falling tree?

Holding: The court held that the tour guide was highly negligent in asking travelers to enter the forest during heavy rain. Since the tour guide was hired by both the travel companies and the local company, the two companies shall bear joint liability, each 10 % liable, while the local company shall bear 80 % of the liability because the accident was mainly caused by the poor management and deficient rescue efforts by the manager of the forest.

Rule: Where any damage is caused by a damaged tree, the owner or manager of the tree shall bear the tort liability unless he can prove that he was not at fault.

#98 Liability for Harm Caused by Objects

Case: Ruiyan Cheng vs. Ivy Real Estate Development Company of Beijing et al.

Facts: The victim went grocery shopping in the neighborhood. While standing on a plastic panel selecting goods, the victim fell into the basement from a 6-m deep light well and died immediately when the panel he was standing on suddenly broke. His family members sued the real estate development company, the property service company, and the shopkeepers.

Issue: When a number of causes contributed to the accident, how the tort liability shall be allocated among multiple tortfeasors?

Holding: This accident was triggered by several indirect causes. The real estate development company (owner) and the property service company (manager) were highly negligent by paving a thin panel and failing to provide warning signs or protective structures; hence, they should take a major portion of the liability. The shopkeepers were not liable because their pasting the words "Grocery" on their own window was just an advertisement. Further, they were neither the owner nor the manager of the well, so they did not have an obligation to warn. Thus, the shopkeepers were not negligent or liable. The victim was also negligent to some extent because he was drunk at midnight when he trespassed into the green area (which was not a passageway). Therefore, the allocation of liability was as follows: the real estate development company 50 %, the property service company 30 %, and Plaintiff 20 %.

Rule: When both the owner and manager of an object are liable to a victim for harm caused by the object, their liabilities shall be allocated with respect to the seriousness of their fault.

#99 Liability for Harm Caused by Objects

Case: Mr. Gao vs. Municipal Engineering Office of Guiyang et al.

Facts: The victim's head was hit by a piece of falling steel tube when he passed underneath an overpass. His injury was appraised as a first-degree disability. The steel tube fell from the truck after the driver mistakenly ran the truck into the guardrail of the overpass. Plaintiff sued the Municipal Engineering Office, the driver, and the owner of the truck.

Issue: Shall the government agency bear tort liability if it was negligent in constructing the overpass?

Holding: The court held that the truck crash was the main cause of the accident. The Municipal Engineering Office was also negligent because it did not comply with the overpass design and install protective measures to prevent falling objects from the guardrail. Thus, the Municipal Engineering Office shall be liable for the victim's damage because of its failure to fulfill its duty of precaution. This damage had several causes that jointly but indirectly resulted in one consequence; thus, the liability shall be shared according to each Defendant's fault. Finally, the court ruled that the driver and the owner shall bear 60 % of the liability jointly and severally, and the Municipal Engineering Office shall bear 40 %.

Rule: When the government agency is negligent in designing, constructing, or managing public utilities, it shall bear tort liability for harm caused by public utilities.

#100 Liability for Harm Caused by Objects

Case: Haiyu Zhang vs. Zhaolin Lin et al.

Facts: Plaintiff's husband worked as a painter on a construction site. One day when he was painting, the balcony above him suddenly collapsed and hit him. He died as a result. Plaintiff sued the general contractor and the subcontractor.

Issue: How shall the damage caused by a falling object in a construction site be allocated between the general contractor and the subcontractor?

Holding: The subcontractor managed the construction and shall comply with the building code to assure quality of the building. So the subcontractor was primarily liable. The general contractor was secondarily liable since he provided the materials for the construction and had the obligation to supervise the construction process.

Rule: Where damage is caused by a collapsing building, structure, or other facility, liability shall be allocated between the general contractor and the subcontractor in accordance with their respective fault.

About the Authors

李响 lixiangfd@gmail.com

Professor **Xiang Li** is a nationally recognized expert in the area of comparative Tort Law. He joined the faculty of the China University of Political Science and Law as Associate Professor in 2006. He also holds a joint appointment with the China-EU School of Law. Professor Li specializes in torts and civil procedure. Additional research areas of focus are: contract, product liability, charity, and copyright law.

Professor Li earned his LL.B. from Fudan University, and his J.D. from University of Minnesota Law School. His research has been published in a variety of outlets in law, legal education, and social policy. His publications include: *Problems in Tort Law (coauthored)*, *Cases and Materials on Products Liability*, *Basic Contract Law*, *The Law of Civil Procedure*, *Class Actions in a Comprehensive Horizon (coauthored)*, *American Copyright Law*, and *Torts: Fundamentals, Cases and Materials*.

靳继刚

Jigang Jin is a litigation attorney with an international law firm (Skadden, Arps, Slate, Meagher & Flom LLP). He specializes in IP and complex commercial litigations, and is based at the firm's Silicon Valley office. Jigang graduated with a J.D. degree from University of Minnesota Law School and a B.E. degree from Xi'an Jiaotong University. He is also the author of a novel.

X. Li and J. Jin, *Concise Chinese Tort Laws*, China-EU Law Series 1,
DOI 10.1007/978-3-642-41024-6, © Springer-Verlag Berlin Heidelberg 2014

Index A

Outstanding Scholars of Tort Law and Their Best-Known Works

(Include, but not limited to)

Xinbao Zhang	*Torts*, China Renmin University Press, 2nd Edition (July, 2010)
	Study On the Constitutive Elements of Tort Liability, Law Press China, 1st Edition (April, 2007)
	Fundamentals of Tort Law, China Renmin University Press, 1st Edition (February, 2006)
Lixin Yang	*Tort Law*, Law Press China, 2nd Edition (March, 2012)
	The Law of Tort, China Court Press, 4th Edition (June 2011)
	Torts and Compensation, Law Press China, 5th Edition (May 2010)
Liming Wang	*Studies In Chinese Tort Law*, China Renmin University Press, 1st Edition (February, 2011)
	Problems for Tort Law, China Legal Publishing House, 1st Edition (June, 2010)
	Tests for Liability in Torts, CUPL Press, 2nd Edition (September, 2004)
Huixing Liang	*Comments on China's Civil Legislation: Civil Code, Property Law & Tort Law*, Law Press China, 1st Edition (June, 2010)
	A Propositional Version with Reasons for Civil Code Draft of China: Tort Law, Law Press China, 1st Edition (December, 2004)
	Medical Negligence Compensation, Law Press China, 1st Edition (September, 2001)
Weiguo Wang	*Civil Law*, CUPL Press, 2nd Edition (March, 2012)
	Principle of Liability for Fault: The Third Thriving, China Legal Publishing House, 1st Edition (March, 2001)
Minan Zhang	*Liability For Infringement of Right of Intangible Personality*, Peking University Press, 1st Edition (June, 2012)
	Tort Liability Law, High Education Press, 1st Edition (February, 2011)
	Vicarious Liability of Tort Law, Peking University Press, 1st Edition (November, 2010)
Jun Wang	*A Comparative Study on Tort Compensation*, Law Press China, 1st Edition (March, 2011)
	Strict Liability in Torts, Law Press China, 1st Edition (April, 2006)

(continued)

DOI 10.1007/978-3-642-41024-6, © Springer-Verlag Berlin Heidelberg 2014

(continued)

Xiao Cheng	*Understanding Tort Law*, China Renmin University Press, 1st Edition (September, 2011)
	Torts, Law Press China, 1st Edition (August, 2011)
	An Overview of the Law of Tort, China Renmin University Press, 1st Edition (January, 2008)
Shaokun Fang	*A Case Study of Tort Liability*, Peking University Press, 1st Edition (August, 2012)
	Civil Law, China Renmin University Press, 2nd Edition (June, 2011)
Zhiqiang Yin	*Cases & Explanations on Medical Liabilities*, Renmin Press, 1st Edition (June, 2010)
	Law of Torts, CUPL Press, 1st Edition (September, 2008)
Shiguo Liu	*Theoretical and Practical Difficulties in Tort Law*, China Legal Publishing House, 1st Edition (August, 2009)
	Tort Law: Perspectives & Problems, Shandong Renmin Press, 1st Edition (January, 2004)
Min Yu	*The Basic Rules of Tort Law in Chinese Civil Code*, Social Science Academic Press, 1st Edition (August, 2012)
	Special Automobile Liability Rules And Comparative Negligence, Law Press China, 2nd Edition (April, 2006)
Youjun Zhou	*Torts*, China Renmin University Press, 1st Edition (April, 2011)
	Lectures on the Tort Liability Law of China, China Court Press, 1st Edition (March, 2011)
	On The Establishment of Liability In Tort Law: Controversies & Cases, Law Press China, 1st Edition (May, 2010)
Xiandong Li	*Torts: Cases & Materials*, CPPSU Press, 1st Edition (October, 2011)
	An Introduction to Tort Law, CUPL Press, 1st Edition (February, 2005)
Xiaoming Xi	*Tort Liability Law: Judges' Handbook*, China Court Press, 1st Edition (April, 2010)
	Tort Liability Law: Typical Case Studies, China Court Press, 1st Edition (February, 2010)
	Tort Liability Law: Issues & Problems, China Court Press, 1st Edition (January, 2010)
	Tort Liability Law: Explanation & Application, China Court Press, 1st Edition (January, 2010)
Zhu Wang	*Advanced Tort Law: Strategies and Difficulties*, China Renmin University Press, 1st Edition (May, 2012)
	Research on Apportionment of Tort Liability, China Renmin University Press, 1st Edition (December, 2009)
Shengping Gao	*China's New Law on Tort Liability: Issues, Legislation & Cases*, Peking University Press, 1st Edition (February, 2010)
	Typical Case Study on Torts, China Legal Publishing House, 1st Edition (February, 2010)
Hui Yao	*Personality Rights in China*, China Renmin University Press, 1st Edition (April, 2011)
	Tort Law: Theory & Practice, China Court Press, 1st Edition (July, 2009)
Mingrui Guo	*Civil Law*, High Education Press, 3rd Edition (November, 2010)
	Torts, Science Press, 1st Edition (July, 2009)
Cheng Wang	*The Tort Law*, Peking University Press, 1st Edition (May, 2011)
	An Economic Analysis of Tort Damages, China Renmin University Press, 1st Edition (June, 2002)

Index B

Selected Primary Authorities of Tort Law in China

(Until January 2013)

Laws

Promulgated by the National People's Congress or Its Standing Committee

Name	Effective date (mm-dd-yy)
Tort Law of the People's Republic of China	07-01-2010
General Principles of the Civil Law of the People's Republic of China	01-01-1987
Product Quality Law of the People's Republic of China	09-01-1993 (Revision in 2000)
Law of the People's Republic of China on Protection of Consumer Rights and Interests	01-01-1994 (Revision in 2009)
Property Law of the People's Republic of China	10-01-2007
Law of Succession of the People's Republic of China	10-01-1985
Marriage Law of the People's Republic of China	01-01-1981 (Revision in 2001)
Law of the People's Republic of China on Industrial Enterprises Owned by People as A Whole	08-01-1988 (Revision in 2009)
Judges Law of the People's Republic of China	07-01-1995 (Revision in 2001)
Public Procurators Law of the People's Republic of China	07-01-1995 (Revision in 2001)
Civil Servant Law of the People's Republic of China	01-01-2006
Lawyers Law of the People's Republic of China	06-01-2008 (Revision in 2012)
Law of the People's Republic of China on the Protection of Minors	06-01-2007 (Revision in 2012)

(continued)

X. Li and J. Jin, *Concise Chinese Tort Laws*, China-EU Law Series 1,
DOI 10.1007/978-3-642-41024-6,

(continued)

Name	Effective date (mm-dd-yy)
Road Traffic Safety Law of the People's Republic of China	05-01-2004 (Revision in 2011)
Railway Law of the People's Republic of China	05-01-1991 (Revision in 2009)
Food Safety Law of the People's Republic of China	06-01-2009
Agricultural Product Quality Safety Law of the People's Republic of China	11-01-2006
Postal Law of the People's Republic of China	10-01-2009 (Revision in 2012)
Pharmaceutical Administration Law of the People's Republic of China	12-01-2001
Mental Health Law of the People's Republic of China	05-01-2013
Labor Contract Law of the People's Republic of China	01-01-2008 (Revision in 2012)
Marine Environment Protection Law of the People's Republic of China	03-01-1983 (Revision in 1999)
Environmental Protection Law of the People's Republic of China	12-26-1989
Law of the People's Republic of China on the Protection of Wildlife	03-01-1989 (Revision in 2009)
Law of the People's Republic of China on Population and Birth Control	09-01-2002
Civil Aviation Law of the People's Republic of China	03-01-1996 (Revision in 2009)
Electric Power Law of the People's Republic of China	04-01-1996 (Revision in 2009)
State Compensation Law of the People's Republic of China	01-01-1995 (Revision in 2012)
Law of the People's Republic of China on the Prevention and Control of Water Pollution	11-01-1984 (Revision in 2008)
Law of the People's Republic of China on the Prevention and Control of Environmental Pollution by Solid Wastes	04-01-1996 (Revision in 2004)
Law of the People's Republic of China on the Prevention and Control of Atmospheric Pollution	06-01-1988 (Revision in 2000)
Law of the People's Republic of China on Prevention and Control of Pollution from Environmental Noise	03-01-1997
Law of the People's Republic of China on Appraising of Environment Impacts	09-01-2003
Law of the People's Republic of China on Prevention and Control of Radioactive Pollution	10-01-2003
Public Security Administration Punishment Law of the People's Republic of China	03-01-2006 (Revision in 2012)
Law of the People's Republic of China on Practicing Doctors	05-01-1999 (Revision in 2009)
Construction Law of the People's Republic of China	03-01-1998

Regulations

Promulgated by the State Council

Name	Effective date (mm-dd-yy)
Regulation on Realty Management	09-01-2003 (Revision in 2007)
Regulation on Work-Related Injury Insurance	01-01-2004 (Revision in 2010)
Regulations on Administration of Business Sites of Internet Access Services	11-15-2002 (Revision in 2011)
Regulation on Protection of the Right to Network Dissemination of Information	07-01-2006 (Revision in 2013)
Regulation on Quality Responsibility for Industrial Products	07-01-1986
Regulation on Safety Management of Hazardous Chemicals	03-15-2002 (Revision in 2011)
Regulation on Safety Supervision of Special Equipment	06-01-2003 (Revision in 2009)
Regulation on Implementation of the Food Safety Law of the People's Republic of China	07-20-2009
Regulation on Supervision and Administration of the Quality and Safety of Dairy Products	10-09-2008
Regulation on Administration of Recall of Defective Auto Products	01-01-2013
Regulation on Administration of Blood Products	12-30-1996
Regulation on Supervision and Management of Civil Nuclear Safety Equipment	01-01-2008
Regulation on Prevention and Control of Pollution Damages to the Marine Environment by Coastal Engineering Construction Projects of the People's Republic of China	08-01-1990 (Revision in 2007)
Regulation on Prevention and Treatment of the Pollution and Damage to the Marine Environment by Marine Engineering Construction Projects	11-01-2006
Regulation on Safety Administration of Explosives for Civilian Use	09-01-2006
Regulation on Safety Administration of Fireworks and Firecrackers	01-21-2006
Regulation on Safety and Protection of Radioisotopes and Radiation Devices	12 01 2005
Regulation on Quality Management of Construction Projects	01-30-2000
Regulation on Safety Supervision over Coal Mines	12-01-2000
Regulation on Implementation of Labor Contract Law of the People's Republic of China	09-18-2008
Regulation on Protection of the Railway Transport Safety	04-01-2005
Regulation on Compulsory Traffic Accident Liability Insurance for Motor Vehicles	07-01-2006 (Revision in 2012)
Regulation on School Bus Safety Management	04-05-2012
Regulation on Implementation of the Road Traffic Safety Law of the People's Republic of China	05-01-2004
Regulation of the People's Republic of China on Road Transport	07-01-2004 (Revision in 2012)

(continued)

(continued)

Name	Effective date (mm-dd-yy)
Regulation on the Emergency Rescue, Investigation and Handling of Railway Traffic Accidents	09-01-2007 (Revision in 2012)
Regulation on Administration of the Work Safety of Construction Projects	02-01-2004
Regulation on Handling of Medical Accidents	09-01-2002
Regulation on Administration of Construction Project Environmental Protection	11-29-1998

Judicial Interpretations

Promulgated by the Supreme People's Court of the People's Republic of China

Name	Effective date (mm-dd-yy)
Notice of the Supreme People's Court on Certain Issues concerning the Application of the Tort Law of the People's Republic of China	06-30-2010
Opinions of the Supreme People's Court on Several Issues concerning the Implementation of the General Principles of the Civil Law of the People's Republic of China (For Trial Implementation)	01-26-1988 (Partially Invalid since 2008)
Interpretation of the Supreme People's Court of Some Issues concerning the Application of Law for the Trial of Cases on Compensation for Personal Injury	05-01-2004
Interpretation of the Supreme People's Court on Several Issues concerning the Application of Law in the Trial of Cases Involving Disputes over Compensation for Personal Injuries in Railway Transport	03-16-2010
Interpretation of the Supreme People's Court on Several Issues Concerning the Specific Application of Law in the Trial of Disputes over Partitioned Ownership of Building Areas	10-01-2009
Interpretation of the Supreme People's Court on Problems regarding the Ascertainment of Compensation Liability for Emotional Damages in Torts	03-10-2001
A Few Provisions of the Supreme People's Court on the Trial of Compensation Cases for Torts Involving Accounting Firms Engaging in the Audit Business	06-15-2007
A Few Provisions of the Supreme People's Court on Trying Cases of Civil Compensation Arising from False Statement in Securities Market	02-01-2003
Notice of the Supreme People's Court on the Relevant Issues concerning the Acceptance of Cases of Disputes over Torts Arising from False Statement in the Securities Market	01-15-2002
Provisions of the Supreme People's Court on Several Issues concerning the Application of Law in Hearing Civil Dispute Cases Involving Infringement of the Right of Dissemination on Information Networks	01-01-2013

(continued)

(continued)

Name	Effective date (mm-dd-yy)
A Few Provisions of the Supreme People's Court on Evidence in Civil Procedures	04-01-2002 (Revision in 2008)
Letter of the Supreme People's Court on the Issue Whether or Not the Parents of a Minor Who has Committed Tort should be the Subject to Lawsuit as Guardians of the Minor in the Case that the Minor Dies	01-20-1990
Interpretation of the Supreme People's Court on Several Issues Concerning the Application of Law in the Trial of Cases on Compensation for Damage in Road Traffic Accidents	12-21-2012
Provisions of the Supreme People's Court on Several Issues Concerning the Trial of Cases of Disputes over Compensation for Vessel-induced Oil Pollution Damage	07-01-2011
Official Reply of the Supreme People's Court of the People's Republic of China on Whether the People's Courts Shall Accept Civil Suits for Mental Injury Compensation Brought by the Victims in Criminal Cases	07-20-2002
Interpretation of the Supreme People's Court on Several Issues about the Trial of Cases Concerning the Right of Reputation	09-15-1998
Resolution of the Supreme People's Court on Several Issues about the Trial of Cases Concerning the Right of Reputation	08-07-1993
Interpretation of the Supreme People's Court on certain issues concerning judicial compensation in civil and administrative litigation	09-21-2000 (Revision in 2008)
Provisions of the Supreme People's Court for the People's Courts to Seal up, Distrain and Freeze Properties in Civil Enforcement	01-01-2005 (Revision in 2008)
Reply of the Supreme People's Court on the Issue of Time Limit for Sealing up, Distraining and Freezing Properties in Civil Enforcement Activities	07-11-2006
Notice of the Supreme People's Court concerning Implementing the 23 Measures for "Justice for the People"	12-02-2003
Reply of the Supreme People's Court on Whether the Aggrieved Party in A Product Infringement Case May Bring A Civil Lawsuit Against the Product Trademark Owner	07-28-2002

Administrative Rules

Promulgated by Government Agencies

Name	Effective date (mm-dd-yy)
Interim Provisions on Giving Punishments for Illegal Acts and Disciplinary Offences in Environmental Protection	02-20-2006
Trial Measures for the Management of Social Aid Funds for Road Traffic Accidents	01-01-2010
Measures for Lump-sum Compensation to the Disabled or Deceased Employees of Entities Involving Illegal Employment	01-01-2011

(continued)

(continued)

Name	Effective date (mm-dd-yy)
Provisions on the Scope of the Relatives to Be Supported of the Employees Killed in Work-related Accidents	01-01-2004
Measures for the Determination of Work-related Injuries	01-01-2011
Measures for the Handling of Student Injury Accidents	09-01-2002 (Revision in 2010)
Measures for the Administration of Drug Recall	12-10-2007
Measures for Operation Management of Urban Rail Transit	08-01-2005
Provisions on the Administration of the Road Transport of Dangerous Goods	08-01-2005 (Revision in 2010)
Provisions on the Administration of Road Freight Transport and Stations	08-01-2005 (Revision in 2012)
Provisions on the Limited Compensation Liabilities of Carriers in Civil Aviation Transport	03-28-2006
Notice on Promoting the People's Mediation Commissions' Mediation of Civil Damages Disputes Arising from Road Traffic Accidents	06-23-2010
Provisions on the Administration of Urban Construction Garbage	06-01-2005
Provisions on the Administration of Food Recall	08-27-2007
Provisions on the Administration of Children's Toys Recall	08-27-2007

Index C

Legal Research Guide: Tort Cases

(Not Binding Authorities in China)

Electronic Resources

The Supreme People's Court of the PRC	http://www.court.gov.cn/qwfb/cpws/
The Official Web Site for China's Judicial System (by Province)	http://www.chinacourt.org/paper.shtml
	http://bjgy.chinacourt.org
	http://tjfy.chinacourt.org
	http://shfy.chinacourt.org
Legal Info	http://www.legalinfo.gov.cn/Case_record/node_40468.htm
Legal Daily	http://www.legaldaily.com.cn/legal_case/node_33788.htm
China Law Info	http://www.pkulaw.cn/cluster_call_form.aspx?menu_item=case
Westlaw China	http://www.westlawchina.com/
Find Law	http://china.findlaw.cn/info/qinquanzerenfa/qqzrfal/
Link Law	http://www.linklaw.com.cn/chinacase/
China Laws	http://www.lawbase.com.cn/
Law Time	http://www.lawtime.cn/cases/judcase_10.html
Oriental Legal Information	http://www.dffyw.com/sifashijian/al/
110 Legal Advice	http://www.110.com/panli/s?a=c&cid=956
Judgment	http://www.panjueshu.com/
Law Library	http://www.law-lib.com/cpws/cpwsml-cm.asp
Public Interest Litigation	http://www.pil.org.cn/
China Civil & Commercial Law	http://www.civillaw.com.cn

(continued)

X. Li and J. Jin, *Concise Chinese Tort Laws*, China-EU Law Series 1,
DOI 10.1007/978-3-642-41024-6,

(continued)

CNKI	http://law.cnki.net/
LLB	http://www.llb.cn/flpc/
Lawyee	http://www.lawyee.net/Case/Case.asp
China Case	http://www.chinacase.net/
Judicial Case Review	http://www.njucasereview.com/web/judicial/

Textual Resources

First author	Book(s)
The Supreme People's Court of the PRC	*Gazette of the Supreme People's Court*, The People's Judicature Magazine (Monthly)
National Judge College	*Digest of Cases in China: Civil Cases*, China Renmin University Press (1993-2012)
	2012 Selected Cases in China Series, China Legal Publishing House, 1st Edition (March, 2012)
	2013 Selected Cases in China Series, China Legal Publishing House, 1st Edition (May, 2013)
The Supreme People's Court of the PRC & The Supreme People's Procuratorate of the PRC	*Judicial Interpretation and Guiding Cases: Civil Cases*, China Legal Publishing House, 2nd Edition (June, 2011)
China Legal Publishing House	A Comprehensive Understanding of Tort Law: Statutes, Explanations & Cases, China Legal Publishing House, 1st Edition (April, 2010)
	Tort Liability Law: Cases-based Explanation, China Legal Publishing House, 2nd Edition (January, 2013)
China Institute of Legal Application	*A Collections of Leading People's Court Cases*, China Court Press (Quarterly)
Haocai Luo	*Comments on People's Court Cases: Remedies in Tort Damages*, China Legal Publishing House, Volume 7 & 8 (March & June 2006)
Xiaoming Xi	*Comments on Guiding Cases of Torts*, China Legal Publishing House, 1st Edition (January, 2010)
	Reference & Guide to Civil Trial, China Court Press (Quarterly)
Wei Zhou	*Digest of Criteria for Judgment and Measures for Justice: Civil & Commercial Cases (1985–2010)*, Peking University Press, 1st Edition (October, 2011)
Yi Sun	*Gist of Civil & Commercial Cases Excerpted from Gazettes of Supreme People's Court: 1999–2011*, China Legal Publishing House, 1st Edition (December, 2011)

(continued)

(continued)

First author	Book(s)
Chunqi Wu, Weijia Wang, Liming Wang, etc.	*Lectures on Law of Torts: Statutes & Cases (Series)*, Intellectual Property Press, 1st Edition (March, 2010)
Baishu Tang	*Judicial Issues and Guiding Cases of Tort Liability Law*, China Legal Publishing House, 1st Edition (August, 2011)
Zhiqiang Yin, Anchao Hu, Wenjing Jin, etc.	*Tort Liability Law: Cases & Explanations (Series)*, Renmin Press, 1st Edition (June, 2010)
Chunqi Wu, Xue Xia, Shiqian Chen, etc.	*Establishment and Calculation of Tort Liabilities: Cases & Materials (Series)*, China Legal Publishing House, 1st Edition (January, 2011)
Shutao Yue	*Torts: Cases & Comments*, University of International Business & Economics Press, 1st Edition (October, 2011)
Yuqing Zhang	*Chinese Tort Law: Comparative Case Studies*, China Commerce & Trade Press, 1st Edition (January, 2013)
Xuguang Wang	*Tort Liability Law: Litigation & Cases*, Law Press China, 1st Edition (December, 2010)
Hongjian Zhang	*Tort Law: Case Illustration*, Law Press China, 1st Edition (January, 2010)
Law Press China	*Tort Liability Laws and Regulations of China*, Law Press China, 2nd Edition (January, 2013)
Xianjie Chen	*Tort Liability Law: Rules & Cases*, China Legal Publishing House, 1st Edition (January, 2010)
Lixin Yang	*Understanding Tort Liability Law Through A Case Method*, Intellectual Property Press, 2nd Edition (May, 2012)
Qingbao Wu	*Legal policies & Guiding Cases of Supreme People's Court: Torts (Volume 5)*, Law Press China, 1st Edition (September, 2011)
Fengbin Hu	*Summaries of Guiding Cases in China: Torts*, Law Press China, 1st Edition (March, 2012)
Xiandong Li	*Torts: Statutes, Cases & Problems*, Law Press China, 1st Edition (April, 2010)

MIX
Papier aus verantwortungsvollen Quellen
Paper from responsible sources
FSC® C105338

If you have any concerns about our products,
you can contact us on
ProductSafety@springernature.com

In case Publisher is established outside the EU,
the EU authorized representative is:
Springer Nature Customer Service Center GmbH
Europaplatz 3, 69115 Heidelberg, Germany

Printed by Libri Plureos GmbH
in Hamburg, Germany